CLOUGH AND REVIE

Roger Hermiston was assistant editor of BBC Radio 4's flagship *Today* programme from 1998 to 2010. Before joining the BBC in 1990, his career as a print journalist included the *Yorkshire Post* (reporter and feature writer) and the *Sunderland Echo* (crime reporter). He graduated from Newcastle University with a degree in politics.

CLOUGH & REVIE

The Rivals Who Changed
the Face of English Football

ROGER HERMISTON

MAINSTREAM
PUBLISHING

EDINBURGH AND LONDON

First published in Great Britain in 2011 by
MAINSTREAM PUBLISHING COMPANY
(EDINBURGH) LTD
7 Albany Street
Edinburgh EH1 3UG

ISBN 9781845966607

A catalogue record for this book is available
from the British Library

Typeset in Dante MT
Printed and bound in Great Britain by
CPI Mackays, Chatham ME5 8TD

1 3 5 7 9 10 8 6 4 2

For Mum and Dad

Acknowledgements

Three people in particular offered me generous and invaluable help in the course of researching and writing this book. Brian Leng, lifelong Sunderland supporter and now editor of the excellent website theRokerEnd.com, gave me his insight into North-East soccer in the '50s and '60s and put me in touch with many characters who came into Clough's and Revie's orbit in that period.

Philip Tallentire, sports editor of the *Evening Gazette*, has taken a great interest in the subject matter of the book and regularly provided me with much vital information on Middlesbrough FC during those years.

Crucial assistance came also from Garry Richardson, my old colleague on BBC Radio 4's *Today* programme; his unrivalled contacts book opened many doors.

I must also thank John Helm, expert football commentator and analyst, for his recollections of Leeds United, Don Revie and Brian Clough in the early 1970s.

Alan Peacock, Clough's striking partner at Boro in the 1950s (and later a Leeds and England centre-forward), is an absolute gentleman. He freely shared his experiences of that time and put me in touch with many of his playing colleagues.

Others I must also thank are Robert Nichols, devoted Middlesbrough supporter and editor of the splendid fanzine *Fly Me to the Moon*; Christine Talbot of the present *Calendar* team at Yorkshire TV, and all those members of the programme in 1974 who helped me recreate the events of 12 September that year; and Jonathan Harvey, another of my old *Today* colleagues, who delved into the BBC archives on my behalf.

I spent a good deal of time in the British Library at Colindale, and the staff there were extremely helpful; equally so were those at the

Royal Society in London and Teesside Archives in Middlesbrough.

Andrew Gordon has been the ideal agent, always calm and thoughtful. He gave me the confidence to pursue the project and always had imaginative suggestions about how best to shape the book. Claire Rose has been a most assiduous and constructive editor.

Finally, I must thank my lovely Eileen for her unstinting encouragement and support along every step of the way.

Contents

Preface

I was the reporter working the night shift for the *Yorkshire Post* in Leeds on Friday, 26 May 1989, when the news came through that Don Revie had died of the crippling, incurable motor neurone disease with which he had been diagnosed two years earlier.

I had about an hour to make some calls, piece together the salient facts of his life and then file my story, which was obviously destined for the following morning's front page. Whatever the wider world may have thought about him by then, Revie remained a hero in the eyes of the city to which he had brought so much football fame and success.

It was obvious where to start. Billy Bremner – 'ten stone of barbed wire', as one writer once memorably described him – had made his debut for Leeds alongside him at the age of 17, and then, when Revie became manager, had made sure his writ ran large on the pitch as his inspirational captain.

Bremner spoke passionately to me that night about the man who became like a father to him. 'The Guv'nor was a master tactician, a superb manager. But more important than that, he was a good guy. He was totally honest and fair, and never badmouthed anyone.'

Bobby Collins, Revie's midfield enforcer in the 1960s, whom Bremner had succeeded as captain, alluded to his empathy with his players, telling me, 'He got the very best out of them and what's more he looked after them.'

Then there was Allan Clarke, his goalscorer supreme, a man who tended to let his boots do the talking. His tribute was characteristically concise: 'Don made Leeds United. It's as simple as that. I have played for quite a number of managers and he was the best.'

Armed with those quotes and having worked in the obvious biographical details of his career as player and manager, I sent the story off to the subeditors. It was a remarkable night on the sporting front: Arsenal were winning the Football League championship in sensational fashion on the last day of the season, defeating Liverpool at Anfield with a last-minute goal from Michael Thomas.

One line in my piece intrigued me: 'Don Revie was brought up in Middlesbrough.' At that time, I was unaware of his connection with the town. Such was the power of his association with Leeds that it seemed to put every other aspect of his life in the shade. As my father's family came from Middlesbrough, it interested me even more.

Years later, when I turned away briefly from making news programmes for the BBC and delved into the world of football in the 1960s and 1970s, I discovered that another complex, controversial football character had been born only a few streets away from Revie. What's more, it was none other than Revie's managerial arch-rival and most outspoken critic – Brian Clough. A story of these two Middlesbrough boys seemed rich in potential.

In Tom Hooper's compelling film *The Damned United* (from the book of the same name by David Peace, a fictional account of Brian Clough's 44-day tenure at Leeds United), there's a scene in which Clough – played by Michael Sheen – is looking forward to the FA Cup encounter between his own side, lower Second Division Derby County, and Leeds, managed by Don Revie and riding high at the top of the First Division.

Clough muses about the similarities between himself and the more experienced Revie, by way of both their personal lives and their footballing careers. He tells his faithful sidekick Peter Taylor:

> We grew up just a few streets apart, you know, in Middlesbrough, close to Ayresome Park. He'll have known my street, Valley Road. Probably bought sweets from Garnett's factory, where me dad worked . . . Best manager in the country, Don Revie. Played for Sunderland, like me, a centre-forward, like me, and England, like me. Peas in a pod, me and Don. Two peas in a bloody pod.

An imagined monologue, but Clough/Sheen's screen speech is firmly supported by the evidence. They *were* born a short distance away from each other in Middlesbrough, in 1927 and 1935 respectively, on either side of the town's (former) Ayresome Park stadium. The historian Richard Overy has described the two decades between the world wars as 'The Morbid Age', a period familiarly associated with poverty, unemployment, the slump and the rise of Fascism. Middlesbrough, one of the 'new towns' of the Industrial Revolution, was ravaged by the Depression more than most because of its reliance on heavy industries, and Revie and Clough both grew up in a climate where jobs were scarce and life was a perpetual struggle.

One of Revie's boyhood contemporaries, the journalist Peter Thomas, described his upbringing more evocatively than anyone: 'His was the harsh background of a Middlesbrough still touched grey and dark by attitudes of Victorian Methodism, where every rich man had his castle and a poor man at his gate.' Not to be the poor man at the rich man's door was what drove Revie on throughout his life.

Through talent, desire and determination both of them went on to become highly successful – if not exceptional – professional footballers: Clough flourished as a free-scoring centre-forward for Middlesbrough and Sunderland, Revie usually in a more deep-lying version of the same position at Leicester, Hull, Manchester City, Sunderland and Leeds United.

Both, too, were capped by England – albeit on just a few occasions. Revie marked his debut in October 1954 with a goal against Northern Ireland; he went on to win six caps. Clough's first game came five years later against Wales; he played only once more, and in neither game did he display anything like his true potential.

Then, as young managers in the early (Revie) and late (Clough) 1960s, they both took clubs languishing in the doldrums (Leeds United and Derby County) and moulded them into championship winners.

So much similarity, then, in background, career path and achievement. But peas in a pod? Emphatically not. These two sons of the Tees had little else in common, and were as different in character as Richard Nixon and John F. Kennedy. A bitter rivalry developed between them, which in turn enlivened and then arguably blighted English football in the late 1960s and early 1970s as their sides fought it out for the major honours.

After Clough had made another of his barbed comments about Leeds when he was Derby manager, it prompted this unusual response from a normally reticent Revie: 'Clough is the last man I would like to be stranded with on a desert island.' The feeling was almost certainly mutual, and that personal animosity often appeared to spread throughout their respective clubs.

These parallels in their professional lives culminated in the remarkable events of the summer of 1974. Revie, who had just led Leeds to another First Division title, decided to leave the club he had nurtured like a family for 13 years to become England manager, after the dismissal of Sir Alf Ramsey. Clough – to the utter disbelief of the football world – succeeded him at Elland Road. Three years later, history repeated itself: when Revie resigned as England manager, one of the four main candidates to be interviewed for his job was one Brian Clough.

Clough, then, was forever following in the footsteps of the older man. To some extent, there was a natural envy on his part of Revie's achievements and a consequent fierce desire to better him. The two men ran their clubs almost as their own personal fiefdoms, but they held very different views on how the game should be played and the role of football in society; those ideological differences also provide an explanation for the bitter clashes.

Temperamentally, too, they were oceans apart: Clough was an extrovert, a showman who was at home in the bright new world of television in the early 1970s, while Revie all too often – in public, at least – appeared to live up to the caricature of the dour Yorkshireman.

Theirs was a gripping enough story even without being fictionalised or put on the big screen, a tale about passionate, driven, extraordinary characters who stood above and beyond their contemporaries, a rivalry in the classical tradition, one that could have leapt from the pages of Homer or Shakespeare.

Then there was my other reason for wanting to write a book about Revie and Clough. I wanted to explore my background and heritage, because the Hermistons were in the first wave of migrants from other parts of the British Isles who came to help build this frontier town in the early nineteenth century. Some of my ancestors on my father's side worked in the ironworks at Eston and helped forge Middlesbrough's pre-eminent place in the Industrial Revolution.

Revie and Clough were outstanding footballers, but my paternal grandfather and father were outstanding local cricketers. My grandfather, Robert Nelson Hermiston, captained Normanby Hall in the 1930s and 1940s, scoring several centuries and thousands of other runs in an aggressive yet elegant style, so much so that he once moved a correspondent on the *North-Eastern Gazette* to write (in an account of a match against Darlington): 'Hermiston has the stamp which puts a batsman into the aristocracy, and would score more runs than he does were it not for a certain casualness of stroke which is often suddenly and quite unexpectedly his undoing.' He was also a choir conductor and a church worker and taught in Middlesbrough schools for 35 years.

My father, Stanley Thomas Hermiston, was born in 1927, the same year as Don Revie. He, too, was an excellent cricketer, and after he left the North-East in the 1950s to find employment in Cumberland he captained his local side, Egremont, to numerous successes, while he himself consistently topped the county batting averages.

My book, then, in its early chapters at least, will have a third character, the town of Middlesbrough itself, a town that invented itself almost out of nowhere and fashioned generations of resourceful individuals with a fierce desire to make something special of their lives, men like Don Revie and Brian Clough – and my grandfather and father.

The book will trace events from Sunday, 10 July 1927 in Bell Street, Middlesbrough, when Donald Revie was born on an exceptionally hot summer's day, and it will finish half a century later in the chill of a December morning in 1977 with Brian Howard Clough coming down the steps of the Football Association's headquarters in Lancaster Gate, west London, having completed the interview for his great rival's job.

Fifty years, then, during which British society underwent profound change, through depression, growing material benefits and choice, war, austerity, increasing prosperity, sexual liberation and finally back to a grim economic climate and a more disturbed, apparently fractured society in the 1970s. Half a century of revolution in football, too, when the rewards for playing and managing at the top level became greater but the divide between the supporter – the working man – and his idols grew wider.

The lives of Don Revie and Brian Clough were, to a certain extent, shaped similarly by their experience of the harsher decades of the 1930s and 1940s. But, 30 years later, all that shared experience counted for nothing as the game of soccer was tugged and twisted in different directions while they fought for influence and achievement. At times, it seemed like an all-out battle for the soul of British football.

Prologue

16 September 1958

Don Revie left Sunderland's Roker Park stadium shortly after 6 p.m. on Tuesday, 16 September 1958 with 15 hours to make a decision that would have the most profound consequences for his professional career and personal life. At the age of 31, with time running out on his playing days, he knew he had to get it right.

He'd just been set a deadline of 9 a.m. on Wednesday to decide whether to leave Sunderland and make the 25-mile journey south to join Middlesbrough, his home-town club, the side he had dreamed of playing for ever since, as a young boy, he'd first listened to the roars of acclaim for a George Camsell goal as he stood in the alleyway behind his home in Bell Street.

Revie disliked deadlines, the pressure to make instant decisions. He was by nature a cautious, meticulous man, who liked to consider, prepare and then make a judgement when everything was firmly settled in his mind.

But for Middlesbrough the courtship was over; they'd pursued their man over several weeks, and now they demanded an answer. In the hour-and-a-half meeting they'd had with him on Tuesday afternoon, they had once more spelled out their admiration for his footballing skills, their vision of how he could help transform the fortunes of their side and their assurances for his financial security.

The Middlesbrough manager, Bob Dennison, and secretary Eric Thomas had impressed him with their enthusiasm and their ambition. There was a clear suggestion, too, that a new house in the area would be part of the financial package. Sunderland had told him that they wouldn't stand in his way, and a fee of around £12,000 had been agreed.

When he was growing up in Middlesbrough, playing his football first at Archibald School then later as a developing teenager for the Boro Swifts side, Revie had no desire to look beyond his native town for a professional career. He was desperate to follow in the footsteps of the forwards he'd idolised, pestered for autographs and watched in wonder on a Saturday afternoon: Camsell, Micky Fenton, Wilf Mannion, great players with flair, imagination and personality. But Leicester City had won the race for his signature, and his career had followed a far different path from that which he'd envisaged as a young, starry-eyed boy.

He was used to change; even before he'd joined Sunderland in November 1956, he'd called himself 'Soccer's Happy Wanderer' (the title of his autobiography), as his search for the best place to display his talents had taken him from Leicester to Hull City and then on to Manchester City.

Now, he was starting to feel, it might be time to move once more. On a personal level, there wasn't much that was wrong with his life. He lived conveniently in a house not far from Sunderland's training ground at Cleadon; his wife, Elsie, had settled into a teaching job in a nearby village, while his young son Duncan was growing up happily.

But as far as the football was concerned, it was an entirely different matter. When he'd first arrived at Roker Park, the side had boasted players of the calibre of Len Shackleton, George Aitken, Billy Bingham and Ray Daniel. True, they were all in the latter stages of their careers, but there was enough quality there, apparently – and with fresh talent coming through from the youth section – to ensure that the club maintained its proud record of First Division status before moving on to bigger and better things.

It wasn't to be. Relegation was narrowly avoided at the end of the 1956–57 season, while a greater calamity was taking place away from the pitch. A Football Association inquiry had found Sunderland – known as the 'Bank of England' club as a result of its spending in the transfer market – guilty of making illegal payments to players. Sunderland's charismatic chairman, Bill Ditchburn, along with director Bill Martin, were permanently banned from the game; two other directors were suspended *sine die*. The club was fined a record £5,000, and manager Bill Murray £200; Murray, a broken man, left the club in June 1957.

For Revie, the problem wasn't the scarring of the club's reputation; it came in the form of Murray's replacement, Alan Brown. Revie could appreciate that Brown had an inventive tactical mind, and there were aspects of his style of management – his closeness to the players, his continual chivvying and coaxing of them, his values of openness and honesty – that he would acknowledge as being of benefit to the side. Indeed, as he always did, he would watch, absorb and store away information that might be of use to him if he was to pursue a managerial career of his own.

No, the problem was that Brown had made it clear, fairly early on, that Revie wasn't going to be part of his plans. And after relegation to Division Two followed in 1958, Brown opted for the energy of youth to restore Sunderland's glory. He instituted a style of play that was complete anathema to Revie, placing the emphasis on hard running, chasing and harrying rather than letting the ball do the work.

For Revie, running twenty yards and then passing the ball five made absolutely no sense; for him, it was far more rewarding just to run five and then pass the ball effectively over twenty yards. Too often now, training was just a grind, a triumph of sweat over skill.

There was a personal antipathy that accompanied the differing footballing philosophies and went beyond the resentment Revie felt at being made surplus to requirements. Deep down, he just didn't like the man.

So, shortly after the start of the 1958–59 season, Revie had asked to be placed on the transfer list. The team had made a dreadful start in the first month and soon found themselves languishing at the foot of the table. As he returned home that Tuesday evening to talk things over with Elsie, Revie was thinking, from a footballing point of view, wouldn't Middlesbrough be a much better bet?

He ran through the pluses and minuses. Yes, Boro had a creaky defence, with a relatively untried goalkeeper in Peter Taylor and a group of defenders who may have had experience but lacked reliability. At least Sunderland had a gifted young centre-half in Charlie Hurley, who promised to be the bedrock of their defence for many years to come.

No, it was the prospect of linking up with Middlesbrough's exciting young forward line that was making Revie think long and hard about a move. Bob Dennison – a decent man of equitable temperament, as far as he could make out, far removed from the forceful and volatile Alan Brown – had emphasised that he wanted Revie to be the old head that would guide his gifted young forwards towards maturity. Dennison had assured him that he would be accommodated in the deep-lying role in which he revelled and which best suited his playing style.

So who would be the recipient of his long, sweeping passes from the middle of the field? On the right wing, 21-year-old Billy Day had already shown he possessed a nerveless temperament, excellent close control, speed and accuracy with his crosses. On the left, Revie was aware of the precocious talent of Leeds-born Eddie Holliday, still only 19 but in many people's eyes destined for international honours.

In the middle, Alan Peacock's height, strength and bravery were making him an increasing handful for defenders. Not yet 21, what Revie liked about him – from the little he'd seen and from what others had told him – was Peacock's unselfishness, his willingness to provide opportunities for better-placed colleagues, his vision in and around the 18-yard box.

Then there was Brian Clough. At the beginning of the season, the 23-year-old centre-forward had been made captain of Middlesbrough, an appointment that had raised many eyebrows, not just because of his relative youth but also because of his aggressive, self-confident – some said arrogant – character.

But in just seven games this season, Clough had scored twelve goals (five of them coming in the opening game against newly promoted Brighton) and led his side to four victories. In the previous two campaigns, he'd hit the back of the net a staggering eighty-two times.

If Revie was to believe that his time at Middlesbrough could be fruitful, he would have to be convinced that he could forge a good working relationship not only with Dennison but also with the young Boro captain. Loud, abrasive types – as he'd learned to his cost with Alan Brown – clashed with his more introverted, thoughtful personality, upsetting his equilibrium and his game.

Nonetheless, he found the prospect of playing with such a natural goalscorer quite enticing. He could help maintain, and hopefully improve, Clough's ration of goals by setting wingers Day and Holliday free through his penetrating long balls out to the flanks; they in turn would provide the crosses for Clough and Peacock to convert in the penalty box. Equally, he could envisage himself supplying incisive through-balls for Clough to race onto and crash into the net with his characteristically fierce, low drives.

Although he'd never walked out at Ayresome Park in the red and white of Boro, he did have fond memories of his appearances at the ground for Manchester City six years previously. He'd scored one goal with a 'grand shot' – as one writer had quaintly put it – in the 2–2 draw in March 1952 and then, six months later, a couple of opportunist efforts in a pulsating 5–4 defeat before a crowd of more than thirty thousand. A hugely superstitious man, he deemed the Middlesbrough stadium to be one of his 'lucky' arenas.

Those were some of the thoughts that swirled around his head as he made his way home to Cleadon that evening. In 24 hours' time, he would either be lining up with his new teammates at Ayresome Park to face Rotherham, playing on the ground just a few hundred yards from where he had been born and brought up, or he would be taking the field with his Sunderland teammates at Hillsborough for a difficult match against league leaders Sheffield Wednesday.

Revie was aware of one other club that might be interested in his services. Leeds United were not a household name in the game, but the presence in their side of the colossus John Charles had made them a force to be reckoned with in Division One. In the last season, however, Charles had departed to Juventus for £65,000, a record transfer fee for a British player, and the team had slumped from seventh to seventeenth in the table. Revie still felt his football warranted a place in the top league, so he wasn't prepared to dismiss Leeds' interest – at this stage, only tentative – out of hand.

The local press were intensely interested in his decision. Subeditors at the *Northern Echo* had already put their back page to bed; the headline in the morning would read 'Revie's 9am Call May Help Put Boro' Back in Division 1'. 'Mandale', the pseudonymous writer of the piece, declared optimistically: 'If Revie's answer is "yes", he will return to his native town riding on the wave of soccer enthusiasm which is likely to promote the sound of clicking turnstiles for tonight's match with Rotherham.'

Fifteen hours, then, before Revie would pick up the phone to Bob Dennison. Could it possibly be a triumphant homecoming? Or was it a mistake to retrace your steps, in life and in football? His heart said the former, but his head remained to be convinced. He needed stability at this point in his career, and he pondered long and hard about whether that would be possible at Middlesbrough.

In particular, his thoughts turned back to Clough. Could the young captain's ambition and drive provide the spark to reignite his own halting career? Or would Clough's blunt, cocky nature disturb and disrupt his ordered playing style?

As he entered his front door, he was beginning to think he knew what his decision would be. But first he had to talk it over with Elsie.

Chapter 1
'An Infant Hercules'

Pity poor Middlesbrough. Conceived in a hurry in the late 1820s, this unadorned child of the Industrial Revolution has always suffered in comparison with the rest of its North-East family, especially its older, fairer cousins Newcastle and Durham.

Many outside observers peering in on the town in the 1930s – when Brian Clough was born and Don Revie was growing up – too often judged it on its aesthetic, rather than human, value. Writers of both fact and fiction invariably depicted Middlesbrough either as some kind of smoking, clanging urban hell or – if in slightly more understanding vein – as merely a desperate, somewhat coarse place overwhelmed by the misery of the Depression.

To catch the prevailing view, look no further than J.B. Priestley and George Orwell. Contrasting figures of the literary left, both were then carving out reputations as perceptive chroniclers of the country's social condition.

Priestley passed through Middlesbrough in 1933 for *English Journey*, his state-of-the-nation book following a pilgrimage through town and countryside, and you might perhaps have expected a fellow Yorkshireman to offer the place some sympathy. Not a bit of it. Pronouncing it to be a 'vast, dingy conjuring trick', he went on to ram the verbal boot home:

> It is a dismal town, even with beer and football. Not long ago I wrote an article in which I attacked a certain industrial town, which I did not name, for its miserable appearance and lack of civilised gaiety. The actual town I was describing was not Middlesbrough, was not even in the same part of the country. But at once an official of that town angrily protested in the

local paper against my writing in such a fashion about Middlesbrough. I did not tell him that I had not had Middlesbrough in mind at all. If the cap fits, I thought, let them all wear it.

George Orwell didn't visit the town as he made his way up north to Lancashire in 1936 to write *The Road to Wigan Pier*, his unromantic depiction of working-class life. But in Orwell's novel *Keep the Aspidistra Flying*, Philip Ravelston, the well-off Marxist publisher, muses about the plight of Middlesbrough and imagines that 'the unemployed huddle in frowzy beds, bread and marg and milkless tea in their bellies'.

To be fair to Orwell, Ravelston's social conscience is clearly troubled by his vision. 'What of the real poor?' he asks. 'What of the unemployed in Middlesbrough, seven in a room on twenty-five bob a week? When there are people living like that, how dare one walk the world with pound notes and cheque-books in one's pocket?'

Orwell and Priestley no doubt embellished these views of the town, for their very different ends; to leave a lasting impact on the page, it is arguably far more profitable to caricature than to analyse soberly. The reality of living and growing up in Middlesbrough in the 1930s was somewhat different – and a little brighter – than their stark assessments. But what was undoubtedly true was that in those days the range of career options open to young working-class men like Revie and Clough were severely limited.

There used to be a saying in the North-East, almost certainly invented around then, that if you whistled down a pit, up would pop a fast bowler. In the footballing world, substitute bowler for centre-half or centre-forward and the same aphorism would apply. The area teemed with talented young boys, eager to embrace their sporting heritage and escape a life of manual labour that was the norm for many.

Nowhere was that more the case than Middlesbrough, where, after the First World War, a succession of gifted working-class footballers emerged to represent both club and country. George Camsell, a powerful and prolific centre-forward, was one, George Hardwick, 'Gentleman George', stylish left-back and captain of England, another, and the incomparable inside-forward Wilf Mannion, the 'Golden Boy' of Teesside, was the cream of the crop.

Mannion is the only Middlesbrough player to have been inducted into English football's exclusive Hall of Fame. But there are two Middlesbrough men who have made it there as managers, and if you'd picked up a loudhailer around the area of the Ayresome Park stadium in the 1930s and 1940s and summoned them both, they might just have come running.

Later on in their careers, the gulf between Don Revie and Brian Clough would seem as wide as the River Tees. But when they were growing up in Middlesbrough, the geographical distance between them was small; indeed, they were just a brisk walk from each other's front door. If you make the journey east to west across town from Clough's birthplace at 11 Valley Road, in Grove Hill, to Revie's home at 20 Bell Street, in the Ayresome area, it'll take you about 15 minutes.

Of course, neither boy made that exact walk; now if they had done, that would be a story to beat all stories. They were of a different generation: Revie was born on 10 July 1927, and Clough followed just under eight years later on 21 March 1935. But to step out on that route is not just to sense the physical closeness of young Don and young Brian as they grew up in Middlesbrough but also to appreciate how their shared environment shaped them. It's also as good a way as any to get a feel for the history of this remarkable town.

* * *

The journey begins at No. 11 Valley Road. A green plaque on the wall outside the 1920s semi-detached council house reassures you that you've come to the right place. It reads: 'International Footballer and Football Manager Brian Clough was born here on 21st March 1935. He was associated with Middlesbrough Football Club at Ayresome Park from 1951 to 1961.'

The Grove Hill estate, of which Valley Road was part, was built in an area that, a century earlier, would have been countryside. Most of the Victorian gentry who lived in or near Middlesbrough had their residences here. Valley Road is on the site of the original Marton Grove Farm, which comprised a large farmhouse and a clutch of other dwellings.

Rewind another hundred years or so to 1728, and two miles south of Clough's home lies the birthplace of Captain Cook, explorer, navigator, cartographer. He was born in the village of Marton, well before Middlesbrough even existed – but it hasn't stopped the locals claiming him as the town's most famous son because of his geographic proximity.

But back to the 1930s, and those three-bedroomed council houses on tree-lined Valley Road would have had a fresh, optimistic feel for the Cloughs and other families, an escape from the privations of the back-to-back terraces that dominated vast swathes of Middlesbrough.

If you step out of the front gate of No. 11 and turn right down the street, you're just 150 yards away from Clairville Common. Back in the 1940s, the Clough brothers would be out there playing football most nights of the week, providing the weather was fine. In those days, there were two cinder football pitches on which some of the leading local sides used to train. Amongst those teams were South Park Rovers, a nursery club for Doncaster Rovers, and Middlesbrough Swifts, who similarly supplied talent for Leicester City.

Young Brian Clough would practise balancing a ball on his feet in the front garden of 11 Valley Road. But when he stepped out to watch football on the common, he would have appreciated the skills of the teenage boys holding their own with the older players in the Rovers and Swifts sessions. Is it too much of a flight of fancy to imagine that, at the age of seven, he cast an admiring glance towards a lean fourteen-year-old playing on the wing for the Swifts, showing an early awareness of how to find space on a crowded pitch and exhibiting good passing skills?

It's not an utterly improbable thought. Certainly Don Revie was playing quite often for the Swifts on Clairville Common in those wartime days, and the impressionable young Clough would have picked up some footballing ideas from the likes of him and a multitude of other talented young players.

But the journey has barely begun. Continue down Valley Road, and then, at the roundabout, turn left into Park Road South. You'll quickly pass the fire station, formerly a site for houses back in the 1950s; Clough's Middlesbrough and England teammate Eddie Holliday, the flying winger, used to live there, just round the corner from his colleague in the forward line.

The feeling of relative affluence on Park Road South, where the trim 1930s detached homes all have sizeable front gardens, derives from its position opposite one of the glories of Middlesbrough: Albert Park.

Strictly speaking, if you took the quickest route to Don Revie's home, you would continue in a straight line down Park Road South. But it's far more pleasurable to cross the road, step away from any traffic and breathe in the fresh air of 70 acres of open, green space.

The man who finished runner-up in a council poll of influential Middlesbrough figures (Captain Cook was first, Clough fourth and Revie nineteenth) was responsible for the creation of this Victorian splendour. Henry Bolckow, ironmaster, was one of the great figures of the Industrial Revolution, the town's first mayor and also its first MP. He recognised that the area needed a 'green lung' to ease the plight of the burgeoning industrial population he had substantially helped to create with his discovery of iron ore in the nearby Cleveland Hills.

Bolckow was a man with a strong sense of civic duty. His 'People's Park' was duly opened on 11 August 1868 by 19-year-old Prince Arthur, the third son and seventh of the nine children of Queen Victoria and Prince Albert, and it was named after his late father. In his speech on opening the park, the young prince said Bolckow had 'stood by the side of the iron cradle in which Middlesbrough was rocked, and had watched over the child with care as it grew'.

Brian Clough would have entered Albert Park from Park Vale Road, running next to Clairville Common, over a little wooden bridge running over Marton West Beck, and then headed straight up the bank towards the bandstand, with a children's play area and boathouse on his right. Another right turn and he would pass the roller-skating rink, which dates back to the 1940s, and from there, he'd reach the central tree-lined thoroughfare that traverses the middle of the park.

Soon you'll observe a bust of Henry Bolckow himself, followed by a memorial to those who lost their lives in the Boer War, before you encounter a seven-foot bronze statue of a very familiar figure.

The sculpture of Clough, which cost £65,000 to make, was unveiled on 16 May 2007. It depicts the young footballer, in his mid-20s, on the way to training at Ayresome Park, boots slung over his left shoulder, face looking intently ahead with the hint of a smile, clearly a spring in his step, with right heel off the ground and left foot in the air.

Clough spent many hours in the park as a boy with his brothers and sisters, but tennis had to be his sport here, as kicking a football around with any serious intent was forbidden. Later, as a young professional footballer, it was the perfect early-morning walk to the stadium just a few minutes away.

You pass the Victorian clock and cannon, then the sundial (which, on a sunny day, tells the time in Middlesbrough, Melbourne and New York), and you eventually reach the front gates of the park. Pass the cenotaph and the Dorman Museum, cross Linthorpe Road, and you're on Ayresome Street and heading for the stadium, just as Clough would have done in the 1950s.

But there's one more significant landmark before you walk a few hundred yards down Ayresome Street, with its tightly packed terrace houses, to the football ground. Rea's Café, on the corner – now the site of a pawnbroker and jeweller – was a vibrant social centre back in the 1950s, a popular meeting place for young men and women because of the quality of its coffee and ice cream. Especially popular, too, for courting couples, because of the seclusion afforded by the separate booths along the length and breadth of the establishment.

It was to here that Middlesbrough footballers naturally gravitated after training, and it was in this place that Brian Clough met his future wife, Barbara, the introduction having been made by Clough's more gregarious colleague, Italian-born goalkeeper Rolando Ugolini.

Continue down Ayresome Street, turn left into Warwick Street, and you'll reach the entrance to a relatively new 60-home Wimpey development – on the site of the famous old football stadium.

Ayresome Park, scene of a thousand great footballing memories from the aforementioned Camsell, Hardwick, Mannion, Clough and the more modern-day heroes such as Maddren and Juninho, was demolished in 1995 when Middlesbrough Football Club decided to move to the glamorous, new Riverside Stadium down by the docks. Fans bemoaned the passing of the great ground, but those inner-city stadiums, set amongst packed, narrow streets, had become an anachronism and allowed no room for expansion.

Nonetheless, as your journey takes you through the estate, along The Turnstile, into The Midfield and finally into The Holgate (named after Middlesbrough's kop end), you wonder whether there's nothing more to remember the old ground by than a clutch of street names. But if you advance slowly and keep a sharp eye about you, you'll spy a number of references to Ayresome Park; it's like an old-fashioned treasure hunt.

First, there's a pair of cast-iron football boots situated at the exact place where the centre spot was marked out each Saturday. Further on, a bronze football marks the old penalty spot, while the nearby goalposts are commemorated by a sculpture of a child's coat slung over a railing. There's little by way of actual preservation, but the old back wall of the Holgate End – together with the section where the pie stall was located – has been kept for posterity.

But the jewel in the crown of this open-air 'museum' is to be found just outside the front door of one of the houses in The Holgate. There, embedded in the lawn, is a curious little sculpture fashioned by South African-born artist Neville Gabie. It's a set of cast-iron stud marks in the shape of the boot of North Korean footballer Pak Doo Ik, and it marks the spot of one of Ayresome Park's most romantic moments.

It happened at 8.10 p.m. on 19 July 1966, when Pak Doo Ik, for one fleeting moment, became the most famous footballer in the world when he drove the ball home from 15 yards, the only goal of the game, to knock haughty Italy out of the World Cup and send the North Koreans – amazingly – into the quarter-finals. Nineteen thousand were there on that remarkable night, but many thousands more have claimed to have been present as the years go by, and the legendary moment remains forever etched on the collective memory of the town. It's also still lodged very firmly in the minds of the North Koreans, who have been back to visit and have made the spot one of their National Heritage sites.

Barely have you left Mr Wimpey than you get to meet Mr Barratt. The old Middlesbrough General Hospital, at the end of Ayresome Street with the main entrance on Ayresome Green Lane, was a massive building stretching over many acres and had a proud history of tending to the town's sick. Seven years ago it was pulled down and a spanking new Barratt development put up in its place, catering for first-time buyers and young families.

It will perhaps, by now, come as no surprise to learn the names of the streets on this estate: Camsell Court, Maddren Way and Clough Close – three generations of Middlesbrough footballers. The town and the game seem inextricably linked.

You're nearing the end of the journey, as the Barratt development is just a couple of minutes from the Revie home. At the end of Ayresome Street, you'll quickly cross a pedestrian bridge over the busy Newport Street, a feeder road for the A66 Middlesbrough bypass, before rejoining Ayresome Green Lane. You'll see Archibald Primary School on your left, where the young Revie was a pupil, and then it's just a few yards before you turn right into Bell Street.

Although hemmed in by those two busy roads at the back and front, Bell Street these days has the appearance of being a tranquil little cul-de-sac. Unlike Clough's house in Valley Road, there's no plaque on the wall at No. 20; indeed, it's the one house on the street that seems to have lost its number plate.

In Revie's day, the little two-up, two-down council houses, built just before the First World War, would have had a uniform look; now, as private dwellings, they have different-coloured front doors, and the odd-numbered homes on the other side of the road have new porches and other embellishments at the front.

But it's easy to imagine the scene in the 1930s, because the alleyway at the back of the houses remains pretty much the same as it was then, a perfect venue for a cricket wicket or a football pitch for the children in the street.

So, from Clough to Revie, from the bright new homes of the 1930s back to the cramped terraced houses of the 1920s – which is where our story really begins.

* * *

Donald Revie was born at 20 Bell Street, in the Middlesbrough West subdistrict, on Sunday, 10 July 1927, the son of Donald and Margaret Emily (formerly Haston), and a brother for twin sisters Jean and Joyce, who were six years old. His father listed his occupation as 'joiner (journeyman)'.

The new addition to the family entered the world on a turbulent day – at least in meteorological terms. Over in Europe, the *Times'* special correspondent in Berggiesshübel, Germany, reported at least 110 deaths and many villages destroyed after severe storms and flooding on the border with Czechoslovakia. 'The catastrophe is the worst of its kind that the country can remember,' he wrote.

Back home, in Middlesbrough, the town had experienced a heatwave. A correspondent for the *Evening Gazette* painted a vivid picture of 'Night Life in the Slums' in the Marsh Road district, not far from the Revie home.

> In certain parts of Middlesbrough, people cannot sleep on hot nights. Driven from their small, overcrowded and badly ventilated houses by the stifling heat, men, women and children may be seen sitting on the doorsteps, or wandering aimlessly around the streets.
>
> Virtually every doorstep and window sill was occupied. Women wrapped in shawls were gossiping; half-clad children were crying; gangs of young men lounged around the street corners.
>
> In some of the four-roomed houses, two families may be

living. It does not appear to be the custom in this part to open
the window at night-time. A large percentage of the windows
are jammed and refuse to be opened. Ventilation is not good.
Hot fumes, gasses and smoke from the neighbouring works
pollute the atmosphere.

The Revies and other residents of Bell Street didn't live in quite the
poverty experienced by those families described in that report, whose
homes were half a mile north on the route from Linthorpe Road to
Marsh Road near the railway station.

Nonetheless, their two-up, two-down terraced houses made for
basic living – even more cramped if inhabited by a large family, like the
Revies' neighbours, the Rhucrofts, at No. 28, who packed seven children
into the bedrooms upstairs. Many households, too, regarded the front
room downstairs – or the 'parlour' – as fit to be used only for high days
and holidays, thus squeezing most activity into the kitchen and two
bedrooms upstairs.

Mavis Barwick – then Longstaff – lived along the street from the
Revies at No. 40 during the 1930s. 'We didn't have a bathroom – we
brought in the tin bath from the back shed into the kitchen once a
week. We washed in the sink in the kitchen, and of course our meals
were cooked there. We did everything in that room! We had a three-
piece suite and a piano in the front room, which was quite chock-a-
block. But to me our house seemed quite luxurious, far better than
houses further down the town.'

Mavis's father would become trading manager at the Middlesbrough
Co-op and later on, in 1956, mayor of the town. The Revies struggled
more than their near neighbours. Don's father was in work in 1927 as
a qualified and skilled joiner but often unemployed in the Depression
years that followed. Revie himself painted a bleak, forbidding picture
of his early years. In *Soccer's Happy Wanderer*, he recalled: 'Unemployment
and its attendant miseries stalked through Teesside in those years.
There was no money; precious few toys for the children. My father was
among that vast army of unemployed.' And in a television interview in
1974, he said: 'We were a very poor family. My father was out of work
for two years and had to go looking for odd jobs; my mother had to
take the washing in to keep us.'

In a 1975 radio interview, he would reflect more deeply on how his
life had been shaped by this tough upbringing:

Yes, I came from a very poor home, but a very warm home. I think poor homes are warm places. I think that when your mother and father can't afford a pair of football boots for you, they can't afford a new pair of shoes – possibly only once a year – and all your trousers have to be patched and your pullovers have to be darned, and you've got to go to the market on a Saturday night to get the cheap things that are left over at the end of the week in order to live for the next seven days, I think it gives you a bit of strength later on in life.

But I think it also gives you a little bit of insecurity, and I think as you go on in life you always feel that round the corner there's a pitfall.

Don Revie Sr, in order to qualify for dole, would have had to pass a means test. Public Assistance Committees put the worker's finances through a rigorous examination, with officials delving into every detail of a family's income and savings. The *Evening Gazette* was full of bitter letters from Middlesbrough residents complaining about the intrusiveness of the test and the insensitive manner of the officials who carried it out. Unemployed men and their families felt offended and humiliated by the experience.

Middlesbrough was suffering, but there had been times of plenty. This was a town created by the Industrial Revolution, built up by generations of migrants who flocked from all parts of the country to work in the iron, steel and coal (exporting) industries. In 1801, it had just 4 houses and 25 inhabitants; by 1901, the population had soared to 91,000, and by Revie's time it was estimated to have reached 130,000.

Victorians had gazed on this frontier settlement, England's equivalent of the gold-rush towns of Victoria and California in the mid-nineteenth century, with no small wonder and admiration.

In October 1862, W.E. Gladstone, then Chancellor of the Exchequer, paid a visit to Middlesbrough and famously described it thus: 'This remarkable place, the youngest child of England's enterprise . . . It is an infant, gentlemen, but it is an infant Hercules.'

The romantic language didn't end there. Around that time, one writer said Middlesbrough occupied a unique position, not just in this country, but around the world. His description of its role was euphoric, almost overwhelming in its lyricism.

The iron it supplies furnishes railways to Europe; it runs by Neapolitan and Papal dungeons; it startles the bandit in his haunts in Cilicia; it streaks the prairies of America; it stretches over the plains of India; it surprises the Belochees; it pursues the peggunus of Gangotri. It has crept out of the Cleveland Hills, where it has slept since the Roman days, and now, like a strong and invincible serpent, coils itself round the world.

But the heavy industries – steel, shipbuilding, engineering – that were the lifeblood of Middlesbrough were the ones hit hardest when the Wall Street Crash of October 1929 set off a ten-year economic slump that affected all advanced Western countries.

Down on the banks of the Tees, the cranes and the derricks stood idle and the blast furnaces no longer scorched the sky. In the centre of town, the picture was of 'eerily quiet streets and men wearing cloth caps and dirty white silk chokers, lolling impassively at street corners, by lamp-posts, on walls, or waiting hopelessly in a long, winding line outside the Labour Exchange'.

Working-class Middlesbrough was a town – visibly at least – dominated by men. The demographer Ernest George Ravenstein, back in the 1880s, noted that its 'rapid growth, the heterogeneous composition of its population, and the preponderance of the male sex, recall features generally credited only to towns of the American West'.

In those small homes on those 'little brown streets', however, the wife's role was crucial. As Lady Florence Bell, wife of Sir Hugh Bell, Middlesbrough's greatest iron founder, observed in her colourful portrait of the town, 'The husband's steadiness and capacity to earn are not more important than the wife's administration of the earnings.'

When a man became unemployed, he was faced with the problems of a loss of occupation and responsibility, but precisely the opposite difficulty faced his wife. She was called upon to carry out her domestic duties with less money, and in many cases had to find some way of earning money to keep the family.

Margaret Revie had much to do while her husband struggled to find regular work. Helped by her daughters, she would bring in bundles of washing from wealthier families in areas like Acklam and would be paid five shillings a basket to clean them. While she was doing the laundry work, she was keeping No. 20 clean and tidy, and encouraging young Don with his football. Then, on 27 November 1939, aged 50, she died after a struggle with cancer lasting several years.

'She wanted me to enjoy my sport; and when she died, it was the greatest tragedy of my life,' Revie recalled. 'Only a boy who has lost his mother knows what heartache it means.' Football was the way out of his grief:

> My Dad used to leave for work at 7 a.m. My sisters Joyce and Jean went to their employment at 8 a.m. There was no point in me waiting around moodily at home. So from eight o'clock until school opened at 8.45 a.m. I stayed in the school yard, kicking my ball against the school wall. In the dull, grey mornings of winter, flicking that ball against the wall helped to pass the time. I didn't feel so lonely . . . I didn't miss my mother so much.

At home in Bell Street, Revie had no shortage of willing boys – and girls – to help him practise his skills. George Tinsley, at No. 44, provided the first decent football for the youngsters to kick about. Previously, Revie recalled, 'We couldn't afford a ball and, as so many youngsters did in those days, I improvised with a bundle of rags tied up in the shape of a football.'

Kathleen Stevens at No. 36 remembers: 'He was up to mischief, like most boys were, and spent a lot of time kicking a football around at the front of the house. But we used to play plenty of other games; in fact, we were outside all the time, in the alleyway behind the houses, and over at the nearby recreation ground. Marbles, hopscotch – we used to take a can full of water and tie it to the front door of a house. Don would do things like that, too.'

Mavis Longstaff, Kathleen's best friend, remembers Don as 'a nice boy, not one of those noisy, tearaway lads . . . I myself was quite a tomboy in those days, and he used to let me take part in the soccer matches in the alleyway. He was the only one of the boys who let me play – the others weren't so keen! I think it was the only thing he was really interested in.'

Don's home was hardly more than a long goalkick away from Middlesbrough's ground. As he remembered it, 'The roar of the crowd at Ayresome Park can be heard quite plainly in Bell Street. I grew up with that roar.'

In those days, footballers were authentic working-class heroes. They came from the streets where the spectators lived, travelled on the same buses around town, drank in the same pubs. They didn't have the money to finance a flamboyant lifestyle; they may have had a little bit more than the people who paid to watch them, but not enough to set them apart and aloof like modern-day players.

Revie recalled waiting patiently at the end of Bell Street for the likes of Wilf Mannion and Micky Fenton to go by on their way to training, hoping for an autograph and a quick word. When he was six, after much pestering, his father started to take him on the ten-minute walk to the stadium to see his heroes in action.

George Scott was brought up in Middlesbrough at the same time as Don Revie. Later, he would become a writer and editor of a small weekly magazine called *Truth*, which aspired to compete with the likes of *The Spectator*. In his evocative memoir *Time and Place* (written in 1956), he remembered the 'Saturday March' of the huge crowds that attended the matches in the 1930s, between thirty and fifty thousand – a fifth of the total population of the town – men, women and children:

> It was to Ayresome Park that the workless thousands of the Thirties took their anxieties and miseries and lost them in the magnification of the Saturday Match into something more important than the Slump, Hitler, Mussolini, the Spanish War or anything that came under the general heading of Politics.
>
> Some incomprehensible, invincible, malevolent Unknown Power had ordered that their lives should be mean, harsh and wholly unromantic. The romance and adventure which others, some few others, might find in their own work, or in books, in the theatre, or in the pursuit of power, the men on the dole found on the fiercely partisan terraces of Ayresome Park. (Where the women found their outlet God only knows.)

For the young Scott, Ayresome Park was an aggressive arena, where the crowds went to see Middlesbrough win by any methods at all. 'That football team was their champion against the ugly bully world. The battle was to be fought without quarter and without scruples. The important thing above all else was that the battle should be won.' He described how the home fans would jeer at any decision taken against 'The Boro' and keep up their psychological warfare against the opposing side for the entire 90 minutes. Savage sarcasm was even directed towards a Middlesbrough player who had lost his touch.

But the crowd's greatest passion and enmity was reserved for Arsenal, a team of remarkable talents representing wealth and privilege.

> They came from the soft south, from London, from the city of government where, it was imagined, all social evil was plotted and directed against places like Teesside. The players themselves enjoyed comforts and amenities such as no other club could afford to provide. They carried themselves with pride and played with a stylistic beauty. They were fine footballers and had a long history of victory.
>
> All these things combined to inflame the hatred of the Middlesbrough crowd and once I saw hundreds of men climb over the barriers, thrust past the police and pour on to the field intending to do injury to the Arsenal team. This was the final explosion of hatred which more often restricted itself to words or at most the throwing of orange peel, cigarette packets or an occasional bottle.
>
> I still remember this spectacle with feelings of fear and horror. This hatred of Arsenal persists, I believe, even now when full employment and large-scale industrial development have changed Teesside from a wasted and dejected place into one of common prosperity.

Such impressions would have been far from the mind of the young Revie. He would return from the match with images in his mind only of George Camsell, Middlesbrough's intimidating centre-forward, who combined physical presence with brilliant opportunism and quick acceleration. In the year Revie first went to watch him, he scored 24 goals in 38 games in Division One. 'I imagined myself in the role of Camsell. I would watch the game with glistening eyes, then come home and play the match all over by myself in the back street, which measured just ten feet across.'

At his school just round the corner, the slight, pale-looking boy was starting to compete on the football field with those several years older than him. At just nine, he was picked for the Archibald School team at outside-right. Later, he would play at inside-left and centre-forward, finishing up as captain of the team.

Hours of practice flicking a ball against the back wall and dribbling it round the iron gratings were beginning to pay dividends. His childhood had been even more difficult than that of most working-class boys of his generation, but his footballing skill had now given him a dream of a brighter future.

* * *

Brian Howard Clough, the sixth child of Joseph and Sarah, known as Sally (formerly Hunter), was born at 11 Valley Road on 21 March 1935, in the Middlesbrough East subdistrict. Joe listed his occupation as 'sugar boiler'. If the Revie family had endured the worst of the Depression, there was no escaping it for the Cloughs either.

Unemployment was slowing, but nationally it was still in the region of 2.3 million. There was some cause for optimism in the South, where employment levels were starting to rise as low interest rates spurred on a house-building boom, which in turn encouraged a recovery in domestic industry.

In the North, however, especially in Middlesbrough, the land of heavy industry, it was still proving to be a long, slow climb out of the abyss. As young Clough was settling into life in the front bedroom in Valley Road, 250 miles away in the House of Commons a debate about Unemployment and Distressed Areas was taking place.

It was a debate of a quality very rarely seen in Parliament today. The importance of the subject prompted contributions from the likes of Prime Minister Stanley Baldwin, deputy leader of the Labour Party Arthur Greenwood and Stafford Cripps, MP for Bristol East and later Chancellor of the Exchequer.

Also on their feet were two local MPs, who reminded the house – and the nation – that much still needed to be done to alleviate the suffering of the people of Middlesbrough and its neighbours.

Harold Macmillan, Conservative MP for Stockton-on-Tees, who advocated a level of economic planning and state help far beyond what his party colleagues would countenance, acknowledged that the country had, albeit haltingly, begun to turn the corner. But in characteristically colourful language, he issued this warning about neglecting the plight of his constituents:

> All the time there is spreading the uneasy feeling that things might be far better still and we might raise our standards much higher. And at the same time over some parts of the country –

like the part I represent, where even in the last month we have had not a decrease but an increase in unemployment – there stalks this frightful shadow of long-continued unemployment, and moral and material decay spreads over the whole community.

More and more people, whether employed or unemployed, are feeling that the standards of living are lower than they should be. They say: 'Why should we tighten our belts in a world of plenty? In a beleaguered city, yes; we share and share alike; but in an open city to starve after the relieving armies have marched in with bands playing and colours flying is not common sense.'

Equally forthright, if not so flamboyant in tone, was Frank Kingsley Griffith, Liberal MP for Middlesbrough West. He suggested there were still 600,000 who had now been out of work for more than six months.

That is a terrible figure and although I freely admit that in Middlesbrough employment is a great deal better than it was and that there has been a substantial improvement, there is still, after the years of suffering through which the locality has passed, a terrible proportion of people, including people whose cases are known to me personally, who have been out of work not for six months but for years. I cannot help feeling that if this problem is merely left to natural development, no ordinary course of revival of trade is going to bring these people back into active work.

If events at home weren't grim enough, the first drumbeats of war could be heard faintly in the distance. On the day Clough was born, the *Daily Mirror*'s front page lead story proclaimed 'Growing Tension Over Europe', with the news that the French were investing £23 million in new air fighters to counter Hitler's recent conscription of half a million soldiers.

In Valley Road, Joe Clough had plenty on his plate with five children (his firstborn, Elizabeth, had died of septicaemia aged four) – and there were to be three additions to the family in coming years – to be paying too much attention to newspaper headlines and political debates. He himself had felt the impact of war. As a private in the King's Own

Yorkshire Light Infantry in the First World War, he was shot in the ankle and suffered deafness because of the explosions and heavy gunfire he experienced at close quarters. He was discharged because of the wounds and left with a permanent limp.

Like many men on Teesside, Joe had been able to find work with ICI at Billingham. If the old industries continued to suffer, the newer, chemical industry was going from strength to strength. In 1934, Billingham became a centre for plastics manufacturing; a few years later, there would be renewed demand for the production of its synthetic ammonia, for explosives.

Eventually, though, Joe settled into work at Garnett's sweet factory, near Ayresome Park stadium, first as a sugar boiler, later as foreman. He was a keen football fan, and he would make sure that the likes of Wilf Mannion and George Hardwick didn't go short of treats.

Joe was a quiet, placid man at home but also a strict enforcer of discipline when he needed to be. 'You never answered back at home,' Brian's brother Joe junior recalled. 'Our mam had a saying "not on the head", but we could be hit anywhere else. Dad certainly did, and he had big bony hands, so his whack was pretty hard and would leave a mark.'

However, the reality was that the Clough household – in common with very many large, working-class families in the north of England – was essentially matriarchal. It was his mother, Sally – or Sal, as she was known – who really ran day-to-day affairs, as well as moulding the characters of her children. Clough adored her.

> She turned that little house into a palace. The front step was scrubbed regularly. I remember how she was so proud of her net curtains and the fact that she managed to keep the same stair carpet for thirty years.
>
> Sunday was the only day of the week we were allowed into what we called 'the other room' – that's where the piano was kept and that was the day the whole family gathered round while Mam played and we sang along, songs like 'Come on to my house – I'm going to give you everything'. And she did.

Thrift, cleanliness, politeness, discipline and loyalty: these were the values and virtues Joe and Sally instilled in their children. Clough had no doubt about their effect on him:

> Anything I have achieved in life has been rooted in my upbringing. Some might have thought No. 11 Valley Road, the end of the terrace, was just another council house, but to me it was heaven. Growing up in a hard-working, often hard-up home I was as happy as a pig in the proverbial.

Such was the reverence Clough accorded his mother that years later, in the front room of his home in Quarndon, Derbyshire, visitors would see her mangle, from those Valley Road days, occupying a prominent place.

The Cloughs were growing up in a world that was changing, and doing so despite the privations brought on by the Depression. In popular mythology, however, '30s Britain has become the Jarrow March, *Love on the Dole*, soup kitchens – a period of unrelenting grimness, the country crippled by rising unemployment and endemic banking failures. A time of doubt, anxiety and fear.

George Orwell wrote: 'What a decade! A riot of appalling folly that suddenly becomes a nightmare, a scenic railway ending in a torture chamber.' W.H. Auden believed the 1930s were a 'low dishonest decade' and Britain was 'a country where nobody was well'.

The historian Richard Overy entitled his book on the period between the two wars *The Morbid Age*, when the idea abroad was that society its very self was in decline, possibly even terminal. He writes:

> Dismay was a mainstream concern, specific to neither class nor region, and even if 'civilisation in crisis' became a populist cliché of the inter-war years, the different ways in which it was explained derived from the serious scientific, medical, economic and cultural descriptions of the present, and were not simply rhetoric . . . the prospect of imminent crisis, a new Dark Age, became a habitual way of looking at the world.

But for middle-class families, and even for optimistic working-class families with a sense of spirit and togetherness like the Cloughs, the '30s were, slowly but surely, becoming a time of opportunity, especially in leisure activities. There was a branch of Woolworths emerging in every town, the cinema (with stars like Charlie Chaplin and Gracie Fields) was now an alternative to the pub, especially for women, dance halls proliferated, greyhound racing was flourishing, lidos were opening and cars were no longer the exclusive domain of the very rich.

Many families were starting to venture out and take paid holidays, albeit on a modest scale. For the Cloughs, it was a visit to the favoured venue then – and now – for many working-class families.

> How on earth Mam and Dad managed to get enough money together to take us all for a fortnight's holiday to Blackpool I'll never know – a rigid regime, I suppose, with careful housekeeping, stretching the resources to the absolute . . . [but] what joy and adventure the youngsters of today are missing as they sit indoors mucking about with computer games and video!

If you lived on the Grove Hill estate in the 1930s and 1940s, you were on the outskirts of Middlesbrough and you could think and feel that you were actually out in the countryside. For those families on Valley Road, the freshness of their surroundings, away from the crowded streets of two-up, two-down terraced houses to the north and west, would have given them a more positive view on life.

Some of Clough's fondest memories were of the garden around the side of 11 Valley Road, where his father grew his rhubarb and sprouts, of finding birds' eggs in the fields nearby, of climbing trees for conkers. These are the recollections of a happy, varied childhood, even if it was in a time of austerity.

Football and cricket quickly moved to the centre of his life – in fact, cricket was the young Clough's first love.

> I would genuinely have swapped the dream of a winning goal at Wembley for a century against the Australians at Lord's. I wanted to be Len Hutton. I spent long, idyllic summers believing I could be just like him. Hutton was, of course, a Yorkshireman, and since I was Yorkshire through and through, he was my boyhood hero.

The question of Middlesbrough's identity never arose in Clough and Revie's day. For them, the town was clearly placed in Yorkshire, land of the Three Ridings and the City of York, the largest of all the historic counties, with the boundary line with Durham clearly marked at its northern edge by the River Tees.

Doubts only began to creep in during the 1960s and 1970s, at a time of local government change. First, in 1968, Middlesbrough, Redcar,

Thornaby, Stockton and other rural areas were brought under one banner: Teesside County Borough Council. It led some enthusiasts for change to claim that 'Teesside' would be the great new city of the area.

Then, six years later, just as Teesside was establishing a foothold, it was abolished under the new Local Government Act. In its place emerged Cleveland County Council, covering a wider area than its predecessor, including the town of Hartlepool and other parts of East Cleveland.

Today, for residents of Middlesbrough, the question of the town's identity is largely a generational matter. Teesside has certainly established itself as a clear reference point for the younger; Cleveland remains on the final line of most people's addresses. But for all those from the 1930s generation – and for very many more – their home is still situated in Yorkshire.

Back then, young Clough was starting to display enthusiasm – and a precocious ability – for football. Even when he was a toddler, on the family visits to Stewart Park on a Sunday, strollers would be entertained by the sight of a two-year-old kicking and heading a football with gusto and a certain youthful expertise.

Joe junior recalled that all the brothers, himself, Desmond and Bill, received a pair of boots for their Christmas boxes, and a proper 'casey' (leather) football between them – bought 'on the drip' from Carey's credit agency in town. They would then head the short distance up the road to Clairville Common, where there were two football pitches, made of cinder, where they could sneak on and play if the older boys and men weren't around. They'd be out most nights if the weather was fine.

Young Brian would go and watch. He'd get the chance to kick around with his brothers when they found the rough common at the top of the field unoccupied; then they'd flatten it out, put down coats for a goal, and have just enough space for an impromptu game. Otherwise, at that very early age, he'd practise in the back garden at Valley Road with a tennis ball at his feet.

Visits to Ayresome Park for the Clough family were few and far between in the late '30s and early '40s. 'We just couldn't afford to go regularly,' said Joe. 'It was a real treat to be able to go and watch a game and have a seat in the Boys' Stand.'

Young Brian may not have been able to go to Ayresome Park every Saturday, but, inspired by his father, he soon had a hero to rival Len

Hutton. Young Don Revie banged his football against the back wall at Bell Street at night pretending to be George Camsell; but young Brian juggled his ball in the front garden at Valley Road, in the manner, he hoped, of the next generation's champion: Wilf Mannion.

* * *

It's interesting to reflect on those choices of hero, because in many ways, Clough's style of play would become more like Camsell's, while Revie played, at least for a good part of his career, in the inside-forward position favoured by Mannion.

Their playing days overlapped for three seasons before the outbreak of the Second World War, Camsell, the old master, in the twilight of his career (he was 37 when war broke out), Mannion, the young pretender, just beginning to make his mark.

Middlesbrough were then a side going places. Each year, they were edging closer to the Division One title: seventh in 1936–37 (the year Mannion made his debut), fifth in 1937–38 and then fourth in 1938–39, the last full season before the war.

In a wondrous four-game spell between 9 March and 10 April 1939, Boro supporters saw the two men propel their side to within touching distance of the title. First, on a Wednesday night at Ayresome Park, Portsmouth were dispatched 8–1, with Mannion grabbing a hat-trick of goals and Camsell two. Then, three days later, the two men scored a goal apiece as the mighty Arsenal were defeated 2–1 at Highbury.

Back at Middlesbrough a week later and two Camsell goals were instrumental in defeating Brentford 3–1. Then, finally, on the following Wednesday, Mannion and Camsell were on the scoresheet again as Boro beat Leicester City 3–2 to go third in the table.

Camsell, born in a Durham mining village, went down the pit at the age of 13 and only took up football when he was spotted taking part in a kickabout while a strike was taking place. George Scott captured the essence of the man perfectly:

> He was built like a bull. Compact of power, bustling, belligerent, predatory. It is not too fanciful to feel that vicariously his effectively militant behaviour compensated the workless in the crowd for their helplessness to find and fight that invisible enemy who had downed them.
>
> His animosity was of an impersonal, single-minded kind; his

ambition, his purpose in life, was to get the ball into the enemy net, and any man who got in his way was to be disposed of with as little thought for feelings as a man will spare for the fly which disturbs the pleasure of his food.

It's easy to see the qualities of startling acceleration and brilliant opportunism that he possessed in the young fellow centre-forward Brian Clough 20 years later.

Wilf Mannion, 'The Golden Boy', who was and still is *the* footballer on Teesside, is fondly remembered today by a statue outside the Ayresome Park gates at the entrance to the Riverside Stadium. An inside-forward – as Revie was, essentially, before he created the role of deep-lying centre-forward for himself – he possessed consummate passing ability, a lethal shot and, above all, masterful dribbling skills. He was the showman, the artist with paintbrush in hand, while Camsell was the workman hammering away relentlessly with his tools.

Both Clough and Revie would later wax lyrical in their memories of Mannion. 'There were times when I got changed in the same dressing-room as Wilf and I couldn't help but stare at him in his training kit in the mornings,' wrote Clough, on meeting him in the early 1950s.

He was skinnier than I was yet there was no more meat on me than a ninepenny rabbit. He was smaller than me – apparently he was only five feet five – but to see him out there on the football field in training, and particularly in a match, I felt as if I was watching somebody who lived on the moon. He seemed that delicate and yet managed to dominate the surroundings totally.

Revie was asked to contribute a piece in the *Daily Mail* in 1974, when he was England manager; Mannion had been discovered working as a labourer and teaboy at ICI's Wilton chemical complex – a sad fate for one of England's footballing legends.

Mannion, it now appeared, was Revie's number-one hero, surpassing Camsell. 'Under the gas lamps I'd dream I was Wilf Mannion. I would dribble round dustbins, lampposts and anything else but I was always Mannion, never anyone else.'

But Revie's description of Mannion at work on the pitch could hardly be bettered:

When he approached people with the ball to take them on, he used to remind me of a ballet dancer. He was so neat and tidy in everything he did. That was his outstanding quality, really, his neatness. He would go at somebody at full pace and without even touching the ball he would sell so many dummies that the opposition would go in all directions and he'd run straight on with the ball.

* * *

I went in further search of the inspirational Mannion, the man who offered Revie and Clough – and generations of other talented young working-class footballers in Middlesbrough – a way out of lives that were seemingly cast in stone.

Coming out of leafy Eston, where my father and grandfather lived, I turned left onto Normanby Road and headed towards South Bank, where Mannion was born and brought up. Visually, it's an unlovely place, although the 7,000 or so residents might wish to disagree. They still rejoice in the area's nickname, Slaggy Island, after the slag heaps that were the waste product of the iron and steel furnaces that used to dominate the area in Mannion's time.

South Bank was built with just one purpose in mind: to house the workers who would serve the shipyards and steel plants on the banks of the Tees. Laid down in the heart of an industrial sprawl, it comprises row upon row of terraced homes, interrupted only by the odd corner shop and pub. It has a uniformity that appears deadening and depressing to the outsider, although, undoubtedly, a strong sense of community has been built up here, a resilience forged in hard times.

Wilf was born in Napier Street. Next door is Hardwick Road, one of four streets in Middlesbrough named after Mannion's club and international colleague George Hardwick; yet more evidence, if evidence was needed, of the reverence in which the town holds its footballers.

I stopped on the other side of the Normanby Road, at the Golden Boy Green Community Centre, named after the great man. The gate to the building and field has his name engraved on it at the top in thin, old-fashioned lettering, and over the railing is draped a cast-iron football shirt with the number 10 etched into it, together with a pair of boots.

A fitting tribute, I thought, and a permanent reminder and inspiration to generations of young sportsmen. Until, that is, I entered the site and discovered that the community centre – a long, warehouse-like building – is boarded up, littered with graffiti on the outside.

Young Jordan, 13, was the only person on the site, riding his bike up and down a skateboard ramp, which is next to a playground with a basketball court. I asked him what he knew about Wilf Mannion. 'Just that he was an old footballer,' he replied. Does he go to the Riverside to watch the Boro? 'No, not really. I'll watch it on TV if it's on.'

He was more interested in finding out if the centre would be reopened. Two local boys ransacked and burned down the building in February 2009. It was a crippling blow to the South Bank community, as the centre had provided advice, practical support and recreation for many people in the area – young and old – over nearly a decade.

I'm not sure there's any startling lesson to be drawn from the arson at the Golden Boy Centre, no easy metaphor for our time. Perhaps just a thought that at the time of Great Depression in the 1930s (as opposed to the Great Recession in 2009), young boys from hard-up families would be kicking a football around in the alleyways outside their homes at 1 a.m., rather than breaking and entering.

Better to return to the excitement and hope of young boys in the 1930s and 1940s. Mannion, Camsell, Hardwick: they were gods of football in Middlesbrough then, and Revie and Clough had embarked on the road they hoped would lead them to the pantheon.

Chapter 2
'This Boy Can Play'

The Archibald School logbook recorded the grim turn of events in a matter-of-fact fashion. '8 September to Dec 11th 1939 – school closed owing to the war' was the entry in the long, spidery writing of one of the teachers.

One of the preoccupations of the staff as they prepared for the looming conflict was to decide which pupils to evacuate – and to where. Discussions on the matter began with parents in July, and by the time war was declared on Germany on 3 September it had been agreed that 48 (out of around 250) should leave Middlesbrough and go to live in homes in the relatively peaceful and secure suburb of York called Clifton Without.

For those children – like Don Revie – who remained, most of the normal rhythms of school life were over. In their place came new disciplines, for example the weekly 'respirator' (gas mask) drills. As the air-raid warnings sounded ever more frequently, the logbook records numerous visits to the 'trenches' (shelters), especially in the summer of 1940. Attendance inevitably declined; on one day, 20 June 1940, after five hours of air raids the previous night, only 41.5 per cent turned up for the morning classes.

The Luftwaffe pilots had many choice targets in their sights when they crossed the Channel and headed towards Teesside. It was an area of major commercial and industrial importance; iron and steel were being produced at Gjers, Mills & Co. and Dorman Long to forge the materials of war, the Furness shipbuilding yards at Haverton Hill built frigates and landing craft for the Royal Navy, and the chemical works at ICI Billingham and a myriad of other engineering plants were also aiding the war effort.

No wonder, then, that Middlesbrough had the distinction of being the first major British town and industrial centre to be bombed in the war, early in the morning – 1.41 a.m., to be precise – on Saturday, 25 May 1940. The Cargo Fleet Ironworks at South Bank and the Dorman Long steel plant at Grangetown took the punishment, but fortunately no lives were lost.

After that, the wailing of sirens and the quick dash to those air-raid shelters became nightly rituals for the likes of the Revie and Clough families. The Revies were more in the line of fire, as they were close to Newport Bridge, which became a clear target for the Heinkel planes and had to be strongly protected with guns, searchlights and barrage balloons.

Mavis Longstaff, Don's neighbour in Bell Street, remembers those wartime experiences: 'Our shelter, a concrete pillbox, was in the middle of the street and we shared it with the family next door but one, the Essens. There were nine of us altogether. I had to sit on a little rocking chair with my little brother strapped to me whilst I tried to nurse him. Sometimes you could be going in and out of the shelter all night. If this was the case, you were allowed to go to school a bit later the next day.'

Archibald School, just a few hundred yards from Bell Street, escaped the bombers. But near neighbour St Paul's School, in Newport Road, was not so lucky; during the night of 11 May 1941, it was totally destroyed by German planes. The entry in the logbook the following day, made by headmistress Miss Gertrude Venables, reads tersely, 'No session, school having been razed to the ground by enemy action.' An extraordinary picture of eight-year-old pupil Desmond Taylor sitting and reading an exercise book amidst the ruins features prominently today in Middlesbrough's Dorman Museum.

The heaviest raids on the town took place in 1942, with the event etched most deeply in people's memories being the attack on the railway station on Bank Holiday Monday, 3 August. Eight people died and fifty-six were injured. But despite the roof, platform and trains being badly damaged, freight trains were running out of the station within twenty-four hours and passenger services just four days later.

The *Evening Gazette* made only an oblique reference to this calamitous event on page four the following day; the main headline was actually 'Russian Army Falls Back in N. Caucasus'. Given the importance of the railway station, the last thing the paper wanted to do was to help the enemy by letting them know the raid had been a success.

Misinformation – or no information – was one strategy on the news front; extensive camouflage was another for Middlesbrough's industrial targets. The ICI works at Billingham, which was high on the Nazis' hit list, was deliberately and skilfully shrouded in an almost permanent smokescreen.

But despite the loss of life, despite the damage to homes, schools and shops, there was a sense that it could have been so much worse. George Scott's verdict was surely accurate: 'We became accustomed to the nervous throb-throb of German aero-engines before the rest of the country. But Middlesbrough was fortunate, despite its highly desirable targets, in escaping any but the mildest injuries.'

It could have been catastrophe 40 years later, however, when a dangerous phase of the Cold War saw a resumption of the arms race. The Soviet Union is rumoured to have placed Middlesbrough as its second most important target in the event of a nuclear attack.

* * *

The slight little boy sits on the front row, to the left of his captain, with his arms folded and a somewhat anxious look on his face. His demeanour isn't shared by the older colleagues on either side of him; big, burly skipper Mick Mendum exudes confidence and solidity – a centre-half, surely – while Dennis Bowley smiles in a relaxed fashion. Behind them, in the back row, goalkeeper Ron Thomas grins cheekily at the photographer.

War, and the loss of his mother after a long struggle with cancer, made 1939 an especially troubled year for the young Don Revie. Football continued to be the primary escape from the sadness he felt at home and the bigger worries pervading abroad.

The Archibald Secondary Modern School team in the picture were no championship winners but a respectable side nonetheless; they finished fourth in the Middlesbrough Schools League in 1938–39. In the next few years, they would pick up a few cups, with the slender, worried-looking Revie displaying signs of real promise at both inside-forward and centre-forward, so much so that he was made captain of the side in 1941.

Football, then, continued in Middlesbrough schools, for the boys who hadn't been evacuated to safer coastal and rural towns in North Yorkshire, such as York, Malton, Helmsley, Pickering, Bridlington and Scarborough. On the professional front, the Football League was suspended on the day war was declared. But while meaningful competition finished for the duration of hostilities, there was a determination that the game should survive in some form or other.

A decision was taken to set up regional football leagues such as the North-Eastern Regional League (1939–40) and the Football League North (all seasons 1940–46). The crowds were massively reduced, with many men off to war, averaging only around three to four thousand at Ayresome Park.

It was often a case of players turning out for whichever club was situated nearest their barracks, so George Hardwick was seen in a Chelsea shirt and Middlesbrough's promising forward Micky Fenton played at Bloomfield Road for Blackpool. Conversely, the red and white of Boro was graced by the likes of Matt Busby of Liverpool, who played nineteen times, scoring three goals.

Of Revie's heroes, Mannion appeared 47 times at Ayresome Park until early 1940, when he went off to join the Auxiliary Fire Service. He was then conscripted to the 7th battalion of the Green Howards and saw service in France (as a Dunkirk evacuee), Sicily and the Middle East. Camsell turned out on 32 occasions, keeping up his notable scoring rate with 21 goals.

Donald Revie may have been impressed by his son's footballing ability, but in the straits of wartime, with his wife having just died, he needed his son to be out learning a trade. So in 1941, at the age of 14, young Don left Archibald School to become an apprentice bricklayer. 'I can't pretend that I liked laying bricks as much as I liked laying on passes for my team-mates on a football field, but my father was quite right,' Revie recalled. 'Every boy coming into the game should make sure that he has some qualified occupation to fall back on if he fails at football.'

Years later, he would take pride in the memory of the trade he was rushed into in his youth, and used it as a life lesson, as his son Duncan recalls: 'Dad was proud of his background and would talk about the difficulties to me, saying, "You don't know you're born, son." He would also boast about the fact that he'd been a bricklayer, and encourage me to get out and do some manual work in the summer holidays – in fact, he put me to work on the Elland Road ground. But actually, as we discovered, he was pretty poor at doing anything of a practical nature with his hands, and he would freely admit that back then he was pretty useless at being a bricklayer!'

When he wasn't struggling on the building site, Revie's footballing education continued at whichever club he could find that would offer him a berth. West Middlesbrough was one of them. Ken Mothersill, now aged 87, remembers a persistent young Revie being picked for his first game for that club: 'We usually met on a Friday night to pick the team, and on this particular night I remember the secretary Ron Elliott's wife saying, "I don't know why you don't pick our Donnie, he always follows your team." Don wasn't playing for a side then, but he got a game for West Middlesbrough, and then he and three of us later went on to play for the Boro Swifts.'

While bringing welcome income into the Bell Street household, Revie continued to search all over his district for new, more challenging football experiences. He had heard about one particular junior side that was developing a growing reputation.

Middlesbrough – or Boro – Swifts were a highly regarded local junior club competing in the Teesside Junior League and in cup competitions like the Magnum Bonum and Ellis cups. Its manager was George Carr, who had been a successful professional footballer with Leicester City; the highlight of his playing career was in February 1925 when he scored the goal that enabled Leicester (then in the Second Division) to knock FA Cup holders Newcastle United out of the competition.

Carr ensured that the Boro Swifts became a nursery club for the Midlands side, identifying young talent for the club and then dispatching them there for trials. The Swifts weren't unique in this form of set-up; for example, Middlesbrough Crusaders (who played in the same Teesside League) were a feeder club for Sunderland, while another club, South Park Rovers, supplied youngsters for Doncaster Rovers.

The deal – if you can call it that – to bring young Revie to Boro Swifts was done by the club secretary, 44-year-old Bill Sanderson, a train driver by day but a man who lived and breathed football every weekend. As Sanderson remembered it 33 years later, when Don Revie was the subject of *This Is Your Life* with Eamonn Andrews, the initial, tentative – and definitely unsolicited – approach to play for the Swifts had come from young Revie himself.

Sanderson used to take football 'classes' on a Sunday after the match the day before. His young protégés would gather round in the front room of his house in Keith Road – not that far from the Clough house in Valley Road. Seated in his former home for the benefit of ITV viewers in April 1974, he addressed his former 'pupil' back in the Queens Hotel, Leeds:

Hello, Don. You remember this room and this blackboard. You

> remember when you were sat over there [pointing to the back of the room] as a very little chap, and you wanted to join the club, and I asked you what you were doing here. You shouldn't have been here, you know, it was a private club, but you wanted to be a footballer, and you thought if you wanted to be a footballer you must play for the Swifts!

Sanderson was clearly impressed by the chutzpah of the youngster and was encouraged to take a look at him. He liked what he saw and, for the princely sum of five shillings, signed up young Revie to play for his developing outfit.

This was to be a defining moment in Revie's life. With hindsight, much of his footballing philosophy took root in that front room in Keith Road and on the Swifts' playing field off Stockton Road – not to mention their training ground on Clairville Common, where a young Brian Clough will have watched them at work on occasions.

Revie himself had no doubt about the extent of Sanderson's influence on the way he thought about football. He would watch in fascination as the manager illustrated his points by moving around brightly coloured corks – used to represent players – on a home-made model pitch. Sanderson would first point out the mistakes the Swifts had made, before running through a variety of moves, particularly for throw-ins, corner kicks and free kicks.

'Sometimes I hear old-timers scoff at these blackboard tactics. Frankly I can't understand why,' Revie wrote in 1955. 'If their only use was to interest young lads in the game, there would still be nothing lost in having these tactical talks. I know from my own experience with the Swifts that these Sunday morning discussions opened up for me new visions of the game.'

The famous Revie 'dossier' of his later years as a manager was born in these times. 'In these days of defence in depth and a defence complex which threatens to paralyse all attacking ideas, it is absolutely vital to discuss the opposition; their strengths and weaknesses; and also for your own team to have their own pet moves thoroughly worked out.'

But also the way his great Leeds side of the '60s and '70s played was in keeping with the principles laid down in Keith Road. 'I came to understand that football is not a game for self-glorification, with players making solo dribbles.

'Football is a team game, with eleven men, by quick inter-passing and changing of positions, trying to outwit eleven other men. The man who hammered that into me was Bill Sanderson.'

For his first few months with the Swifts, Revie had to bide his time, watch and learn. He spent most of it as 12th man, carrying the side's kit. But he did force his way into the team for the 1941 Ellis Cup competition and was in the Swifts semi-final line-up that lost to Cleveland Works, the eventual winners. A contemporary report of the match noted, 'such was his ability that, despite his tender years, he didn't look out of place'.

Young Don was prepared to give up most things to further his footballing prospects – he even managed to miss his sister Jean's big day. She recalled: 'My wedding was arranged on a particular Saturday afternoon, and at that time Don was 14 years of age and playing for the Swifts. However, instead of being a guest at my wedding, he slung his football boots over his shoulder, walked through the parlour and said, "Well, I'm off. See you after the match!"'

When he began to play regularly, it was mainly on the right wing, with a gifted young inside-forward called Freddie Watkin alongside him.

Ken Mothersill played left-half for the Swifts, and remembers young Don had all the attributes of a winger. 'He was good-looking, tall, blond, the picture of a young athlete. He was very fast out there on the touchline – his pace was definitely his trademark.'

One of Don's opponents, Frank Stephenson, centre-half for Middlesbrough Crusaders and captain of the North Riding XI, recalls that Revie had a particular skill: 'He had this unusual knack of being able to float the ball across from a corner so that it would hang in the air for a forward to be able to head it. It was a special skill for someone of that age, and a bit like – in this generation of players – what David Beckham does now.'

Revie relished the service he received from Watkin, who would send the ball on its way to him with slide-rule accuracy. 'You can take it from me that Freddie had everything to become another Raich Carter or Wilf Mannion. My partner was one of the greatest inside men I have ever seen,' was his fulsome tribute.

Revie himself moved infield after his initial start on the wing. His displays were beginning to attract attention, and the assistant editor of the *Evening Gazette*, Ernie Thompson (known in the paper by his acronym ELT), was an early admirer and made this assessment: 'Even when so young, Don had superb ball control, a strong and accurate shot, but above all, he was a dominating general who could read a game and employ the tactics necessary to beat his rivals.'

Thompson regarded the Boro Swifts as the finest junior side he'd seen in 25 years, and he was determined that Wilf Gillow, then the Middlesbrough manager, should go and watch one of their games.

Gillow, an avuncular character who more often than not had a pipe in his hand, had himself been a talented all-round sportsman. He played for Blackpool and Preston at football and represented Middlesbrough CC at cricket in the North Yorkshire and South Durham League until well into his 40s; his major claim to fame was that he once fielded as substitute for England in an Ashes Test match at Old Trafford.

Thompson's recollection, in 1968, was that Gillow liked what he saw of the Swifts. 'He was exceedingly enthusiastic about the skill of the two inside-forwards, Revie and Watkin, and although the latter was a tiny boy, he would have signed them both.'

What ELT said next, in his article for the *Gazette*, prompted a question that has never been properly answered – and almost certainly never will be. 'How they [Revie and Watkin] came to join Leicester City and not Middlesbrough is a story which cannot be told in this article,' he wrote enigmatically.

Given that the Middlesbrough Swifts were so closely allied to Leicester City, it shouldn't necessarily have come as a surprise that Revie preferred the Filbert Street club to his home-town team. But it was to people who knew him back in Bell Street.

Mavis Longstaff, for one, was certain that Don wanted to stay at home. 'He was desperate to play for Middlesbrough. It was all he ever wanted to do. But they weren't even interested in having him in the boys' team. He fully expected that by the time he finished with the Swifts he would at least get a trial with Boro, but he got nothing, so he went to Leicester. Familiarity breeds contempt, perhaps, in the case of the Middlesbrough management and Don.'

Revie himself, in his autobiography, had a somewhat different story when describing the background to his move into professional football:

> It was almost by chance that I became a Leicester City player.
> For two seasons the Swifts had swept all before them. Billy
> Forrest, a former Middlesbrough left half [who was then
> coaching the juniors], had asked my father if I would like to go
> for a trial with Middlesbrough.

At this point George Carr, the Leicester City scout, came along. The Swifts became a Leicester nursery, and in the August of 1944 Freddie Watkin and myself were invited to go to Filbert Street.

Watkin and Revie were both offered terms, but the former decided to forsake a footballing career and returned to Teesside. Revie signed, but only with assurances that he could continue his apprenticeship as a bricklayer. His father, Donald, worried about the uncertainty of the profession that his son was now about to pursue, had been adamant that he should have an alternative career.

'[Don] negotiated his own signing as a 16-year-old with Leicester City rather than his home-town club, Middlesbrough. [It was] a negotiation he carried out with the tenacity and shrewdness of a 30-year-old,' recalled Peter Thomas, the *Daily Express* columnist who grew up with Revie and later ghosted many of his articles.

So at the age of just 17, Revie joined Leicester City as a part-time professional. A well-worn cliché, perhaps, but it undoubtedly was a dream come true for this soccer-mad boy who had spent hours dribbling around the lamp posts and up and down the alleyway at the back of Bell Street.

On the day he travelled down late at night from the North-East to begin his new life – 18 August 1944 – the world was turning. The *Daily Express* reported that Hitler's armies in the west and south of France were on the run in the face of massive Allied attacks. 'Only 23 Miles from Paris', the headline proclaimed. There was a clear end in sight after five years of war.

From Middlesbrough to Leicester it was 130 miles, the other side of the world for a teenage boy who had never travelled further than Redcar, a few miles up the coast, for a rare day out with his mother, father and sisters.

'I was lonely, very lonely,' Revie reflected. His train arrived in Leicester in the early hours of Saturday, and he wandered for hours and hours around the town, his football boots tucked in a brown paper bag underneath his arm; he didn't dare to eat in case it put him off his game, and indeed he was so nervous that the thought of food barely entered his mind.

He was due to make his debut that afternoon on the right wing against Wolves, and eventually, apprehensively, he made his way to the players' entrance at Filbert Street. Once he was there, his worries started to ease. Septimus Smith, Leicester's outstanding inside-forward, greeted him with the words 'You from the North, son?' When answered in the affirmative, he responded, 'Good. Stick with me and we might be able to make a player of you, then.'

Revie had met the second great influence on his footballing career. He was now on his way in the game – and in the world.

* * *

Twelve-year-old Don Revie may have worn a burdened look in his school football team photograph, but young Brian Clough, with the flicker of an enigmatic smile, looks assured and self-confident in the Marton Grove line-up ten years later, in 1949.

The side assembled was due to play in the Dorman Cup final on 7 May against Middlesbrough Junior Technical School at Ayresome Park. The 14-year-old Clough sits in the centre of the front row, arms folded, with the air of a captain about to lead his side into battle.

He wasn't actually – formally at least – in charge of the team, although he wasn't shy about giving advice to his skipper on the field. The team had merely lined up in the photograph roughly in the positions they would take up on the pitch. Goalkeeper little Keith Harkin was in the middle at the back, with his full-backs and centre-half on either side of him. The front row was the forward line, Clough, who was centre-forward, surrounded by his inside-forwards and wingers.

When he'd first been picked for the team, Clough had been regarded as a right-half or a centre-half. But he'd always had an inclination to join the attack and was relieved and happy when Mr Fred Dodsworth, who was in charge of the side, decided to switch him to the forward line.

Football team systems had a greater simplicity about them in 1949; put simply, they generally all had two full-backs, three half-backs and five forwards (the pyramid formation). Upfront, most sides would have two fast or tricky wingers and a centre-forward to score the goals. The two inside-forwards were playmakers and would see-saw depending on the flow of play behind the front three. The wing-halfs were also playmakers, charged with turning defence into attack. The centre-half was the pivotal defender, and the full-backs alongside him would operate the offside trap when feasible.

There were variations on this at club and international level, but it was a straightforward arrangement of the players that had stood the test of time. Then came the events at Wembley on 25 November 1953, when the Hungarians revealed a new way of playing, shattering English football's complacency; a certain Don Revie was foremost in ensuring that the lessons of that day were learned. But more of that later.

Clough and his teammates had done well to reach the final by defeating the fancied Lawson School side, from Cargo Fleet, in the semi-final. But the tech side proved too much for them at Ayresome Park in front of a crowd of around 500 cheering family, friends and schoolmates. Marton Grove lost 3–1, and their small, aggressive – some said cocky – centre-forward failed to get on the scoresheet. 'After the teams had got over an attack of the "Ayresome Nerves",' reported the *Evening Gazette*, 'Marton Grove were outclassed for most of the first half by a bigger and faster combination.'

Keith Harkin, however, had no doubt about his colleague's potential. 'At school, Brian was first of all a centre-half, and he was good in that position, but when he moved to centre-forward you could see what an excellent footballer he might be.

'I played with and against him in youth football, and I can vividly remember one match when I was in goal for Tollsby against Grove Hill, who Cloughie played for. At half-time we were 3–0 up, and we congratulated our centre-half, saying he had Cloughie in his pocket. Forty-five minutes later, the score was 3–5, and Cloughie had scored all five – diving headers, balls he should never have reached, all manner of goals!'

George Littlefair, left-half, was standing at the back on the far left in that photograph of the Marton Grove team but reckons he was probably dropped from the cup final side. He lived just a couple of hundred yards away from Clough on Bishopton Road, and the promising young centre-forward would come knocking on his door quite often, asking him to come and play on Clairville Common. There was a very good reason for his call: 'We struggled to get a good ball. Sometimes we would have to play with one made of rags. But one Christmas my brother sent me this amazing football all the way from Bombay in India – although, strangely, it was stamped as being made in England.

'Anyway, it was called a "T" ball, and it was a genuine cowhide, top leather specimen. I remember taking it down the town to Jack Hatfield's sports shop on Borough Road, and asking him to blow it up. His eyes nearly popped out of his head when he saw the quality of it!'

Clough was relishing his football, inside and outside school. In the classroom, however, it was a different matter. He was bright and alert and interested in the world, but translating all that into academic success proved difficult. He failed his 11-plus, the only member of the Clough family to do so.

Bill, his older brother, has said he was unable to concentrate on anything for long periods and rarely completed his homework. Keith Harkin, who was in the same year, recalled: 'He wasn't a good scholar. In a class of around 40, he would come somewhere in the midfield. I can't remember him shining in any subject at all.'

In his autobiography, Clough reflected that being made head boy at Marton Grove was, in some large measure, compensation for his academic failures. For his mother, it gave her 'more pleasure, pride and satisfaction' than Derby winning the league title in 1972. Clough recalled:

> I enjoyed being head boy because it gave me a certain amount of power . . . I wasn't a belligerent head boy but I didn't mind telling another kid what he should have been doing. I actually enjoyed standing at the top of the stairs and warning the late arrivals – 'It's gone nine . . . you're late . . . and if it happens once more this week . . .'

Keith Harkin remembers that Clough took his responsibilities as a senior member of school perhaps a little over-zealously. 'As a prefect, Cloughie was a little bit of a bully with the young kids in that role. I think it went to his head a bit. He laid the law down to young kids – stop running, take your hands out of your pockets and so on – but he would be the first to be running and to have his bloody hands in his pockets, to put it bluntly!

'I got on with him – we went to the same youth club together, Marton Grove, and played junior football together. But he was a cocky so-and-so at school, and on umpteen times he was lucky he didn't get a good thumping.'

A final word on Clough's time at Marton comes from his sister Doreen: 'The headmaster, Mr Turnbull, wrote to Mum and said he'd never had a prefect like him, and could he keep him on. That speaks for itself, doesn't it?'

In 1950, leaving school meant a limited range of options for boys like Clough who had failed to make it into grammar school. On

Teesside, there was still a dependency on steel-making, the manufacture of chemicals and, to a lesser extent, shipbuilding. Any diversification of light and heavy industries would have to wait a few years; in the first year of the new decade, many roads still led to ICI at Billingham, where there were jobs for life and career paths predetermined almost to the smallest detail.

At his mother's insistence, Clough applied for a 'nice job' as a fitter and turner at ICI. From his description, you'd think his introduction to the giant works was like entering an industrial underworld, a cross between Fritz Lang's *Metropolis* and George Orwell's *1984*:

> I turned up for my first day at work feeling utterly bewildered. I was frightened. It was the first time I had been away from home on my own and for a few moments, before stepping through them, I just stood and looked at the big metal gates.
>
> They were the biggest I'd ever seen. I know it's a cliché, and you've heard it many times before, but to a boy not yet 16, with his sandwiches and bottle of pop in his pocket, they really did represent the gates of hell.

There was no fooling the authorities at ICI over his technical knowledge. 'He was useless doing anything practical,' wife Barbara later recalled. 'They gave him some bolts, locks and keys to put together, and he didn't have a clue what to do.'

So a fitter he couldn't be; a minor office job was the only alternative. Clough was given the title of 'junior clerk', but he knew what that really meant. He was a glorified messenger boy, running errands from department to department. Later, he would be recruited to do what was described as 'work study' – essentially helping to fill in overtime sheets.

Amidst the humdrum nature of work at ICI, there was the odd opportunity for him to show off his natural gifts. His colleague Peter Lax recalled: 'We junior clerks used to go to education every other Tuesday and sometimes they'd organise debates, one side of the room against the other. It was hopeless. No one else could get a word in edgeways!'

These were uncertain times for Clough. He clearly had talents, but none of them fitted neatly into the working life with which he'd been saddled. At this stage, a career as a footballer remained a long way off.

In fact, for some 18 months after leaving school Clough played little soccer as he adjusted to his new job and his new way of life. It was a period of turmoil for him, bringing with it some measure of disenchantment. But then he joined Marton Grove Youth Club and the bug bit once more. 'I think it was while I was playing for them that I realised just how much in love with the game I really was,' he recalled.

It was certainly learning the hard way, as week after week Marton were hammered by just about every other club in the Middlesbrough Junior League. In one particular match, Marton were thrashed 20–1 by South Park Rovers, the Doncaster Rovers nursery team. So little of the ball did Clough enjoy at centre-forward in those months that he decided to drop back to his original position, at right-half, so he would at least be more involved in the game.

But relief – and family help – was at hand. Three of his brothers – Joe, Des and Bill – and sister Doreen's husband, Sid, were playing for a village club called Great Broughton in the Cleveland League. Brian joined them, aged 16, and made the 12-mile trip out of Middlesbrough to play on Saturday afternoons.

The Great Broughton side was managed by the larger-than-life village postmistress Nancy Goldsborough, who held the job not necessarily because of her tactical acumen but supposedly because of her administrative skills – she was said to be one of the few villagers who could write!

It was certainly a tough environment for young Brian to cut his teeth in senior football. His opponents were, in the main, no-nonsense farm workers, and there was strong rivalry between the neighbouring villages, with no quarter asked or given. The pitch was a flattened farm field and this truly was football in the raw.

The Clough family dominated the side, with Des perhaps the pick of the bunch; a centre-half, he went on to play for Bishop Auckland and captained Whitby Town. But there were two other sets of brothers in Reggie and Billy Holmes and Malcolm and Peter Lax. So there were only two places available for Great Broughton villagers!

Not surprisingly, with all these quality 'ringers', the Great Broughton team enjoyed a good deal of success. In Clough's second season, he banged the goals in left, right and centre and established some form of scoring record. In one cup tie against Skinningrove, he was on the score sheet *ten* times in a thumping 16–0 victory.

Before the games, the older Cloughs would enjoy a pie and pint in the Black Horse pub before changing in the Temperance Hall. After the game, it would be tea before a blazing coal fire, then the bus journey back to Middlesbrough.

Clough's reputation was growing. Every opportunity that arose – and there were many – he would play football. Towards the end of the 1952–53 season, while still attached to Great Broughton and Marton Grove, he was also turning out for Marske Rovers (Ellis Cup) and Acklam Steelworks (Magnum Bonum Cup), besides playing for his own section team in the interdepartmental competition at ICI Casebournes, where he was then working.

For one three-week spell, he played every day bar Sundays. 'Towards the end,' he told the *Evening Gazette* in 1957, 'I was so tired I was almost falling asleep at work, much to the annoyance of my boss, who advised that I should give a little less time to football and more to the job for which I was being paid!'

The next important stop on Clough's footballing journey was at Billingham Synthonia, of the amateur (with some semi-professionals) Northern League. It was through Peter Lax, his friend at ICI, that he joined the club for a busy month from April to May 1953, in which he played five games.

Billingham Synthonia is a club with a rare name and an interesting history. Its origins – if you follow them all the way back – lie with David Lloyd George, Minister of Munitions at the outbreak of the First World War. He was worried that Britain was lagging dangerously behind Germany in the production of TNT (the major basis for explosives). What he needed was a chemical company to match the Germans' BASF and supply industrial quantities of synthetic ammonia for shells for the war effort.

That badly needed chemical company – Brunner, Mond & Co. – didn't materialise until after the First World War. Then, the ammonia being produced was for more peaceful purposes, its major use being in the manufacture of nitrogenous fertilisers. Brunner Mond merged with Nobel Explosives, United Alkali and British Dyestuffs Corp to form the new Imperial Chemical Industries Ltd (ICI) in 1926. With its site at Billingham, it quickly became established as the largest factory in the British Empire, employing more than 10,000 people.

So Billingham Synthonia – the football section of the sports club built for the workers – is the only football team to be named after an agricultural fertiliser (synthonia is a contraction of synthetic ammonia).

It has another claim to fame simply in terms of soccer prowess.

Three seasons before Clough arrived, in 1950–51, the club went the entire season without conceding a goal at home in the Northern League, notching up thirteen victories and one draw. Harry Armstrong was between the posts for the bulk of those games; incredibly, in the last game of the season, at home to Bishop Auckland, he saved a penalty!

So it's a club rightly proud of its traditions – and proud, too, of its association with Brian Clough, who joined them as an up-and-coming youngster. In one of the rooms underneath the giant main stand, the wall is covered with pictures of notable days and famous visitors – the Duke of Edinburgh on an ICI visit in 1956, Stanley Rous opening the new ground in 1958 (the pitch Clough played on in 1953 became the massive headquarters of ICI) – and there's a plate commemorating a match between a Northern League representative team and a joint Juventus/Liverpool line-up. In amongst it all is a framed page outlining Clough's Billingham Synthonia career, with particular prominence given to his goalscoring debut in a 2–1 win away at Evenwood Town on 11 April 1953.

The Synners' historian is 82-year-old Jackie Weatherill, who has kept a record of every game the club has played since joining the Northern League in 1945 – and he's seen the vast majority of those.

He's worked for the club ever since the war. One of his first jobs was to hand the players a towel as they got out of the old communal bath, and he remembers the grass being mown by horse-drawn cutters. These days, he still cleans the dressing-rooms and makes the teas for the players and referees at half-time.

He has a newspaper report of Clough's first game for Synthonia at Evenwood. The reporter wrote: 'With the looks of an adolescent, Clough combines the skill, vigour and guile of a veteran campaigner. The greatest blow to Billingham so far as he is concerned is the fact that soon he joins the forces.'

Two days later, Clough made his home debut, also against Evenwood, at the Recreation Club ground. The match report of that game the next day is again approving of Clough's performance – even though he didn't score – referring to his 'masterly touches'.

After those two games in three days, Clough turned out three more times for the Synners, scoring a goal in a 9–2 rout of Stanley United but being on the losing side away at Bishop Auckland (1–4) and at home to Penrith (1–3).

But, of course, while all this experience was invaluable, Clough's dream – like Revie's – was to agree professional terms with

Middlesbrough. The story of how he came to do so is – as they say – the stuff of legend.

George Camsell, Revie's boyhood hero, was at that time in charge of Middlesbrough juniors. At the urging of Ray Grant, head teacher at Hugh Bell Secondary School and a Boro scout, he went to see Clough play for Great Broughton but came away unimpressed by what he'd witnessed and reluctant to sign the Grove Hill boy.

Grant wasn't giving up. He persuaded Middlesbrough to let Clough play in a trial game against Huddersfield at Heckmondwike. Grant, in Tony Francis's book *Clough: A Biography*, takes up the story:

> I respected my friend's [Camsell's] original opinion, but I knew there had to be something to this lad. Brian had a quiet match, then he produced something which made me take notice.
>
> Our outside left, Albert Mendham, decided to bypass him and hit a ball out to the other wing. He struck it with terrific power. As it was passing behind Brian – or so it seemed – the Huddersfield defenders moved over. Brian, who was facing the opposition goal, turned around and flicked the ball at right angles up and over his shoulder.
>
> With the defence flat-footed, he burst through the middle, and from the edge of the penalty area, hit a screaming left-foot shot into the top corner.
>
> I thought: good heavens, that's either a complete fluke or he's a genius. Later it was obvious that he was blessed with a touch of genius. I sent a message to the club: 'Ignore previous report from George Camsell – this boy can play!'

Ray Grant's recommendation did the trick, and Clough was invited to sign by Boro on a £1 per week retainer and £7 if he was selected to play. 'I'd known for a long time that I really wanted to be a footballer . . . I didn't need asking twice. I didn't need to talk terms,' he recalled.

There was delight in the Clough household – especially for his mother. 'She had followed him and encouraged him all the way. The story goes that she filled in and signed the forms to get him to Middlesbrough – it cost £10. She then took them herself to Ayresome Park,' remembered sister Doreen.

The forms were signed about a week before Clough set off to do his two years' National Service with the RAF, first at Dumfries, then at Watchet in Somerset.

At first, while based up in Scotland, he played quite a few games for Middlesbrough, with the club arranging for 48-hour passes through an accommodating commanding officer. Clough was scoring a few goals for the reserves but wasn't entirely happy. Because of a surfeit of centre-forwards, he was slotted into the inside-left position and that irked him. In his by now familiar forthright way, he persistently asked to be given a chance at centre-forward, but his pleas went unanswered.

Despite his outward self-confidence, the Clough of those days still retained real doubts about his true worth as a footballer. That wasn't helped when he failed to win RAF representative honours. He played for his station team in a small Somerset league and several cup competitions, picking up a fair number of trophies – but that was as far as it went. Burnley's left-winger Brian Pilkington, who was in the RAF at the same time, remembers being picked in the national side ahead of Clough, who had to make do with being a reserve. Pilkington would later make his England international debut on the same day in 1954 as Don Revie.

But Clough was making progress in the game, albeit not as swiftly as he would have liked. He was still getting games with Middlesbrough, and he had moved up the ladder from being fifth-choice centre-forward to the reserve side.

There was a long way to go. But he was out in the world, and he was doing what he felt he did best – and getting paid for it.

Chapter 3
'I'll Be That Man in a Thousand'

In 1953, the British were just starting to feel good about themselves again after the years of austerity. In February, the Clough household – with father Joe working at Garnett's factory – would have rejoiced at the end of sweet rationing. Meat remained the last foodstuff to be restricted, and that would end in a year's time.

The enthusiasm for football remained undimmed, and in May families across the country packed into front rooms to witness one of the great FA Cup finals, with Blackpool – and, above all, Stanley Matthews – clawing their way back from a 3–1 deficit against Bolton Wanderers in the last 22 minutes to win 4–3.

Then the following month, when Brian Clough was heading off to Dumfries to start his National Service, the nation was in a state of royal fervour. Children clutched their free mugs, mothers scrubbed the front steps till they were spotless and families hung up the bunting and laid out the trestle tables in the streets in preparation for Coronation Day.

Tuesday, 2 June, the date of Queen Elizabeth II's coronation, was the moment British television came of age. There were just 2.5 million television sets in the country at that time, but it's estimated that a staggering 20 million people watched the Queen that day; another 12 million tuned in on the wireless.

Just to improve the national mood on that momentous occasion, the highest peak in the world, Mount Everest, was scaled for the first time by a British Commonwealth team led by the New Zealander Edmund Hillary, with the redoubtable Nepalese Sherpa Tenzing Norgay as his companion at the summit.

★ ★ ★

At his home in the North-West, 26-year-old Don Revie no doubt rejoiced with the best of them. But as he cast his mind forward to the new football season in a couple of months' time, his mood might well have darkened.

No one could doubt that he'd now established himself as a highly capable professional footballer, playing in the best league in the country – or indeed the world. On one level, his worth could be calculated in simple financial terms: Hull City had paid £19,000 to take him from Leicester City in 1949, and two years later Manchester City were prepared to pay £28,000 to bring him to Maine Road to be a key part of their new era as a Division One side.

But, as he re-evaluated his career to date, he knew that he could – and should – have achieved a great deal more. As it often did, his mind went back to that approach from Arsenal in September 1949. What an opportunity! The aristocrats of the football world, under manager Tom Whittaker, were still the side to beat. The year Revie was asked to join them, they'd slid down the table as far as fifth, but last season, 1952–53, normal service had been resumed and they'd finished champions once more.

Revie couldn't rid himself of his self-doubts, his constant worry about just how good he was and whether he could hold his own in the very highest company on a football field. That caution, that fear, combined with a reluctance to move from the North to London, meant there would be no journey to the marbled halls of Highbury.

Now, after two seasons with City, where had that choice left him? Fifteenth in the table in the team's first season back in 1951–52 was just about excusable. But last season's desperate struggle for survival, which ended in 20th place and just a point away from relegation, was dismal and not remotely what he'd anticipated when he'd joined the club.

This season, in the hoary old phrase, would be make or break. He was 26 years old, yet to win anything, yet to play representative football, yet to influence the game in any truly significant way. His horizons seemed to be narrowing; back in 1944, all had seemed possible.

* * *

Septimus Smith, so-called because he was the seventh son born in his family, had been Revie's mentor in those early wartime days at Leicester. A North-Easterner, from Whitburn in County Durham, he was a gifted player who found time and space easily and could thread through a defence-splitting pass. A one-club man, the only surprise, given his obvious talent, is that he played just once for England, in 1935 against Northern Ireland at Windsor Park.

He was tough on the Middlesbrough teenager because he felt he'd spotted an unusual talent and didn't want it to go to waste. Revie's tiredness, loneliness and insecurity were such that he would often cry after long, arduous training sessions with Smith, ones that were usually punctuated by robust criticism.

But he was absorbing the lessons Smith was teaching him, which were summed up in these four sayings:

- When not in possession get into position.
- Never beat a man by dribbling if you can beat him more easily with a pass.
- It's not the man on the ball but the man running into position to take the pass who constitutes the danger.
- The aim is to have a man spare in a passing move, then Soccer becomes easy.

Find space, pass the ball, support the man. Simple principles, ones that would be the hallmark of Revie's Leeds side 25 years later.

If Smith was Revie's coach and tactical mentor in his early days at Leicester, then Scotsman Johnny 'Tokey' Duncan, who took over as manager from Tom Mather in 1946, was his pastoral guide. Eric Thornton, in his book *Leeds United and Don Revie*, recalled how Duncan pursued the boy from Bell Street:

> Uncle Jock, as he was always known to everybody in the family circle, had first heard of the boy from someone living near to the Middlesbrough club. He kept his ear very close to the ground, saw him in action, and recognised that this youngster with the lean build of a greyhound, and almost the speed to match it, was improving fast.
>
> So remembering the doggerel of Alice's Walrus, he knew when the time had come, and introduced him to Leicester's payroll.

Revie would recall how Duncan would wait at the ground on Tuesday and Thursday nights for his young apprentices to return from their day jobs – bricklaying, in his case. He'd then take them to his house – there were usually eight or nine of them to fit in – and feed them with his own special recipe of Scotch broth.

To supplement their diet and build up their strength, he'd also send eggs and sherry round to their digs, and big bags of oats so they could have porridge with milk every morning before training. Revie had lodgings in Thirlmere Street in those early days, where he was well looked after by a genial couple, Mr and Mrs Meadows.

'Johnny Duncan taught me the importance of looking after the players' welfare, trying to get "inside" them and not just treat them as numbers. He tried to make us feel part of a family, and I always thought at the time that if I ever became a manager that's the way I would approach the job,' recalled Revie.

Duncan inspired loyalty and a large degree of affection in his charges, but they also knew that if they didn't pull their weight in training they would feel the lash of his tongue. He was an admirer of clever inside-forwards, and when he had played for Raith Rovers in the 1930s he had partnered one of the very best – Alex James, who went on to great things with Arsenal. Leicester may have been in the Second Division, but they had one or two handy players, mainly forwards – like centre-forward Derek Hines and Jack Lee, an England international and also a first-class cricketer.

Revie's progress was steady and sure. He played in 33 wartime games and in 1946 seemed set fair for a regular place in the side, with the opportunity of teaming up on the right wing with the experienced Septimus Smith. Then came the moment that looked almost certain to snuff out his football career.

It happened in a home game against Tottenham Hotspur. Revie went in for a challenge with Ronnie Burgess, the Spurs and Wales wing-half, and came out of it with his ankle broken in three places and a joint dislocated. The injury was so severe that specialists at the Leicester hospital thought he would never play again.

Revie's account – in his 1955 autobiography – of hearing that news is, you might think now, a touch melodramatic. But, given the enormity of his predicament, he can surely be forgiven for that.

> I turned my face away and gripped the blankets. Then I heard Johnny [Duncan]'s soft Scottish brogue again saying: 'The doctors say it's a thousand to one against you ever playing again, Don.' Johnny was looking straight at me again. 'What say we make you the man in a thousand, son?'

> At nineteen, a youth, with all his hopes of Soccer stardom lying shattered, finds it hard to fight back the tears. I just looked up at Johnny and muttered: 'I'll be that one man in a thousand if you say so, Boss.'

Revie's leg was in plaster for two months, but, remarkably, within five months he was back on the pitch again. After his comeback match with the reserves, he headed straight for the Turk's Head Hotel in Leicester, where he ordered a double whisky and delivered it to Matthew McCleary, the orthopaedic surgeon who had saved his career. Twenty-eight years later, when Revie appeared on *This Is Your Life*, Mr McCleary was one of the guests.

Revie initially struggled to find his form after his long lay-off, which was almost inevitable. He had to endure a short period of barracking from the Filbert Street crowd that proved extremely disconcerting for one who was so naturally sensitive.

But he battled through the rough patch, and off the pitch he was being helped through this difficult period by Johnny Duncan's niece Elsie. They became close over the next 18 months and would marry on 17 October 1949, at the Robert Hall Baptist Church, Leicester. 'We got married on a Monday, the traditional footballers' day off, we spent our honeymoon round the corner from his digs and he was back training on Tuesday morning!' she recalled later.

Elsie was a proud Scot, born in Lochgelly, Fife, and football shaped her life. Her father, Tommy, was a player who moved south from Raith Rovers to Leicester City as part of an unusual transfer deal: he and his brother Johnny were both signed on the same day by Peter Hodge, the former Raith manager.

Tommy Duncan died at the age of 39 and Johnny became something of a surrogate father to Elsie. She was a teacher by profession, having graduated from Moray House teacher training college in Edinburgh. As her husband would move from club to club, so Elsie would have to get to know a new set of pupils every few years, until she was able to settle down at Leeds Girls' High School in the 1960s.

· Being the daughter of a footballer and niece to a football manager helped Elsie appreciate the stresses and strains of the profession. Revie knew how vital it was to have a partner who could give support but also a tough dose of reality. Elsie provided both, as he admitted in a television interview in 1974:

I owe her an awful lot, because she had a fantastic education, which I didn't have, and she could tell me an awful lot I didn't know about. She is a driver of people, and if I was ever down in the dumps she would never sympathise with me, ever, but urge me to get back on my feet. Having said that, she feels what I'm going through very much, and sometimes I think that on a Saturday she goes through it more than I do.

If marriage was the most significant event in Revie's life in 1949, on the football pitch real achievement beckoned at last after years of flickering promise. Leicester struggled in the Second Division, despite much pre-season optimism after finishing ninth in 1947–48. But in the FA Cup, it was a different matter altogether. They embarked on a glorious run, defeating Birmingham City 2–1 (in a second replay), Preston North End 2–0, Luton Town 5–3 in a replay (after a 5–5 draw in the first match) and Brentford 2–0. The lowly side from Filbert Street had made it to the semi-finals, where mighty Portsmouth – already crowned First Division champions – were waiting for them. Pompey were the overwhelming favourites, the bookmakers giving them odds of 8–1 on.

★ ★ ★

On 26 March 1949, the day of the semi-final at Arsenal's Highbury stadium, Revie overslept and nearly missed the team coach, which was due to receive a civic send-off before heading down to London.

He still felt tired when, after the team had exchanged pleasantries with all the dignitaries at Town Hall, the coach eventually set off down south. But comforted by the thought that Joe Louis, when he was heavyweight boxing champion of the world, used to like a long sleep before all his big fights, he lay back and closed his eyes. 'We had all to gain and nothing to lose in the semi-final. What was the use of worrying? I had caused enough upset for one day.' So, in a frame of mind he would rarely be able to recapture in the stress-filled years ahead, he arrived at Highbury relaxed and ready to perform.

Several spectators had to be treated at the side of the pitch by St John Ambulance members before the start of the game, as an excited crowd of around 50,000 surged down the terracing. The Portsmouth president Field Marshal Viscount Montgomery acknowledged the cheers from his vantage point in the directors' box, and so, amid great expectation among the Pompey fans and some trepidation among the Leicester faithful, the match got under way.

It was testament to Sep Smith's careful analysis of the strengths and weaknesses in the opposition sides that Leicester had been so well prepared for all the obstacles in their way on this cup run. This game would be no different, and while Leicester were nearly run off their feet in the first quarter of an hour, they steadied themselves and began to get a foothold in the match.

The British Pathé News commentator quaintly summed up the nation's expectations for Leicester: 'They've got two chances – a dog's chance or no chance at all!' But the film shows Ken Chisholm sweeping a ball out to the right edge of the penalty area, where Mal Griffiths centres low and hard across the face of the six-yard box. The ball is neatly stunned dead by centre-forward Jack Lee, leaving Revie to smartly steer the ball with his left foot past the Portsmouth keeper Reg Butler from eight yards.

Pompey's swift right-winger Peter Harris promptly equalised when he ran onto a through pass past a static defence and crashed the ball past the Leicester keeper from 15 yards. After that, Portsmouth's class began to tell and their long, raking passes were a constant threat to Leicester's suspect back line.

After the interval, Leicester rallied, and in their best spell of the match they regained the lead when Jack Lee wriggled away from two Pompey defenders on the right to centre for Chisholm, who tucked the ball away with his left foot from the edge of the penalty area.

Portsmouth threw the proverbial kitchen sink at Leicester, and Harris was guilty of a glaring miss when, from no more than eight yards, with the goalkeeper nowhere to be seen and just a defender on the line to cover, he somehow contrived to push the ball wide of the post.

It was then that Sep Smith's 'dossier' proved its worth. He'd noticed that Portsmouth's keeper had a curious habit of palming the ball over an opponent's head when he was challenged and then running round him to catch it.

Smith had urged Revie to sit back a few yards when the ball was pumped into the penalty area and Butler had to come out and deal with it. Sure enough, when a ball was swung in and Jack Lee went up to challenge Butler, the Pompey keeper palmed the ball over Lee's head. But Revie had anticipated it all; he'd positioned himself to receive the ball from the punch and promptly chipped it back past the defenders and into the net.

It was an astonishing victory, and with two goals – and much clever prompting in between – Revie rightly received many of the accolades. Most knowledgeable critics reckoned it was only a matter of time before the 21-year-old schemer would be on his way to a bigger club.

As it turned out, that day at Highbury was the high point of his Leicester career. Two weeks before the cup final against Wolves, Leicester played West Ham at Filbert Street in a league game. Revie challenged for the ball in midfield with Dick Walker, the West Ham centre-half, and went tumbling to the ground with blood pouring from a nose injury.

The nose looked swollen but nothing more than that, and Revie turned out to play three days later against Blackburn Rovers. He made it through that match despite some pain and travelled with the team to Plymouth for the Saturday fixture.

Once in Plymouth, Johnny Duncan, sensing that the injury was starting to affect Revie, took the decision to leave him out of the side and rest him up for the final. Then, late on Saturday night, in his hotel room, his nose started bleeding profusely. He was rushed off to hospital to be seen by a specialist, who diagnosed the problem as a burst blood vessel but nevertheless managed to stem the flow of blood.

By Tuesday, the rest of the Leicester squad had left Plymouth for Skegness, where they were set to undertake some special training ahead of the cup final. On that day, Johnny Duncan decided that Revie, still in discomfort and with the nose bleeding once more, should be taken back to Leicester by car to be examined by specialists at the town's infirmary.

It was a hellish eight-hour trip, with Revie continuing to lose huge amounts of blood and becoming 'as weak as a kitten'. He had to be carried into the hospital, where he was instantly given blood transfusions. He was later told that if he'd been on the road for another hour he almost certainly would have died.

Leicester, without Revie, lost the FA Cup final at Wembley (their very first appearance at the home of football) to Wolves 3–1. Their fight for survival in the Second Division proved successful – just; a point against Cardiff in the last game of the season left them in 19th position.

Revie was sent to Ireland to recuperate. It cost him a place on an England summer tour that would have been reward for his outstanding form throughout the season. When he returned, he discovered that Johnny Duncan had made him captain for the 1949–50 season. But rather than rejoicing in his elevation, he worried that people might accuse him of nepotism because of his forthcoming marriage to the manager's niece. Revie wanted to be seen to be making a success of his career purely through his own ability, and in any case he sensed this was the time to move on, although in the course of the next few months he turned down that Arsenal approach, after much soul-searching, and then also rebuffed Manchester City's advances.

The team he eventually decided to join, in November 1949, was Hull City, who paid £19,000 for his services. Revie's decision to join a club with no great history and tradition was based on the prospect of playing for – and for a while, with – one of the legends of North-East soccer, Raich Carter, the 'Silver Fox'.

* * *

Raich Carter and Don Revie should have been a football marriage made in heaven. The Old Master and the Young Apprentice, one of the most skilful midfield players of the pre-war generation nurturing the talents of one of the best to emerge post-war, North-Easterner (Sunderland) handing the torch to North-Easterner (Middlesbrough). Sadly, it didn't turn out like that.

Carter was soon to turn 36 in the autumn of 1949 and all too aware he was nearing the end of his illustrious career. As a player, he had achieved it all. He was just 22 when he captained Sunderland to the league title in 1936. A year later, he led the Wearside team out at Wembley for the FA Cup final against Preston North End, scoring the second in a 3–1 victory. He played thirteen times for England, scoring seven goals, and would undoubtedly have gained many more caps had the war not intervened.

Carter took over as player-manager at Hull City in 1948 and immediately guided them out of Third Division North, taking them up as champions. As well as dominating the league (they won their first nine matches) they enjoyed an excellent cup run, culminating in a thrilling match at Boothferry Park against Manchester United, which the Tigers were unlucky to lose by a single goal.

All this recent achievement, together with the added comfort of remaining in the North, would have helped persuade Revie to opt for a career with a Second Division side rather than Arsenal. But the thought that his game might reach even greater heights with Carter to advise him would have been a further significant factor.

But, almost immediately, there was a surprising clash of playing styles. Carter liked to play more directly, aiming to supply defence-splitting balls; Revie preferred a more deliberate passing game. Carter played deep so as to be better able to open the game out; that left Revie lying upfield all the time, with none of the creative work to do. He felt uncomfortable and out of place.

Eventually, Revie was moved to right-half, where he was able to make a far better contribution. But the Hull supporters never really warmed to him. Ernest Hecht would later set up an independent publishing company, Souvenir Press, that worked closely with Revie and Leeds United, producing the club's football annuals in the late 1960s and early 1970s. But in the early 1950s Hecht was at university in Hull and a close observer of events at Boothferry Park. 'Carter bought him [Revie] as his new protégé, and you could see he was a very good player but somewhat lost in Carter's shadow. But the fans didn't like him at all, as he was perceived as being a "milkie" because he wouldn't go into hard tackles.'

That observation about Revie's deficiencies in the defensive side of the inside-forward's game would be levelled at him from time to time in the rest of his playing career. It wasn't his prime duty – no one expected him to be a Nobby Stiles type; he was valued instead for his passing ability and vision. But one wonders whether the criticism stayed with him to such an extent that – in later years as Leeds manager – he would be determined to ensure that his side would not be described as 'milkies' or 'high jumpers', and he perhaps overcompensated accordingly.

Whatever the reasons, Revie's career at Hull never scaled the heights. Neil Franklin, the great England centre-half who had played in Colombia at a far higher salary than he could expect to receive at home at the time of the maximum wage, had returned to Britain and was brought to Hull early in 1951, an indication of the team's ambition. But Raich Carter got into a bitter dispute with the board of directors, and left the club in September 1951.

By then, Revie had realised that his goals in the game were unlikely to be realised at a club that was now teetering on the verge of another drop into Third Division North. When Manchester City came to pay court to him once more, the prospect of First Division football looked most appealing.

Revie moved to Maine Road in October, with City manager Les McDowall paying £28,000 for him, a very large sum of money for a player who appeared to have lost his way after promising so much as a youngster at Leicester City.

But Revie wasn't McDowall's only big-money signing. He also paid out £25,000 for Sunderland's Ivor Broadis, a clever, tricky inside-forward. They joined the likes of Ken Barnes, a powerful, attacking wing-half, Roy Paul, a more defensively minded half-back who was the side's charismatic, inspirational captain, and German goalkeeper Bert Trautmann.

Poor Trautmann. Captured by the British and imprisoned in a POW camp at Ashton-in-Makerfield in Lancashire, not only did he face open hostility from the City fans for his nationality (season-ticket holders threatened a boycott) but also because he was attempting to fill the shoes of Frank Swift, considered at the time to be City and England's greatest-ever keeper. It's to his eternal credit that he surmounted all obstacles and was himself revered as the years went on for his courage and ability.

With such a line-up, surely Revie's career would now ignite? Not so, and his first few months at Maine Road must have given him a dreadful sense of déjà vu. Substitute Raich Carter for Ivor Broadis, and another clash of the talented inside-forwards was taking place.

Once again, Broadis lay deep to do the midfield scheming; once more, Revie did likewise. 'We got in each other's way. As at Hull, I went upfield and found I couldn't play the role of goal grabber. Maybe the reason is my brand of football needs time and space to flourish properly,' recalled Revie in *Soccer's Happy Wanderer*. 'I am no speed merchant. I have never pretended to be anything but a schemer and an accurate passer of the ball.'

Once again, Revie had to cede the position and make do with a role at half-back. Broadis would receive his first England cap that season; Revie ended it in frustration, suffering with a groin injury.

In the following season, 1952–53, there was little improvement for either Revie or his Maine Road colleagues. Manager McDowall tinkered with the team to devise a formation that would better suit his group of undoubtedly talented players, but all too often City looked a side with a strong defence and an impressive attack – and nothing in between to link them.

It ended up in a desperate struggle against relegation. A 6–0 defeat to Cardiff, who had previously failed to score a league goal for ten weeks, was a humiliating experience. Derby, already relegated, also hammered City. But then they rescued themselves with a 5–0 victory over Blackpool, who were obviously easing up with the cup final (Matthews' game) just a few days away. Eventually, with a deep sigh of relief, they scrambled to safety in 20th place.

And so to the summer of 1953. Revie had turned down Arsenal only to tread water in Division Two and the lower reaches of the First Division. Expert judges in the game reckoned he had it in him to compete with the very best, but he was tired of hearing the word 'potential' attached to his name.

His managers weren't giving free rein to his ability. He knew there was much more he could offer – but how on earth was he going to be given the opportunity?

* * *

The day the course of Revie's career was altered irrevocably was 25 November 1953, and the man who did most to change it was a 31-year-old Hungarian named Nándor Hidegkuti.

The match, between England and Hungary at the Empire Stadium, Wembley, was billed as the 'Match of the Century' by the British press. What seemed like the usual hyperbole could be justified on several counts: Hungary were ranked first in the world at the time on a points basis, and England were third (Argentina lay in between); Hungary were the Olympic champions and on a run of 29 matches without defeat; England, on the other hand, had never been beaten in a home international by overseas opposition.

But this was more than a clash of two very fine sides; it was also a collision of two very differing footballing styles and, indeed, philosophies. England's tried and tested 3–2–2–3 'WM' formation, created by Herbert Chapman at Arsenal in the 1920s, had been the blueprint for the majority of British clubs for the past few decades. It featured five defenders and five attackers: three backs and two halfs in defensive roles, and two inside-forwards assisting three attacking forwards (two wingers and a centre-forward).

The England side was comfortable with the system and certainly had the players to make it work. At the back, Alf Ramsey was a superb full-back with excellent technique and anticipation; Billy Wright, captain and right-half, was a model of consistency and had more than 100 caps to his name; in attack, the apparently ageless Stanley Matthews would supply the crosses for the powerful number 9, Stan Mortensen.

The only problem for England – well, actually, the speed, skill, fitness and flair of the Hungarians made for a multitude of difficulties – the *major* problem for England was that Hidegkuti had number 9 on his back, like Mortensen, but didn't behave remotely like a conventional centre-forward.

He lay deep in midfield, and helped orchestrate attacks rather than being the focus of them as Mortensen, or indeed any orthodox centre-forward of the day, would expect to be. Harry Johnston from Blackpool, one of the most reliable centre-halfs in the country, was used to competing against big, robust centre-forwards who battled fiercely with him in the air and on the ground but largely within the confines of the penalty area. He just didn't know whether to follow the roving Hidegkuti or to continue to mark the territory where he should have been.

He opted for the latter, and Hidegkuti was given the freedom of Wembley. With his constant movement around the field, exquisite ball skills, incisive passing and consummate finishing, he masterminded England's beating. He himself scored a hat-trick, Ferenc Puskás two and József Bozsik the other. England replied through Jackie Sewell, Stan Mortensen and Alf Ramsey, but 6–3 didn't really reflect the yawning chasm that now clearly existed between the two nations.

It would be wrong to ascribe the Hungarians' overwhelming control purely to the new deep-lying centre-forward role adopted by Hidegkuti. All his colleagues were fluid in their movement, supremely fit, utterly confident and relaxed with the ball at their feet. If ever 'Total Football' existed, it was on that fogbound night in front of 105,000 astonished spectators and many more watching on television.

Before the kick-off, Billy Wright looked down at the opposition's footwear. 'I noticed that the Hungarians had on these strange, lightweight boots, cut away like slippers under the ankle bone. I turned to big Stan Mortensen and said, "We should be all right here, Stan, they haven't got the proper kit."'

While Wright was making a mental note of their boots, Puskás picked up the match ball and juggled it on his left foot, flicked it into the air, caught it on his thigh and then let it run down his shin and back onto the centre spot. There were some jeers from the crowd, who thought Puskás was showing off; in fact, he was only doing what came naturally.

One goal of the six – the third – still has the power to make you gasp with incredulity, even after fifty-eight years and the likes of Pelé, Maradona, Cruyff, Best, Messi et al. in the meantime. The build-up is often forgotten, but it was a sweet, flowing seven-man move out of defence, the ball being moved effortlessly with short passes, flicks and then a longer pass down the right flank.

When the ball was eventually played into the area to the edge of the six-yard box, Puskás controlled it adroitly, shadowed all the while by Billy Wright. Let the victim describe what happened next:

> Puskás was in the inside-right position when he received the ball. I thought I was perfectly placed to make a tackle, but as I challenged he pulled the ball back with the sole of his left foot and all in the same movement fired a left foot shot inside Gil Merrick's near post.
>
> I tackled thin air and the next day that great reporter Geoffrey Green wrote in *The Times* that I was like a fire engine going in the wrong direction for the fire. It was a perfect summary. Puskás had completely hoodwinked me. In all my 105 internationals I did not see a better executed goal.

For those British football managers and players, like Revie, who thought deeply about the game, it was an exciting moment. Revolution was in the air, and the tactics, training methods, every aspect of the way they'd previously prepared and played the game would need to be rethought.

The British being the British, change would be slow in coming. While the lessons taught by the Hungarians were no doubt being absorbed, the rest of the 1953–54 season saw no fundamental changes to the style of play of Division One clubs.

Revie's dissatisfaction at Manchester City continued. He played mostly at wing-half, but was also asked to fill in at other positions. 'It isn't exactly conducive to happy relations when one is switched around like a yo-yo,' was his curt assessment of the role – or roles – given him in the side.

Despite all that, he did manage to win his first representative honours, playing for England B against Scotland B at Roker Park in March 1954. Then a groin injury curtailed his progress and ruled out a possible inclusion in the full England squad; his place, much to his chagrin, went to his City colleague Ivor Broadis.

Manchester City stumbled towards 17th place in the table. But far more interesting developments were taking place in the reserve side, where centre-forward Johnny Williamson – a good friend of Revie's –

was trying out a Hidegkuti-type role, lying deep behind the other four forwards.

Whether by accident or design, it seemed to work and the reserves embarked on an extraordinary run of 26 matches without defeat by the end of the season. Food for thought, indeed, for City's first-team boss, Les McDowall.

You might have expected Revie to be enthusiastic about the experiment. But his instinctive caution, at this stage, held sway over the more innovative side of his nature. He believed it wouldn't work at the highest level because backs and wing-halves would cover and tackle too quickly.

So when the 1954–55 season started, Revie and his colleagues were in for a surprise. Asked to start pre-season training two weeks earlier than normal, they were startled to be told the emphasis would be on as much ball practice as possible. The normal pre-season routine involved plenty of stamina work, loads of running; now City's players were being asked to prepare more like Continentals.

Then McDowall delivered his bombshell. Without mentioning the name Hidegkuti, he outlined a plan for the side that was clearly, in essence, the same method of playing as that created by the Hungarian maestro. A deep-lying centre-forward or midfield schemer would have licence to wander all over the field, demand the ball and set attacks in train. It would need someone with a lot of stamina, but if it was backed up by hard-working wing-halves and inside-forwards, McDowall assured his players, it had every chance of working.

He turned to Revie, and made it crystal clear that he was the ideal man to fulfil the role. Revie was excited at the prospect but worried. He felt the plan would fail if keeper Trautmann just banged long kicks up the field; it would falter, too, if full-backs, feeling under pressure, also resorted to hitting long hopeful balls out of defence. But, as he weighed the pros and cons in his mind, he knew that City couldn't continue in the mediocre, stereotyped fashion of recent seasons. It was definitely worth a go.

The 'Revie Plan', as it would eventually be known (a misnomer in many ways, because, as we've seen, Revie wasn't its architect, although he was its executioner), had its first outing on 19 August 1954, at Deepdale. It was a disaster; Preston thumped Manchester City 5–0, and the scoreline could have been much worse if it hadn't have been for the heroics of Bert Trautmann. One Tommy Docherty, Preston's 26-year-old Scotland wing-half, particularly revelled in the uncertainty in the City ranks and carved out numerous openings for his teammates.

But the die was cast, and despite the initial failure McDowall and City persevered with the new system. Slowly but surely, it began to produce results, with Ken Barnes, the most industrious of wing-halfs, doing much of the fetching and carrying for Revie. The backs, including Roy Paul, Dave Ewing, Jimmy Meadows and Roy Little, were asked to be far more flexible and mobile than in the past, and they responded superbly, too.

Revie was now a zealot for the system; read his 1955 autobiography and you'll find four chapters on the subject, complete with diagrams. He played down his role, claiming, 'It was not Don Revie who made the team play. I was only in the position which you might describe as the linksman; or chief ball distributor from defence to attack.'

But as City moved up the First Division table, people were sitting up and taking notice, including the England selectors. They wanted to completely reshape the national side after the humiliation at the hands of the Hungarians, followed by an indifferent World Cup campaign in Switzerland, which culminated in a 4–2 quarter-final defeat at the hands of Uruguay.

For England's first game in the British Home Championship against Northern Ireland on 2 October, no fewer than seven new caps were awarded. In came Don Revie, Johnny Haynes (Fulham), Ray Wood and Bill Foulkes (Manchester United), Johnny Wheeler (Bolton), Ray Barlow (West Bromwich Albion) and Brian Pilkington (Burnley).

Pilkington, aged 21, a clever left-winger, was the man who kept Brian Clough out of the RAF National XI; he would later play with him in an England B side. He was lucky to have been posted to RAF Kirkham, just down the road from Burnley, so he had hardly missed a league match between 1951 and 1953.

He found out about his selection after stepping off the bus on his way home to Preston. 'The *Evening Post* billboard said something about "New England Team Announced", so I bought a copy and discovered I'd been selected. Then when I got home there was a formal letter waiting for me.

'It came as a bit of a surprise, although I'd played for England B, as well as representing the Under-21s and the Football League. I didn't know Don very well, but when we met up as a squad and got talking he seemed a nice chap and helpful, on and off the pitch.'

Pilkington's father, William, and one of his brothers, Bill, sailed over from Fleetwood on Friday to watch him make his debut at Windsor Park on the Saturday. They had the pleasure of watching him help make England's opening goal. *The Times* described it thus: 'From Pilkington's touch, Haynes made his first telling pass inside Montgomery to Revie, and followed this by moving cleverly to receive Revie's return. With a sidestep to an Irish tackle he was free to beat Uprichard with a low shot.'

A minute later, and Revie had a debut goal to treasure. A fluent move between Matthews, Nat Lofthouse, Revie and Haynes, and back again to Revie, allowed City's new deep-lying centre-forward to shoot low across Norman Uprichard's body and into the net. England were home and dry, 2–0.

Despite the win, the verdict on the side's performance was fairly damning. 'Football Headache For England; New Combination a Failure in Spite of Belfast Victory' read one headline. Wheeler, Barlow and Pilkington were discarded, joining the ranks of one-cap wonders.

'I thought I'd done all right,' recalls Pilkington. 'I expected to play again, to be honest. In those days there was a selection committee, and if they liked your face you probably stood a better chance. I don't know. You just have to take it on the chin. They think they're picking the best team – let them get on with it.'

The jury was still out on Revie's ability to compete at the very highest level. He himself was brutally honest in his assessment of his performance that day: 'I was a flop. It was my own fault. I played too close to Stan [Matthews], and there were times when I must have got in his way.'

He missed the next few international games but was back in the side to play Scotland at Wembley on 2 April 1955. It was a memorable match for a variety of reasons, and not just the scoreline, an emphatic 7–2 victory for England.

Duncan Edwards won his first cap at the age of 18 years, 183 days, the youngest England player of the twentieth century. Meanwhile, one of the oldest, Stanley Matthews, aged 40, showed no sign of letting up; his wing play – helped by some incisive passing from his inside-forward partner Revie, wearing the number 8 shirt – destroyed the Scots again and again.

Revie tapped in from close range for England's third, and had a hand in goals from Wilshaw and Lofthouse. Dennis Wilshaw, the twenty-eight-year-old quick, left-footed centre-forward from Wolves, scored no fewer than four, three of them in just thirteen minutes in the last twenty-five minutes of the game.

Finally, Tommy Docherty, who'd put a spanner in the works of the 'Revie Plan' back in August, scored the goal of the game, albeit only a consolation, a rasping 30-yard free kick that fairly flew into the top left-hand corner of the net.

On that day, it looked as if a long and illustrious England career beckoned for Revie. Instead, there would be only four more caps spread over the next eighteen months. His last match for his country that season was a disappointing 1–0 defeat against France in Paris in May.

By October, he was ensconced in his deep-lying role for his club, but for England he had to be content with an orthodox inside-right position, alongside Nat Lofthouse, for the away fixture against Denmark in Copenhagen.

It was a triumph for Revie, arguably his best display in an England shirt. He scored twice (one a penalty), as did Lofthouse, and they tore the Danish defence to shreds. Three weeks later, he earned his fifth cap, against Wales at Ninian Park, a match England lost 2–1 but might have drawn had Revie's astute back-heel in the closing minutes been converted by Tom Finney; his shot rattled the crossbar, and the Welsh had their first win over England since 1938.

Finally, almost two years to the day since his debut, and on the same pitch, the curtain came down on Revie's international career. Stanley Matthews' 11th (and last) goal for his country gave England a great start in the match against Northern Ireland at Windsor Park on 6 October 1956; but Jimmy McIlroy equalised and, if truth be told, England were lucky to escape with a draw, with Irish captain Danny Blanchflower – later a fierce critic of Revie the manager – in inspirational form.

Revie played for England at a time when there was stiff competition for places in the forward line. Johnny Haynes, the Fulham schemer and one of the most accomplished passers of a ball the game has ever seen, was a natural competitor for his place, and Haynes tended to get the nod.

But if his England career had started and then stuttered, Revie was continuing to reap the rewards of City's new system and his freedom at the hub of it. The club finished seventh in Division One in 1955 and made it all the way to Wembley for the FA Cup final against Newcastle. Derby, Man United, Luton, Birmingham and Sunderland (1–0 in the semi-final) were all seen off comfortably enough, with just one goal conceded on the way.

But Newcastle were formidable cup warriors, having won in 1951 and 1952. On that day in May, they got off to an electric start, with

Jackie Milburn heading home Len White's corner kick after just 45 seconds – the quickest opening goal (then) to have been scored at Wembley.

City responded well, and for a while the 'Revie Plan' seemed to be functioning smoothly, with its namesake prompting effectively. A terrific flying header from Bobby Johnstone brought City level just before half-time, and there was some cause for optimism.

But the match turned, principally for two reasons. City's full-back Jimmy Meadows, who had already been finding Newcastle's dazzling winger Bobby Mitchell a handful, was forced to go off with a twisted knee that he had actually sustained after just 20 minutes – and there were no substitutes in those days. In addition, the Newcastle defence was getting wise to the 'plan', pushing out early and catching City's forwards offside as Revie tried to thread the ball through to them.

The elusive Mitchell grabbed a second for Newcastle, squeezing the ball past Bert Trautmann from a narrow angle, and George Hannah completed the scoring after yet more smart work from the winger.

The wags had dubbed the final 'The Gaudies v. The Geordies' because of the flashy tracksuits on display that day from City's players. Revie put the defeat down to the simple fact that Newcastle had an extra man for the final 45 minutes: 'The plain truth is, that I believe it is impossible to win a Cup final at Wembley with ten men – especially against such doughty and experienced opponents as Newcastle. Wembley might be perfect to play on . . . but [it's] extremely tiring when you have to do all the chasing.'

Despite the disappointment of a cup final defeat, and City fading away somewhat in the league, it was the season Revie finally fulfilled his huge promise. It was rounded off when he received the coveted Footballer of the Year award, voted for by the Football Writers' Association, in succession to Tom Finney.

Brian Glanville, combining a career as football writer and novelist in those days, never had any doubts about Revie's qualities: 'He was an extraordinary player. I even remember watching him for Leicester reserves at Highbury back in the 1940s and he looked good then. Technically he was very accomplished, he had excellent ball control, and he used the ball so well. If there was a chink in his armour, it was that he wasn't particularly fast; but he didn't need pace on days like that semi-final against Portsmouth in 1949, when he absolutely destroyed them.'

This should have been the time when Revie sat back, basked in the warm glow of his achievements and contemplated the prospect of an even better season ahead. At 28, he was now at the height of his powers, confident and experienced. With hindsight, though, this was the beginning of the end of his time in Manchester, even though greater glories lay ahead in 1956.

★ ★ ★

When City's players returned after their summer break they were surprised not to find Revie alongside them. Revie believed he had struck an agreement with trainer Laurie Barnett that he could take his first extended holiday for six years, and so he booked a fortnight's break in Blackpool. At the last moment, City backtracked and ordered him back for early pre-season training. Revie, who felt he needed – and deserved – a longer rest, refused to comply and stayed away, although he trained while on holiday and when he did eventually return was half a stone lighter.

The damage had been done, though, as far as manager Les McDowall and his board of directors were concerned. Revie was suspended for 14 days without pay (costing him £27), and the club hierarchy quickly made the facts – as they saw them – known to the newspapers.

Revie, furious, retaliated with a press offensive of his own. It began back home in Middlesbrough; the *Evening Gazette* reporter managed to grab a quick word with Revie, who revealed he'd swiftly put in a transfer request: 'They have turned me down and I am not prepared to say more. The news, I must say, has come as a very big shock, but it will be a day or two before I decide what my next move will be.'

Revie was relegated to the reserves, and 26-year-old Bobby Johnstone took over his pivotal role in the side, which may have been McDowall's intention in any case. For the rest of the season, Revie was in and out of the side, ultimately playing in only about half of the matches. Both Johnstone and Ken Barnes regretted his demotion and felt McDowall was tinkering around far too much with the side; he even experimented with a sweeper.

But there was to be one final, glorious twist to Revie's City career. The side had once more enjoyed an excellent cup run, culminating in a 1–0 semi-final victory over Tottenham Hotspur. Their opponents on Saturday, 5 May 1956 were Birmingham City, who had comfortably disposed of Sunderland 3–0 in their semi-final.

Birmingham were the clear favourites. They'd been streets ahead of their opposition in the games leading up to the final, while City, more often than not, had to scrap for their victories.

Revie had just displayed tremendous form in City's 4–2 win over Portsmouth in the last league match of the season. McDowall still wasn't sure he wanted to pick him for the Wembley match, but, with Manchester's right-winger Billy Spurdle unexpectedly laid low with an attack of boils and Bobby Johnstone doubtful with a calf injury, the way was surely open for Revie to secure a place.

Journalist Eric Thornton was an eyewitness to the drama that followed on the morning of the match. In his book *Leeds United and Don Revie*, he picks up the story:

> We lolled around in the lounge of the Oatlands Hotel in Weybridge. Don, a match winner if ever there was one, crossed and re-crossed his legs, took a spot of fresh air outside, then returned and rejoined the others once more.
>
> I went upstairs, opened a line to Manchester, and waited. Suddenly the place came to life. McDowall opened his bedroom door and said, with a half-smile: 'Revie's in, Johnstone switches and don't mention the injury.'
>
> I slipped downstairs, McDowall followed, and we looked across at Revie. He seemed to be fearing the worst. So I gave him a half-hidden thumbs up, but he shook his head in disbelief, then knew it was true as the team was read out.

What Revie felt was a massive surge of relief. The reprieve granted, he went out and played the game of his life, although it will always be remembered as Trautmann's final because of the astonishing courage City's goalkeeper showed in playing the final 17 minutes of the match with a broken neck.

The highlights show Revie losing the ball in midfield in an early exchange; he's slow to react to a ball played up to him. But that's soon forgotten in a virtuoso passage of play just two minutes later. Revie picks up the ball in the wide open spaces in the centre of Wembley's immaculate pitch. With no one within ten yards of him, he's free to fashion a move pretty much as he pleases. He doesn't hesitate and surges forward from midfield before sweeping a beautiful 40-yard pass out to Roy Clarke on the left wing.

Revie doesn't rest on his laurels. He races forward into the penalty area, and when Clarke's cross comes over he has the presence of mind to deftly back-heel the ball into the path of Joe Hayes, who, with his defender unbalanced by Revie's cheeky bit of skill, fires the ball into the net with his left foot from 15 yards.

A wonderful goal and one Revie almost seemed to have worked out from the moment he picked up the ball, unmarked, in midfield. Vision, quick thinking, smart footwork: the elements of his work.

Birmingham equalised just after the interval when Noel Kinsey's shot went in off Trautmann. But Revie was in charge and played a key part in the build-up to the second goal, scored by Jack Dyson after a neat pass from Bobby Johnstone. For the third, Revie could take no credit; Trautmann's long punt upfield found the duo of Johnstone and Dyson free of the Birmingham defence, and this time Johnstone crashed the ball home to make it 3–1.

Then came Trautmann's sickening injury, sustained when Birmingham's inside-forward Peter Murphy's knee collided with his neck as he came out to smother the ball. Trautmann, knocked unconscious, came round to feel a wave of pain shooting down his neck and shoulder. For the next five minutes, he reeled around the goalmouth like a drunk, bending over in agony and clutching his neck with his left hand. But still he somehow managed to make a number of saves and challenges, with the other defenders taking goalkicks for him.

Trautmann would recover, in time, from his injury. A place for him in City folklore was assured, but Revie stands beside him. Perhaps he was relaxed because he just didn't expect to play – relaxed in a different way from his preparation before the FA Cup semi-final seven years earlier.

Whatever the reason for his exceptional performance, he had a winner's medal at last, the first of his career. McDowall bowed to the evidence just laid out before him, and when the players returned for the 1956–57 season Revie was restored to his playmaking role.

But City started disastrously, losing six games in succession in September and October, and McDowall quickly reacted as he had done a year earlier by pulling Revie back to right-half and switching Johnstone to deep-lying centre-forward.

The cracks had only really been papered over in the relationship between McDowall and Revie. The wanderer wanted to be on the move again, his standing in the game now likely to bring him substantially increased earnings in any transfer deal.

That deal was done in November, with a £24,000 move back to his native North-East, to Roker Park, where he had started on the first rung of his England career back in 1954. He was 29, at the peak of his footballing ability, and he was confident Sunderland could bring the best out of him again.

Chapter 4
'Clough Must Change His Style'

Don Revie may have left the town at the age of 17 to achieve footballing fame, but the people of Middlesbrough undoubtedly felt pride in his achievements. He could never be compared with the likes of Camsell, Hardwick and Mannion, who had worn the red and white shirt with distinction, but nonetheless he was still 'one of them'. In a place with a history of just over a hundred years, heroes were too rare to be discarded just because they had made their real mark elsewhere.

For 20-year-old Brian Clough, back from National Service and about to embark on a full-time professional career, Revie's election as Footballer of the Year in 1955 would have been an inspiration.

'At that time there was definitely a touch of hero worship,' according to Duncan Hamilton, who got to know Clough well in later years as a journalist in Nottingham and wrote a memoir about their relationship, *Provided You Don't Kiss Me*. 'He would have admired Revie for being an FA Cup winner, a famous man who had made it to the top from a town that for most people was just a dot on the map.'

As he prepared for the 1955–56 season, Clough's own path to fame and glory was far from straightforward. The man in possession of the number 9 shirt at Middlesbrough was Charlie Wayman, a former miner who was approaching the veteran stage at 33 but was still reckoned to be one of the best goalscorers in the Football League; his tally of 105 goals in 157 appearances for his previous club, Preston North End, bore testimony to that.

But should Wayman be injured or lose form, there were two other rivals to Clough waiting in the wings. One was 28-year-old Ken McPherson, Hartlepool born, brave and particularly good in the air, who had scored six goals in nineteen appearances in the previous season. The second was Doug Cooper, not yet 19, a local lad from Eston, a big, bustling centre-forward who had been a prolific scorer for Middlesbrough's junior sides. A number of shrewd judges at Ayresome Park expected greater things of him than of Clough.

Peter Taylor, a 27-year-old goalkeeper who arrived at Middlesbrough in August 1955 for a fee of £3,500, was not one of them. The first time he faced Clough on the pitch, in a pre-season Probables v. Possibles match, he was won over at once:

> I was impressed immediately by the way this crew-cut unknown shielded the ball and how cleanly he struck it. Above all, I admired the arrogance of his play.
>
> I've never been backward about voicing my opinions, but when I suggested, 'That lad can't half play,' the other players merely shrugged, but Brian himself sidled up after a while. Someone told him I was singing his praises and that was how our friendship began.

Taylor described how he was so taken with the young centre-forward from Grove Hill that he even suggested to his old boss at Coventry, Harry Storer, who was by then in charge of Derby County, that he should sign him. He took Clough to meet Storer in secret at Hartlepools United's ground – in flagrant contravention of FA rules – but Storer, despite Taylor's passionate recommendation, decided not to pursue the matter.

Clough, not the most patient of men, nevertheless knuckled down in the reserves, so much so that by mid-September he'd already notched 15 goals. Finally, Bob Dennison, the Boro boss, decided the time was right, leaving out McPherson and pitching in Clough for his debut against Barnsley at Ayresome Park.

The headline the day before the game read 'A Second Camsell Makes His Bid for Fame'. For any young, aspiring centre-forward at Middlesbrough, the Camsell reference was de rigueur. In his enthusiasm to promote Clough, the writer – under the pseudonym 'Talk of the Town' – had mistakenly given his age as 19 and also claimed he'd been spotted by Camsell, which was far from the real story of Clough's recruitment to Boro, as we've heard.

Nevertheless, a young goalscorer always attracts plenty of attention and Clough was now firmly in the spotlight. His first appearance at Ayresome Park was a little underwhelming – Boro were held to a 1–1 draw in front of a crowd of nearly 25,000, inside-forward Arthur Fitzsimons rescuing a point with a goal in the 83rd minute. Clough himself had one vivid memory of that day:

> At the very moment I walked towards the dressing-room door, on my way out with the rest of the team, Dennison said to me: 'It's up to you now.'
>
> That was wrong. He should have cuffed me on the back or shoulder and said, 'Good luck, son. I know you'll do well.' He sent me out on a downer when he should have put me at ease. It was a mistake I never made in 28 years as a manager. When footballers go out onto a field they have to be relaxed, not frightened. Sometimes that frame of mind is difficult to achieve, but they simply have to relax.

Clough began to settle down a little once he'd scored his first goal, in Boro's thrilling 4–3 home victory against Leicester City on 8 October. Seven more appearances followed that season, with a couple more goals against Lincoln City and Bristol City.

Another exciting young forward had burst onto the scene in the closing weeks of the season who may at first have appeared as a threat to Clough but who would soon become a formidable partner. Alan Peacock, a strapping eighteen-year-old, scored two goals in a 4–2 away win at Nottingham Forest and wore the number 9 shirt on six occasions.

Middlesbrough finished the season in 14th position. If there was something positive to take forward, it lay in the introduction of a group of exciting young forward players: Clough, Peacock, Billy Day, a pacy 19-year-old right-winger from South Bank, and Derek McLean, a hard-working 23-year-old inside-forward. The future of the club looked much brighter than it had done for several years.

One man on his way out of Ayresome Park was Rolando Ugolini, the goalkeeper Peter Taylor was brought in to replace. It would be an important loss to Middlesbrough, perhaps not on playing grounds, because the 33-year-old keeper was probably past his best, but because he was a character in the dressing-room and liked by the supporters on the terraces. He'd come to Boro from Celtic in 1948 and chalked up 335 appearances; consistently good on the pitch, he was a man who raised the spirits off it.

One of the iconic football photographs of the 1950s shows Wilf Mannion leading his side out onto the Ayresome Park pitch, ball clasped between his hands, looking intently towards the pitch, mind concentrated on the task ahead. Ugolini, dark, rugged face with jet-black hair, grasping his own ball, has an equally purposeful air as he follows his skipper out from the players' tunnel.

The picture – one of a number for a feature entitled 'The Team Is the Town's Concern' – was taken by George Douglas for *Picture Post* on 3 November 1951, as Middlesbrough prepared to take on championship leaders Arsenal in front of a 35,000 crowd.

The two men are flanked by commissionaires as they walk out, and there's a man in a flat cap and raincoat sitting facing them on the wall, shouting some words of encouragement. Close by, a mother, with her young son perched nervously on the wall, watches in anticipation as the heroes step out. All around the players stands a sea of men, some with flat caps or hats, nearly every one wearing a shirt, tie and jacket.

It's a lovely day, with the promise of a great game. The Golden Boy is striding out towards an afternoon of golden sunshine and the prospect of many memorable moments on the ball.

A touch of madness is a prerequisite for a goalkeeper, so it's often said, and Ugolini was one of life's eccentrics. But although he clowned around both on and off the pitch, his basic ability was in no doubt; he was agile, brave and commanding in his penalty area.

He certainly took no nonsense from opposing forwards, and he tells the story of how he put a stop to a tactic of Don Revie: 'Don was one of those guys who stood next to goalkeepers and backed into them. In fact, he may well have started the whole trend. Anyway, on this particular day, he did it once, and I warned him about it. When he repeated it a second time, from a corner kick, I squeezed him very hard at the side of his body – you know, where the fat area is – and he started squealing like a pig. He told the referee I'd nipped him, and I told him not to talk silly. Then he lifted his shirt to show a big black-and-blue mark. But he didn't back into me ever again!'

Indeed, after that, Ugolini and Revie became good friends on the players' golf circuit. Revie was virtually a scratch golfer in those days, while Ugolini played off just three.

$$\star \ \star \ \star$$

Talk to any Middlesbrough player from the late '40s through the '50s about the Ayresome Park crowd and the one name that constantly springs to their lips is 'Big Astor'.

Astor Garriques was a man you couldn't fail to miss – or, more especially, to hear – whether you were playing on the pitch or watching on the terraces. He had a big, booming voice that sounded out across the ground, silencing conversations in the crowd and bringing everyone to attention. It quickly earned him a variety of sobriquets on the same theme, including 'The Mouth of the Tees' and, quite simply, 'The Voice'.

Astor stood out like the proverbial sore thumb for other reasons: he was easily over six feet tall, burly – and black. To be one of just a handful of black men in a sea of 30,000 white faces would have been intimidating for most, but not Astor. He had a captive audience, perfect for a man who was a fireman at ICI by day but a comedian in the pubs and clubs in Middlesbrough – indeed in the whole of the North-East – by night. His impromptu gags kept the crowd entertained when the action on the pitch was less than compelling. Just after the war, he once rolled up his sleeve and told them, 'You lot have got rid of your khaki. I've got mine for life!'

Charlie Williams, a black footballer for Doncaster Rovers who later went on to become a famous TV comedian himself in the 1960s, recalled playing at Ayresome Park and hearing a loud voice booming out from behind the goal as he raced towards it, 'This place ain't big enough for the two of us!'

Astor would target many of his choicest comments at Middlesbrough's own black player, Lindy Delapenha, a Jamaican-born winger who was a crowd favourite for his speed, physical presence and fierce shot. Astor would call Delapenha 'our kid' and urge him on to greater things.

This son of exotic parentage – his father, Joseph, was French West Indian, his mother, Bertha, Russian – can lay a powerful claim to being Britain's first black comedian. There were a few others around in the North at the time – Charlie Williams, Josh White, Sammy Thomas – but Astor hit the clubs before any of them did.

His material was, by today's standards, utterly politically incorrect and – as perhaps a black man felt he had to be in those days – self-deprecating. Astor would, unusually, climb down into the audience and walk around, and he'd say to them, for example, 'If you don't laugh at my jokes, I'll eat you up. I've had a missionary for my tea before!'

His son Garth, as a young boy, used to travel around the clubs watching his father's act. 'When he walked into a pub, people would stop and look up at him in awe. He was always very dapper, very smartly dressed, always in a suit. Two-thirds of the time, he didn't even use the microphone. He could play the trombone, but he also used to like to play the drums, and he'd do that for about half a minute then look up and tell the audience, "You're surrounded!"'

Astor's almost celebrity status in Middlesbrough was down to the unique character of the man. But his story tells you something else about the character of the town, indicating a tolerance that was perhaps rare in England at the time, especially in big Northern urban centres.

Middlesbrough, however, was different from places like Newcastle, Sunderland or Durham. It had always been a melting pot, since its birth, with immigrants coming to the town from the British colonies, the East Indies and the United States.

Garth Garriques reflects, 'Dad had no problems in Middlesbrough if you're talking about racial prejudice. There were quite a few black people in the town, but there were also Irishmen, Scotsmen – it had a very cosmopolitan feel to it. People in this part of the world were easy-going and enjoyed good crack together.'

Historians who believe that's too romantic a view of Middlesbrough's social integration often point to the Cannon Street Riots of 1961 as evidence of stresses within parts of the community. Cannon Street was where Astor lived for a spell. There were scenes of widespread disorder there in August 1961 after John Joseph Hunt, an 18-year-old apprentice moulder, was killed in a fight with a sailor, Hassan Said. Said was later charged with Hunt's murder. The Middlesbrough magistrate at the time, Alfred Peaker, told the rioters:

> I have no doubt that this affair started through some individuals visiting public houses and then trying to whip up feeling against some of these coloured people living in the Cannon Street area. The evidence shows that the coloured population were quiet and peaceful and never did anything at all to give any provocation. But they were attacked.

Back at Ayresome Park, Garth Garriques remembers the time his father had another of his habitual crashes on his motorbike: 'He signed himself out of hospital so he could go and watch Middlesbrough play on the Saturday. Brian Clough was playing, and at half-time he came out of the dressing-room, walked over to Dad, brought him a cup of tea and signed the plaster cast on his legs!'

Astor's 'our kid', Lindy Delapenha, was not the first black man to play professional football in England, but he was the first Jamaican to do so, and he was certainly Middlesbrough's first black player. A pacy winger with a ferocious shot, he very rarely encountered racial abuse from his home fans. The Ayresome Park faithful took him to their hearts not just because of his skill but also because of his ability to laugh at himself.

'If anything happened on the field that I didn't do the right way, I would somehow try to defuse it with a sense of humour, and in the end most of the fans ended up laughing about whatever it was. I think that technique worked at away games, too, at places like Anfield, where the Spion Kop appreciated a player with character.'

But Delapenha admits there were some grounds where he took some stick. 'Once or twice, I might be called a black bastard, and I'd give them the finger, you know, but it didn't happen very often.'

His best friend and roommate for most away matches, Rolando Ugolini, himself an immigrant from Lucca in Italy, thinks Delapenha played down the level of abuse he received. 'It was very hard for Lindy. At away matches, they used to call him everything under the sun. It was terrible at times. Away from the pitch, they wouldn't say anything to him when I was with him, because I could handle myself. If anyone said anything bad about the Italians, I'd fire back and . . . bang!'

* * *

Clough, perhaps encouraged by his new mentor Peter Taylor, startled manager Bob Dennison by putting in a transfer request towards the end of the 1955–56 season – the first of many during his period at Middlesbrough. It may just have been a ruse to get a wage rise; Taylor reckoned Clough was earning just £11 and a few pence for a fortnight, after stoppages.

Typically, Clough used the local media to plead his case, as he would do consistently over the coming years. 'The trouble is I feel no further forward now than I was when I played for the senior team near the beginning of the season,' he told the *Evening Gazette*. 'I want to improve all the time and I think that any big improvement will come quickest if I move from Ayresome Park.'

The request was turned down, the pay rise was eventually forthcoming, and Clough embarked on a remarkable goal spree. He came of age in what he would refer to as his 'Golden Year', the 1956–57 season, when his cockiness, sometimes out-and-out arrogance, were justified by his displays home and away.

The scoring started in the first away game, at Bury on 21 August, when he struck two second-half goals in a 3–2 defeat. Four days later, at Barnsley, he hit two more in a 3–1 victory. By 1 December, after 20 league games, he'd scored 20 goals and Boro were up into fourth position.

Opposing centre-halfs knew they were facing something special, the sort of threat they'd not often encountered before. Allenby Chilton, formerly of Manchester United and England, faced up to Clough for Grimsby Town at Blundell Park. Grimsby won 3–2, but Clough scored both goals for Middlesbrough, and Chilton commented after the game: 'He is a grand young player. He scored two and might well have scored two more. I cannot see any reason why he should not have a great future in the game.'

On the terraces, Boro fans revelled in the fact that they had a centre-forward in the George Elliott/Andy Wilson/George Camsell tradition. Alan Keen, later to become a scout for the club and after that an MP, was one of those spectators who looked on admiringly. 'His instinct always was to go for goal,' he remembers. 'It didn't matter whether there was one or two defenders in front of him. He was a very direct player. He was expert at finding the corner of the net with his shots, which were invariably hit all along the ground. He also specialised in diving headers. Once he started scoring goals for the club, he never seemed to stop.'

Delapenha was one of those who originally thought young Doug Cooper might turn out to be a better player than Clough. 'But Peter Taylor used to ram it down my throat about how good Brian was and – as was often the case – Peter was right and I was wrong. Brian was so mature in his mind for a youngster and, to my surprise, I learned a lot from him. He found the open spaces well, and you could always find him with the ball because he was such a clever mover around the field.'

Delapenha wasn't having a bad season himself, and he'd notched up eight goals by the beginning of December. His on-field relationship with Clough was a good one – principally, no doubt, because Clough appreciated that Delapenha was, in his words, 'making the bullets for him to fire'.

'I remember one game in particular at Leyton Orient. I hit a fierce shot at goal, which the keeper parried but only just across the side of the goal, giving me the clear opportunity to try and score again. Instead, I turned it back across to Brian and he hit it into the net. And do you know what he did next? He came over to me, held up my right arm above my head and ran back with me all the way to the halfway line, keeping my arm above my head, letting people know it was really my goal, not his. Now, I appreciated that very much. He was arrogant, yes, but also fair.'

Clough had an almost mystical view of the task of scoring goals:

> I loved the feeling that came with every goal. When you're a goalscorer, the penalty area is sacred ground. When you are in that 'box' every eye is on you. Everyone in the other team is trying to stop you. I revelled in that responsibility. I make no apologies for jumping in the air and flinging my arms sky high each time I scored.

Away from the hallowed turf, the trio of Clough, Delapenha and Taylor were spending a lot of time together. They tended to travel around the countryside, as Taylor, a Midlander, was less than impressed by the leisure opportunities in the town:

> Middlesbrough of the mid-'50s was a place where you could see hundreds of men shuffling on the pavements of the main streets on Sunday mornings, gazing expectantly at the town hall clock. At the first stroke of noon, they had vanished into the opening doors of pubs. What drab pubs, too. Many in the Middlesbrough of those days were sawdust-on-the floor alehouses that refused admission to women.
>
> Emptying pint pots seemed the chief preoccupation of Middlesbrough's shipyard workers and steelmen; after that came football, horses, dogs and pigeons.

You might regard what Taylor, Clough and Delapenha did instead of supping pints to be equally dull. Such was Taylor and Clough's obsession with football that they'd hop into the back of Delapenha's little Morris Minor – later he acquired a Morris Minor 1000 – and persuade him to drive them all around Cleveland and beyond looking for a match to watch.

It could be any kind of game, from schoolboy Under-13 to North-East Wednesday League matches. Almost anywhere, it seemed to Delapenha, that they found a green field and a ball being kicked about, they'd get him to stop the car, then they'd climb out and start analysing what was before them.

Sometimes they would spend a few hours informally coaching schoolboys at Redcar, picking up a little money from the headmaster along the way. 'I guess that was the start of their path to management,' says Delapenha, 'although whether they had that specifically in mind at the time I wouldn't know. I was the only one with a car at the time, so I had to do the work, but I didn't mind; I liked them. Brian was a likeable rogue and Peter – well, I know a lot of people who didn't get on with him because they felt he was sly, but we got on well because we were racing people. We loved horse racing and used to go to events together in the area.'

Back on the pitch on a Saturday, Boro couldn't maintain their excellent form of the first three months and their championship challenge slowly fizzled out. Lindy Delapenha's form suffered, too, and a bright young right-winger called Billy Day took his place.

The rave reviews that Clough consistently commanded, however, now thrust him into the international arena. On 6 February 1957, he was selected to play in his first representative match, for England B against Scotland B at St Andrew's, Birmingham.

With barely 30 seconds gone in the game, Clough had made an impact. He whipped the ball across the pitch and into the path of Brian Pilkington – the man who had beaten him to a place in the RAF XI and who had made a full England debut alongside Don Revie two years earlier – and the Burnley left-winger ran onto it and rocketed a first-time drive into the net.

Ten minutes later and Clough had his own goal, crisply converting a cross after Alf Stokes of Tottenham Hotspur had cut the ball back from the byline. Further goals followed from Preston's Peter Thompson and Harry Hooper of Wolves – Clough having a hand in the latter – and England ran out comfortable 4–1 winners in front of a remarkably large crowd of 39,376. Proof that it was a serious footballing occasion was the televising of the second half of the match.

Cliff Mitchell of the *Evening Gazette*, by now established as Clough's cheerleader-in-chief, was ecstatic at the turn of events. 'Breath-Taking Debut by Clough' blazed the *Gazette* headline. Mitchell wrote: 'It was a superb display by a 21-year-old who must surely be destined for the game's highest honours. And not before very long.'

But the accolades came not just from the local press. The *Daily Express* headline was 'Clough's The Boy!' and reporter Bob Pennington mused: 'How's that for a boy in his first season as a league regular and having his first taste of representative football with two stitches under his eye? Crew-cut Clough can thank an ice-cool temperament and an ice-pack for this fantastic start to what looks like a long England career.'

Three weeks later and Clough was picked for England again, this time for the Under-23s against Scotland in Glasgow. He performed indifferently in a 1–1 draw, after being asked to play in an unfamiliar deep-lying centre-forward role more suited to the likes of Don Revie. In the subsequent Under-23s match in May, he kept his place. But despite his headed goal, England succumbed 2–1 to the Bulgarians in Sofia.

A few weeks before that appearance, Clough rounded off his domestic season with a remarkable display in the final home match against Huddersfield Town. The score stood at 1–1 after forty-five minutes, but Boro let rip after the interval and ran out 7–2 victors, with Clough scoring four to bring his season's tally to forty goals in forty-four games. Middlesbrough ended up a highly creditable sixth in the table, eight places better than the previous term. Promotion to Division One now looked a distinct possibility.

Cliff Mitchell, in his end-of-season report, had little doubt that the 'most important single factor' to explain Boro's improvement was Clough's contribution. 'His success has been largely due to his fierce shooting, accurate heading and indomitable spirit,' he concluded.

Clough's penchant for using the media – even in those early days – was evident in the final weeks of the season when he wrote a piece headlined 'It's Hard Not to Hit Back at "Clog Brigade"'. He described how some of the 'methods of restraint' used by opposing defenders had tempted him to use similar 'over-vigorous' tactics in response. The message to referees was clear: give me greater protection.

Despite niggling opponents, a worry about the inconsistency of his England performances and a developing concern about Middlesbrough's defence, Clough could be more than satisfied with his achievements. He'd finally broken through and was clearly a major talent to be reckoned with; Peter Taylor didn't need to do any more explaining on that subject.

★ ★ ★

The 1957–58 season was almost an exact replica of 1956–57. Middlesbrough finished a place lower in the league, 7th, scoring 83 goals as opposed to 84 the season before. More worrying – and a statistic Clough wouldn't fail to point out – the defence conceded 74 goals compared to 60 the previous term.

Clough's phenomenal goalscoring continued, this time with 42 goals in 42 league and cup matches. In two matches he hit the back of the net four times – during a 5–0 thrashing of Doncaster Rovers at Ayresome Park, then a 5–2 beating of Ipswich Town, again at home.

You couldn't argue with that sort of record, could you? Well, actually, undercurrents of dissatisfaction were just starting to develop in one corner of the Middlesbrough dressing-room, created by Clough's perceived selfishness and also his close relationship with Peter Taylor.

Brian Phillips, a no-nonsense centre-half who had arrived at Boro in 1954 from non-league Altrincham, finally established himself as a regular in the side in 1957. Later on, in the early 1960s, he would be jailed and banned from football after a widespread bribery racket was discovered in the English game.

At first, he got on well enough with Clough. They'd come out of the forces at the same time – Phillips had been in the RAF police. But the relationship quickly soured. Clough was fed up with the Boro defence leaking so many goals and even started to wonder if it was deliberate.

Phillips disliked the young centre-forward's cocksureness, but he was also suspicious of the Clough–Taylor friendship. 'Cloughie and Peter Taylor always used to have their heads together,' he remembers, 'and they did spend a lot of time with the manager, Bob Dennison. There was always something in the air. At times, the two of them seemed to be running the show.'

There was an encounter between Phillips and Clough at the training ground that did nothing to cool the simmering resentment that existed between the two men. 'It was a practice match, forwards against defence – no prisoners taken – and Cloughie was niggling away, holding my shirt every time the ball was getting played up from the back. I said, "Look, Clou," – that's what I used to call him – "stop holding my shirt, I'm sick to death of this." He told me to shut up and carried on doing it. Anyway, the ball gets knocked up again, he comes to turn on me with the ball, and I went right through him with a crunching tackle.

'He was squirming on the ground and said, "Wait till I get up." I told him, "Listen, when you get up, I'll bloody well still be here, don't you worry." The training session was brought to a halt and Clough taken away to receive treatment.'

Phillips' view of Clough wasn't shared by everyone in the dressing-room, although some of the older players were starting to become irritated by him. But up-and-coming youngsters like Billy Day and Alan Peacock looked up to him and relished the opportunity to play alongside such a natural goalscorer.

Peter Taylor recognised how divisive a figure Clough was:

> I remember a winger complaining to the Middlesbrough training staff that Brian had knocked him off the ball before an open goal and scored himself. Brian's answer, when questioned about it, was undiluted Clough – 'Well, I'm better at it than he is.'
>
> That was his outlook on almost everything: 'I can do it better. What's more, I'll prove it.' He seemed pushy, a know-all and arrogant – but never forget that arrogance is an asset in a footballer. Anyone could see how Brian might upset people, yet I liked him. He was clean-cut; there was nothing treacherous in his nature and, unusually for someone so full of himself, he could stand a little ribbing.

By April, all eyes were starting to turn towards the World Cup in Sweden. Clough picked up his third Under-23 cap against Wales in Wrexham, scoring England's goal in their 2–1 defeat. Opinion was divided on whether Clough had done his full England prospects any good. The *Daily Express* praised the determination he showed for the goal, shrugging off three defenders and driving the ball low into the net; but the *Daily Mail* reckoned Clough 'did himself no good at all. He was pocketed by the match's strong man, Mel Charles, from the word go. There was hardly a peep out of Clough all evening.'

Nonetheless, he was picked for the England party to tour behind the Iron Curtain in May, with games against Yugoslavia in Belgrade and Russia in Moscow. It looked to be a straight choice for the number 9 berth between Clough and Derek Kevan, the big, hard-working West Brom centre-forward, with the latter the man in possession.

It was a fascinating trip for young Clough on the cultural front; in Moscow, he got to see the ballet *Swan Lake* and the opera *Prince Igor*. On the football front, it was immensely disappointing, as he was forced to sit out both games, the 5–0 defeat by Yugoslavia and the 1–1 draw with Russia. Maybe today he would have had a run out as substitute, but, of course, they weren't allowed back then.

For the readers of the *Evening Gazette*, Clough was diplomatic: 'I suppose some people will be saying I must be the most disappointed man in English football. That's how it goes sometimes in professional sport. The big breaks don't always come your way when you most hope they will.'

Later on he would reflect more candidly on his exclusion: 'Derek Kevan was a big, willing centre-forward, not blessed with quickness or outstanding ability to put the ball into the net. It was not simply a disappointment that Kevan was selected ahead of Clough. It was a crime.'

Unfortunately for Clough, England manager Walter Winterbottom thought Kevan had shown enough form on the trip to book his place for the World Cup, to link up with young Bobby Charlton; Spurs centre-forward Bobby Smith was also included as a back-up. So there was no room for Brian Clough in the 20-strong squad.

Of course, Clough had every right to feel frustrated given his goal record the previous season – albeit in Division Two. But wise judges, even in his native North-East, still had to be convinced that he was worth a full England cap.

George Hardwick, former Middlesbrough and England full-back, wrote a critical article that was headlined 'Clough Must Change His Style'. Hardwick's argument was that Clough had misguidedly adopted a bulldozing, tearaway sort of game, worrying goalkeepers and forcing defenders to make errors in the same way that Derek Kevan did; in other words, if you can't beat them, join them.

He wrote: 'I say Brian must change his style. I have already said he has England potential; now is the time it must be developed.' His recommendation? Hours of coaching in ball jugglery in the Continental style, learning all the tricks a Len Shackleton might possess. 'He can do it, for he has a natural, delicate feel of the ball. The only thing he needs is concentrated work with the ball.'

Hardwick's role model for Clough was a young Dutchman, Roel Wiersma, who had honed his rough skills to become the 'best centre-half in Europe' and captain of Holland. He concluded his piece by saying that English coaches must pan out across the world to find new techniques and ideas to bring back and instil in British players.

Clough would have been chastened by that analysis of his game from one of his Middlesbrough heroes. But he was always quick to learn and would have absorbed the advice and been prepared to act on it.

But his unsatisfactory summer was to end with some unexpectedly good news. At the beginning of August, Boro manager Bob Dennison announced a change in the club captaincy. Bill Harris, the team's skilful Welsh international right-half, had been given the captain's job shortly after arriving from Hull City in March 1954. But Dennison felt he needed a more assertive leader. 'Bill is not the type to shout at players on the field and I know he is happier when he is allowed to get on with his own job,' he said. 'That is one of the reasons why I have appointed Clough. He has almost three years' league experience behind him and I am sure he has the aptitude for the job – so that age does not matter.'

Clough was only 23. To those who said he was too young, he replied, 'Age, I think, does not carry a great deal of importance, for if a comparative "youngster" is able to do a job, or at least have a crack at it, then why not give him the chance to prove himself?'

For those who argued that it was folly to hand the responsibility to a centre-forward, mostly stuck at one end of the field, he had this response: 'If it is inspiration that is needed from a captain, I do not think there can be any greater inspiration than when, after being on the defensive for a long period, someone goes through and pops one in at the other end.'

Clough was naturally excited about the season ahead. Long a critic of what he regarded as Middlesbrough's pedestrian training routines, he assured readers of his column in the *Gazette* that new methods had been introduced, with the emphasis much more on ball work. Perhaps he was taking George Hardwick's advice to heart.

The new Clough era started in extraordinary fashion on 23 August at Ayresome Park. Brighton, newly promoted, got the hiding of their lives. Bill Harris put away two penalties, and Alan Peacock grabbed two as well. As for the new skipper – he scored a mere five.

Peacock, for one, wasn't getting carried away with the result. 'Remember,' he says, 'they'd just come up, it was their first game in the new division, and they weren't the greatest of sides.'

But the crowd of 32,367 had had their appetite whetted for the eight months to come. A fresh start with a dynamic new captain, nine goals – it engendered a kind of feverish optimism.

With a couple of additions to the squad – perhaps experienced players who could guide the highly promising set of youngsters in the forward line – promotion would surely be secured this time round. All was set fair for Middlesbrough's return to their rightful place in the First Division.

Chapter 5
'Give It a Real Go for Walter'

It had been an extremely difficult decision to make. Don Revie wanted to leave Roker Park, of that there was no doubt. Back in November 1956, when he'd arrived, the club's horizons had seemed boundless. Now, two years later, those high hopes had been dissipated, first by financial scandal and then by relegation to the Second Division for the first time in the club's proud sixty-eight-year history.

Revie's relationship with the new manager, Alan Brown, initially one of mutual, if grudging, admiration, had very definitely turned sour, and he saw no real hope of improvement to it. Brown had made it abundantly clear that he would like to move out most of the older players, and Revie was the first to acknowledge that they hadn't done themselves any favours by the team's shocking start to the season, the latest calamity being that 5–0 thrashing at Swansea.

So it was obvious that he had to start his wandering again. But to Middlesbrough? He'd go back to great acclaim, he knew that. On each occasion he had returned to the town, he'd been greeted with much enthusiasm; he was especially touched by the reception he always received at Archibald School, where he had been educated to the age of 14, and where there was a cup in his name that the boys played for every year. He'd be able to keep a closer eye on his dad, Donald, who still lived in the little two-up, two-down terraced house in Bell Street where Don had been born.

But . . . instinctively, it just didn't feel like the right choice to make. He respected Bob Dennison, the Boro manager, as a decent, fair man with whom he'd enjoy a much calmer relationship than he did with Brown. He appreciated that he'd be given the free role he coveted in the middle of the field. He recognised, too, that the club had some very talented youngsters who could be expected to reach maturity this season or next.

But it wouldn't be First Division football. He was 31, he wasn't over the hill, and he felt he could still flourish in the highest company. He might not win his England place back – he was realistic enough to accept that – but there was still plenty left in the tank.

He had had no offer of the captaincy from Dennison. He wouldn't necessarily have expected it, especially as the new skipper, Brian Clough, had scored twelve goals in his first seven games in the job. It seemed that the young man was thriving on the responsibility.

But he knew from the North-East footballing grapevine that young Cloughie, despite his obvious ability, was starting to become something of a divisive figure at Ayresome Park. It may just have been jealousy, of course – how was he really to know? – but some of the older players appeared to resent Clough's blunt approach and what they perceived as his selfishness on the pitch. Mind you, he'd take a slice of that selfishness if it meant a goal every game from your centre-forward.

The problem with Middlesbrough was that there were a few too many uncertainties: Dennison's authority (or lack of it), Clough's abrasiveness and the potential for dissent in the club, and a creaky defence. There was no guarantee his home-town team would get promoted this season, despite an encouraging start. He really needed to be playing First Division soccer *now*, before it was too late.

Middlesbrough weren't the only suitors. He knew a number of other clubs had been asking about his availability ever since he'd put himself on the transfer list. Cardiff City was one, and he was aware that Leeds United, in particular, had been tracking him for some time.

But could Leeds really be the answer? The Elland Road club, having lost the services of the great John Charles the season before, had now sacked Revie's old mentor Raich Carter and had appointed as acting manager Bill Lambton, the current trainer-coach, whose name meant nothing to Revie.

So, a First Division club, yes, but one, apparently, with big debts, a poor headquarters and now turmoil in the management. And yet . . . something indefinable intrigued him about Leeds. They had some promising younger players, he'd been told, including a raw, rugged centre-half named Jack Charlton. There just might be something to build on . . .

Anyway, one thing was now clear in his mind. There would be no homecoming to Middlesbrough. He knew his decision would disappoint many people back in the town, in the Ayresome area, his old Boro Swifts colleagues. But in his gut he felt it wouldn't be the right thing to do. It was now 9 a.m., and he had to ring Bob Dennison to break the bad news.

★ ★ ★

The news of Revie's rejection of Middlesbrough made page one of the *Sunderland Echo* that afternoon, Wednesday, 17 September. The headline read 'Revie Says "I'm Not Going"', and the pseudonymous writer 'Argus' had managed to grab a quick word with the Sunderland player. 'I've told Mr Dennison I'm not going,' was Revie's brusque comment. When asked whether he still wanted to leave Roker Park, he replied delphically, 'No, I don't think you could say there has been any change . . . yet.'

In Middlesbrough, there was surprise, and a measure of annoyance. The *Evening Gazette* reported the decision in critical tones:

> Don Revie got the chance he has been waiting for today – the chance to leave Sunderland – and he turned it down. He had only to say the word and he could have played for Middlesbrough tonight instead of Sunderland but, surprisingly, he refused to sign for the Ayresome Park club.
>
> His decision was as big a shock to Wearside folk as was his eve-of-season transfer request. Revie . . . would not give his reasons for turning down the chance he was waiting for so impatiently.
>
> He had been offered a house by the Ayresome Park club, but apparently made up his mind without inspecting it.

After talking to Dennison, Revie set off with the Sunderland squad for the evening match against Sheffield Wednesday at Hillsborough. Twelve hours later, he must have wished he hadn't bothered; a crowd of 33,398 saw Wednesday hammer Sunderland 6–0, with Redfern Froggatt scoring a hat-trick for the home side.

Ironically, Dennison himself was in the crowd for the match, not back at Ayresome Park where Middlesbrough were entertaining Rotherham. After Revie's rejection, he'd turned up to watch his next target, the home side's skilful inside-forward Albert Quixall, who'd just lodged his own transfer request. Dennison must have been impressed by what he saw. Quixall scored a goal and had a hand in a couple of others. But Dennison was set to be disappointed over Quixall, too; shortly afterwards, he opted to join Manchester United.

Back in Middlesbrough, minus Revie, Clough's side – despite a goal from the new captain – suffered a surprising defeat by Rotherham United, a side they'd comfortably disposed of 4–1 away only a week earlier. It was Boro's second successive beating, and the gloss of their sparkling early-season form was starting to wear off.

Wing-half Ernie Whalley conceded a needless penalty after ten minutes, and the night got much worse for him minutes later when he crumpled up after a midfield challenge. He was stretchered off with a dislocated cartilage and it was always an uphill task for Boro after that, 1–0 down and reduced to ten men. They conceded a sloppy second just before half-time, and although Clough's speed enabled him to slip his marker and shoot past the advancing keeper after 55 minutes, there was no retrieving the match.

Middlesbrough's defensive frailties were starting to be exposed. Sunderland's woes in that department had been all too obvious for some time, with 5–0 and 6–0 beatings in the last two matches. The forthcoming Tees–Wear derby, at Ayresome Park on 11 October, looked tailor-made for the creative talents of Don Revie and Brian Clough, who would face each other on the pitch for the first time.

★ ★ ★

In those days, if you were walking through Albert Park at around half past nine on a weekday morning, more often than not you'd come across two pairs of young men separated by a distance of ten yards.

The more serious-sounding discussion would come from the first couple, who would be talking intently, gesturing to each other, arguing at times. A greater air of levity came from the second grouping; they would wear perpetual smiles and their conversation would be punctuated by bursts of laughter.

Brian Clough, Peter Taylor, Billy Day and Eddie Holliday would walk to training each day across the park. Billy Day recalled those early-morning journeys to work:

> Brian and Peter would walk together in front, while Eddie and
> I would follow on behind. Brian and Peter would generally
> always talk about football. The two were very friendly and very
> much in tune, and I guess these were just the very beginnings

of their partnership. Eddie and I – now, we would just talk about the dogs the night before, or the racing to come in the afternoon!

Three of those four men, together with Clough's striking partner Alan Peacock and young inside-forward Alan Rodgerson, were the participants in an extraordinary meeting three days after the defeat at home to Rotherham.

The gathering took place after breakfast in the team hotel just a few hours before Middlesbrough were due to play Charlton Athletic at The Valley in South London. Alan Peacock takes up the story: 'It was known that Walter Winterbottom, the England manager, would be coming to watch the game. Anyway, Peter Taylor comes over to me and says, "Peachy, there's a meeting upstairs, can you come up and join us?" I went up, opened the door, and there was the forward line – Eddie, Alan, Brian and now me – with Peter the only other person present. It was very strange.

'Peter closed the door, and he and Brian started to speak. They said we want you to do this and that, give it a real go – essentially, asking us for extra effort to feed opportunities for Brian so he could make the best impression possible before Walter Winterbottom.

'When I came down after the meeting, Billy [who hadn't attended] said, "Where have you been?" I said, "I've been to a meeting," and he replied that he didn't think there was a team meeting. I said, "No, there wasn't. I've been to Cloughie's room!" Anyway, it didn't work, we lost, and next week three of us were dropped!'

The records show that Middlesbrough lost 1–0 that day to move down to seventh in the table. Eddie Thompson, in the *Evening Gazette*, reckoned Clough's showing that day had been 'his worst for a long time and would be best forgotten'. For others, however, the punishment for a poor display was immediate. The side for the home match against Bristol City the following week did not include Peacock, Rodgerson, Day or Holliday. The *Evening Gazette* reckoned the first two had definitely been dropped; Day had, in any event, been unable to get leave to play from his army superiors in Germany, while Holliday had developed tonsillitis.

That game with Bristol ended in a disappointing 0–0 draw, and when Boro lost 3–2 away at Cardiff the following week, it was just one draw and four defeats in five games.

Clough and Taylor were forthright, opinionated men with clear ideas, even then, about how the game should be played. It may well be that manager Bob Dennison and trainer Harold Shepherdson encouraged Clough, as captain, to promote his views to the team on his own and without managerial interference. Nonetheless, the meeting at Charlton was highly irregular, and, while the younger players may not have been unduly perturbed by events, it had the capacity to stir dressing-room unrest.

So neither Sunderland nor Middlesbrough went into the first Tees–Wear derby for five years in the best of form or spirits. Brian Clough, without a goal in three games, needed to galvanise his side again to get it back on the title trail. Don Revie's ambitions were more limited; of course he wanted a win for his side, but perhaps more important was a good personal performance to keep himself clearly in the shop window, so he could soon make his way out of Roker Park.

* * *

Boro manager Bob Dennison had an injury scare to contend with on Saturday morning the like of which, you might think, would be unlikely to occur today.

His young, gifted 19-year-old inside-forward Alan Rodgerson – a former England schoolboy international – had fallen off his bicycle on Friday night. He'd been returning home at the end of an afternoon learning his trade as an apprentice electrician when his machine hit a kerb and he was thrown off.

He required six stitches to a deep gash above his left eye, but he was patched up and the Boro medical team pronounced him fit to play. Heading was not one of his strengths, so he was unlikely to put any pressure on the wound.

But two other players had failed fitness tests for the home side: inside-forward Derek McLean, a regular that season, who had a pulled thigh muscle, and Joe Scott, usually a reserve, who had a twisted knee.

So, on a blustery, autumnal day in Middlesbrough, with the threat of rain, the sides lined up as follows:

Middlesbrough
Taylor

Bilcliff   Stonehouse

Harris   Phillips   Dicks

Taylor   Rodgerson   Clough (c)   Peacock   Burbeck

Grainger   Revie   Kichenbrand   Anderson (c)   Bircham

Pearce   Hurley   McNab

Ashurst   Hedley

Bollands
Sunderland

Referee: Mr L.N. Teake (Rotherham)
Middlesbrough manager: Bob Dennison
Sunderland manager: Alan Brown

The Iron Man's Approach

Sunderland's players went into the game with a run of poor results behind them and uncertain about their futures. Manager Alan Brown clearly wanted to make major changes in the coming season, with the accent on youth. Some of the more experienced players, not just Don Revie, had started to look elsewhere for employment.

It would be wrong to suggest that Revie's two years at Sunderland were a consistently unhappy period. True, the team was under-performing on the pitch and he and Brown clearly didn't see eye-to-eye on training methods, but for the most part he rubbed along well with the majority of his teammates. They recognised the quality of football he brought to the side. If a pass of his went astray, it was more often than not because his colleagues weren't on the same wavelength, because they didn't have the vision that he possessed.

Left-winger Colin Grainger was one of Revie's closest colleagues at Sunderland. They both stayed at the Seaburn Hotel while their new houses were decorated and would room together on away trips. 'Off the pitch, he was a likeable man – a real gentleman. I remember that he was a devil on the poker table. He seemed to win all the money all the time! On the pitch, Don was always a good user of the ball, he was never one for racing around the pitch and closing people down. Give him the ball and he would control it and distribute it; he was a very "articulate" player. He had a brilliant physique, tall with stocky shoulders and strong legs.'

'Don was a gentleman,' recalls goalkeeper Johnny Bollands. 'He was an excellent player and a funny man at times, with a nice sense of humour.'

However, not everyone agreed with that assessment. Len Shackleton, North-East football's 'Crown Prince', who was just finishing his career at Sunderland, has told this story about him:

> It was actually when Don Revie arrived at the club, and he was in the dressing-room bragging to the lads about his latest trick. He was flicking a sixpence up in the air, catching it on his foot and, after about the third attempt, flicking it back up in the air and catching it in his blazer pocket. Ray Daniel was having a go, because his ego was enormous, but he couldn't manage it because you've got to practise it.
>
> So, after a few days Revie says to me, 'Hey, Shack, are you not going to have a go?' He must have imagined I would be keen to have a go the first time he demonstrated it, but I didn't want to, not until I had practised it first! So I practised at home for a few days using a half-a-crown.
>
> Then, one morning when all the lads were in the dressing-room getting ready for training, I said to Revie: 'Hey, Revie, have a look at this, will you, what about this?' I wasn't flicking it a foot and a half in the air as Revie had, but right up to the ceiling, catching it on my foot, and then lobbing it back up into my blazer pocket. That was great – stealing the thunder from Revie, 'the show-off'.

As much as the big egos clashed in the dressing-room, they clashed more with the manager. Shackleton had no time for Alan Brown and his methods; Revie had long since ceased to have a good working relationship with him. Were these just the gripes of old pros unwilling to learn new tricks? What manner of man was in charge of Sunderland on that day in October 1958?

Brown, the son of a painter and decorator from Consett, Co. Durham, was passionate about the game, his feelings for it sometimes bordering on religious fervour. Indeed, on one occasion, in apparent seriousness, he described football as 'one of the biggest things that happened in Creation'.

In 1933, at 16 years old, he joined Huddersfield Town as a trainee, hoping that in addition to football the club would help support his further education, not something his own family could afford to do at the height of the Depression. However, Huddersfield showed no inclination to help him, and Brown quickly realised he was viewed as nothing more than a member of the ground staff. His experience as a young, lonely, often ignored player would make him determined never to allow junior apprentices and young professionals at any clubs he had responsibility for in the future to suffer in the way he had done.

He decided to leave the game to pursue a career in the police force. In his two and a half years on the beat, one of the incidental skills he learned was how to dig ditches – 'as well as any Irish navvy', he would often proudly proclaim. It happened when he was spending days on end undercover, keeping watch over a house reputed to be a brothel. Appreciating the benefit this bout of hard labour had for his own fitness and discipline, he later incorporated it into training schedules for his Burnley and Sunderland sides.

Brown left the police to return to football – and to Huddersfield. After the war, he played for Burnley as captain – helping them to promotion and an FA Cup final – then for Notts County. He was a good, solid defender, an unremarkable player but a natural leader of men.

A step into management seemed inevitable, and he took over at Burnley in 1954, his greatest legacy there being the creation of an excellent youth set-up that stood the club in good stead for a decade or more.

Alan Brown was brought to Sunderland to help restore confidence and self-respect after the illegal-payments scandal of 1957. What he brought to the job was a profoundly moral outlook, a keen sense of the right values to instil in his young players; if they adopted the wrong ones, as he saw it, they would be quickly discarded.

During his spell at Sunderland, Brown joined Moral Re-Armament, a Christian evangelical movement based in Switzerland. The association was based around what it called 'The Four Absolutes': absolute honesty, absolute purity, absolute unselfishness and absolute love.

On the pitch, he demanded discipline from his charges, and woe betide anyone who argued with the referee. Off it, he detested a shabby appearance and unkempt hair, preferring his players to look like clean-cut army recruits. Brown's was a holistic approach. He wanted to know what was going on in every nook and cranny of the club and the players' lives. If, as a player, you respected his views and his methods, you could live with this intrusion. If you couldn't, life was difficult.

Don Revie couldn't accept much of what Brown was preaching, although if you examined his management style later at Leeds, you'd find something of the Brown approach incorporated into it.

Sunderland's goalkeeper that day, 23-year-old Johnny Bollands, had just returned to the team after the side's 5–0 and 6–0 thrashings the month before. He remembers the Brown regime with little affection. 'Alan Brown was a maniac. Sorry to speak ill of the dead, but there it is. He was an arrogant man and particularly cruel to the younger boys. His training regime was unbelievable. In the close season, he'd have us joining the labourers in helping build a new gymnasium. We were wielding picks when we should have been kicking balls around. He'd have the younger boys lapping round this huge playing ground and they'd collapse with exhaustion. He'd just say, "Leave them." I thought that was wrong, for young boys; it would have broken their hearts.'

Brown's approach seemed to split the squad at that time. The older players resented it, while some, like Bollands, considered it too harsh. However, others, especially youngsters like Len Ashurst, left-back that day, and Colin Nelson, his understudy, respected it and felt they benefited from it.

In his autobiography, *Left Back in Time*, Ashurst admitted: 'All the staff and most of the players were frightened to death of the manager, so much so that not one player dared to tell him over a long period of time that he had a piece of cotton hanging down from the back of his light-coloured mackintosh.' But, despite the fear factor, Ashurst acknowledged the strength of Brown's personality and the (positive) application of his dictatorial methods: 'Brownie formed an unbreakable bond with his players. We understood him as a man who knew what he wanted.'

Colin Nelson, then a 20-year-old on the verge of the first team, had nothing but admiration for the 'Iron Man', as the press had taken to calling him. 'He was a stern man, but a lovely fella. If you did it for him, he'd back you all the way. In pre-season training, he was always at the front. He never asked you to do anything he wasn't going to do himself. If you could ask Brian Clough [later to play under Brown] today, he'd say exactly the same, and it's no secret that he based much of his managerial strategy on what he learned from Alan Brown.'

The Sunderland side that day wasn't yet really Brown's team. The process of weeding out the old stars and introducing the younger generation like Charlie Hurley, Jimmy McNab and Ashurst was by no means complete.

Quite where Don Kichenbrand and Colin Grainger fitted into his long-term plans, no one could be sure. Kichenbrand, South-African born, was a marauding centre-forward signed from Glasgow Rangers early that year to help in the unsuccessful fight against relegation.

Known affectionately as 'The Rhino' by the Rangers fans, Kichenbrand had enjoyed his time at Ibrox Park, averaging nearly a goal a game and once scoring five goals against Queen of the South, on the occasion of the first-ever floodlit match in Scottish league history. However, he'd always lived a little fearfully on the edge of discovery at Rangers. He was a Catholic at a club with fiercely Protestant affiliations, something he certainly didn't advertise in his time there.

'We used to call him "Kitchen Sink"!' recalls Johnny Bollands. 'He used to run with the ball as though his legs didn't belong to him. Open the gates at Roker Park and he would have run out and kept on running.'

Supplying the crosses for Kitchen Sink was Grainger, an unconventional footballer, to say the least. By day, he was a dashing left-winger (with seven England caps) who scared full-backs to death with his pace and dribbling skills; by night, you could find him singing ballads – in the style, say, of Englebert Humperdinck – in the biggest concert venues in the north of England.

The soccer-playing crooner was headlined as 'The Voice with a Kick In It', sharing bills with the likes of Jerry Lewis, Danny Kaye, Max Bygraves and, on one evening later on in his career, in June 1963, with a young up-and-coming band called the Beatles. 'It was at the Southern Social Club in Manchester. They'd just had a number-one hit, "From Me to You", and a number-one album, and they were just months away from bringing out "She Loves You". They were still only kids and full of themselves. When I wandered into their dressing-room, Ringo was playing with a big yellow Dinky toy!' Grainger was earning only £20 a week from football, but in the clubs he could often expect to get £50 to £75 a night. The previous year, he had broken box-office records at the Sunderland Empire when he performed with comedian Bobby Thompson in a week of sell-out shows.

Back on the pitch, his international career had got off to a stunning start in May 1956, when, against a gifted Brazilian side (who would go on to win the World Cup two years later), he scored with his very first touch of the ball. It came in the fourth minute, when he slid in at the far post to turn in a clever pass from Johnny Haynes and put England 2–0 up.

Grainger went on to give the talented Brazilian right-back Djalma Santos a torrid time. But the highlight of that game was the duel on the other side of the pitch between Nílton Santos (no relation), one of the greatest attacking left-backs ever to grace the game, and the evergreen Stanley Matthews.

'I remember standing next to Stanley just before the game started,' says Grainger, 'and he asked me if I was nervous. "I certainly am," I replied.

'"Don't worry," he said, "I am as well. I'm always nervous when I play here, Colin."'

Matthews, who had been recalled at the venerable age of 41, betrayed no worries once the whistle blew and went on to produce one of the finest displays of his much-garlanded career. It culminated in the closing minutes with a perfectly flighted cross to the back post for his new wing partner to head the ball home to secure a 4–2 victory.

A couple of weeks later, Grainger helped England to another memorable victory, against West Germany in Berlin, in a game that will be forever remembered as 'Edwards' Match'. The young Duncan Edwards from Manchester United, just 20, bestrode the Berlin pitch like a colossus that day, tackling like a lion, attacking at every opportunity and topping it off with a cracking goal.

Grainger played his part, scoring England's third and helping his country overcome the world champions in front of a 100,000 crowd – half of whom were soldiers from the British-occupied zone of Berlin.

With cultured inside-forward Stan Anderson, who had been made Sunderland captain, helping Revie supply the passes to Kichenbrand, Grainger and another promising youngster, 19-year-old winger Clive Bircham from Herrington, Durham, the Wearside team had the firepower to rise above their lowly league position and give Boro a game.

Dennison's Attacking Style

If Alan Brown was the modern – albeit forbidding – face of the football manager, in control of all playing matters and much more besides, Bob Dennison was more akin to the old type, the secretary-manager.

Brian Clough described him as a 'kindly, old-school type of manager'. Dennison arrived in July 1954, a difficult time in Middlesbrough's history, to say the least. The previous man in charge, Walter Rowley, had resigned earlier that year on health grounds, and the club had effectively been without a manager for several months.

Dennison, who had been in charge at Northampton Town for six years, was taken on as secretary-manager. Up to that point in time, the routine was that the board of directors met on a Thursday morning to pick the team to play on a Saturday; it had been the case since day one at Ayresome Park, back in 1899. The system changed and Dennison started to select the side, but he continued to undertake the secretarial duties until Harry Green was appointed to that job in 1960.

In 1954, Dennison had his hands full. He had inherited a club with big debts, the star player Wilf Mannion wanted away and the supporters were demanding an instant return to the First Division.

Nothing in his footballing past had prepared the mild-mannered Dennison for any of that. Born in Amble, Northumbria, he joined Newcastle United as a 17-year-old in 1929 but went on to play just 11 games for the club. He then moved on to Nottingham Forest, Fulham and Northampton, before hanging up his boots at the close of a largely undistinguished career in 1948.

His tenure as manager at Ayresome Park started disastrously. With Mannion departed to Hull City, and after a 2–2 draw against Plymouth Argyle in the opening game of the season, Middlesbrough contrived to lose the next eight games in a row. Things did pick up eventually, and the club finished the season in 12th position.

Dennison steadied the ship in the next few years, and by the time the 1958–59 season came along he'd gained a measure of respect for his efforts. An undemonstrative, somewhat inarticulate man, there was certainly a feeling in some quarters that he was starting to cede control of the dressing-room to Clough and Taylor. Equally, he was applauded for his introduction of good, young talent, particularly in the forward line.

One of those bright youngsters, Billy Day, had lost his place after the Charlton game and was yet to win it back. But Alan Peacock was back in favour and had scored one of the goals in the previous game against Cardiff City.

Day felt that Boro, in those days, were a fast, attacking team, at their best early in the season when the pitches were still in good condition. He recalls: 'Wingers had to stay wide, strikers had to be running in formation. I would go down the right wing and cut the ball back low into the penalty area for Cloughie, unless it was overcrowded, then I'd put my foot through the ball and Alan knew it would be in an area for him at the far post. Those were my instructions every game – I could have done it blindfold!'

Dennison had decided to accentuate Boro's attacking strengths and hope they covered up the defensive weaknesses. So his novel formation contained *two* centre-forwards, Clough and Peacock.

'Cloughie didn't like other players in his space. He'd literally push players like Derek McLean and little Arthur Fitzsimons away if that happened!' recalls Peacock. 'But although Cloughie and I were always within striking distance of each other, we never seemed to get in each other's way. Our partnership worked.'

In the creative department, Boro relied a lot on Welshman Bill Harris, who had great control and vision and was a terrific passer of the ball, especially over long distances; he also had a fierce shot.

But Dennison clearly believed Harris needed some support and the team needed a wise head to guide it through difficult games – hence his determination to try to bring Don Revie 'home'. Alan Peacock reckons Revie would have been a perfect partner for Harris and creator of goals for Clough and himself. 'He would have been a great acquisition. With Billy [Day] and Edwin [Holliday] wide, Revie spraying the ball about and Brian and myself on the end of things, it would have been a great team to play in.'

On that weekend in October, Day (who in any case was unable to get leave from the army to join the squad) and Holliday were still absent post-Charlton, so Carl Taylor and Ron Burbeck made up the forward line. Taylor was a young, Cumbrian-born winger who had made his debut in November 1957 in place of Lindy Delapenha; he'd made only sporadic appearances since then. Burbeck, an England youth international, was a more than adequate replacement for Holliday, a left-winger who hugged the touchline and swung over a good supply of crosses for Clough and Peacock.

Defensively, Ray Bilcliff, 27, and Derek Stonehouse, 25, solid enough players, occupied the full-back berths. Veteran Ronnie Dicks, 34, nicknamed 'The Handyman' because of his versatility (he played in every position for the club), was at left-half that day, with Brian Phillips – Clough's adversary – at centre-half.

Two teams, then, with impressive attacking credentials, if a little shaky or inexperienced in defence. It promised to be an exciting game, with many intriguing personal duels contained within it. Above all, the Boro faithful were eager to compare and contrast the 'Old Master', Revie, Footballer of the Year and England international, with Clough, the 'Young Pretender', the man whose avalanche of goals would surely propel him towards an England place any day soon.

The Match

A large contingent of Sunderland supporters had made their way 25 miles south to swell the crowd of 36,973. Their first surprise was seeing their side in a new strip – the famous red and white stripes were retained, but it was now a very narrow red stripe on a white background.

The visitors easily had the better of the opening exchanges, with Revie orchestrating most of the attacks. First, he sent Colin Grainger free down the wing with an incisive pass, making himself available inside the penalty area for the return ball. Grainger, however, unnecessarily tried to go past Ray Bilcliff first and was promptly stopped in his tracks.

A minute or so later and Grainger set off on a mazy run, beating three opponents before his shot was blocked by Brian Phillips. The Sunderland winger remembers the match with affection. 'Not wishing to be immodest, but I had a very good game. I always liked to play against Bilcliff. Some full-backs you preferred to others. He wasn't slow, but I knew I could take him to the cleaners.

'It was a good pitch that day. Mind you, Ayresome Park was always a good pitch, big and wide, so it lent itself to wingers. I never had a bad game at Middlesbrough. I loved the place; I loved the environment.'

Not long afterwards, Revie slipped a ball through for the galloping Kichenbrand to chase, but Peter Taylor came quickly out of the Boro goal and smothered the ball at the centre-forward's feet.

Middlesbrough remained on the back foot for the first 15 minutes and young Stan Anderson joined Revie in making some excellent opportunities for his forwards.

Jack Hedley intercepted one Ron Burbeck centre and played the ball promptly to Anderson. His delightful pass sent the galloping Grainger free once more, and from his perfectly flighted cross Kichenbrand rose to beat Brian Phillips and head narrowly over the bar. It was the closest effort yet.

It was all Sunderland, and Brian Clough was making very little impact, starved of service from his inside-forwards and shackled by the impressive young Charlie Hurley. The nearest Boro came was a speculative drive by Alan Peacock that he dragged well wide of the left post.

Hurley approached all his encounters with Clough with relish:

He was a very, very good goalscorer. I used to change my game when I played against him. He was very outspoken and it was always Clough versus Hurley – who's going to win? And I knew at the end of those games that I was going to win because I looked at Cloughie and I forgot about playing all the football and the clever stuff and just concentrated on him; he was 'the boy' down there. I kicked him an awful lot of times. He wasn't that good in the air, but you couldn't give him an inch.

Sunderland thought they had the lead after half an hour when Revie's clever pass split the home defence and Clive Bircham raced through to beat Peter Taylor and put the ball in the net – only to be given offside.

Just before half-time, Middlesbrough had their best opportunity yet. Johnny Bollands lost control of the ball from a corner, and when Alan Rodgerson sent the ball forward towards goal Jimmy McNab – who had wisely taken up position on the goal line – headed behind to safety.

Half-Time: Middlesbrough 0, Sunderland 0

The home side came out after the interval knowing they needed to step up their game after their lacklustre display in the first 45 minutes. Dennison would have told them to shut out the flow of probing passes coming from Revie's boot; he would also have told Clough to move around the pitch more, or withdraw to a deeper position, in order to evade the attentions of the determined Hurley.

When Bill Harris floated in a free kick from five yards outside the penalty area, Peacock succeeded in diverting it into the Sunderland net. However, referee Teake had spotted a handball from the lanky Boro centre-forward, and the goal didn't stand.

Clough continued to have one of his most ineffective games of the season and had so far failed to have a shot on goal – a most unusual occurrence for him.

Then he was sent on his way towards goal by Harris, only to be thwarted by Johnny Bollands, who came out, dived at his feet and took the ball off him before he could shoot.

Bollands, who was justifying his place back in the team with every minute that passed, recalls Clough's growing frustration: 'We had words, actually. Brian was a very good player but a very hard one. He often used to follow through with his foot on the goalkeeper, rather than jump over you. It happened on that day and I said, "Come on,

Brian, let's just have a game of football." I can't remember what he said back. Brian would swear at you if you saved a shot of his. I'd just reply back, "That's what we're there for, Brian!"'

Sunderland were worried when Anderson needed attention for an ankle injury early in the second half, but he recovered and continued to thread clever passes through the Middlesbrough rearguard.

It was by now fast, furious, end-to-end stuff, typical derby fare. The home side had come much more into the game, and a couple of dangerous crosses from Carl Taylor flashed across the Sunderland six-yard box, without Clough or Peacock managing to get a foot on them.

They were to be young Taylor's last meaningful contribution to the game, because soon afterwards he suffered a serious injury. 'I actually ruptured my thigh,' he says, 'which I only discovered after the match. Len Ashurst had won a tackle against me, and I was chasing him back. He went to strike the ball and hit me in the thigh as I was coming up on him. But, of course, there were no substitutes, and I just kept playing on, as you did in those days.'

Revie continued to stand out, finding time and space and manipulating the ball in his characteristically elegant way. He then created the chance of the game for Kichenbrand, threading a long pass through the middle from his deep-lying position and giving the burly centre-forward the opportunity to beat Taylor from just ten yards out. Kichenbrand wastefully screwed the ball wide.

Finally, with about five minutes left, Brian Clough had his first shot on goal. He hit the ball sweetly from 15 yards, but Bollands, diving to his left, brought off a fine save.

There was one final salvo from Sunderland in the dying seconds of the game. Revie glided through the Boro defence and sent in a terrific shot, which Peter Taylor did exceptionally well to save, deflecting the ball towards a colleague. He then picked up the rebound practically on the line.

Referee Teake blew his whistle immediately afterwards. In a game with plenty of openings, it was a major surprise that the scoreline remained blank.

Full-Time: Middlesbrough 0, Sunderland 0

Post-match analysis from the *Sunderland Echo* gave great credit to Charlie Hurley for snuffing Clough almost completely out of the game. It added: 'Anderson and Revie gave excellent service in attack . . . while

Grainger maintained his recent improvement and Bollands was again in great form.'

From the home perspective, Cliff Mitchell, writing in the *Evening Gazette* on Monday, grudgingly acknowledged the impact Revie and Anderson had had on the game: 'Sunderland's two inside-forwards were far from brilliant, but they were adequate. They saw to it that their centre-forward, Kichenbrand, received some accurate passes, along the ground, and it was not their fault that the South African failed with the chances he was given.'

With similar support, Mitchell reckoned, Clough might have won the game for Boro. That was an optimistic gloss on affairs, but Revie's refusal to join Boro the month before still left the side short of vital creativity. 'Wish manager Bob Dennison the best of luck, you Middlesbrough supporters, in his quest for a ready-made inside-forward!' Mitchell wrote.

* * *

For Revie, his impressive display that day was not quite his last hurrah. On 22 November, he played a key role in Sunderland's first away win of the season, a crushing 4–0 victory at Rotherham. But, within days of that game, he was gone.

His departure was hastened by an incident in the Sunderland dressing-room after the Rotherham game. Len Ashurst, left-back that day, recalls Revie asking Alan Brown if he could head off to visit relations who lived nearby, and so not return to Roker Park on the team coach with the rest of the side. The others watched on aghast at the ensuing confrontation, described by Ashurst in his autobiography:

> Alan Brown flatly refused, probably knowing he would provoke a reaction from Revie, as was often his wont. A verbal slanging match ensued at which stage Revie lost it. He pushed Brown into a corner of the dressing-room and as the two of them traded blows, Stan Anderson, who had not played in that match because of injury, Don Kichenbrand and Charlie Hurley dived into the action and eventually parted them.
>
> Brown was a hard man, something which all the players had confirmed to them, if they didn't fully realise it already, when, after having dealt with Revie in the Millmoor dressing-room, with blood spattered all over his face, he faced the speechless

players: 'If anyone else starts trouble, then you know what you will get.'

There was clearly no way back for Revie after that. Leeds United had firmed up their interest in him, and the directors of the two clubs spent some time in protracted negotiations over the transfer fee, which was eventually dragged down from somewhere near £20,000 to £14,000. The sum total of all Revie's transfer fees now amounted to a healthy £76,000.

He will have breathed a sigh of relief that he was now able to move on. He was probably thankful, too, that he was able to pack in his part-time job as a carpet salesman for George Tait, the Newcastle-born businessman and director of Darlington Football Club. The *Daily Mirror* reported that Revie rushed so fast to Leeds to sign for them that he forgot to take his boots. He went straight into the side on Saturday, 29 November and made an immediate impact.

Leeds beat Newcastle 3–2 at Elland Road, and Dick Ulyatt of the *Yorkshire Post* wrote euphorically: 'Revie made deft through passes, just in front of his teammates, of a type no Leeds forward has made or received in the 25 years I have been watching them.'

The wanderer was settling in to his latest club well. Clough, meanwhile, had the task of lifting his side and preventing them from slipping back towards mid-table mediocrity.

He was feeling impatient. He knew there was talent at the club – especially among the forwards – but why did the defence continue to leak so many goals? Did enough people at Middlesbrough share his fierce ambition, and would they take the tough decisions and make the effort needed to achieve real success, or were they just content to drift along as they were?

Chapter 6
'Some of the Lads Don't Like You'

Three months after their encounter on the pitch at Ayresome Park, Brian Clough and Don Revie were both captaining their clubs, in different divisions but not dissimilar circumstances.

At the end of January 1959, Middlesbrough found themselves in 15th position in Division Two. For their ambitious – and impatient – young leader, that was nowhere near acceptable. With twenty-eight goals – including two hat-tricks to add to the five he scored on the opening day of the season – Clough had contributed more than his fair share to the side's cause. But the defence, comprising goalkeeper Peter Taylor (who had just been dropped and replaced by Esmond Million), Bilcliff, Phillips and Stonehouse, had already shipped 43 goals.

Fifty miles away at Elland Road and Leeds were encountering similar problems. Revie had taken over as skipper after just six weeks at the club, the unanimous choice of the players as successor to Wilbur Cush, the Northern Ireland international who had enjoyed a successful World Cup the year before.

January had been a dismal period for Leeds, with defeats in the league at the hands of Burnley and Preston and a 5–1 thrashing by Luton Town in the FA Cup. Under Revie's new captaincy, however, the side had finished the month with a 1–0 home victory against Leicester City.

Revie was deployed at right-half, inside-right and inside-left in the course of the season; where there was a gap, or a perceived weakness, he was inevitably the man called upon to fill it. He'd lost a good deal of his pace, but his mind was as quick as ever. What he couldn't do much about was United's creaky defence, where the strapping centre-half Jack Charlton did a great deal of the good work but – in Revie's eyes – had the potential to do much better.

Clough was starting to store up problems for the long term with his style of leadership. Whereas the Leeds players had been, as one, delighted to have in charge a player of Revie's experience and stature within the game, Clough's colleagues had a different perspective on their new leader.

Most of the younger generation – Alan Peacock, Billy Day, Edwin Holliday – were in thrall to Clough, to the strength of his commanding personality and his skill on the field. They were also too busy merely establishing themselves in the game to worry about the politics in the dressing-room. But some of the older players had resented Clough's appointment, didn't appreciate being bawled out on the pitch or in the dressing-room and had noted a tendency of the new captain to sulk when things weren't going his, or the side's, way.

As for Clough, he was starting to harbour dark suspicions about the number of goals his defence was leaking. Could the rumours of match-fixing that were beginning to do the rounds, players betting against their own side and deliberately conceding goals, possibly have any basis in fact at Ayresome Park?

So 1959 would be a taxing year for both men. For Revie, the goal appeared a limited one: survival for Leeds in the First Division and a chance from then onwards to help rebuild the club. For Clough, despite the tensions under the surface at Middlesbrough, it was a year of tremendous personal opportunity, with the chance, as long as he continued to bang in the goals, of establishing himself as an England international.

* * *

The most important day of what would ultimately prove to be a turbulent year for Brian Clough came on Saturday, 4 April, when he married Barbara Beatrice Glasgow, a 21-year-old shorthand typist who lived in Gifford Street, just three-quarters of a mile away from Valley Road on the other side of Albert Park.

With perhaps just a touch of the braggadocio for which he was famous, Rolando Ugolini claims credit for introducing the couple a few years earlier in nearby Rea's Café. 'Brian wasn't all that confident socially around that time, believe it or not. Anyway, we'd always go to the café for an hour or so after training, and one day he spots this girl on the other side of the room and says, "She's nice – she's lovely." I said, "I'll introduce you to her," and he says, "No, no," because he was a little shy. Anyway, I introduced him to the girl, whose name was Barbara, and they finished up going out together and he married her!'

Clough recalled: 'Rea's caff . . . was where I spotted the girl with a smile that seemed to light up the entire North-East. It was where I first saw Barbara and the rest, as they say, is my extreme good fortune.'

The wedding was held at St Barnabas Anglican Church and the reception afterwards at Linthorpe Hotel. Then there was a dash on for Clough to make it to Ayresome Park on time for Boro's three o'clock kick-off against Leyton Orient. On the pitch, the bridegroom celebrated his big day by scoring Middlesbrough's last goal in a 4–2 victory.

Middlesbrough finished the season in 13th place, disappointing to say the least with the talent at their disposal. But Clough, despite his responsibilities, had another extraordinary year of goalscoring, 43 in 43 games.

When the 1959–60 season started, his advocates in the press waged a ceaseless campaign to persuade Walter Winterbottom and the England selection committee to pick him. In fact, they really didn't need to have bothered; his performances were such that it was becoming nigh on impossible for the England manager to ignore him.

It came to a climax in September and October. On 19 September, Clough scored all three goals as Middlesbrough beat Charlton Athletic at Ayresome Park to go second in the table. With Clough and Peacock knocking in the goals – and even centre-half Brian Phillips grabbing one in a 2–1 away win at Liverpool – dressing-room dissent was in short supply at that point.

Four days later, at Windsor Park, Clough lined up for a Football League side against the Irish League. He proceeded to state his case for inclusion in the full England side with a stunning display of the centre-forward's art. He opened the scoring just before half-time and then, in a fourteen-minute spell after the interval, astonishingly scored four more.

There was now no doubt. 'Brian Clough has made it,' declared the *Daily Express*. 'The Middlesbrough boy showed England's selectors one of the most incredible feats of opportunism that soccer has ever witnessed at Windsor Park. He shot his way into the England team, for after this he must be a certainty. His first three goals were the finest examples of chance-taking I have seen.'

The *Daily Mail* proclaimed, 'Here was his answer to those selectors who for so long have rated him no more than a successful goal-getter in the Second Division,' while even the more sober *Daily Telegraph* opined, 'Clough played brilliantly and his five goals should satisfy the most sceptical of England's selectors about his ability.'

For Cliff Mitchell on the *Gazette*, it would be nothing more than a national dereliction of duty if his man didn't now get his chance: 'If Clough is not in England's team next month (injuries permitting of course), there'll be an uprising on Teesside!'

He needn't have worried. Almost immediately, Clough received his call-up for what might best be described as an experimental squad. Billy Wright, indomitable centre-half and captain, had finally departed the international scene in the summer after 105 appearances for his country. Johnny Haynes, who had more or less cemented his place as the team's principal creator, was absent on this occasion through injury.

Into the group of players for the first time came Clough, his Middlesbrough colleague Eddie Holliday, another bright young winger in John Connelly, from Burnley, full-back Tony Allen (Stoke City) and centre-half Trevor Smith (Birmingham City). Ronnie Clayton, Blackburn Rovers' right-half, had the unenviable task of succeeding Billy Wright as captain.

There were two matches to play, the first against Wales at Ninian Park on 17 October, and then a more taxing game at Wembley eleven days later against Sweden, World Cup runners-up to Brazil the previous year. Walter Winterbottom made it clear from the outset that – barring injuries – the new recruits would have both games in which to make their mark.

There was eager anticipation in many quarters in advance of the games, primarily because of the exciting new forward talent about to be unveiled. If Connelly and Holliday could produce anything like their club form, then Clough and Jimmy Greaves, the brilliant nineteen-year-old forward from Chelsea who himself had played just three international games, would have a field day latching on to their crosses from the flanks.

However there were cautionary voices. The absence of a proper 'schemer' like Haynes was bemoaned, as was the lack of a 'grafter' in the forward line; it was also suggested that Clough and Greaves were a little too similar in style and approach to make an effective partnership.

The side's task was to give the country a bright new start, erasing the memory of an indifferent Home International tournament the previous year and a dismal tour of the Americas in May. Eric Todd of

The Guardian was clear about what was expected of the team at Ninian Park: 'Nothing less than victory by at least three goals will be regarded as expiation, complete or partial.'

★ ★ ★

Whether Walter Winterbottom actually wanted Brian Clough in his squad for those games is a moot point. Strange as it might seem these days, back then the FA's international selection committee still picked the side – and then handed it over for the manager to manage. Winterbottom will have had a voice in the selection discussions, but his was just one of many.

Just as Don Revie had a Burnley winger – Brian Pilkington – alongside him for his England debut five years earlier, so Brian Clough also had one for his. John Connelly, aged 21, played on the right wing, the opposite side to Pilkington, in a very gifted Turf Moor side under the astute management of Harry Potts.

Connelly was then only a part-time soccer player. His father insisted he keep his trade as a joiner in the Bank Hall pit in north-east Lancashire, just in case football didn't work out for him as a profession. But by October 1959 young Connelly's speed, skill and toughness – he would never allow a full-back to rough him up – were duly noted and, just as important in those days, the gentlemen of the press had observed his talent and were beginning to give him regular, favourable notices.

Connelly, now looking back over half a century, found his introduction to international football an exciting but strange and somewhat unsettling experience. 'I learned I'd been selected to play for England from a man called Noel Wild, a reporter from the local paper, the *Nelson Leader*. He tracked me down to where I was working that day, near Todmorden, came over to me and said, "Did you know you've been picked to play for England?" All hell then broke loose in local circles, the paper photographed me sawing a piece of wood or some stunt like that, and I was a celebrity all of a sudden.

'I then had to make my way by train to Porthcawl, where the team was staying ahead of the game. I was all on my own, and I'd never travelled further than Burnley in my life before! Anyway, I made it to the hotel, and when I stepped into the lobby I saw a group of people stood round listening attentively to someone, and I assumed at first it was the manager, Walter Winterbottom. Then I looked a little more closely and thought, no, he's a bit young for Winterbottom. I then realised it was Brian Clough! It was the first time I'd ever come across him in the flesh, and right from that moment you could sense he was a born leader.'

Perhaps it was all just nervous energy. Clough's memories were a little different: 'At the team hotel I felt nervous and vulnerable, 24 years old but a young 24 and hardly a man of the world.'

He may have been telling his new colleagues how he was hoping the side would perform at Ninian Park, but he had little time to get to know their playing styles and approaches. In those days, England players assembled a couple of days before the game, but the main training session was little more than a 'get to know you' affair as opposed to the detailed practice of free kicks, corners and throw-ins that took place at well-run, successful clubs like Burnley. All that would change under Alf Ramsey, but in 1959 there was still a distinctly amateurish feel to the whole set-up.

The game at Ninian Park was played in appalling conditions of driving wind and incessant rain. In his match report, Tony Pawson of *The Observer* reckoned the game was a 'tale of two halves, with England's bright promise and easy authority of the first swept aside by the fervour of the Welsh rally in the second'.

Connelly, who had been testing his full-back with some penetrating runs, was the provider of England's goal after 26 minutes, firing in a shot that was parried by Welsh keeper Jack Kelsey only for Jimmy Greaves to turn in the rebound.

Kelsey, of Arsenal, kept Wales in the match with a series of superb saves. Clough missed the easiest of chances when he deliberated too long after Eddie Holliday had left him poised in front of an open goal. Then, with less than a minute on the clock, England were left to rue their misses when Cliff Jones, the Spurs winger, floated the ball over and Graham Moore from Cardiff headed Wales level.

In the post-match discussion, it was generally judged that Connelly and Holliday had impressed on the wings, and plaudits also came the way of Tony Allen for a stout display at full-back.

As for Clough, opinion was divided. Tony Pawson felt 'he rarely positioned himself properly to receive a pass' and had also 'lacked his usual certainty near goal'. Roy Peskett from the *Daily Mail* argued that 'Clough was not so mobile or challenging as an England centre-forward should be'.

But the verdict wasn't completely negative. Desmond Hackett in the *Daily Express* wrote: 'Clough, having finally forced himself into the

England team, tried his best to get the chaps together. It was a pretty good best, too. Certainly good enough to keep him in the England side to play Sweden on 28 October.'

Connelly remembers it as a game of missed opportunities. 'Actually, Wales had a decent side in those days, even if the Charles brothers weren't playing on that particular occasion. I think we did quite well, but we just couldn't put the ball away. I remember getting to the byline and smashing one across but Brian being unable to anticipate it and get on the end of it.

'He shouted, "To me feet, to me feet." The problem was, I'd never seen him play before, so I didn't know that's how he liked the ball to be delivered to him. At Burnley, I was used to hitting the ball to the near post for Jimmy Robson while Ray Pointer hung back, or vice versa; I knew instinctively where to find them. I just hadn't had enough time to get to know Brian's style.

'He was certainly a talker, both on and off the pitch. Whereas we would listen to Winterbottom, Brian would put his point across, and say, "This is how I like things to be done." I could be wrong, but I suspect that might not have gone down well in certain quarters.'

Clough's willingness to have his say may well have irritated Winterbottom, who may have been surprised that a 24-year-old debutant should be so forward with his views. But that wouldn't matter as long as Clough could translate a first display of fleeting moments of promise into a more rounded and convincing performance against the Swedes.

The match at Wembley, in front of an 80,000 crowd, started so promisingly. After just eight minutes, England crafted a delightful goal. Don Howe of West Brom started the move from the back, Greaves continued with a quick pass out to the right to Connelly, who pushed the ball to Clough and then ran intelligently into the middle to side-foot the return into the net.

Clough and Greaves had shots saved soon afterwards, while a header from Connelly flashed wide of the post; it looked like a goal feast might be on the cards. But slowly, methodically Sweden got a grip on the game with their clever forwards Agne Simonsson and Henry Thillberg pulling England's defence apart.

After half-time, they reaped their just rewards, helped by a nervous performance in England's goal by Eddie Hopkinson of Bolton Wanderers. Goals from Simonsson, Rune Borjesson and Bengt Salomonsson put Sweden in complete control before Bobby Charlton scored a late consolation for England.

Donald Saunders of the *Daily Telegraph* and *Morning Post* was scathing about England's efforts: 'Sweden won much more handsomely than the narrow margin of victory indicates. They pitilessly exposed our type of football as old-fashioned, devoid of ideas, lacking in basic skill.' Desmond Hackett agreed: 'England were made to look foolish by the part-timers of Sweden. This youngest-ever England were infants in the basic arts of soccer, and they finished like a team who could be beaten by Millwall – without Millwall being particularly proud. It was pitiful. It was frustrating.'

Clough's one powerful memory of that day was of embarrassingly failing to convert a chance to level the match after his shot had hit the bar:

> When I moved in to try and finish off the rebound I finished on the deck instead, rolling on the line with the ball trapped against my midriff. I couldn't get a foot or a head to it, even though it just needed knocking over the line.
>
> Some would call it fate. I called it a bloody nuisance. There were to be no further chances for me. I was cast aside at the age of 24 by a manager who, in my opinion, didn't know his job.

You could argue – as Clough did – that Winterbottom lessened his chances of success by partnering him in the middle of the attack with a forward like Greaves, who was so similar in method and style. Then, from Clough's narrow perspective, there was the added complication of Bobby Charlton – not the traditional schemer that he liked to play with but another forward who wanted to occupy similar territory on the field to Greaves and himself.

Equally, there's a simpler explanation for Clough's 'failure', if it can be considered such after just two opportunities. Great goalscorer that he was, he may simply have lacked the subtlety of approach and the all-round game required to thrive at the very highest level.

Whatever the assessment, it had been a disappointing and chastening few weeks with the England party. His early-season optimism, already dented, was to receive a hammer blow when he returned to Ayresome Park.

* * *

When pondering any question of corruption at Middlesbrough

Football Club in the late 1950s, it's all too easy to put two and two together and make five.

However, it is a fact that three of those who played for the club at that time were later convicted in court of offences of corruption related to the game.

Esmond Million made 52 appearances in goal – mainly as understudy to Peter Taylor – between 1956 and 1962. In July 1963, he was found guilty under the Prevention of Corruption Act of being party to an attempt to fix a match between Bristol Rovers and Bradford Park Avenue. He was fined and later banned by the FA from playing football or managing a club.

Brian Phillips, centre-half and Clough's adversary in the Boro dressing-room, was convicted of the same offence as Million in July 1963 and also fined and banned from the game. Then, on 26 January 1965, he was found guilty of conspiracy to defraud by fixing matches and jailed for 15 months.

Kenneth Thomson played 84 times for Middlesbrough between 1959 and 1962; he took over as captain when Clough relinquished the role in the summer of 1960. Like Phillips, he was convicted in January 1965 of conspiracy to defraud by fixing matches and was jailed for six months.

Thomson and Phillips were lesser lights in the trial at Nottingham Assizes, which saw eight footballers jailed. The big fish were Peter Swan, Sheffield Wednesday and England centre-half, and club colleagues David Layne and Tony Kay. All three were jailed for betting against their own side in a league match against Ipswich Town.

The man behind it all was Jimmy Gauld, a former inside-forward at Mansfield Town, who over several years systematically interfered with matches in the Football League, enticing players into betting on the outcome of fixed matches. He was jailed for the longest stretch, four years.

All this was in the future. It should be stressed that Phillips, Million and Thomson were never accused of and never charged with anything in connection with their time at Middlesbrough.

But back in 1959 rumours of football matches being fixed and players betting against their own teams were starting to emerge around the country. It will have been against that backdrop that Clough started to wonder why, when he was banging in so many goals at one end, did so many continue to be leaked at the other?

'I sensed a nasty smell. There was something wrong, something obvious even to a blind man. It struck me as simple, straightforward incompetence at the time, but I came to wonder if it might be something sinister.'

Clough's suspicions would reach their height a year later on 22 October 1960, when there was a remarkable result at The Valley: Charlton Athletic 6, Middlesbrough 6 (Clough 3). He couldn't believe that his defence could be quite so incompetent, and in his 2004 autobiography he recounted how he took his concerns first to Bob Dennison and then to director Harold Thomas, who was a solicitor. But neither man was prepared to take the matter any further.

In October 1959, though, Clough had a more immediate problem. Only days back from international duty, he was shocked to discover that he had a full-scale dressing-room revolt on his hands. The older pros like Ray Bilcliff, Bill Harris and Brian Phillips, together with new recruit Willie Fernie from Celtic, resented Clough's style of leadership – as they saw it – the chivvying, the bullying, the brash approach, the sulks when things weren't going so well for both him and the team. For these experienced players, Clough had stepped over the line that separates self-confidence and arrogance; too much of the latter was now permeating the training ground and the dressing-room.

And while they might have appreciated his witty one-liners, they also took exception to Peter Taylor's overweening influence on Clough and Dennison. The suspicion, whether unfounded or not, was that this triumvirate, not the manager alone, was effectively picking the team.

Mind you, to suggest that the growing discord in the Middlesbrough dressing-room was something unique to the club would be naive. Ron Reynolds, goalkeeper at that time for First Division championship challengers Tottenham Hotspur, summed it up well:

> Clubs are actually a hotbed of Machiavellian political intrigue, packed with manipulators so cunning they could give lessons to weasels. And that shouldn't come as any surprise – after all, a football club is the same as a political party, where everybody wants the unit to be a great success, but they all want the credit as individuals for achieving it.

According to one of the younger players, a jocular – and entirely unjustified – remark Clough directed towards him about his drinking habits, after training one day in October, was a provocation too far for many of the Middlesbrough side.

It became clear by Monday, 2 November, when the team travelled up to Edinburgh for a friendly match with Hibernian, that something serious was afoot. Even the younger players like Alan Peacock, who had been away on army duty and was blissfully unaware of what was going on, finally woke up to the situation.

'I remember the game with Hibs on that Monday night. I remember somebody playing the ball through to me and I ran on, took it past the goalkeeper but was forced wide of the goal. I looked up, squared it across and Cloughie knocked it in. In those days, there was no taking your shirt off to celebrate or anything like that, so I just went to shake his hand. But I was the only one congratulating him – everyone else turned away from him. A little later, some of them said, "What do you think you're doing? Why did you pass it to him?"'

The gulf that had opened up between Clough and a section of his team was illustrated by their respective activities in the hours before the Hibernian game. The 'card school' remained at the hotel playing all day, while Clough, Taylor, Dennison and vice chairman Eric Thomas went on a visit to Edinburgh Castle.

The plotters made their move almost immediately on the return from Scotland, handing over a round-robin letter to trainer Harold Shepherdson to deliver on their behalf to the board of directors. The letter – which to this day no one will admit to drafting – had the signatures of eight or nine players.

Then on Wednesday, 4 November, a meeting was held with Bob Dennison, chairman Wilf Gibson and Eric Thomas present, along with all the players.

Ray Bilcliff said he didn't like the way Clough spoke to him during the match and the way he sulked afterwards if the side was beaten.

Brian Phillips claims his objections about Clough were more tactical. 'All I said was that I didn't think it was a good idea for a centre-forward to be captain.' Clough, however, remembered Phillips raising the tension by saying simply, 'Some of the lads don't like you.'

The meeting brought a rupture in the friendship between Clough and the team's hard-working inside-forward Derek McLean. McLean was a friend of Clough's off the field. The two men went to each other's weddings, and he and his wife, Marion, used to go dancing with Brian and Barbara at Saltburn at weekends. Yet he, too, had signed the round robin.

Clough's recollection, two years later in the *Sunday Sun*, was that

McLean accused him of shouting at him on the field. 'He came up to me later and apologised and asked me to shake hands. I refused. Now I wish I hadn't.'

McLean, more than 50 years later, regrets his involvement in the whole episode. 'It seemed to come to a head over the way Brian and Peter closeted themselves together. They rarely mixed with the other lads, and on one particular away trip you never saw them apart, on the train or in the hotel. Over the years, I've regretted signing the round robin. Looking back, it seemed to me to be over nothing much, really. My relationship with Brian certainly cooled after that, which was a shame.'

Lining up on Clough's behalf that day were Peter Taylor, Billy Day and Eddie Holliday. Clough recalled Taylor telling the gathering, 'You all knew Brian when he was a youngster. Can you honestly say that he has changed?'

The cracks were papered over. Wilf Gibson urged the rebels to 'see how things go' and asked everyone to pledge not to go to the press with the story.

It was remarkable that such a tale of dressing-room discord should remain within the four walls of Ayresome Park for as long as it did. But the story did eventually leak, and the Teesside public woke up on Wednesday, 18 November to the front-page story 'It's "all together now" for the Boro' and an attempt by Cliff Mitchell to put the best gloss on the misfortune.

His version of events was that 'some of the players had, apparently, taken exception to Brian Clough's attitude – a "lone wolf" who did not always train with them, was one reported complaint. And a change in the captaincy was mooted.' But Mitchell, ever hopeful, informed his readers that the 'Ayresome Park storm in a teacup' had blown itself out. He'd been assured by Clough: 'The spirit in the dressing-room is good. We are all fighting for one thing, promotion, and I want to play my part in that fight.'

That apparent resolve lasted no longer than 24 hours. The page-one headline on Thursday, 19 November read 'Clough (I've Changed My Mind) Asks for His Transfer'. Clearly the captain's mind was in a state of turmoil. Clough told Mitchell: 'I apologise very sincerely for any trouble I might have caused. When I told you that yesterday, I meant what I said. But I got back home last night and I got to thinking. It was all boiled up inside me and I decided that there was only one way out – ask for a transfer.'

By Friday, there had been further developments. Billy Day had joined Clough on the transfer list, while three of the rebels had sought – and had apparently been given – assurances that manager Dennison wouldn't victimise them for their actions.

Players from different factions continued to jostle anonymously on the pages of the *Gazette* for prominence for their side of the story. A stream of bland, reassuring – but clearly disingenuous – statements from the board attempted to calm the situation.

Eventually, over the following week, the febrile atmosphere started to cool. Publicly, Clough acknowledged that 'some of the lads had raised one or two good points'. The idea of players with grievances going to the directors to discuss them was deemed to be a positive step that would 'undoubtedly help team spirit'. It was back to business as usual, if you believed everything you read.

But, privately, Clough was seething. Later, he would tell the readers of the *Sunday Sun*: 'I can't fully describe my feelings. I was hurt, angry, confused, all at the same time. When I got home [that first night], I felt miserable and depressed.'

It would be another 18 months and 64 goals before he left Ayresome Park, but the seeds of his departure were undoubtedly sown in that week in November.

Whatever the accusations about his brashness or his selfishness, none of his critics could deny his remarkable strength of character. When he took to the field for Boro's home match against Bristol Rovers on 21 November, some elements in the 25,000 crowd even barracked him. But after 14 minutes, any criticism was silenced by Clough curling a terrific shot into the net from 25 yards. He added two more to complete yet another hat-trick, and Boro won the match 5–1.

★ ★ ★

On 23 January 1960, a partnership was formed that would plot a course for the great days of Leeds United Football Club. Don Revie, captain and inside-right, had a little 17-year-old Scottish winger playing outside him for the first time that day. His name was Billy Bremner.

Leeds' scouting system was sharper than most north of the border, and they had identified Bremner's talent when he was a schoolboy playing for Gowanhill Juniors in his home town of Stirling. Bremner went on to represent Scotland at schoolboy level, but although big London clubs like Arsenal and Chelsea were interested in him, they ultimately rejected him because, at 5 ft 5 in., they considered him too small to make it at the top level.

Leeds had the foresight not to be bothered about the lack of inches; what they saw was a young player bubbling over with energy and enthusiasm – and no little skill. They also perceived a toughness and a will to win unusually well developed in one so young.

By this stage of the season, manager Jack Taylor knew he was in a relegation battle but nonetheless was determined to blood the gifted youngster. So Bremner travelled down with the squad to London for a match against Chelsea, and the captain quickly took him under his wing.

Revie knew Bremner was homesick. He remembered the loneliness and apprehension he had felt as a youngster at Leicester City and how Johnny Duncan had gone out of his way to try to settle him down and make him feel comfortable. He was determined to follow his example at Leeds United. Bremner was in for an instructive weekend.

> It was Billy's first game, he was just 17, and I thought that being the captain and senior player I should share rooms with him that night. I always got down on my knees every night and said my prayers, and it gave me a sense of security. I prayed for the good health of the family first, and then I'd thank the Lord for what I'd had out of football and how fortunate I'd been.
>
> So I made Billy go down on his knees with me that Friday night before the Chelsea game. The next morning I made him get up around nine o'clock and go for a good walk, and do some deep breathing exercises.

It must have worked. Leeds beat Chelsea 3–1, with two goals from John McCole and one from Noel Peyton. The *Yorkshire Post*'s verdict was that the debutant 'was no star, but he can be well marked on the credit side'.

'He used the ball speedily, generally accurately and always intelligently . . . Revie and Cush nursed him well out of their rich experience, and on a rainswept slough of a pitch the lightweight boy came through well.'

Bremner played ten more games before the end of the season, scoring twice. One of his goals was in a 3–3 draw with Birmingham City on 9 March at Elland Road. The right-wing partnership was clearly working well that day – Revie scored the other two.

There were only 8,500 spectators for that midweek match against Birmingham, the lowest crowd at Elland Road that season. The average attendance for the entire campaign only just topped 13,000.

By mid-April, Leeds were in a desperate fight for survival with the likes of Birmingham and Nottingham Forest, and defeats by Everton and Blackburn Rovers decided their fate. They were relegated, back in the Second Division after just four years in the top flight.

The superstitious side of Revie nagged away at him, even telling him that his spell as captain had brought Leeds bad luck and hastened their departure from the First Division. He resigned the captaincy at the start of the 1960–61 season, handing over to former Manchester United defender Freddie Goodwin.

As the new season progressed, Revie featured less and less on the team sheet. Ever since those Sunday morning lessons in Keith Road with the Boro Swifts, Revie had been an unusually thoughtful footballer. He had, of course, been instrumental in the introduction of one of the major tactical changes in the British game with the 'deep-lying' centre-forward role at Manchester City.

Eric Thornton recalled a conversation with Revie back in 1954, after he'd just won his first England cap, that showed quite clearly where his eventual interest would lie:

> Always a quiet thinker, even when others around him were talking clap-trap after big games, he was peering ahead even immediately after winning a first 'cap'.
>
> Which is why I'll never forget as the plane from the Belfast international touched down at Ringway one cold autumnal night, he suddenly turned to me and said: 'I've been thinking how I'd like to have a crack at managing when the playing days are over.'

He'd watched and learned from managers like Johnny Duncan, Raich Carter, Alan Brown and Walter Winterbottom. Now, perhaps, the time had come to follow in their footsteps.

The opportunity came early in 1961, as Leeds were reaching the end of another mediocre season. Two offers had already come Revie's way, one from Chester to be their player-coach, another from Tranmere Rovers. Then, in February, Bournemouth came knocking on his door; this time he was attracted to the job of player-manager, even though the club was struggling in the lower reaches of Division Three.

Revie asked influential director Harry Reynolds to write him a reference for the Bournemouth job. Reynolds did so – but tore it up before he sent it, baffled by what he was doing. Why was he signing away the best asset Leeds United possessed on the playing side?

Lord Harewood, who had just been made president of the club, claims some credit for shaping Reynolds' thinking. 'He said to me, "I've had this letter from Revie to ask if I would recommend him as player-manager for this club down south." I said, "For goodness' sake, why don't we have him as manager here?" He was an excellent player and a very bright and intelligent man.'

Financial reality may also have played a part in the final decision. If they were forced to let Revie go, the Leeds board wanted a substantial amount of compensation for the loss of his services. Bournemouth, however, weren't prepared to pay.

A few weeks later, Jack Taylor was prompted to resign and Reynolds persuaded the board to offer Revie the job. He admitted later, 'I'd been thinking about the chance of a manager's job for some time, and kept wondering which club might be the right one for me, but this one suits me down to the ground.'

Harry Reynolds, who became club chairman a few weeks later, was a remarkable man. Born in the back streets of Holbeck in inner-city Leeds, he worked on the railways as a young man before first building a brief career as an on-course bookie, then dabbling in second-hand cars and motor-wrecking. After the Second World War, he made his fortune buying and selling steel. With his new-found wealth and status, he took up riding to hounds with the Bramham Hunt, bought polo ponies and then went into pig breeding.

But this self-made squire had a vision for Leeds United Football Club, and it was one that was not to be deflected by the club's huge debts of £237,000 and looming bankruptcy. That dream required the club to have a young, innovative manager to shape it, and he was convinced from very early on that Don Revie was that individual.

With a three-year contract in his pocket – albeit not on financial terms he was entirely happy with – Revie decided to head across the Pennines for advice on how to approach his new job.

He called on Matt Busby in his office at Old Trafford. The Manchester United manager was impressed by Revie's initiative: 'His first question was, can you enlighten me about the snags in the game, and I thought, that's a very good, quick thinker, because he wants to be prepared for all the problems before he meets them. I got a tremendous impression that here was a man who was bursting to succeed and bursting to build a great side.'

Busby generously outlined his football philosophy to Revie over several hours. The new manager was all too aware of how Busby had built up a cadre of young players – 'the Busby Babes' – who had been schooled by him from an early age and prepared meticulously for life in the top echelons of football. He resolved to copy Busby's approach, and gather around him a group of talented young players whom he could mould for success.

One player on the Leeds staff who could not be considered 'young' any more was Jack Charlton. He was nearly 26, a player of great promise, but with plenty of rough edges that still had to be knocked off. Revie's ascendancy, he believed, was not necessarily good news for his own prospects, as he recalls: 'I remember one day we had a practice match on. I was charging up the field for corner kicks, venturing into areas a centre-half wouldn't normally go in matches. Don came up to me and said, "If I was manager of this club, I wouldn't play you, because you spoil it for everybody. You're always running forward wanting to get goals, and you're always running with the ball. You're not doing things right as a centre-half." I just swore back at him. Three weeks later, they made him manager!'

In fact, Revie would go on to revitalise Charlton's career in the next couple of years, acknowledging the big man's waywardness and volatility but also recognising his natural ability and determined to unlock all the potential that still remained stubbornly hidden away.

Leeds finished the 1960–61 season in 14th place in Division Two. Crowds had dwindled, the ambition of a few seasons ago had evaporated and there was a general air of neglect around Elland Road. Plenty of work, then, for the new manager to get his teeth into – and there was no more willing worker than Don Revie.

* * *

Just as Don Revie resigned the captaincy at Leeds ahead of the 1960–61 season, so Brian Clough did likewise at Middlesbrough. Although he'd eventually led his side to a creditable fifth place in the table, he remained scarred by the events of November and the players' revolt against him. So he now resolved to concentrate purely and simply on scoring goals. He was succeeded as skipper by centre-half Ken Thomson, who had joined Boro from Stoke City for £9,000 soon after the revolt.

Clough being Clough, however, events didn't run smoothly. The summer was spent wrangling with Bob Dennison about a new contract, which wasn't signed until the verge of the new season. While the impasse existed, Clough stayed away from the club for six weeks. He only started training in mid-August and, not being match fit, consequently missed the first two games of the new season.

In an interview with the *Daily Mail*, the wounds from the November debacle still showed. 'Their round robin letter nearly broke my heart. So I asked for my cards. If it hadn't been for my wife, I might have quit football.' He went on to say that he was now content and focusing on his football. There was, though, an ominous tone to his final remarks: 'But I don't want to endure another nine months like last season, with so many old spinsters bickering behind the scenes. Indeed, if we can't all row together I want no part of the Middlesbrough programme.'

His teammates will have taken all that with a pinch of salt. Alan Peacock says: 'I remember him saying to us once, I'm writing about you this week, and I'll be slagging a few players off. Don't take any bloody notice – I'm just getting paid for it!'

Brian Phillips, one of the 'ringleaders' of the players' protest, was put on the transfer list and was certain it was a consequence of the events of November. 'I was forced out, and it was wrong. I felt very aggrieved towards Clough, and I know he was involved in getting me out. The thing that really annoyed me was that shortly after I left for Mansfield, he went too. I feel sad about Boro. As far as I'm concerned, I put as much into the club as anyone.'

Ronnie Dicks and Carl Taylor also reluctantly left Ayresome Park around this time, and the rifts between the players were still evident. Ray Robertson had just taken over covering Middlesbrough for the *Northern Echo*. 'In those days, remember, there were few motorways, and we used to travel hundreds, thousands of miles in a year by train. I would travel with the team and Cliff Mitchell of the *Evening Gazette*.

'We travelled in the Clough compartment – because there was a Clough compartment, and an anti-Clough compartment. Some players were still in favour of him, some against. In those early days – before I got to know him properly – I was a little intimidated by him because he was such an outspoken, abrasive character. I would hardly dare open my mouth because I could be pounced upon!'

If there were still differences between the players, they didn't show markedly on the field. Clough was back in the old routine; by the end of 1960 he'd already rattled in twenty goals in twenty-one games, and

Boro were fifth in the table. He'd finished the year off with two late goals against Liverpool at Anfield to give his side an unlikely 4–3 victory.

But, as in previous years, Boro just couldn't find the momentum to propel them into a promotion place. In February, Clough scored a hat-trick away at Portsmouth and then followed that up with two more goals in a 3–0 defeat of Leeds – minus Don Revie – at Ayresome Park. But there were defeats away at Norwich, Huddersfield, Ipswich and Lincoln, and in the end they had to settle for another fifth place and the same number of points – 48 – as the previous season.

Clough finished with 34 goals from 41 appearances. But it was clear by now that his days at Middlesbrough were drawing to a close. He wanted to get away, and the club were less inclined than before to hang on to him. There had been rumours a year before that Fiorentina of Italy might be on the verge of making a bid for him. But, realistically, the interest was coming from closer to home, with newly relegated Newcastle considering an offer.

Clough made no bones about it in yet another signed piece, this time in the *Daily Express* in May: 'Newcastle United are reported to be interested in me. That thought doesn't depress me. Because I'm interested in Charlie Mitten and Newcastle, and every other manager and club in the business who is interested in me. I want to get to another club and be happy. Not frustrated.'

In the end, this open invitation was taken up by the Wearsiders, not the Tynesiders. Sunderland had been consolidating after the upheavals of 1957 and 1958 and had finished one place behind Middlesbrough in the Second Division table in 1961.

Unbeknown to Clough, a deal was struck between the two clubs while he was on a cruise in the Mediterranean with Barbara. Alan Brown, the Sunderland manager, was on holiday himself in Cornwall when the directors agreed terms but quickly abandoned his break and headed for Southampton docks.

There, he waited at the quayside for the Cloughs to disembark. When they did, he called them over and tipped the porter for carrying their cases. Clough recalled: 'Mr Brown lifted our cases onto a trolley, turned to me and asked: "Will you sign for Sunderland?" I presumed he had asked Middlesbrough first, so I didn't think to ask. With Barbara standing behind me I said "Yes", just like that. Brown said: "Fine. I'll see you at Roker Park in a week's time."'

Brown had his man for £42,000 – a big fee in those days. Clough didn't even bother to look at the small print of the contract, so desperate was he to get away from Ayresome Park after all the travails of the past 18 months.

He was 26, at the height of his powers, with plenty left to do in the game and an international career to resurrect. In Alan Brown, he would find a hard taskmaster but a kindred spirit, a manager whose values of order, discipline and loyalty were ones close to his own heart. It was a relationship that would prosper right from the start.

Chapter 7

'From Butlins to the Kremlin'

Nineteen sixty-one was a tense year in which a young, inexperienced American president was put to the test and global peace severely threatened. It was 12 months when the Cold War, in all its manifestations, looked likely to turn hot.

On 17 April, goaded by Fidel Castro and urged on by the hawks in his administration, President Kennedy encouraged a clandestine invasion of Cuba, known as the Bay of Pigs, which failed disastrously within hours.

On 13 August, the White House received the startling news that barbed-wire fences up to six feet high had been put up by East German troops during the night, and Berliners awoke to find themselves living in a divided city. A wall would soon separate east from west.

Then, on 30 October, the Soviet Union detonated a 50-megaton hydrogen bomb, known as Tsar Bomba, over Novaya Zemlya. It remains the largest-ever man-made explosion.

In the narrow world of professional football, an earthquake of sorts struck on 18 January that year. A personable, articulate, bearded man with a long chin had finally won the battle on behalf of his fellow players and compelled the 'masters' of the Football League to give the 'serfs' their financial freedom.

Jimmy Hill was a decent enough player, a wing-half for Fulham with an eye for goal. But his role as chairman of the Professional Footballers' Association will almost certainly be his greatest legacy, because on that day in 1961 he forced the lifting of the maximum wage, the cap on players' wages (then set at £20 a week) that had lasted forever and a day. Hill had finally dragged football, kicking and screaming, into the modern age.

Players were still not able to join a new team if and when they wanted, as the clubs controlled their contracts in the old 'retain and transfer' system. But the first major skirmish in the war with the Establishment had been won.

The consequences were immediate, right there in Jimmy Hill's dressing-room at Craven Cottage. Tommy Trinder, Fulham's comedian chairman, always on the lookout for some good publicity, declared that his England inside-forward Johnny Haynes would now be paid £100 a week. Rival chairmen throughout the land ran for cover.

Ultimately, the lifting of the maximum wage would make the highest class of footballers into not just sportsmen but celebrities. They would have lifestyles far removed from the men and women who supported them on the terraces.

But any thoughts of the consequences of this new development in terms of greater social mobility for footballers, even a new social order, were way off in the distance. For the moment, there was expectation that the short-term benefit would be the eradication of the financial 'irregularities' that had besmirched the game for many years. Players from high-profile clubs like Sunderland, where they'd been paid 'boot money' and received other perks in contravention of the maximum wage, had faced the threat of suspension over receipt of such payments; now there was far less reason for these illicit handovers of cash.

For players like Brian Clough, 26 years old, at the peak of his career, coveted by many clubs for his unique goalscoring ability, it was a golden opportunity to negotiate a new contract that would provide him and his family with greater financial security.

Up and down the country, players began to tussle with managers over their remuneration – healthy discussions in the new 'free' market of football but not without drawbacks for team harmony. In some clubs, team spirit was fractured and player pitted against player, as Ron Reynolds, Southampton's goalkeeper, recalled:

> The only time I ever had words with Ted Bates [the manager] was when the maximum wage was lifted. I believe I'm right in saying the increase we were offered was one pound to twenty-one pounds. It could have been twenty-two, but certainly no more. Not quite Johnny Haynes, the first hundred-pound-a-week player, was it? Had it been across the board, it might have been accepted, but of course Terry Paine couldn't help bragging about the money he was on. We knew they'd given him forty-five pounds.

The Southampton players, aggrieved at this disparity, confronted Bates ahead of the first match of the season against Plymouth Argyle: 'Unless we get some satisfaction, you haven't got a team for Saturday! About an hour and a half before the game started, Ted relented and we were all put on twenty-five pounds.'

Johnny Haynes' playing equivalent today, Frank Lampard, signed a five-year contract with Chelsea in 2008 widely reported to be worth £33 million, with his weekly salary reaching £140,000 by 2011. A small token of his gratitude should, by rights, head the way of Mr Jimmy Hill.

★ ★ ★

Don Revie and Brian Clough headed into their second pitch encounter on 9 September 1961, with their teams struggling to make an impact in the season's early matches in Division Two.

Leeds had started their campaign promisingly, with victories against Charlton at home and Brighton away, young Billy Bremner on the scoresheet in both games. But a crushing 5–0 defeat by Liverpool – orchestrated by the impressive Ian St John – brought them down to earth and was followed by a draw against Brighton at home (another Bremner goal), then defeats against Rotherham (home) and Norwich City (away).

Revie, now aged thirty-four, was increasingly certain in his own mind that there was one year, at most, left of his playing career. But he wanted to try to continue for just a little longer while younger players were bedded into the side.

He turned out for Leeds in the 2–0 defeat at Carrow Road on Wednesday, 6 September. The *Yorkshire Post* reported on Friday, 8 September that he was eager to return to his old stamping-ground at Roker Park for the next fixture: 'Revie is to play against his old club. He does not consider two first-team games in four days too great a strain for him, even bearing the additional responsibility he shoulders as team manager. "I have been hard training for a month," he said last night, "and am quite fit."'

On and off the pitch, Revie's task was proving an enormous one. Attendances were low (around 12,000 for those first three home games of the season), and the club was sliding alarmingly into debt. He had taken over what he would later describe as a 'dead club'; 'there were players here who didn't care whether they played or not'.

He had a very clear idea of how he intended to turn things around at Elland Road. It was less a plan, more a revolution, not just a change of playing personnel but a transformation in the whole ethos of the club. He wanted the training methods and structure completely overhauled, and he sought a totally different approach from the players, not just in terms of their commitment to the game but also by way of their behaviour and lifestyle on and off the pitch.

In turn, he would look after them properly, not scrimping and saving on hotel bills; they would be made to feel part of a big club that was going places. He wanted, too, to have them far better prepared for games, to make them fully aware of the strengths and weaknesses of the opposition.

But revolutions take time. Fidel Castro's in Cuba had taken a couple of years; Don Revie's at Leeds would need at least a similar period. His chairman, Harry Reynolds, needed no convincing that Revie's planned upheaval was the right way forward at Elland Road. But it would require a large outlay of money from him and the other board members that couldn't be forthcoming in just one year.

There was one early visible sign of the Revie Revolution. To help lift the despondent air that enveloped the club, he decided to change the team colours. Out went the old blue and gold, and in came an all-white strip, deliberately imitating the great Spanish side Real Madrid (with the likes of Di Stéfano, Puskás and Gento) that had won five European Cups in a row between 1956 and 1960.

Forty years of Leeds United history was discarded, but, remarkably, very little was made of it at the time either on the terraces or in the boardroom – although there were a few derisory cheers when it was first announced over the tannoy at Elland Road. Revie was a man who needed his good-luck charms, but he also believed the brightness of the new white strip would stand out and contribute to his side's psychological domination of opponents.

Revie had an imagination that stretched far beyond the short-term improvements that were required to make Leeds United a more successful football club. His son Duncan, then a young boy, remembers standing on the centre circle at Elland Road with his father: 'When he took me out onto the pitch and we looked round the stadium, it was an absolute pigsty. But Dad just glanced round and said to me, "Son, in the future this will be a 60,000 all-seater stadium. You'll go to football matches at 11.30 in the morning, there'll be private boxes, there'll be sponsorship, there'll be logos on shorts, private areas where you go for lunch before the match and even shopping malls next to the ground." And I looked at him and thought, "You're bloody mad, Dad!" But he'd seen what the future could bring.'

Over at Roker Park, Brian Clough wasn't yet dabbling in visions. His simple objective was to score plenty of goals for his demanding new manager to justify his £42,000 price tag. He would later say his time at Sunderland had been the happiest of his professional career, but back in October 1961 he still had everything to prove.

He hadn't started well. In the first game of the season, Sunderland lost 4–3 away at newly promoted Walsall, and in the dressing-room Clough, along with other senior players, took a verbal lashing from Alan Brown for the slipshod performance. Two wins and two more defeats followed, so by 9 September Sunderland were keeping company with Leeds near the foot of the Division Two table.

Clough may have needed time to convince Alan Brown, but right from the start he endeared himself to the Roker fans. Brian Leng, these days editor of theRokerEnd.com, a website devoted to the memories and exploits of former Sunderland players, was then just a soccer-mad 14-year-old. He was in a group of boys who used to hang around the stadium waiting for the players to arrive in the morning, then cycle after them when they headed off to the Cleadon training ground.

'I used to watch him practise his penalty-box shooting, and it was an awesome sight to behold. He'd get four of the youth-team players to throw balls at him from all sides, so he could work assiduously on his volleying and half-volleying. He'd consistently smash the ball in the net from all angles.

'He was slim, and he wasn't tall and didn't really look like a footballer. But he had immensely strong thigh muscles that enabled him to generate so much power in his shots from such a short backswing.'

Young Leng was also witness to the Clough insistence on good manners: 'He came out of the players' entrance one day, and this lad handed him his autograph book and asked him to sign it – not in any rude or brusque sort of way. Cloughie listened and then pushed the boy's book away to one side. Another lad then approached him – with some trepidation – and said, "Can I have your autograph, Mr Clough, please?" Clough immediately picked up the pen and signed it, telling the other boy, "That's the way to ask!"'

* * *

So, as they lined up on Saturday, 9 September, Sunderland and Leeds both badly needed points to drag themselves away from the foot of the table. Clough needed goals for his confidence and self-esteem; Revie wanted to know if he still had the legs to effectively prolong his playing career.

Leeds' regular centre-half, Jackie Charlton, was out injured, his place taken by Freddie Goodwin, with Willie Bell coming in at left-half.

For the home side, wing-half Stan Anderson, right-winger Harry Hooper and right-back Colin Nelson all passed fitness tests and took their places in the side.

Sunderland
Wakeham
Nelson   Ashurst
Anderson (c)   Hurley   McNab
Hooper   Fogarty   Clough   McPheat   Overfield

Johanneson   Peyton   McCole   Bremner   Mayers
Bell   Goodwin   Revie
Hair (c)   Smith
Humphreys
Leeds United

Referee: Mr W. Crossley
Sunderland manager: Alan Brown
Leeds United manager: Don Revie

The Players
Colin Nelson, Sunderland's right-back that day, was a singular man. He had made his debut on 25 October 1958 at Bristol City, but three years later and established in his position, he still only played part-time. With foresight unusual in footballers of that generation – or indeed any generation – he'd planned an alternative career from the age of 15.

The career he chose was pharmacy. It required a commitment to study on Saturday afternoons, so his football career was effectively put on hold for two years in his late teens. Then, when his pharmaceutical apprenticeship was finished, Nelson's father contacted Alan Brown – who he knew had been tracking the progress of his son over the years – and the Sunderland manager promptly picked him for a reserve game against Middlesbrough. Soon after that, he was in the first-team squad.

Being part-time meant he trained just two nights a week, Tuesday and Thursday. He was a naturally fit man, but nonetheless it was hard work keeping up the required levels of stamina and skill. His Saturday routine before a home game would startle the professional footballers of today.

'I would normally have a lecture in Newcastle on Saturday morning between ten and midday. Helpfully, they'd let me leave the lecture hall at 11.50 so I could run down to Newcastle Central Station in order to catch the twelve o'clock train. When I got off the train at Sunderland, my brother used to have a meal of steak and toast ready for me. Then I used to run to the bus stop, get the bus to as near to the ground as I could, then walk the mile and a half to the ground to prepare to play. Tell that to today's players and they would cringe. Even after I'd left college in Newcastle, I'd go and work in the shop on a Saturday morning, then run out in front of 40,000 people at Roker Park in the afternoon.'

Nelson had been a teammate of Don Revie's just briefly before he left for Leeds. But he remembers Revie encouraging him in his football a few years before that: 'When I was a young lad, I used to practise at the front of the house because there was a brick wall. I played with a tennis ball, and I used to throw it up and practise controlling it. One day, I was in my usual routine when I heard a voice from behind me say, "That's the way, lad. That's the best way to improve – go for a small ball!" It was Don. He lived in Cleadon at the time, just over the railway, near me. I know he rated me; he tried to sign me after he took over at Leeds, but Alan Brown told me I couldn't go.'

On that day, of course, Nelson's loyalties lay with the new addition to the Sunderland forward line. 'I got on well with Cloughie. I could only take him as I found him. I took all his bravado and bluster with a pinch of salt, and he was fine with me. But there was certainly a mix of opinions about him. I can remember being in the dressing-room one particular day, and one of the players said, "Brian, I love you to bits when you're scoring goals, but I hate you otherwise." Straight to the point!

'On the pitch, he had the knack of being in the right place at the right time. I remember playing at Middlesbrough one day and the keeper had hold of the ball, so we all went upfield and left him, but Brian just stood there in front of him, continuing to harass him. Then suddenly you heard a big roar; the keeper had dropped the ball and Brian had stuck it in the back of the net.'

Three years on from that game at Ayresome Park, Alan Brown's 'young guns', Len Ashurst, Jimmy McNab, Charlie Hurley and, of course, Stan Anderson, were still in the side and developing as players. They were the core of his team and would continue to serve Sunderland well for many years.

In the forward line, Clough had two excellent wingers to provide the crosses for him: 28-year-old Harry Hooper, an England Under-23 international, and Jackie Overfield, who'd come from Leeds the previous season. High hopes were invested in 19-year-old inside-left Willie McPheat, while inside-right Ambrose 'Amby' Fogarty was a Republic of Ireland international.

Colin Nelson's task that day was to subdue Leeds' most potent attacking threat, 21-year-old left-winger Albert Johanneson, a black South African who was one of Revie's first signings after he'd impressed on a three-month trial earlier in the year. 'I had some good tussles with Albert,' recalls Nelson. 'He was a bit quick. He used to push the ball past you and run, but fortunately I was one of the quicker ones and was often – but not always! – able to catch him.'

Albert Johanneson was following in the footsteps of Roy Brown of Stoke City, Charlie Williams of Doncaster and Lindy Delapenha of Middlesbrough, all black players trying to achieve prominence in British football at a time when the colour of their skin marked them out as distinctive, unusual performers. In fact, to their credit, Leeds had two black wingers at that time; 27-year-old Gerry Francis, formerly a shoe-repairer in his native South Africa, played on the right wing.

Johanneson, who came from a township in Germiston, South Africa, had been recommended to Leeds by a local schoolteacher. Prime Minister Daniel Malan was entrenching the apartheid system when Johanneson was growing up, and when he arrived in England he was unsure of himself and the rules governing his behaviour and his life. In his autobiography, Eddie Gray, the fellow left-winger who would later take his place, recalled: 'Having been conditioned to apartheid, he believed he would not be allowed in the bath with the white players. On the pitch he was subjected to a lot of heavy tackles, not to mention racial abuse.' But at Elland Road the supporters had warmed to him immediately. He was judged entirely on his merits, and his explosive pace and dazzling sidestep lit up a side that was lacking in flamboyant personalities.

Bremner had by now moved from the wing to inside-right, a more natural position for him. Leeds expected the goals to come from Irish-born centre-forward John McCole, an accomplished player who had scored 21 in the previous season. Noel Peyton, a Republic of Ireland international, occupied the inside-left berth, while Derek Mayers, a new signing by Revie from Preston North End, was at right-wing.

Grenville Hair, right-back and captain, had been at Leeds since 1948 and in the first team since 1951. Quick in the tackle and an excellent passer of the ball, he might have won international honours had he plied his trade with a more fashionable club.

Eric Smith (Celtic) and Willie Bell (Queen's Park) were two rugged defenders whom the previous manager Jack Taylor had brought to the club after raiding the Scottish leagues. Smith had been astonished by what he had found at Leeds when he arrived the previous year:

> The club was fifth rate and the players were undisciplined. It wasn't their fault. Jack Taylor had let the thing go. I thought beforehand I was coming to a top club. I found out otherwise in the first three or four days. We would go on long training runs and at the end, some players, quite senior players, would walk in with ice lollies in their hands.

Completing the line-up was another of Taylor's signings, the former Busby Babe Freddie Goodwin, a robust wing-half who moved over to centre-half in place of Charlton for this game, and 21-year-old goalkeeper Alan Humphreys, signed from Shrewsbury and given a baptism of fire in Leeds' relegation season. Revie was beginning to have doubts about Humphreys' sureness and consistency and was casting around for a replacement. He'd had good reports from scouts about a 16-year-old from Swansea named Gary Sprake.

The Rivalry

In the 1960s and early 1970s, clashes between Sunderland and Leeds United were invariably bitter in spirit and often violent in deed. Take the fierce, highly personal rivalries between Don Revie, Alan Brown and Bob Stokoe, add the natural contention between two Northern sides with partisan, committed sets of supporters, and the concoction was a witches' brew that would often poison the encounters.

Those sour meetings had their origins in 1960 and 1961. In his autobiography *Left Back in Time*, Len Ashurst recalled being ordered to 'deal with' Revie when the former Sunderland man brought his Leeds side to Roker Park in October 1960:

> Brownie, who had taken something of a dislike to Revie during his time at Sunderland, wound us up before the game and specifically picked out Revie for personal attention ... Very early on in the game, somehow my over-exuberance found my left boot hovering a few inches from Don Revie's face as he lay on the ground in front of the main stand by the players' tunnel. He had gone down in a tackle from my fellow assassin Jimmy McNab, who had taken him off by the knee.
>
> A snap decision was required; do I engage, as the consequences would inevitably result in scarring Don Revie for life as well as me being sent off? I went against the immediate impulse coursing through my veins and pulled away, much to the disappointment of a packed house at Roker Park and probably to the annoyance of Alan Brown.

Brown's ruthless tactics backfired that day. Leeds won 3–2, with goals from McCole, Peyton and Francis, and Revie played a prominent part in the victory.

Then, on 25 August 1962, it was Leeds' turn to dish out some similar treatment. In the 26th minute of the match at Elland Road, young Willie McPheat darted out to challenge for the ball. The *Sunderland Echo* reported matter-of-factly what happened next: 'There was an opponent's foot over the ball as he cleared, however, and he went down badly injured.'

McPheat collapsed in agony with a broken leg and was rushed to hospital; he never played for Sunderland again. He played a smattering of games for Hartlepools under Brian Clough in 1965 and 1966 before finishing his career in Scotland with Airdrieonians. But he wasn't the same player after that summer day in 1962.

And the opponent whose foot was over the ball? That was Bobby Collins, the little Glaswegian whom Revie brought from Celtic late in the 1961–62 season to add guile, toughness and leadership to the Leeds team from the middle of the field. Resentment over what they considered to be not just a rash but a particularly brutal challenge still lingers today in the minds of the Sunderland supporters who watched that game all those years ago.

Johnny Crossan, who joined Sunderland just a couple of months after that incident, recalls the ferocity of the clashes: 'They were violent. They were pretty tight matches, too, and it led to some hectic battles. Revie was very good at saying little things that got people's hair up, you know. He'd say about me, "That Irishman can't play." Leeds also had this tactic – the whistle would blow, the match would begin and they'd go and "do" one of the opposition players early on because it would be too soon for the referee to want to send anyone off.'

It has to be said that Leeds weren't the only side in those days that got a stiff – euphemistically speaking – tackle in early, while the referee was minded to exercise some leniency. Most of the hard men around the country would use the same ploy.

In the 1963–64 season, when both sides were promoted to the First Division, there were two particularly fiery matches played in just three days at Christmas. After one challenge on the Sunderland goalkeeper Jim Montgomery, Charlie Hurley grabbed Leeds centre-forward Ian Lawson by the throat and it took Len Ashurst, Jimmy McNab and Martin Harvey to drag him off.

Johnny Giles felt that Leeds were as much sinned against as sinning:

> We were no angels, far from it ... We were young and inexperienced, and Sunderland knew full well that we could be vulnerable to physical and verbal provocation. They intimidated the Leeds players throughout with such jibes as 'You're a bunch of scrubbers', 'That was a rubbish tackle', and we eventually lost our heads. I am not condemning Sunderland because I have done this sort of thing myself. Let's face it, most professional footballers have.

Those particularly ferocious games lay ahead. But even by September 1962 there was a sharpness to these confrontations that kept spectators on the edge of their seats as much as the quality of the football.

The Match

At Roker Park in front of a crowd of 30,737, bright sunshine, a fresh breeze and a perfect playing surface presented ideal conditions for the two sides. The home team began with a flourish, Overfield picking up a loose ball from Eric Smith before making ground down the left wing and whipping in a low cross that Clough unfortunately overran.

Soon afterwards, Sunderland attacked again down the right, McPheat feeding Fogarty, who delivered a delightful cross for Clough to head towards goal. There wasn't enough power or direction in his effort, however, and Humphreys was able to pull off a decent save.

Clough was, even this early in the game, making an impressive impact. He knew he had much to do to convince the Roker crowd of his worth, but he was clearly on his mettle. After just seven minutes, he silenced the doubters.

Under pressure on the left wing and facing his own goal, he played an incisive ball down the line for Jackie Overfield. The winger slipped inside full-back Smith and played a short pass through the middle, just on the angle of the box. Amby Fogarty squared the ball across to Clough, who fired it emphatically past Humphreys from ten yards and into the back of the net.

A flowing move, started and finished by Clough, proving he wasn't merely a poacher in the penalty area but could also play a part in the creation of a goal.

Leeds rallied, as they had to, and good covering by Ashurst prevented Revie from threading a pass through to Mayers, who would have been clean through on goal. Soon afterwards, Peyton broke free with only keeper Peter Wakeham to beat. Wakeham parried well, and when Peyton followed up to put the ball in the net, McNab stole in to intercept it and clear the danger.

By now, the game was flowing back and forth. Billy Bremner broke through in the inside-right position and fired in a rising drive that Wakeham did well to turn over. At the other end, Clough – who had displayed an excellent understanding with winger Overfield – mis-hit his shot and rolled the ball wide when put through again.

Such were the chances coming his way that it was no surprise when Clough doubled his, and his side's, tally after 31 minutes. Grenville Hair failed to control a through ball by Fogarty, the ball ran loose and Clough was onto it in an instant. He dribbled round keeper Humphreys and slotted the ball easily into the net.

There was no stopping the new recruit. He next turned past the statuesque Goodwin and hammered in a right-foot shot that Humphreys did brilliantly well to grasp just inside the post.

There was just time for another superb save by Humphreys from a Fogarty shot, and a Clough volley that sailed over the bar. Leeds were like a boxer on the ropes, desperately waiting for the bell to sound for the end of the round.

Half-Time: Sunderland 2, Leeds United 0

Revie decided on a tactical switch at the start of the second half, with wingers Mayers and Johanneson swapping positions. The latter had been utterly ineffectual in the first 45 minutes, unable to escape Nelson's attentions.

Clough carried on his good work of the first half by holding the ball up under pressure from Goodwin before playing it sweetly out to Hooper on the right wing. He was quickly back in the middle for Hooper's cross, pulling the ball down and shooting, only for Humphreys to save once more.

Revie tried to pick Leeds up and bring them back into the game, and it needed an excellent intervention from Hurley to stop him in his tracks inside the penalty area.

But there was no stopping the Sunderland onslaught. McPheat held off three fierce tackles before laying on yet another chance for Clough; Humphreys stopped his first shot, only for Clough to follow up and drive the ball into the net. Referee Crossley, however, disallowed the goal for a reason that wasn't immediately clear, denying Clough his hat-trick.

As an attacking force, Leeds were nowhere to be seen by now, and they had another lucky escape with about ten minutes to go. Stan Anderson, despite apparently having suffered a nasty leg injury earlier in the half, was back in the fray and latched on to a centre from Overfield, crashing a left-foot drive onto the post.

Then, with seven minutes left on the clock, Leeds gave themselves a chance, with a goal completely out of the blue. John McCole reacted well when Bremner's effort was blocked, placing a right-foot shot just inside the upright, well out of Peter Wakeham's reach.

Sunderland, however, finished the game as they'd spent most of it – on the offensive. After McPheat was brought down just outside the area, Clough's free kick was deflected away as it headed towards the dangerous Hurley, lurking at the far post. Then, in the final action of the match, Hooper curled a free kick straight into the arms of Humphreys after Clough had been brought down.

Full-Time: Sunderland 2, Leeds United 1

Brian Clough's display that day was arguably one of the best of his career. He ran the Leeds defence ragged, and if Walter Winterbottom had been watching, he would surely have had second thoughts about adding the young centre-forward to his list of England discards. Clough

FROM BUTLINS TO THE KREMLIN'

had scored three, four, even five goals in a game before, but on that day his game rose to a higher plane.

The *Sunderland Echo*'s Argus was unstinting in his praise:

> Brian Clough, spearhead of a side pulling together splendidly in a promotion-class display, touched his brightest form as a Sunderland player.
>
> Incredibly, the two [goals] he cracked home in the seventh and thirty-first minutes turned out to be his only reward for the finest exhibition of centre-forward play seen at Roker Park for years.
>
> He was in tune with everyone around him, making good service look extra good and doing his share of the foraging too. Over the 90 minutes he was so often in the finishing position that it became almost a personal duel between himself and a brave, inspired keeper in Alan Humphreys.
>
> Clough's work was not confined to the goal-front, however. He was just as successful in setting up attacks from the deep position, producing several brilliant reverse passes to both wings.

Roy Ulyatt of the *Yorkshire Post* was no less complimentary: 'Clough on this form was the best centre-forward I have seen this season, distributing the ball with great care and imagination.'

For Don Revie, there was a good deal of thinking to be done, both about his own performance and that of his side. His experienced defence looked slow and ponderous, and his swift wingers Johanneson and Mayers never really featured at all, shackled effectively all game long by Sunderland's full-backs Colin Nelson and Len Ashurst. Young Bremner was bound to have a quiet game now and then as he learned his trade. As for Revie himself, two games in four days had proved wearing, and if he was going to continue playing, he'd almost certainly have to ration his appearances.

Revie hadn't had a bad game, and there was a spell in the second half when he'd dragged Leeds out of their stupor and initiated a few dangerous attacks. But young Willie McPheat had worked tirelessly to ensure that his influence was merely peripheral, and he'd just about succeeded.

On the evidence of this game, Sunderland had the potential to be promotion challengers; for Leeds, a long, hard seven months lay ahead.

★ ★ ★

In typically blunt and expressive language, Clough had described his switch from Middlesbrough to Sunderland as 'like moving from Butlins to the Kremlin'. Yet, after the benign regime of Bob Dennison, who had given him free rein, he found he also thrived under the 'tyranny' of Alan Brown.

Clough – like most of his colleagues – found it difficult building any sort of personal relationship with Brown. But he'd learned the nature and value of discipline from his mother, Sally, back in Valley Road, and Brown's version of it, although tougher and far crueller, was what he came to respect.

Clough recalled: 'I remember him [Brown] telling me when we first met, "You've probably heard that I'm a b— . . . Well, I am." Yet he restored my faith in football after it had been sapped from me at Middlesbrough, and he taught me the true meaning of the word "professionalism".'

Alan Brown irritated the Sunderland supporters at the start of the 1961–62 season by altering the famous strip of red and white shirt and black shorts. He changed the colour of the shorts to white to signify a new era for the club, a burying of the past glories of Shackleton, Carter et al. – a similar psychological ploy to that of his detested rival Don Revie?

The fans' indignation was soon assuaged as Clough began to bang in the goals with the same sort of regularity as at Middlesbrough, and the side steadily climbed the table. Sunderland's home form was exemplary – 37 points out of a possible 42 – but they were found wanting on their travels.

Eventually, it all came down to the last match of the season, on 28 April, when a victory was needed at Swansea to gain promotion. The home side, third from bottom of the table, were safe from relegation but chose this day to battle as hard as they had done for many months.

Before a crowd of 18,100 – 2,000 of them Sunderland supporters – Clough put the visitors ahead in the first half with an opportunist goal, firing home superbly from inside the penalty box after the ball had fallen to him in the wake of a goalmouth melee.

Sunderland sat back on their lead and were punished for their tentativeness when centre-forward Brayley Reynolds – who had given Charlie Hurley a difficult afternoon – equalised for Swansea after 66 minutes. Despite his goal, Clough was well held by Swansea's Welsh international centre-half Mel Nurse. Manager Alan Brown admitted afterwards that his side had been rendered tense by the occasion, unable to play their natural free-flowing football.

Bitter disappointment at the last, but Clough could look back with satisfaction on his first season at Roker Park. Despite Brown dropping him for five games, he still finished up with thirty-four goals, virtually one every match.

The Sunderland manager was determined to get the very best out of his principal asset. For the 1962–63 season, he recruited inside-forward Johnny Crossan from Standard Liège of Belgium for £30,000, giving him the job of being Clough's creator-in-chief.

Crossan was an outstanding player, inventive yet also hard-tackling. He'd been forced abroad in 1959 when on the verge of being transferred to Bristol City from Coleraine; an Irish League committee had found him guilty of receiving illegal payments while an amateur at Derry City and suspended him permanently from Irish football. It proved a blessing in disguise, as Crossan was able to prove his worth first at Sparta Rotterdam, then at Standard Liège, where he won a league championship medal. The Belgian side even reached the semi-final of the European Cup in 1961–62, when Crossan came up against the giants of Real Madrid – Alfredo Di Stéfano, Ferenc Puskás and Francisco Gento.

Real Madrid won the first leg 4–0. Crossan had the dubious privilege of man-marking Di Stéfano. Despite the scoreline, the Irishman felt he'd done a reasonable job, and he played even better in the return leg, hitting the woodwork twice in the first half before Real ran out 2–0 winners.

When Alan Brown asked him to sign for Sunderland in October 1962, he made it perfectly clear why he was bringing him to Roker Park. 'Mr Brown brought me to provide ammunition for Brian Clough,' says Crossan. 'He told me, I want you to do this, that and the other – and this guy Clough will put them in the net. Never was a truer word spoken. My job, basically, was to make more chances for Brian.' It was important, therefore, that the two men, vital cogs in the Sunderland machine, should build up a good relationship on and off the field.

Crossan found it hard to settle in the area at first. It was a shocking winter, with many games postponed, and he was stuck – as he saw it – in the Roker Hotel on the seafront with his wife, Barbara, and young son Johnny, waiting to move into a new house. Back at Roker Park, he was trying to get the measure of Clough.

'It was a few games into the season, and I didn't think I was doing all that badly. We were all sitting in the dressing-room when Cloughie shouts to me, "Young man, do you realise this club has paid £30,000 for you to get goals for me and since you arrived you've not created one chance!" But I quickly realised this was just his way. What I liked about Brian was that he might give you a bit of stick during the game, but then when it was all over he would forget about it. He was a terrific player. When people say, well, he wasn't a great player because he didn't score his goals in the First Division, I find that hard to understand. There's an old adage in football: if you can score goals, you can score them anywhere. Brian would have scored them anywhere.'

Crossan and Clough quickly became firm friends. They would often meet up in an Italian café called Morelli's near the Seaburn Hotel, and on Monday nights they'd play games of solo, accompanied by journalist Vince Wilson, while their wives went out to the pictures. Clough also introduced Crossan to cricket, and the two of them would head off in the summer months to Bramall Lane and Scarborough.

As the 1962–63 season progressed, and the Crossan–Clough partnership developed, promotion looked more likely than not. By Boxing Day, Sunderland sat in second position, four points behind Chelsea and three points ahead of third-placed Plymouth Argyle.

Clough's latest goal – incredibly, his 28th of a season that was only halfway through – was in the 2–1 win over Revie's Leeds United at Roker Park four days before, in front of a crowd of 40,252, who sensed that, at last, this was going to be their year. It was his seventh goal in five matches against Leeds for either Middlesbrough or Sunderland; he definitely felt he had the Indian sign over the Elland Road club.

Jack Charlton was centre-half for Leeds that day, having missed the game 12 months earlier through injury. 'He hadn't had a kick all game, then suddenly he scored a goal. That was Cloughie. He wasn't really ever someone you felt you had to watch out for as a defender because he was always there next to you in the box. He took up a position in the area where 90 per cent of the time defenders would get the ball but the other 10 per cent the ball would fall to him, and that's when he was dangerous. He was a poacher.'

When Boxing Day dawned in that grim winter (the coldest since 1795, according to the Met Office), Sunderland's home fixture with Bury looked unlikely to go ahead. The North-East was at the mercy of a piercing wind, driving sleet and ice under foot; the Roker Park pitch was very hard and it seemed likely that referee Kevin Howley would call off the match by lunchtime.

Bury's player-manager Bob Stokoe telephoned the ground from Scotch Corner to check that the game was still on. When the Bury team arrived, they found the ground staff attempting to melt the ice with braziers. The surface appeared soft on top but it remained, for the most part, rock solid underneath.

Nonetheless, the game got under way. Bury took an early lead, then Clough took the ball into the penalty area and the visitors' goalkeeper, Chris Harker, whipped his legs from under him. Charlie Hurley strode up to take the penalty but squandered the opportunity to draw level by blazing the ball a couple of yards wide; he was only taking the spot kick because the usual taker, Harry Hooper, was injured.

Then, five minutes later, Len Ashurst played a hopeful ball forward towards the Bury goal. It looked to have too much weight on it for Clough to reach, but he was a game chaser of lost causes and didn't give it up. He described what happened next:

> The rest is crystal clear, as if it happened yesterday. I sprinted across the heavy, muddy surface towards the ball, my eye on it the whole time. I was never to be distracted in circumstances like that. I sensed an opportunity to score another goal, to add to almost 30 I'd already scored that season.
>
> Suddenly it was as if someone had just turned out the light. The Bury keeper, Chris Harker, had gone down for the ball, and his shoulder crunched into my right knee. I was slightly off-balance, with my head down. If I'd seen him coming I might have been inclined to kick his head off, but I didn't see him. My head hit the ground, and for a second or two I didn't know a thing. Only blackness.

Instinctively, Clough tried to get to his knees, but he collapsed; his cruciate ligament had been ripped apart by the collision. He heard the words 'Get up, get up' from a nearby Bury player. Then he listened to a familiar voice tell referee Kevin Howley, 'Come on, he's only codding.' Bob Stokoe uttered his rebuke in the heat of the battle and with no knowledge of the gravity of Clough's injury. But Clough never forgot and certainly never forgave Stokoe for the comment. In later years, he would tell people he'd put a picture of Stokoe up in the bedroom for his children to throw darts at.

Clough was stretchered off, in shock and pain. In the treatment room, as physio Johnny Watters was gingerly taking off his boot, Alan

Brown arrived from the directors' box to see the extent of the injury. When he asked if his centre-forward might be able to return to the pitch, Watters took him aside and, out of Clough's hearing, whispered, 'Finito,' to the manager.

Without him, and despite Johnny Crossan stepping into his shoes and scoring 15 goals in the remainder of the season, Sunderland missed out on promotion. They succumbed once more on the last day of the season, this time through a 1–0 home defeat to Chelsea.

For Clough, this was a dreadful time, the career-threatening injury being accompanied by family grief: 'I had stitches in my face, my knee was giving me hell inside a plaster encasing my entire right leg, the surgeon couldn't tell me whether I would play again, and my wife arrives to announce she has lost the baby I didn't know we were having. It was not exactly the best moment of my life.'

After the plaster came off three months later, Clough began a gruelling eighteen months of rehabilitation. Most of the time, he was on his own, trotting, running and kicking up and down the empty terraces at Roker Park. Month after month of pain, graft and solitude. It was the darkest period of his life, and he took it very badly. When he wasn't training, he tried to keep away from the ground. But when he did meet his teammates, bitterness at his plight would often show through and he would lash out verbally.

In December 1963, surgeons had written him off as a footballer and he had been warned he might be crippled for the rest of his life if he attempted a comeback. Publicly, Clough was defiant, telling the readers of the *Evening Gazette*, 'The tragedy is I'm now otherwise perfectly fit. I can kick a ball just as hard and just as accurately as ever. But what's the good of feeling like that if doctors say I can't ever go into another game?'

It may just have been bravado and unwillingness – perfectly understandable with his whole career on the line – to face facts. Yet he soldiered on with the training and the rehabilitation, and by April 1964 there was just a glimmer of hope that he might get back on the pitch. His desire to return was now even greater because, finally, he had the chance to play at the top level. Sunderland had won promotion, finishing two points behind the Division Two champions, Don Revie's Leeds.

Alan Brown kept encouraging him, urging him to keep on training throughout the summer while everyone else at the club was setting off on their holidays; he even accompanied him in those sessions on occasions, trying to give Clough hope when he probably knew himself

The forward line that steered lowly Second Division side Leicester City to the FA Cup final in 1949. From left: Mal Griffiths, Don Revie, Jack Lee, Ken Chisholm and Charlie Adam. (© Getty Images)

Don and Elsie Revie after their wedding in October 1949. (© *The Times*/ NI Syndication)

The Clough brothers in the all-conquering Great Broughton side of 1953. On the back row, Joe (third from left), then Desmond, Brian, Bill and brother-in-law Sid Elder. (copyright unknown)

On tour with England – Revie with Billy Wright and Stanley Matthews in 1955. (© Getty Images)

Harmony – but only briefly – at Sunderland between Revie, manager Alan Brown (centre) and coach George Curtis. (© Getty Images)

The goal machine: Clough cracks home one of his 204 for Middlesbrough, against Blackburn Rovers at Ayresome Park. (© Press Association)

Astor Garriques, 'The Mouth of the Tees', fervent Boro and Clough fan by day and comedian by night. (courtesy of Garth Garriques)

that realistically there wasn't a great deal. Clough's contract was up for renewal at the end of July, but he set off on two weeks' unpaid leave and told Brown he would sign on his return.

When he came back, Brown had left to become manager of Sheffield Wednesday; club secretary George Crowe was in temporary charge while the Sunderland board looked for a successor. Clough just returned to his lonely vigil running up and down the terraces. He went so far as to sell his car, walking everywhere to supplement his training. At home – and even out at a restaurant, or at the cinema – he'd religiously strap a weight to his ankle and lift his leg for ten minutes every hour.

But the true test of the repaired knee could come only through playing matches. Clough started the 1964–65 season in the reserves and scored a goal against Grimsby in his first match back. When he notched a hat-trick in the next game, he began to dream the impossible.

Then, on Wednesday, 2 September, he was picked to play in the home match against West Bromwich before a crowd of 52,000 – his first-ever match in the top flight. He didn't score in a 2–2 draw, but four days later that elusive First Division goal came – almost inevitably – in a 3–3 draw against Revie's Leeds United, for whom Jackie Charlton was the opposing centre-half.

Achieving that milestone meant a great deal to him, and he retained his place for the third match in a week at Roker Park, against Aston Villa, which ended in yet another draw (2–2). But, deep down, it was becoming increasingly clear to him that he wasn't the player he had been 18 months previously. The knee was unstable, and his strong quads and upper-thigh area – responsible for his key attribute, his powerful shooting – had wasted away. His reactions, too, had slowed down.

The decision to retire a few weeks later, at the age of 29, was ultimately a joint one taken by the doctors, the club and himself. 'Perhaps, with more time, I could have made it,' he pondered later. 'But time is the one thing you can't afford in football. Sunderland had bought a £45,000 centre-forward ... they didn't want one with a gammy leg. And so finally I had to accept that I was finished.'

It was a devastating moment for a man with a wife and two young children, who wasn't really qualified for anything beyond the world of football. What on earth could he do next?

* * *

Don Revie's 18-year playing career had come to a more natural end than Clough's, 30 months earlier at Huddersfield Town's Leeds Road ground on 3 March 1962.

He hadn't played since the 2–1 defeat at Swansea on 21 October, realising he needed to devote all his energy to motivating and managing the side with a critical eye from the sidelines – as well as searching for new players to keep Leeds afloat in Division Two.

The prospect of Division Three football was a distinct possibility by March. The Elland Road side was stranded at the foot of the table and the transfer deadline was approaching; some new faces were needed to provide fresh guile and spirit to a team that was in a rut of indifferent performances.

One of the first to arrive was Ian Lawson, who was only Burnley's reserve centre-forward, yet Revie had somewhat desperately splashed out £20,000 for him, knowing how much he needed a goalscorer.

Lawson made his debut that March day, partnering Jack Charlton, who'd been pushed up from his normal position at the back. Charlton got on the scoresheet, but a crowd of more than 16,000 saw Huddersfield win the West Yorkshire derby 2–1. The only glimmer of hope on a depressing day was that relegation rivals Bristol Rovers, Brighton and Charlton Athletic all lost.

And so the curtain finally came down on Revie's illustrious career, although the end wasn't heralded at the time, as he kept open the option of another appearance in the event of an emergency.

In eighteen seasons, he'd represented five clubs – Leicester City, Hull City, Manchester City, Sunderland and Leeds United – played 474 games and scored 100 goals. For England, he'd scored four goals in six appearances. All that, plus an FA Cup winner's medal and the satisfaction of being voted Footballer of the Year in 1955.

Reflections on those achievements would have to wait. Right then, he took one of the biggest decisions yet as manager by paying Everton £25,000 for their 31-year-old inside-forward Bobby Collins. It was the highest transfer fee paid in Leeds United's history, and it was the highest fee ever received by Everton. At the time, there was incredulity in the football world that Revie had staked so much on Collins, despite his impressive career with Celtic and Everton and ten international caps for Scotland.

Harry Catterick, Everton's manager, was starting to rebuild his side – which had finished fifth in Division One the previous season – and had made it abundantly clear to Collins that he had no part in his future plans at Goodison Park. Yet Revie perceived that in the stocky, diminutive (5 ft 4 in.) Glaswegian, here was the inspirational player he needed to help bind his disparate group of old-timers, young tyros and those – like Jack Charlton – who had simply lost their way a bit. What Revie saw in Collins was a consummate passer of the ball and also a ferocious battler in the middle of the field.

Despite making the drop to the Second Division, Collins sensed the potential at Elland Road:

> I could see that Don had the makings of a good side because in those days there were some very fine youngsters awaiting their chances, and they included Gary Sprake, Norman Hunter and Paul Reaney.
>
> Don Revie talked my language, which is particularly important to a player, and, in addition, he was always insisting that the only way to play the game was to play it simple, which is a fact I have always believed in.

His new colleagues recognised his value straight away. 'What marked him out, and what made the difference to the Leeds United sides he played in, was his commitment to winning,' recalled Jack Charlton in his autobiography. 'He was so combative; he was like a little flyweight boxer. He would kill his mother for a result! He introduced a sort of "win at any cost" attitude into the team.'

Collins' impact on the pitch was immediate; he scored on his debut in the 2–0 win against Swansea City at Elland Road on 10 March. In the last ten games of the season, Leeds lost just once, but they went into the last match of the campaign, at Newcastle, still needing a result to ensure survival.

With Collins dominating proceedings in the centre of the field and Johanneson tearing the Newcastle defence apart, the visitors coasted to a comfortable 3–0 win once the left-winger had opened the scoring in the 37th minute. Leeds were safe, and Revie now had some breathing space to lay the groundwork for the revolution at the club he'd promised chairman Harry Reynolds.

In the 1962–63 season, Reynolds and his board of directors continued to dip into their pockets to finance the next stage of that revolution. Their most notable acquisition was John Charles, who was persuaded to sign – once more – for the Elland Road side after a series of long, protracted negotiations.

Leeds paid £53,000 for their former idol, now 31, only to discover he was unfit and unable to readapt to the quicker pace of the English game. He made just eleven appearances, scoring three goals, before returning to Italy, this time to Roma. The only consolation for Reynolds was that he actually did a reasonable piece of business on the deal; Leeds sold Charles for £70,000.

The Charles affair was baffling. It seemed to go against Revie's philosophy of building the club up from the bottom by attracting and nurturing the best of the teenage talent. With hindsight, a far more significant event that season took place on 29 September in Leeds' home match with Southampton: the debut, at just 15 years and 289 days, of Peter Lorimer.

Lorimer became Leeds' youngest-ever player that day, joining five other teenagers in the side and pointing an optimistic way forward to the future. It was one of John Charles's last matches for the club, and, ironically, he turned in probably his best performance in his brief spell – albeit at emergency centre-half. Lorimer picks up the story on the day before the game: 'I was sweeping the stands at 11 a.m., as you had to do as a youth player in those days, when one of the coaching staff came and told me the gaffer wanted a word with me. The first thing I thought was what have I done wrong? But Don told me I was in the side for the match the next day. He said, "I know you're only 15, but I think you're ready, so go and get yourself showered." He packed me off to stay overnight with Syd Owen [coach]. Don had actually rung my mum and dad to tell them I was playing – before he told me! – and they were put up in a local hotel.'

The 'Charles Effect' had certainly brought the spectators flooding back to Elland Road, and there were more than 25,000 there that day. If Lorimer felt understandably a little awestruck, it wasn't evident in a remarkably assured display from one so young.

'I was so lucky to play with the great John Charles, who I'd only ever heard of. Wonderful man, wonderful player, and he was terrific that afternoon. Then there was Bobby Collins, too – all these guys I'd read about, some of them 15 years older than me. I had to pinch myself that I was actually playing with them! I thought I did well. Jack Charlton got a broken nose in the first five minutes of the game and was taken off to hospital. There were no substitutes in those days, of course, so John Charles went back to centre-half and we played virtually all the game with ten men.'

Lorimer wouldn't play again for another two years, but the presence in the side of Norman Hunter, Paul Reaney, Terry Cooper and Gary

Sprake – who was only 16 when he made his debut in the away fixture against Southampton on 17 March – was evidence of Revie's determination to give youth its day.

Leeds ended that season of transition in fifth place, finishing confidently with a 5–0 thrashing of Swansea City at Elland Road. Schooled by Collins, they were developing a tough, resilient streak and proving very hard to beat.

They carried that philosophy into the 1963–64 season. Revie now felt he just about had the right squad to make it into the First Division, with the possible exception of another creative player and a goalscorer. The former, Johnny Giles, arrived early in the season from Manchester United; the latter, Alan Peacock, joined Leeds from Middlesbrough for the final three months of the season.

Revie's excellent relationship with Matt Busby helped secure the signing of an unsettled Giles for £33,000. Just 23, he was already an experienced international, having made his debut for Eire a few days before his 19th birthday; but Busby had left him out of the side at the beginning of the season.

Giles was an outstanding footballer who could operate on the right wing or at inside-forward; initially at least, Revie placed him on the wing. When Peacock arrived, the two of them quickly built up an excellent understanding. Giles said of the tall, angular centre-forward: 'I rated Peacock highly. Quite apart from his heading power, he was an accurate passer of the ball, and one of the most astute positional players I have seen.'

Peacock, by now an England international, had spent several successful years in tandem with Brian Clough in a freewheeling but inconsistent Middlesbrough side. What he saw at Elland Road opened his eyes, he remembers: 'Bob Dennison at Middlesbrough was a great guy, but he didn't really have much tactical awareness. When I'd been at Leeds a few weeks I thought, wow, I've wasted years at Boro. Revie had everything mapped out, his methods were clear and innovative, and the side responded exactly to the way he wanted them to play. I'd never had that kind of leadership at Middlesbrough.

'The style they played at Leeds then was great for me. Revie said, "I want you to be the main man upfront, you just get yourself into the right positions and we'll get the ball to you." And they did, of course – especially Johnny Giles. At Ayresome Park, we reckoned Bill Harris was something special at wing-half, but Johnny Giles could put the ball exactly where you wanted it. He was also one of the hardest men I've played with.'

With the steel and creativity of Giles, Collins and Bremner, a developing, youthful defence led by the ever-improving Jack Charlton, and Peacock's goals, Leeds were now serious contenders. On 7 March 1964, they beat Southampton 3–1 at home to begin an astonishing sequence of results. In their last ten matches, they won eight and drew two, taking the championship on the last day of the season with a 2–0 victory at Charlton Athletic, Peacock scoring both goals.

Leeds had lost just three games in their promotion campaign. Revie was now one of the most talked-about and coveted young managers in the business. The previous year, he'd been forced to dismiss as 'ridiculous' the suggestion that he might be a possible successor as England manager to Walter Winterbottom. The Leeds board felt they had acted swiftly at that time to secure their man, giving him a contract extension that would see him through to March 1967.

But that didn't stop the rumours – or indeed the offers – coming, and barely had Leeds begun their new life in Division One when some old acquaintances from the North-East came calling.

Chapter 8
'It's Us Against the World'

In the end, it was his heart that ruled his head. Don Revie knew his critics in the press wouldn't see it that way, of course, but that was the truth of the matter.

When his old club Sunderland, in the shape of chairman Syd Collings, came knocking on his door in mid-September 1964, he was sorely tempted to take up their offer. They weren't the first, of course; a number of other clubs had approached him in the last couple of years as they'd seen the massive improvements he'd wrought at Elland Road. Their inducements – including a salary worth twice what he was getting at Leeds, plus the attractive fringe benefits of a Jaguar car and a new luxury house – had been extremely tempting.

But he'd turned them all down, not only because he was satisfied with the current side he was building at Leeds but also because he was tremendously excited about the crop of youngsters he was nurturing who were nearly ready to take their places in the squad. He felt this was now *his* club to mould as he saw fit, and he relished the freedom Harry Reynolds had given him.

The Sunderland offer, though, initially seemed almost too good to ignore. A five-year contract worth £6,000 a year was reason enough, of course, to contemplate the move. It would give him the extra security of tenure Leeds had denied him, plus the additional money to better look after the needs of his immediate family – Elsie, Duncan and Kim – and the wider group of elderly relatives he was increasingly caring for.

On the flipside, of course, if he looked at the league table, he'd see Leeds perched at the top but Sunderland disastrously placed at the bottom, without a win so far. The major problem was that the Roker Park club had been leaderless since the departure of his nemesis, Alan

Brown, in July. George Crowe, the club secretary, a decent, hard-working man, had stepped in to manage the side temporarily, but he could only be expected to accomplish so much. A replacement was obviously needed quickly, otherwise it would be too late to successfully manage the transition back into Division One.

Then there was the plight of Brian Clough. He had chosen to bring Clough's former Middlesbrough colleague Alan Peacock to Elland Road earlier in the year, and the tall centre-forward had played a crucial role in Leeds' successful promotion campaign, scoring goals and leading the forward line intelligently. But Revie had always kept a close eye on the progress of his fellow townsman. He knew Clough had rubbed many people up the wrong way with his cocky approach, but he liked players with self-confidence and a touch of arrogance.

Despite all his skill and ability, he knew his own weakness as a player had been mental rather than physical, those moments when self-doubt crept in and affected his performance on the pitch. Clough had never appeared to harbour real self-doubt, and moreover he'd been an instinctive and prolific goalscorer. But Revie knew he'd struggled to regain fitness after his horrific knee injury on Boxing Day 1962, and the word now was that his career might well be over. How would he manage that situation?

But, like Leeds, Sunderland did have their own group of good, combative young players, of whom he'd been all too well aware through the ferocious encounters between the two clubs in recent years. He felt sure there was enough skill and spirit within the club to enable them to pull away from the bottom of the table.

He didn't know too much about the whys and wherefores of Brown's departure. He'd heard it was all about a dispute over money; but why would you want to dispense with the services of the man who had just brought you promotion? All it did was reinforce, in his own mind, the need to win the best possible deal for yourself to guard against the whims and prejudices of the boards of football clubs.

Aside from the length of the contract, the money and the playing potential, he would be returning to his native North-East, the heartland of English football, and to a club of a size and prestige that Leeds couldn't match. Those were the attractions placed before him.

And yet . . . deep down, he knew he didn't really want to leave Elland Road. When the story of the Sunderland offer had broken in the *Yorkshire Evening Post* – as he knew it would – he'd been surprised, and greatly gratified, by the coverage. Under the back-page headline 'Revie for Roker Bombshell at Elland Road', reporter Phil Brown had written, 'Elland Road today was as sad a soccer ground as I have ever known.' That emotive description encompassed both his own likely departure and Harry Reynolds' serious car crash on Tuesday, which had left him in Barnsley hospital with head injuries.

On that day, Wednesday, 16 September, his decision on whether to leave Elland Road was still in the balance. Before his accident, Reynolds had assured him that he would win round the rest of the board and have a new, five-year contract for him to match the Sunderland offer. There would also be more money on the table, although it was unlikely to rival the £6,000 a year Syd Collings had offered him.

But nothing had yet been finally settled. Meanwhile, the side was preparing to play Blackpool at home that evening. It had all the makings of a difficult match, given the 4–0 thrashing the Bloomfield Road club – inspired by little Alan Ball – had administered to Leeds nine days earlier.

He wandered into the locker room at Elland Road, wondering whether to pick up his kit in case the worst came to the worst and he was about to leave the club. There he came across a group of recently signed apprentices, and as he talked to them about his leaving, he could see they were distressed at the prospect; some even had tears in their eyes.

He was affected quite deeply by their response, and it helped clarify things in his mind. He was fond of preaching the benefits of loyalty; indeed, he was now asking the Leeds board for greater loyalty in him. But where did that leave *his* loyalty towards these young boys, many of whom he'd recruited to the club from school, promising their parents he'd look after them and develop their careers?

He left the locker room to prepare for the match against Blackpool with his mind made up. If Leeds would offer him the security of a five-year contract, he would not desert these young boys and the club just as it was on the threshold of great achievement . . .

* * *

While Harry Reynolds was recovering in hospital and final negotiations with the board had yet to conclude, Revie hadn't been able to say anything definitive to reassure the players in the dressing-room that evening.

If they thought he was on his way out, then their 'farewell' performance for him was outstanding. For a midweek game on a wet evening, there was an excellent crowd, of 35,973, and Leeds, marshalled splendidly by Bobby Collins on his 100th appearance for the club, swept Blackpool aside 3–0. Collins himself scored twice, 20-year-old Norman Hunter the other one, and Leeds could afford the luxury of Billy Bremner missing two penalty kicks. After all the shocks of the day, it was a resilient, often inspirational display.

Revie's new contract was agreed after final discussions overnight and first thing the following morning. He called the players together and told them to ignore all the paper talk – he'd started a revolution at Leeds and would be there to see it through.

The headline in the *Yorkshire Evening Post* on 17 September summed up the mood perfectly: 'Don Revie Stays – So Everybody Is Happy'. Vice chairman Percy Woodward, in the absence of the injured Reynolds, spoke for the board:

> Naturally we were all upset and rather surprised at the unexpected turn of events, but now everything has turned out all right and I am quite thrilled about it.
>
> Don has got what he wanted – a five-year contract and the salary increase for which he asked, and I am sure he is just as pleased as we are. He didn't really want to leave. We knew that.

For public consumption, Revie spoke of his relief at the agreement and his desire to mould his group of gifted youngsters into league champions in the not-too-distant future. Privately, he must have reflected on the advantages the Sunderland approach had brought him. Yes, of course it had given him job security and greater financial benefits, but nearly as importantly it had provoked a ringing public endorsement from the board. From now on, Revie felt, he was in complete control of his destiny at Elland Road.

* * *

On the day Sunderland's attempt to woo Don Revie to Roker Park was being made public, Prime Minister Sir Alec Douglas-Home was – finally – firing the starting pistol for the 1964 general election.

The British political parties had been conducting something of a phoney war ever since the spring, when it appeared very likely that the

Conservative government would go to the country in May. But Douglas-Home, wanting more time to establish a relationship with the electorate after the unexpected departure of Harold Macmillan through ill health in October 1963, decided to let the full five-year term run its course.

Brian Clough could easily have been one of those bright young Labour politicians fighting the Tories in their heartlands, inspired by Harold Wilson's vision of a more modern, scientifically led nation, forged in the 'white heat of technology'.

In December 1963, as he continued his rehabilitation from injury and pondered what – if any – future he had left in the game, Clough was approached by the Stokesley Labour Party and invited to go on a shortlist of prospective Labour candidates for the Richmond (Yorks) constituency.

It was – inevitably – Peter Taylor who had stirred Clough's interest in politics six years earlier after he had joined Middlesbrough from Coventry. Taylor was not an archetypal professional footballer; he had a trade-unionist upbringing, and liked to go and watch the powerful orators of the left, like Aneurin Bevan. As his friendship with Clough blossomed, he widened the horizons of his young friend, and that included introducing him to politics. Taylor recalled taking Clough to hear Wilson, fellow Yorkshireman and then the rising star of the Labour Party, at a working men's club one Sunday afternoon. The audience numbered barely fifty, but Clough was impressed and learned a trick or two about holding a crowd's attention.

However, when the Stokesley Labour Party approached the injured centre-forward in 1963, they were to be disappointed with his response. 'All I can say is that, unfortunately, he cannot allow his name to be put forward and he does so with great regret,' secretary Ron Jones told the *Evening Gazette*. The Richmond Divisional Labour Party (of which Stokesley was part) denied the move had been just a gimmick aimed at sprinkling some stardust over the impossible task of unseating Conservative MP Timothy Kitson, who had a 15,000 majority. 'He is a member of the Labour Party and a sincere and convinced Socialist,' secretary-agent George Atkinson told the paper.

He was right about the latter. Clough's political views were in line with the vast majority of Middlesbrough's army of working-class men – instinctively Labour. With Taylor's encouragement, he had begun to grasp, however broadly, some of the big issues of the day. But Atkinson got it wrong about Clough's membership of the party, because, despite

171

many forays into the political arena in the coming years, he wasn't actually a paid-up member then and didn't become so until the 1980s.

Instead of taking the chance to traipse round Wensleydale and Swaledale and pound the streets of Northallerton, Richmond and Great Ayton looking for votes, Clough remained in a slough of despond in Sunderland in the autumn of 1964. There were some vague thoughts about a career in teaching – he would certainly have provided the inspiration a schoolchild requires – but nothing more than that. Football was all he really knew, and football now seemed to have turned its back on him.

Until, that is, 'Gentleman' George Hardwick appeared on the scene at Roker Park in quite extraordinary circumstances.

* * *

Nowhere is the reverence in which Middlesbrough people hold their footballing heroes better illustrated than in the Blue Bell Lodge Hotel in Acklam. Step inside the front entrance to the bar and restaurant area, glance around the walls and you're transported back to a bygone age.

Owner Ron Darby has turned his comfortable hostelry into something akin to a shrine to his great friend George Hardwick. Everywhere you look – if you have inquisitive eyes that can evade the usual paraphernalia of a modern pub area with its fruit machines, prominent satellite TV, etc. – there are photographs, at work and at play, of a smiling, debonair man, who, in the 1940s, was football's equivalent of Clark Gable.

There are pictures of George shaking hands with rival skipper Johnny Carey in the famous Great Britain v. Rest of Europe match at Hampden Park in 1947, opening the new Middlesbrough Municipal Golf Course with Labour MP Manny Shinwell, in robust action on a grey day in a game against Scotland. Upstairs at the hotel, the main conference room is named the Hardwick Suite.

It used to be said of George Hardwick that he was as hard as the ironstone mined in the pit where his father worked as an electrician before it closed during the Depression. 'I was a cruel captain, the players were frightened of me . . . I was never off their backs,' he would later reflect.

Off the pitch, Hardwick moved in different circles from the average professional footballer; he was friendly with some of the leading actresses of the day, including Shirley Eaton, Kay Kendall and Margaret Lockwood. But his matinee-idol looks – his moustache was a conspicuously unusual touch when facial hair was a novelty on the football fields of England – might have been mocked by the no-nonsense denizens of Ayresome Park had he not possessed the talent and toughness required of a top player. Those qualities propelled him towards the England side, earning him 13 caps and the distinction of being the last man to captain his country on debut.

After finishing a successful career at Middlesbrough and then Oldham Athletic (as player-manager), Hardwick stayed in the game, taking over as coach of the Netherlands national side in 1956. Such was the young talent at his disposal in Holland that he was able to pursue his theories of Total Football (it wasn't called that then, of course), instilling ideas of flexibility and movement on the pitch that anticipated the style of play demonstrated by the great Dutch sides of 1974 and 1978, Cruyff, Neeskens et al.

On leaving the national side, Hardwick managed PSV Eindhoven successfully for a season before returning to Teesside. Initially, he set about developing a new career in the motor trade, but he was brought back to football once more when Middlesbrough manager Bob Dennison invited him to work as a part-time coach with the youth side.

When Dennison left Ayresome Park in 1963, Hardwick drifted back to journalism, while retaining a job as an oil consultant. He'd written about the game, on and off, for several years, having his own column in the sports section of the *Evening Gazette*. In his capacity as a columnist, he'd crossed swords with Brian Clough on occasions, once, as we have seen, advising the young centre-forward – having watched the technically adroit Dutch youngsters at work – that his ball skills needed improving if he was ever to make the grade at international level. Clough was irritated and responded in his own captain's column the following week.

Hardwick, because of his stature and connections in the game, tended to have the inside track on most goings-on in the North-East clubs. He was, for instance, one of the first to spot the tensions that existed between Don Revie and Alan Brown and to predict the parting of the ways that followed.

In November 1964, Hardwick was in the press room at Roker Park, collecting information for his column, when George Crowe approached him and told him the chairman wished to see him. Hardwick was delighted, presuming that Collings was about to give him a scoop for his column with the name of the new Sunderland manager. In fact, he was stunned to be told that the chairman wanted the new manager to be . . . George Hardwick!

'You could have knocked me down with a feather,' he recalled. 'I was the main character in the exclusive story I'd hoped to scoop . . . the chairman said simply that the club would be pleased if I accepted the position. To say I was taken aback by Mr Collings' offer was a complete understatement. However, it was not a bad offer for a part-time journalist.'

Hardwick was aware that the likes of Don Revie, then Tommy Docherty, Bob Dennison and others had been offered the job and turned it down. But Sunderland were now back in the First Division – although struggling badly at this early stage of the campaign – and a great challenge was there to be accepted. He elected to work without a contract and to be judged by results at the close of the season.

If moving the first team up the table was obviously his number-one priority, Hardwick also knew he had to do something about Clough. 'When I took charge of Sunderland, Cloughie was hanging around the place like a miserable and persistent North Sea fret. His much heralded comeback had failed, and although he was training to keep himself physically fit, he had no focus in his life. But I was determined to give him one.'

Clough had pondered alternative careers once he knew his days as a professional football player were over. Teaching was one, journalism another. He certainly knew how to sniff out a fresh story and find a new angle for an old one, as he'd demonstrated in his columns in the *Evening Gazette* and elsewhere. He had a curiosity about the world that would have benefited him in the job; whether he had the writing skills was another matter entirely.

Hardwick called Clough into his office and told him he wanted him to train the youth players. He enrolled him on an FA coaching course at Durham so he could obtain the required formal qualifications and then sat back and watched as Clough's enthusiastic, motivating direction on the training ground began to reap results.

Clough revelled in his new role:

> The truth was that I'd developed an instant liking for being in charge. The challenge of management was not just to my liking, it was one I knew I could meet and conquer. A coaching

qualification hadn't proved anything like as much as the reaction
of those young men at Roker Park, the ones who put in practice
what I'd been telling them all week. They were the ones who
convinced me I could be a manager.

The training methods that Hardwick had pioneered back in Holland
were now adapted, with relish, by his protégé. Out went the constant
stamina training so beloved of Alan Brown, the endless, mindless
lapping of the pitch. In came games of five-a-side and six-a-side, skills
training, more variety – anything, in short, that involved the players
getting better acquainted with a football, the essential tool of their
trade. As Clough put it: 'They would see little enough of it on a
Saturday so it was common sense to make sure they had plenty of it
during the week.'

He was helped by the fact that Sunderland had an excellent crop of
youngsters in that period – including Colin Todd and John O'Hare,
both of whom would join Clough at Derby County a few years later.

O'Hare, the elder at 18, was playing for the reserves – although he'd
also made his first-team debut in August against Chelsea – but trained
and played with the youth team during their successful cup run. 'When
Clough had still been playing,' he recalls, 'I used to watch him a lot,
because I'd play in the Northern Intermediate League in the mornings
and then be able to watch the first team play in the afternoons. He was
an incredible goalscorer, that's really all you had to say about him, an
amazing finisher.

'When he was put in charge of the youth team, he took to the job
with relish. It seemed to me like he enjoyed his job, and he was certainly
enjoyable to be with. He was quite different, really, in his approach to
how we trained, with a lot of ball work, shooting, all that sort of stuff,
instead of the laps or half-laps of the field that we'd been used to.

'At that time, I was more of an inside-forward or midfield player, but
he used to tell me to go up and play centre-forward, which soon became
my position. So he helped shape my career. He had lots of confidence
and lots of arrogance about himself. He had this fierce desire to do well,
and it didn't surprise me that he went into management fairly quickly.'

Clough's Sunderland side reached the semi-finals of the FA Youth
Cup in 1965, losing to Arsenal. The interest shown in the competition
in those days is demonstrated by the phenomenal crowd at Goodison
Park for one of the legs of the final – 30,000 – in which Everton defeated
Arsenal 3–2.

Hardwick was so impressed with what Clough was achieving that he started to tell the directors he could envisage a future role for him as his assistant with the first team. The idea horrified the Sunderland board, many of whom had come to resent the presence of this forthright, undiplomatic young man. In any event, they'd made up their minds that Hardwick had to go at the end of the season, despite only 168 days in the job and the principal objective – survival in the First Division – having been achieved.

Once Hardwick was on his way out, his protégé inevitably followed. The new man in charge, Ian McColl, who'd been manager of Scotland for five years, made it abundantly clear he wanted his own men around him, and Clough's time at Sunderland was brought to an abrupt end.

Hardwick was appalled by the train of events – perhaps even more so for Clough than for himself. 'Cash in on the insurance money you've received for an injured player and then discard him. Very caring. The whole sorry situation left me feeling sick in the pit of my stomach.'

The stark realisation that he was unemployed with a young family to support, his whole *raison d'être* stripped from him, left Clough in a dismal state of mind. 'I went berserk for a while, drank heavily and was hell to live with,' he admitted a few years later. 'I'm ashamed now. It wasn't very manly. I lost heart, which was something I'd never done as a player, and I nearly went off the rails. But nobody else could know, could appreciate how hard it hit me.'

He'd find solace in heading off to Acklam Park, Middlesbrough or North Marine Road, Scarborough to watch the great Yorkshire cricket side of the early '60s – Close, Illingworth, Trueman, Sharpe, Binks, Wilson, Padgett, Nicholson and a young, bespectacled opening batsman named Geoffrey Boycott, who'd recently attracted the attention of the England selectors.

Clough and Boycott started a lifelong friendship during this period. Clearly, they shared a similar, working-class background, both with a strong mother at the heart of the family. Both were blunt (to the point of rudeness), both were perfectionists, completely, often ruthlessly dedicated to gaining success in their respective sports. They both understood and appreciated each other's profession: Boycott had been a decent footballer, having had trials with Leeds United, while Clough's boyhood hero was Len Hutton.

Boycott remembers Clough being totally absorbed in the game when he came to watch Yorkshire. 'Back in the early '60s, when he'd finished training at the club, he used to come down to the ground and watch the final two sessions of play. And he used to really sit and watch – it wasn't just a social activity for him, he studied the game closely and really understood it. He'd say to me, what do you think of such-and-such a bowler, and I'd reply, "I don't think he's that good," but he would say, "No, no, he's got something in him," and very often he'd be right. He could see things others couldn't, sense things, in a nutshell. He loved his cricket, and I loved him being there; he could make you feel ten feet tall. He would want to talk cricket with me, when I'd want to talk football!'

At the start of the 1965–66 season, Sunderland arranged a testimonial for Clough. Whatever the directors thought, there was no doubting the affection of the Wearside fans. A crowd of 31,898 turned out on Thursday, 28 October to watch their champion centre-forward for the last time. He obliged by scoring both Sunderland's goals, the second a penalty that would have been highly dubious in anything other than a friendly match.

Clough came away from the game with more than £5,000 in his pocket, but, more importantly, he had a new job to go to immediately. Earlier in the month, he'd been offered the manager's post at struggling Hartlepools United of the Fourth Division, perennial losers who had had to seek re-election to the Football League no less than six times in the previous seven years.

Ernie Ord, the Hartlepools chairman, had first approached George Hardwick to see if he might be interested in the vacancy at Victoria Park. Hardwick wasn't, but he 'did suggest the name of a young man who I thought had real managerial potential. That name was Brian Clough.'

Independently, it seems, Clough's chief advocate in the North-East press, Len Shackleton, who was by then working for the *Sunday People*, made strong representations to Ernie Ord on Clough's behalf.

The recommendation from these two greats of the game worked, and Ord offered Clough the job. Shackleton, who knew Clough well, was shrewd enough to realise that he'd be better equipped to take it on with the helping hand of his old friend and colleague Peter Taylor. Shackleton had observed the dynamic between the two of them when they were together at Middlesbrough and sensed that they would work well together in what would clearly be a testing assignment.

Taylor was by then a successful manager in his own right, albeit at Burton Albion in the Southern League. He needed some persuading to take a substantial pay cut, move his wife and two children from their new home and disguise his effective new role as joint or assistant manager by taking the job of 'trainer' (Hartlepools wouldn't countenance too many titles).

But Taylor had always felt a football club could be more swiftly and effectively built by two men rather than one, as long as they shared the same philosophy of the game and complemented each other's strengths and weaknesses. 'Against all the logic, I promised Brian I'll come. We shook hands on it, and that's how we started,' Taylor recalled.

So it was that Brian Clough's managerial career started on Friday, 29 October, the day after his testimonial game at Roker Park. At 30, he was the youngest manager in the Football League, and he and Taylor had just 24 hours to prepare their new charges for a match away at Bradford City.

* * *

In their famous encounter in the Yorkshire Television studios almost a decade later, Don Revie admitted to Brian Clough that he sent out his early Leeds sides with an utterly pragmatic approach. Without the necessary experience or resources, there was no attempt on his part to start trying to emulate the cultured approach of the side – Real Madrid – whose white-coloured shirts he had symbolically adopted for the dawn of a new era at Elland Road.

'The first four or five years – I've always said this – we played for results,' Revie would tell Clough. No sooner had he put the phone down after rejecting Sunderland's advances than newly promoted Leeds put together an astonishing streak of results that pushed them high up the First Division table.

Between 17 October 1964 and 20 March 1965, they played twenty-two league games, winning fifteen, drawing six and losing just one. They were winning 'ugly', with four successive 1–0 victories in late November/early December, over West Bromwich Albion, Manchester United (away), Aston Villa and Wolves.

But it would be wrong to say the Elland Road fans were simply forced to endure dull, attritional affairs. In the space of five days in March, the home crowd were treated to crushing successes against Burnley (5–1) and Everton (4–1). With Bobby Collins, Billy Bremner and Johnny Giles exhibiting their undeniable flair and skill alongside a steely, combative approach, Leeds were showing the country they could entertain as well as stifle.

Nonetheless, it was their defensive qualities, first and foremost, that enabled them to compete at the top of the table with Manchester United and Chelsea. At the heart of their defence, Jackie Charlton, now in his 30th year, had been transformed into arguably the most effective, consistent centre-half in the land.

Such was his confidence that he started to embark more regularly on those characteristically lolloping journeys into the opposition penalty area – witness the two goals he scored in the demolition of Burnley at Elland Road. At corners, he would take up a threatening position at the near post, standing straight and erect like a lighthouse, blocking the sight and movement of opposition defenders and occasionally flicking the ball on with his head to his own onrushing forwards.

Bedding in alongside Charlton were three of Leeds' bright new generation of players: Gary Sprake in goal, Paul Reaney at right-back and Norman Hunter at left-back. Sprake was already a full international for Wales, having made his debut in 1963 at just 18; Hunter and Reaney were, by now, turning out regularly for England Under-23s.

Big Jack was shown at his resolute best in two FA Cup semi-final matches against Manchester United in late March that followed Leeds' drubbings of Burnley and Everton. The first match, at Hillsborough, was a squalid contest played on a gluepot of a pitch, with entertainment at a premium. Chances were few and far between, and the rough edge to the game ultimately provoked a senseless bout of fisticuffs in the second half, with many players involved from both sides.

In the replay, four days later at Nottingham Forest's City Ground, tempers had calmed and the football started to flow more readily. Best, Bobby Charlton, Law and co. looked set to overwhelm Revie's men in the early stages of the second half, but Leeds – marshalled superbly once more by Jack Charlton – weathered the storm.

Then, just as extra time looked likely, Leeds won a free kick inside the centre circle. Johnny Giles looped a high ball into the Manchester United penalty box, and, improbably, Billy Bremner was the man who got to the ball at the far post, twisting and directing his backwards header past keeper Pat Dunne for the winning goal.

For Jackie Charlton, the aftermath of the match provided him with one of the most vivid and memorable moments of his time at Leeds: 'I went back into our dressing-room and there was booze all over the place. I sat down, and Don came over and sat next to me and said, "I've got some news for you. I didn't want to tell you before the game because I thought it might put you off, but you've been picked to play for England against the Scots at Wembley next month." I said, "Me?" and he said, "Yes." All the lads went, "Well done, Big Jack," and I thought, I've got to tell our kid. So I wandered over to the Man United dressing-room – which was like a morgue – and I went across to him and said, "You'll not believe this, but I've been selected to play for England with you against the Scots. What do you think of that?" And he just looked up at me, wearily, and he said, "I'm pleased for you," and then looked down at the ground again. I heard one of the other players say, "Now f— off out of here," so I left.'

The Charlton brothers were to see a good deal more of each other in the next three weeks. First came that match against Scotland, in which Bobby scored England's opening goal and Jackie acquitted himself well on his debut. Bobby – with a typically rasping drive from the edge of the area – and Jimmy Greaves put England 2–0 up early on, before a deflected left-foot shot from Denis Law pulled a goal back for the visitors before the interval. England were then reduced to nine men through injuries to Ray Wilson and Johnny Byrne (still no substitutes allowed at that time), and Ian St John's close-range header levelled the scores on the hour.

After that, England clung on for a draw, with Jackie gamely assisting his more experienced colleagues, his captain, the immaculate Bobby Moore, and the redoubtable Gordon Banks in goal.

Then, the following Saturday, 17 April, the brothers lined up opposite one another again for yet another Leeds–Manchester encounter, this time a crucial league match at Elland Road. Leeds stood proudly at the top of the table, three points ahead of Manchester and Chelsea. A win and they knew they would be within sight of the title in their first season back in the First Division.

Revie's team was missing Billy Bremner, not for the first time out suspended for a series of bookings. Bremner undoubtedly deserved much of his punishment, but opposition teams knew how to rile him and provoke his fiery temper, and at this time he was far too easily drawn into their trap.

Without him, Leeds struggled on that day. Before a massive crowd of more than 52,000, the match was a scrappy affair in windy conditions, with a bumpy, rock-hard pitch making control of the ball difficult. The only goal of the game came after 14 minutes. Manchester's full-back Tony Dunne fed Denis Law on the edge of the Leeds penalty area, and when he swiftly transferred the ball out to John Connelly, the left-winger's first-time, scuffed shot went through Norman Hunter's legs and past Gary Sprake in goal. Bobby Collins was unable to wrest control in the middle of the field and develop Leeds' passing game. Manchester United created a series of chances they were unable to convert, but they held out comfortably for the narrow win.

Connelly, who'd moved to the Manchester team from Burnley in 1964, derived plenty of satisfaction from his winning goal but also took wicked pleasure from another incident in the game: 'Don Revie didn't take to me for some reason or other – I never knew why. Leeds could be a very niggly and aggressive side in those days; when I meet up with Norman Hunter and Jack Charlton these days, you wouldn't think they were the same people I used to play football against! Anyway, on that day I remember Revie coming to the touchline in his mac and shouting abusive things at me and telling his full-back [Paul Reaney] to get stuck into me. So the best part of the game wasn't the goal I scored but the moment when the ball landed just outside the Leeds dugout, where Revie, Les Cocker and the rest of them were seated. I hacked at the ball and it flew towards the bucket of water stood in front of them, hitting it and spraying the contents all over them. I got as much enjoyment out of that as I did scoring the goal!'

It was now nip-and-tuck for the title. Leeds crashed to a 3–0 defeat at Sheffield Wednesday two days later, on Easter Monday, but bounced back with a 2–0 home win against the same side the following day, followed by an impressive 3–0 away win at the other Sheffield side four days later. But with Manchester United having a vital game in hand, Revie knew his side needed to win at Birmingham on Monday, 26 April, to have any chance of the title.

It proved to be one of the more frustrating days of his managerial career. The Midlands side, bottom of the table, were 2–0 up at the interval, and added a third shortly afterwards. Leeds, sluggish and bereft of ideas, looked down and out, but belatedly stirred themselves. Goals from Reaney, Charlton and Giles (a penalty) incredibly drew them level, but despite coming close in injury time, they couldn't quite force home a winner.

The league title was now lost to Matt Busby's men, and five days later Bill Shankly's Liverpool ensured this was to be a season of great progress but no achievement. Leeds lost 2–1 after extra time to Liverpool in their first-ever FA Cup final, a somewhat flattering scoreline for a tired team who had plainly come to the end of their tether.

Bremner scored a superb half-volleyed goal to take the game into the extra period, but Ian St John's winning header was no more than Liverpool deserved. Too many of the Leeds team failed to play up to their potential on the day, and it was an especially galling experience for left-winger Albert Johanneson.

The South African was the first black player to take part in a Wembley final, and his pace and strength were expected to be a crucial part of the Leeds attack. But the occasion – or the tight marking of full-back Chris Lawler – proved too much for him, and he looked sadly out of sorts and out of place.

It was an anticlimactic end to Revie's first season as a First Division manager. But what a season! The Double had been a distinct possibility with a month to go, and the players could console themselves with the thought that they were now well and truly established with the leaders of the game, Liverpool, Manchester United and Chelsea. Revie had taken his young side a very long way in such a short space of time.

* * *

In an uncharacteristically vivid turn of phrase, Don Revie once said of Eddie Gray, 'When he plays on snow, he doesn't leave any footprints.'

Leeds' famed Scottish scouts had identified the talent of the fleet-footed young wing-half (he became a winger only later) – as they had similarly done with Peter Lorimer – at a very early age. The boy from a big council estate in the Glasgow suburb of Castlemilk was aged 15 and due to take his exams when Revie, who knew up to 30 other clubs were vying for his signature, decided he had to act quickly.

Gray recounts how he was plucked from his Scottish surroundings and taken down to Leeds: 'Don Revie said to my mother – this was in May, and I wasn't supposed to leave school until July – "I'm taking him to Leeds tomorrow." She told him, "I don't think you can do that. He's still at school for the rest of the term," but he replied, "Don't worry, just get him ready and I'll take him to school in the morning and sort it out."

'So he picked me up and drove me to my school – it was in quite a rough area of Glasgow – went in, asked where the headmaster's study was, tapped on the door and went in, telling me to stay outside. A little while later, he came out, I left the school that day and we headed off to Leeds. To this day, I don't know how he managed to swing it – he never told me! So I left school at the age of 15 without sitting any exams. My mother said to him, "What about his education?" and he replied, "Don't worry about that, he's going to be a footballer." And that was it.'

Gray's parents weren't the first Revie had persuaded to release their boy into his effective care, assuring them that he had a big future in the game. He had great physical presence and deployed enormous charm in these situations, and he almost always got his man.

At the time Gray came down from Scotland, Leeds had actually filled their quota of apprentice professionals, so Revie had to bend the rules a little – he certainly wasn't the only manager in the country doing this – to make sure young Eddie and young Peter Lorimer earned some money while they were doing their training.

'Peter was a printer and I was a motor mechanic or a joiner – I never remember which,' says Gray. 'Well, that's what we were supposed to be, that's what the employment forms said, presumably with our "phantom" names on them. I think there may actually have been a printing company across the road from the ground. But we never did any work! Yet I think we received something like three times the amount of money the apprentice professionals were getting. Don asked us to keep quiet about that!'

Gray made his debut on 1 January 1966, at home against Sheffield Wednesday, just 16 days before his 18th birthday. He crashed a 25-yard shot past Wednesday's England keeper Ron Springett to help Leeds to a 3–0 victory, and the press understandably waxed lyrical about this potential star in the making.

However, with hindsight, the words of the seasoned *Yorkshire Post* correspondent Richard Ulyatt had a prophetic touch: 'Gray played with the flair of a born footballer . . . If this boy has the luck all footballers need – luck to avoid serious injury – and is not overwhelmed by the head-turning praise of himself he is likely to read and hear, he should become a brilliant footballer.'

Gray was one of the least conceited footballers, despite having a dazzling set of skills that included immaculate close control, dribbling ability that made the ball appear as if it was on the end of a piece of string, a glorious, deceptive body swerve and a fierce shot. But despite making a total of 454 appearances for Leeds in a career stretching over 18 years, he waged a constant battle against injury. Ankle, shoulder and thigh injuries over the years hampered his effectiveness, so much so that he couldn't train as much as other players for fear of breaking down. He also had to change the way he played, choosing to try to wrong-foot opponents rather than beat them with sheer pace (which he certainly possessed) to allow for his injuries.

It was injuries – not necessarily young Gray's – that cost Leeds dear in seasons 1965–66 and 1966–67. The most severe blow came in October 1965 when Leeds were playing Torino – then an impressive Serie A side – in the second leg of an Inter-Cities Fairs Cup tie in Turin, defending a 2–1 lead from the Elland Road match. Torino's left-back Fabrizio Poletti went 'over the top' in a tackle with Bobby Collins, and such was the ferocity of the challenge that he broke the Scotsman's femur, the biggest bone in the body. Normally, it would take something like a car crash to shatter that part of the anatomy.

Billy Bremner was in tears on the pitch at the plight of his midfield partner. 'The foul was quite the worst that I have ever seen and when I realised what had happened, I must admit that I lost my head completely and snarled at the player, "I'll kill you for this." Believe me, I really meant it at the time, too.'

Incredibly, Collins did make it back for the last game of the season, against Manchester United, and started the 1966–67 campaign before an ankle injury sidelined him and his appearances started to dwindle, but he was clearly never the same player again. Revie had set his sights (ultimately to fail) on signing Alan Ball from Blackpool as his replacement, and Collins was eventually granted a free transfer to Bury in February 1967.

Collins was by far the worst casualty, but his actual replacement as playmaker, Johnny Giles, also missed a good part of the 1966–67 season with a thigh injury. It was galling for Revie, as Giles had settled in as Collins' successor so well. Then there was Alan Peacock, exactly the kind of centre-forward Revie had been looking for, an accomplished leader of the line, good at bringing others into play, a brilliant header of the ball and a goalscorer; yet he continued to spend long spells on the treatment table with recurrent knee injuries.

Leeds finished the seasons 1965–66 and 1966–67 without a trophy – but it felt to them, and it looked to the outside world, as if it was now only a matter of time. In 1965–66, they were runners-up to Liverpool in the league and losing semi-finalists to Real Zaragoza in the Fairs Cup. The following year, they slipped to fourth in the league behind champions Manchester United, but reached the final of the Fairs Cup, this time succumbing 2–0 on aggregate to Dinamo Zagreb.

Revie's side had gained respect and much admiration for their rapid progress. But there was a degree of distaste for their 'professional' tactics on the pitch and the perceived siege mentality of the club.

Eddie Gray acknowledges the over-zealous approach adopted in those days, but says the Elland Road side were by no means the only ones:

'When I first came to Leeds, they were playing – and this wasn't just Leeds – a type of game that was foreign to me. It was nasty, and the game was quite nasty in those days. Every club had a player that was feared and did the "enforcing" job. The game was a tougher one to play for the type of player like me, because people would try and kick you. You *knew* they were going to try and do it. Teams would say in the dressing-room, first time he gets it we'll give him a right good whack to unsettle him. So you had to have a mindset, knowing it would happen.'

It is one of the more remarkable statistics in football history that Eddie Gray, despite all the punishment meted out to him in more than 450 games for his club, was never once booked. Not once did he strike back, not once did he feign injury or play-act. If he was badly fouled, he merely picked himself up and got on with the job of finding a way through the opposition ranks. Mind you, if there was retaliation to be done, there were certainly those in the Leeds side who were quite happy to carry it out.

Though undoubtedly acknowledged for their resolution and the developing skill of their young players, nonetheless Leeds were unloved. The pattern of their relationship with the British sporting public was set in those days and never really altered until perhaps the 1973–74 season.

Lord Harewood, club president and a good friend of Don Revie and his wife Elsie, felt the Leeds supporters revelled in their side's reputation. 'Leeds were not at all the hardest club, in my opinion,' he says. 'People liked to talk about it that way, as did the press, and quite a lot of Leeds fans liked it because they liked to be behind a club that was feared as much as a club that was loved. They didn't mind the thought that it was "us against the world". Don didn't mind the "us against the world" attitude either. But he did resent Leeds being described first and foremost as a dirty side – because we weren't.'

By June 1967, the club was on a sound footing on all fronts. The massive debt of £250,000 had been erased and Leeds were now in profit. For that to continue, gates of 38,000 plus were regularly required, but such was the consistency of the performances on the field that Harry Reynolds felt confident that target would be achieved.

The Revie Revolution had transformed a failing, ramshackle club into an elite outfit now regarded as one of the best in Europe. All that was missing was a piece or two of silverware.

★ ★ ★

While Don Revie was going head to head with the likes of Matt Busby and Bill Shankly at the very top of the Football League, Brian Clough – with Peter Taylor's not inconsiderable assistance – was scrabbling for survival with Hartlepools United at the bottom rung of the ladder.

If they had been anything other than the supreme pragmatists that they were, Clough and Taylor might have come away from their first week at Victoria Park thinking management at this level wasn't such a difficult job after all. They emerged with a 3–1 win from their first game in charge, at Bradford City, two goals from Jimmy Mulvaney and one from George Wright giving the Pools their first away victory of the season. A week later, Crewe were soundly beaten 4–1 at home – two goals apiece for Ernie Phythian and George Wright – and Hartlepools were out of the bottom four and the re-election zone. But a strong dose of reality quickly followed, with four successive defeats and then a humiliating 6–1 reverse away at Tranmere on New Year's Day 1966. There was a huge amount to be done, both on and off the field.

As a town, Hartlepool suffered from being the North-East's poor, little, unsophisticated relation to the bigger, wealthier, more stylish cousins like Newcastle, Sunderland, Durham and even Middlesbrough. There's always been a self-deprecating, sometimes self-mocking side to the character of Hartlepudlians, best illustrated by the perverse pride taken in the legend of the hanged monkey.

During the Napoleonic Wars, so the story goes, fishermen from Hartlepool watched a French warship founder off the coast, and the only survivor was a monkey, which was dressed in French military uniform, presumably to amuse the officers on the ship. The unsophisticated fishermen assumed that this must be what Frenchmen looked like, and, after a brief trial, summarily executed the poor animal. Opposition supporters – in particular those from local rivals Darlington – used to taunt the Hartlepools fans by calling them 'Monkey Hangers'. Over the years, it became less of an insult and more a description to be worn as a badge of pride.

Hartlepool is also the home of Andy Capp – or rather of his creator, Reg Smythe. In the late 1950s, Hugh Cudlipp of the *Daily Mirror* asked Smythe, the paper's resident cartoonist, to create a character that would help boost Northern readership. He came back with Andy Capp, in the famous words of Cudlipp himself a 'workshy, beer-swilling, rent-dodging, wife-beating, pigeon-fancying, soccer-playing, uncouth cadger, setting an appalling example to the youth of Britain'. The popularity of Andy was such that his adventures were chronicled in the *Mirror* six days a week in the early 1960s, and he was exported successfully around the world, appearing in at least 34 countries and 700 newspapers, with text in 13 or more languages.

Hartlepool, then, was a town that could laugh at itself and its lack of pretension. In the past, the football club hadn't been lacking in spunk – the sort of fortitude that prompted the directors to pursue (unsuccessfully, as it turned out) Kaiser Wilhelm II for compensation after a Zeppelin bombed Victoria Park in November 1916, destroying the main stand. But being in the bottom four in the bottom division in six years out of seven had sapped the spirit of everyone connected with the club. Clough and Taylor wanted the laughing to stop as far as Hartlepools United were concerned. They aimed to end this culture of resigned failure as they went about learning how to build a football club from the bottom up.

The ground was dilapidated, the players were unmotivated at best, lazy at worst, debts were piling up and they had to work with a chairman – Ernie Ord – with whom they didn't always see eye to eye. Their answer was to roll up their sleeves and get stuck in – literally, in some instances, when helping plug the leaks in the roof of the stadium, painting the stands and cutting the grass.

Clough took his players out and about in the community, to pubs, clubs and workplaces, to foster a sense of togetherness and raise money. He toured the town himself, lecturing every night for a fortnight in February 1967. He took lessons to obtain a Public Services Vehicle licence so he'd be qualified to drive the team bus. In his most brazen publicity exercise, he announced he would forfeit a month's wages to help reduce the club's debt. Clough was already a master at manipulating the media, and giving up his salary was just one of tens of different stories he produced to help push Hartlepools into the spotlight.

If he was the 'goods in the shop window', Taylor was working overtime in the back office to bring in players of a certain calibre who could help stave off the threat of re-election. He concentrated his efforts in the Midlands, the area he knew best. John Gill, a brawny centre-half from Mansfield, was his biggest-money signing, for £2,500. Wing-half Tony Parry came from Taylor's former club, Burton Albion, for £200, and others included goalkeeper Les Green (also Burton Albion), Terry Bell (Nuneaton Borough), and John Sheridan and Tony Bircumshaw (Notts County).

One man who cost nothing was little left-winger 20-year-old Michael (Mick) Somers, who came on a free transfer from Torquay United. Somers' story is one of great promise, high expectations,

187

disappointment, then a cruel twist of fate – a salutary tale for all young boys hoping to fulfil their dream of becoming a professional footballer and playing at the top level.

He was a talented youth player in Nottingham, playing while working as a motor mechanic in a local garage, when he was spotted by a Chelsea scout and asked to go for a trial at Stamford Bridge. Somers impressed the then manager – one Tommy Docherty – enough to be asked back for another trial game. Once more, he caught the eye, and he was offered terms as a professional for one of the glamour clubs of the First Division, where the likes of Peter Bonetti, Terry Venables, Bobby Tambling and Barry Bridges plied their trade.

But it didn't quite work out, and after a number of months Chelsea released him and he went to play for Torquay United in the Fourth Division. That was where Clough and Taylor – who had met him and knew him from Nottingham days – came calling early in 1966. Their charm and persuasion worked, and Somers was a Hartlepool player by the start of the 1966–67 season.

'Cloughie was an arrogant bastard,' recalls Somers, 'but you could see he was so honest, he called a spade a spade, which in football counts for a lot, really, because the amount of back-stabbing that goes on is unbelievable. Everybody respected him for that. I thought, well, this bloke is going to go a long way. In training, when we had a kick-around, I could tell he used to be a first-class goalscorer. He used to stand in the penalty area and get John McGovern on the right wing, and me on the left, to float crosses over for him, and some of his volleying and finishing was fantastic.'

The Hartlepool players were a ragged bunch when Clough arrived. One of them was arrested at the ground for non-payment of maintenance. Another, who had been suspended, was given £5 out of his own pocket by Clough and responded so badly that he was transferred before the end of the season.

Somers lived in lodgings with four other players, and one of them, Tony Parry, was a gifted player but a wayward character who liked a drink or two. 'Cloughie knew what he was up to,' says Somers, 'and came up with a novel way of stopping him going out on a Friday night before the game. He'd come round to our digs, summon him to the door and say, "Right, young man, come with me," and he'd then take him to the Clough home and get him to spend the whole evening babysitting his children!'

But in the 1966–67 season, with Hartlepools moving steadily up the table as the Clough/Taylor effect started to reap rewards, Somers suffered a knee injury playing against Notts County. Clough wanted him back playing quickly, as the club was still in with an outside chance of promotion, so he quickly sent Somers to Sunderland to be seen by the same surgeon who had operated on his own knee. He was playing again within a few months but never felt entirely confident of his fitness.

'I don't really blame Cloughie, but I was rushed back too soon after the operation. I did play 32 games the following season when we got promoted, but the knee never really felt right. I played one game at the start of the 1968–69 season, then I got injured again, and the surgeon said I should think about packing it in because otherwise I'd end up having my leg damaged beyond repair. I thought, I'll never be able to kick a ball about with my grandchildren, so I took the surgeon's advice.'

So Mick Somers played his last match as a professional footballer on 17 August 1968, at the age of 23. The following year, Clough brought his Derby team to Victoria Park for his testimonial match, and a good crowd of around 6,000 came to watch. These days, he's a successful plastering contractor in the Mapperley area of Nottingham.

After staving off the prospect of applying for re-election in 1966 by finishing eighteenth, Clough and Taylor took Hartlepools to the dizzy heights of eighth in 1967. Their relationship with Ernie Ord deteriorated as the little millionaire – he was only five feet tall – grew jealous of the attention Clough received from an adoring North-East press, while both Clough and Taylor took exception to constant interference from Ord in their jobs.

But life became easier when Ord was replaced as chairman by a more benign figure, Councillor John Curry, who was the Conservative Group leader on West Hartlepool Borough Council. Clough had needed Curry as an ally in an effort to see the back of Ord, so much so that he swallowed his political principles during the local elections of 1965 and campaigned for Curry.

Life was certainly looking rosier now that they had the freedom to make decisions as they pleased. But then, in early June 1967, their old friend Len Shackleton got in touch again to recommend they should go for the vacant manager's job at Second Division Derby County.

Clough was initially reluctant to contemplate a move. He felt he'd started a project at Hartlepools and wanted to see it through to promotion and beyond. But Taylor was determined to go, tempted by a higher grade of football, decent money to wheel and deal in the transfer market and a move back to his home territory. Eighteen months at Hartlepool had been a wearying, frustrating experience, despite the achievement in building a useful side from a standing start.

The deal to take them to Derby was done in a meeting with the club's chairman, Sam Longson, at Scotch Corner on the A1. 'It took Shackleton and me hardly any time at all to convince the impressionable Longson that I was his man,' was Clough's recollection of the meeting.

Derby had done little of note since being promoted from the Third Division ten years earlier under Taylor's old mentor Harry Storer. It would require another big rebuilding job by Clough, but the experience at Hartlepools would stand him in good stead.

As a man, and as a manager, his character and style were now fully formed. He was still only 32, and there would be embellishments aplenty to come. But the core of what he was about, his philosophy, his methods, were all there to see if you looked hard enough. The young dictator was ready to conquer new territory.

Chapter 9
'The Most Superstitious Man in the World'

O ne of the bestselling books of 1969 was a novel that featured a compelling, dominating central character. He was a man who had worked his way up society's ladder from humble beginnings, created a business empire of his own out of next to nothing, then developed into a despot who would stop at nothing to gain more power.

Despite his obvious ruthlessness, he did have redeeming features. He was the benevolent patriarch of a large extended family whose every need he catered for; he knew the names – and the foibles – of all of them, and was especially attentive with gifts of flowers or chocolates on the days that really mattered – births, christenings, birthdays and weddings.

He also lived his life by a very clear code of honour that valued, above all else, hard work, loyalty and, of course, family. It was a very personal code, however, and its moral boundaries were stretched to the limit – and way beyond – on many occasions.

The man was Don Vito Corleone, and the book was *The Godfather*, written by Mario Puzo and three years later brought to the screen by Francis Ford Coppola with Marlon Brando in the leading role.

The juxtaposition of Mafia boss Don Vito and Don Revie in the late 1960s and early 1970s was a heaven-sent opportunity for writers looking for a fresh perspective on the Leeds manager. 'The Godfather of Elland Road' was a title they could bestow on him with some relish and even a little validity – having swiftly put aside, of course, any suggestion of criminal comparisons.

Revie's grip on Leeds United was partly the product of a somewhat obsessive mind that wished everything to be totally planned and under control. But it was also because of his own personal experiences back in the 1940s and 1950s.

When he was at Leicester, Revie had learned at first hand just how lonely and disorientating life could be for a young apprentice footballer away from home for the first time. He knew he had been luckier than many, as his manager Johnny Duncan had, when he could, taken a keen personal interest in his welfare. But there had still been long periods of isolation and introspection for the young Revie, and as his career had progressed at Hull City, Manchester City and Sunderland, what he'd found most lacking was a human relationship with his managers.

He was determined that if he was ever to manage a club, he would devote as much time to what happened to his charges off the field as on it. Consequently, he treated his Leeds players as if they were his sons. No aspect of their lives was neglected – how to dress and behave, how to look after their money, how to conduct their relationships. There was even a spiritual adviser who would make regular visits to Elland Road.

In 1970, Revie wrote what was, effectively, his footballing credo, his manifesto, a revealing five-page document entitled 'What I Expect from My Players'. It was published in that year's edition of *The Park Drive Book of Football*. It didn't deal so much with performance on the field but concentrated instead on advising players how to carry themselves away from it. Was it perhaps a riposte to the barrage of criticism the club faced for its supposed roughness on the pitch and insularity off it?

> Any new boy should combine courage, hard but fair play and complete confidence on the field, with courtesy, good conduct, manners and humility away from it.
>
> We inculcate into the lads a knowledge of dining out, checking into and out of hotels, how to travel in comfort, even how to reply to toasts and many other things. In addition there is emphasis upon religious advice if they want it and talks on girlfriends, male and female fans etc. Everything and anything in fact.
>
> The idea behind all this is to insure [*sic*] that so far as is humanly possible every lad on the staff has, within a short time of joining Leeds United, been taught sufficient to feel

comfortable in any sort of company, able to enter any hotel he wishes and also made aware of the temptations as well as the honours and awards that can come his way.

If you dealt with all those matters satisfactorily, Revie reasoned, you would free players from worries and they'd be better prepared for their 3 p.m. appointment on a Saturday afternoon.

The players' reliance on their manager was illustrated by the case of Billy Bremner, who when he developed a sharp pain in the side of his stomach the night before a match decided to ring Revie with his concerns rather than his doctor. The Leeds manager had to organise for his own GP to visit the Bremner household.

In return for all this pastoral work, Revie demanded that the players knuckle down to his set of rules and his regime and, of course, strictly observe his footballing philosophy. The vast majority of them, beguiled by his charm and attention and respectful of his knowledge of the game, were more than happy to do so.

The 'Godfather' was omnipresent at Elland Road. John Helm, football correspondent and then sports editor at Radio Leeds, recalls, 'He always made a point, every day, of saying good morning to everybody at the club, partly so everyone knew he was at the ground. It was like putting the flag up the pole!'

Revie didn't work alone, of course. He gathered around him a group of tried and trusted lieutenants, including Maurice Lindley (assistant manager), Syd Owen (head coach), Les Cocker (trainer), Bob English (physiotherapist) and Cyril Partridge (reserve-team manager).

With good staff and good players, the other attribute a manager needed – apart from a little luck – was the ability to understand the minds of the individuals in his charge. 'I think a manager has got to be a bit of a psychologist,' Revie explained, 'knowing when to get the best out of players, when to rollock them, when to lift them, when to coax.'

His son Duncan saw evidence at home of the motivational force his father could exert on people. 'He was an amazing manager of people, including his own family. If you were getting too big for your boots, he'd have you back down on the floor in 30 seconds. Equally, if you were down on the floor, he'd have you up to the ceiling in the same time. He was a magnificent man. He was my hero, as well as my father.'

Eddie Gray said he understood when Revie was angry or upset

because he'd come into the dressing-room, look in the mirror and flick back his hair. 'Then you knew you were in trouble, that he wasn't happy with the team.'

Norman Hunter recalled being five minutes late on one occasion and Revie said nothing to him but merely glanced down at his wrist and turned his watch round ever so slightly. 'I can't ever remember him really raising his voice. But he had this air about him. You knew he laid the rules down and you knew you had to abide by them.'

Having succeeded as a player at the very top level of his sport, with all the attendant pressures, clearly gave Revie the self-confidence and authority that he exuded at Elland Road. Once he'd gathered men around him that he could trust, then he was able to create the family atmosphere he so desired.

But underneath that mask, he was a man who was deeply superstitious and who suffered from feelings of shyness and insecurity. Being uncomfortable with others was something he ascribed to the lack of a decent education, as he explained in a BBC radio interview in the 1980s:

> I'm a rather shy person deep down. I think shyness comes basically from one's background. I think that if you've had a good – or reasonably good – education, then you're never shy when you walk into a room . . . if you haven't had one, you're afraid to step forward in certain company when you walk into a room and they're discussing something you know nothing about. I think this is where your shyness comes out.

He was doubly determined that his son and daughter should have the education he could never have. When Duncan was underachieving at Leeds Grammar School (glorying too much in the achievements of a famous father and not concentrating on his work), he was quickly removed and enrolled at Repton public school in Derbyshire.

Duncan remembers his first day there: 'When Mum and Dad drove me there – I was 12 or 13 – I ended up crying on the steps, and Dad was crying, too. Mum just looked at me and said, "You get yourself in there, now," pointing to the school entrance, and she looked at Dad and said, "And you get yourself back in the car."

'I was miserable at the time, but of course it was the best thing I ever did, and I started at last to concentrate on academic work. Dad was absolutely adamant about it. "I can give you money," he said, "I can give you happiness, but an education is the richest thing you can have in life." Later on, on a TV programme, he was asked what was the proudest moment of his life. Was it leading Leeds out at Wembley, winning two league titles, becoming England manager? "No," he replied, "the proudest moment of my life was watching my son Duncan graduate from Cambridge." That was lovely.'

The superstitious streak that ran deep in Revie's character was also a legacy of his Middlesbrough childhood. He explained how it all started:

> This came from my mother. I was going down to the shops one day with her when I was very, very young, and there was somebody painting in the street, he was up a ladder and painting the bedroom windows up above. My mother made me walk round the outside of the ladder instead of underneath it, and to this day I'm probably the most superstitious man in the world.

It led to him having a 'lucky' new light-blue mohair suit made each year. He would wear it for every match until the season's end – even if the seat of his trousers started, embarrassingly, to wear out. There'd be a 'lucky' tie to accompany it, and in the pockets of the jacket there'd invariably be a charm or two.

Once out of the door and heading for the ground, he'd never, ever turn back for anything, even if he'd left the bag he was travelling away with. Elsie – or someone else if she wasn't there – would be sent back to recover it.

With Leeds United, he'd always sit in the same seat in the team coach, and once at the hotel he'd try to sit in the same seat in the dining room. As a matter of course, he'd also take a stroll out of the hotel to the nearest set of traffic lights, then walk straight back again.

On a Thursday morning, he had a ritual of helping the physiotherapist massage the players' legs and backs; but it would only be certain players and certain legs and backs.

Turning to the behaviour within the dressing-room, it's a wonder the side was ever ready to take to the pitch at three o'clock. Certain players would have to put their left boots on first, some were to carry balls out while others couldn't and there was a strict order to the line-up when they walked out.

All this, plus a fear of ornamental elephants and a firm belief that certain birds brought bad luck. The latter eventually led to the removal of the peacock from the club badge. Even Revie's wife couldn't escape the rituals. Elsie watched the team at Elland Road in the same suede, fur-lined coat for five years.

Of course, sportsmen have been superstitious souls since time immemorial. In ancient Rome, gladiators were careful to put their dominant foot forward when entering the arena, a practice – some say – that left us with the expression 'putting your best foot forward'. But Revie, at least in the first four or five years, made it into an art form. The crowning moment of this superstitious frenzy came in 1967 when he resolved to lift a gypsy curse he was convinced had settled on Elland Road and had been responsible for the side's run of near misses in the league, FA Cup and Fairs Cup.

It's thought that Revie's faith in gypsies began when he was a boy in Middlesbrough, observing his mother, who never turned one away from their door in Bell Street. Then that belief strengthened when a gypsy gave him a piece of tree bark to carry as a charm on the eve of the FA Cup final in 1956 – a match in which he excelled in the winning Manchester City side.

Anyway, Revie received a letter telling him of the gypsy encampment that used to exist on the site of Elland Road before the football stadium was built. Once they had been forcibly evicted, the writer informed Revie, the gypsies had nowhere to go, so they put a curse on the ground and its future inhabitants. Revie acted immediately:

> I was told only a practising gypsy could take the curse off, so I had a word with the Vicar – Rev. Jackson – about this, and he said it's very possibly true. So I then found a gypsy in Blackpool – Gypsy Rose Lee – sent a car for her and she came to the ground.
>
> She insisted – and I'll never forget this – on all the doors of Elland Road being locked. No one was to be allowed inside the ground except her, and me. She then went to all four corners of the ground, then to the centre circle, scattered some seeds and did certain other things I can't reveal. But it worked. We won something at the end of that season.

That 'something' was the League Cup, which Leeds won in March 1968 by beating Arsenal 1–0 at Wembley – their first major trophy. After that, the superstitions, the rituals lessened in number, although they never entirely went away.

In June 1971, a reporter from the *Yorkshire Evening Post* managed to track down the gypsy who had apparently worked her magic for Revie. Her name was actually Gypsy Laura Lee – the 40-year-old daughter of Gypsy Rose Lee – and she was, by then, living in a caravan in a farmyard at Cayton, near Scarborough.

Gypsy Laura told the paper she'd known Revie for six years and done many readings for him. She would say no more than that about their relationship. 'Gypsies are like priests and doctors. They have a code they must stick to,' was her rationale. On the nature of the curse plaguing Leeds United, she said:

> Generally, curses befall the very wealthy. In this case there was the smell of a curse – and curses do have smells – in the dressing-rooms at Elland Road, and obviously something was wrong . . . One thing I can tell you now is that within three years Leeds United will be at the top of the football world. Their hoodoo has ended.

If there was an illogical bent to Revie's character, it was more than compensated for by the practical side of his nature, which made his Leeds United team one of the best-prepared in modern British football.

Every detail was taken care of, nothing was left to chance. Once the week's training – rigorous, innovative, constantly changing – had been done, the players would leave their families and head to a hotel on the Friday night before the game, a comfortable place like the Craiglands Hotel in Ilkley or the Mansion House in Roundhay Park, Leeds, where Revie wanted them both to relax and to focus on the game the next day.

Relaxation came in the shape of games of carpet bowls and bingo, strange occupations, perhaps, for young men with an eye for current trends, fashions and styles, but which nonetheless seemed to work as bonding exercises. The focus came with thick, elaborate dossiers on their opponents, which the players were expected to read, absorb and then discuss on the morning before the match.

Over the years, the dossiers became a stick with which to beat Revie. Some time later, Norman Hunter admitted, 'Looking back, they were a bit boring and tedious.' But at the time they were an innovation that fascinated the rest of the football world and which many sought to copy.

Alan Keen was scouting for Middlesbrough in the late 1960s and immediately saw the value of the Revie dossier. 'When I started scouting, you'd rarely see fellow scouts watching the opposition and making any notes. I'd make quite a few myself, analysing dead-ball situations, who was running off the ball where and plenty of other stuff. Then, a couple of years later, I saw other scouts actually making diagrams of what happened at corner kicks! The whole culture had started to change, and it was Revie who started it. There was a lot of interest, because it had never been done before. But there was criticism, too, because it was primarily a destructive tool, there to stop the opposition from playing rather than being about the state of your own play.'

The dossiers could run to many pages, with a detailed résumé of the opposition side's last game, a breakdown of the performance of each player – strengths and weaknesses – and some psychological, as well as tactical, tips.

Here's an extract from the opening of the dossier that prepared the Leeds side for their trip to Anfield on 2 September 1964, compiled after Liverpool's 2–2 draw with West Ham at the same venue on 15 August:

> Liverpool took the field first and proceeded towards the Spion Kop end. This being the end they prefer to defend in the first half, an advantage may be gained by getting out first when we play there.
>
> Use the right-hand goal for warm-up and should we win the toss elect to stay as you are at K.O. [kick-off]. Shankly has devised his team tactics to cover some deficiencies in his playing strength. Both full-backs lack pace and our wingers must seek the ball behind them.

The dossiers could read at times like a policeman's notebook, but they came to life with their succinct, quite sharp individual assessments. The compiler on this occasion noted of Ron Yeats, Liverpool captain and centre-half: 'Does a solid job without any frills. Takes no chances with his clearances, and hates every opponent.'

In the event, the preparation ultimately came to naught, because Leeds lost the match 2–1! But from that season on – 1964–65 – Revie was a firm believer in this scientific approach and invested heavily in it.

Following a match, Revie and his side would sit down for what they termed 'pull each other apart' sessions. The players were encouraged to voice criticisms of one another's mistakes on the pitch, with the firm instruction that it should not lead to the bearing of any future grudges. A dangerous strategy in a club anything less than utterly harmonious, but in the Leeds 'family', it seemed in those years to have nothing but positive benefit.

Off the field, Revie's insecurity and innate shyness were well masked. The front he presented to the world was a confident one, as Eddie Gray remembers. 'Any room that he walked into, he'd be centre of attraction. He was a powerful character, a big bear of a man; he was the boss, and he carried that demeanour wherever he went. If he had any fears about mixing socially, he was very, very good at hiding them. He could talk with anybody. Lord and Lady Harewood, for example, absolutely loved him.'

For Gray, the difference between the two managers he worked for – albeit one for nearly nine years, the other for just forty-four days – was abundantly clear. 'Don was very comfortable in his environment at the football club. Brian Clough was the funniest man on television at one point – Don would shy away from that. It was a closed shop for Don at Leeds, but Brian wanted to invite everyone into his world and get everyone to think his way of thinking.'

On the touchline at matches, Revie was as tense as they come. He would be utterly absorbed in the spectacle, mentally kicking every ball and rarely able to just sit back and let his players get on with business.

If he had an Achilles heel, it was his over-sensitivity to criticism, fair or unfair. He could rarely let it go and would sometimes resort to ringing up individual reporters or editors to complain.

Away from the game, he found it very difficult to completely relax. He was a brilliant, natural sportsman, a very good snooker player and an even better darts player. Most summer holidays were spent playing golf. Entirely self-taught and – in his son's words – with 'a swing like a busman', he brought his handicap down to two, shooting scores in the low seventies around formidable courses like Lytham St Annes. In his playing days, he won the Professional Footballers' Golf Championship.

But Revie found it almost impossible to switch off during the football season. Sometimes he would go to Harewood Hall for a meal – invariably roast beef or steak, his favourite food – and watch *Match of the Day* afterwards. Even when he tried to escape the game, his friends in it would unwittingly drag him back to it, as Ian St John, Liverpool and Scotland inside-forward (and a contender for the Leeds manager's job when Revie left for England), amusingly recounts.

'Don liked to socialise on a Saturday night after the game, have a meal and a few drinks. Bill Shankly, on the other hand, didn't drink at all but lived and breathed football every minute of the day and just loved talking about the game. So, as Don described it, the phone by the side of the bed would often ring very late on a Saturday night and it would be Shanks on the end of it.

'"Hello, Don, good result you had today."

'"Thanks, Bill."

'"Don, we were terrific!"

'Don would then sit back and listen for the next 20 minutes or so while Shanks regaled him with a detailed rundown on the Liverpool match. The conversation would then end with Shanks saying, "Well, Don, it was very good to talk to you," and putting the phone down. Don hadn't said a word!'

Revie gave generously of his own time to young up-and-coming coaches and managers. Most of them would make a beeline for Leeds at some point or other to watch and learn, and Lawrie McMenemy, first a coach at Sheffield Wednesday, was one of the regular visitors. He recalls: 'I'd get tickets for the game at Elland Road, where his wife Elsie dominated the guest room, passing the tea round and keeping everybody happy. She was very much a football woman. Then after the match Don would always make a point of coming in and singling out the young coaches and giving us a good deal of his time. Later, he kept an eye on me when I became manager of Doncaster. Don, Shankly, Bill Nicholson, Joe Mercer were in one set of managers, while Cloughie, Bobby Robson and myself were the next generation. Don was always keen to impart advice, and I was eager to listen.'

For seasoned football watchers in the late 1960s, Revie was an utterly paradoxical figure. He himself had been a player of the mind rather than of physical contact, gliding through games silently, often in the shadows, yet emerging to decorate them with play of touch and subtle deception.

Tommy Docherty played against Revie on a number of occasions – most famously in the Preston North End side that put the 'Revie Plan' to the sword on its first outing. 'I've always thought Don played a little like Paul Scholes [Manchester United and England] plays today – very creative, supported the attack and a wonderful passer of the ball,' he says. 'Don was a big tall man, over six foot, and he had a lovely touch. But when it got a bit robust he wasn't very keen, as I found out early on. He didn't appreciate a little Glaswegian snapping at his heels!'

Yet the Leeds sides he put out were not in his stylish image. Skilful, yes, but rugged often to the point of brutality. Those who admired Giles' supreme passing ability, Cooper's pace and crossing skills, Madeley's unhurried elegance in whatever position and Bremner's all-round virtuosity were often alienated by the team's ultra-physicality and propensity to nag at and argue with referees (often, misleadingly, in the name of 'professionalism'). Revie's Leeds could seem a Jekyll-and-Hyde side.

Revie himself freely admitted, 'I'd always felt if I'd been harder, I would have been a better player.' So for much of the 1960s his band of outstandingly gifted players, with iron in their souls, would make sure the dirty work – metaphorically and actually – was done first, before the flowing football followed.

As his caution evaporated, Revie would 'let his players off the leash' and enable them to perform more joyously, putting the accent on their skills first. Then came true greatness as a side.

* * *

For Duncan Hamilton, author of the memorable memoir about Brian Clough entitled *Provided You Don't Kiss Me*, a glance into the offices of Clough and Don Revie told you all you needed to know about their respective characters and styles of management. He's describing the rooms as they were a few years later, in the mid-1970s.

'If you walked into Clough's, it looked like a Steptoe and Son junkyard in terms of the vast amount of paper and debris. Nothing was planned; the office was in a complete mess. He'd be sat there in a rugby shirt, with a pair of old trainers and tracksuit bottoms. You walked into Don Revie's office, and not only was he sitting there in his England blazer, with a white shirt and perfectly knotted tie, but his desk was absolutely immaculate. It had the blotter, the pencils were lined up, everything was in its place and the whole office was spotless. I've always thought that if you wanted to know about the approach of the two men, it was reflected in the state of their two rooms. Revie's was almost obsessively neat and well planned, and you could see everything had to be just so for him. He was perfectly courteous and very helpful to me, treating me as if I was the football correspondent of the *Sunday Times* rather than from a humble provincial paper.'

If Don Revie appeared to share character traits and values with one particular, flawed cultural icon of the late 1960s, Brian Clough seemed more like an amalgam of some of those working-class heroes – usually, but not always, 'Angry Young Men' – who seemed to come fizzing out of the pages of numerous books and plays in the late '50s and early '60s.

For Clough, perhaps read Joe Lampton, the brash, pushy, articulate, ambitious anti-hero of John Braine's first novel, *Room at the Top* – minus the cruelty and the adultery, of course. Or possibly Arthur Seaton, the rebellious factory worker in Alan Sillitoe's *Saturday Night and Sunday Morning*, like Clough, always a man with a pithy quip on his lips: 'What I'm out for is a good time. All the rest is propaganda.' Or maybe, to bring the literary comparison directly into the sporting arena, Clough shared some of the characteristics of Arthur Machin, the rugby-league player in David Storey's *This Sporting Life*, an uncompromising, selfish individual on the field of play.

Those men had an attitude born of a decade, the 1950s, that bred a more questioning type of working-class man, the sort who aspired to go places in society and achieve things that their fathers could not have dreamed of. Sir Michael Parkinson was one of them. 'I was thinking about this when attending Keith Waterhouse's memorial service last year,' he says. 'There was a lot of us who came out of Yorkshire at that time who hadn't been to university and who started work very early – whether it was in newspapers, like Keith and I, or in other professions. It was an extraordinary generation. Keith represented it but so did Brian. He was perhaps the first bright, articulate maverick [from Yorkshire], the one who challenged authority all the way through, felt he knew more than football chairmen and wasn't afraid to say so.'

Middlesbrough fundamentally shaped Brian Clough. All the poverty he viewed around him there had propelled him onwards as a sportsman. He felt football was his best way out – in fact, his only way out, really, after failing the 11-plus, which initially handicapped him in the search for a job and rankled with him for the rest of his life. In *Room at the Top*, Joe Lampton despises his home town: 'No dreams were possible in Dufton, where the snow seemed to turn black almost before it hit the ground.' Clough cherished his memories of family life and sporting achievement in his home town, and the values it brought him, but, like Lampton, once out he wanted to divorce himself from it and make sure he never slunk back to it.

By 1967, the Brian Clough the world saw was increasingly self-assured. With the North-East behind him, he now seemed even to have shrugged off his Middlesbrough accent as well, speaking in a peculiar style all of his own, elongating the vowels in a kind of North Country drawl. It would be much imitated in the coming years.

Unlike Revie, who felt his lack of a good education so keenly that he remained uncertain when stepping out of his comfort zone of football, Clough was never fazed when asked his opinions about the world – indeed, he was eager to give them.

Sir Michael Parkinson sensed there was something unique about his fellow Yorkshireman. 'Cloughie was born with this innate sense of himself. The part of our brain that contains doubt and uncertainty – well, he didn't possess it. He was a born performer, perfect for the developing television age, a complete natural for the screen, who would talk about anything. The only trouble was that he never shut up. He didn't listen a lot – he was so certain that whatever he said was right.'

Geoffrey Boycott observed the Clough character over many years of friendship and came to this conclusion: 'Brian was an extrovert/ introvert. In a sense, he had a dual personality. After I'd had my cancer, I delved a little into Chinese feng shui, and, to my eyes, Brian was a typical pig – the 12th sign of the Chinese zodiac. He liked a very nice home life, with his wife, his kids, his mother and father round and about him, the children brought up well. But when he was out on stage he was the life and soul of the party. He totally changed from the quiet, introverted man at home to the extrovert at the football ground or in front of the TV cameras. He was two completely different men in those environments.'

This desire for the limelight was also identified by Jack Charlton when he joined Clough at dinners or on TV panels commenting on England matches and World Cups. 'Brian would always be late. Now, whether he would do it on purpose or not, I can't be sure. But he would always be sat in his car somewhere close to the place he had to appear. Everybody would be sat down having their soup served and then Brian would suddenly appear through the door – and everybody would stand up! He always made an entrance, no question about that.'

Clough exuded optimism on his arrival at Derby, keen to focus supporters' minds on the future rather than hark back to the fading glories of an FA Cup win in 1946 and great old players of the past like Raich Carter and Peter Doherty.

For a few months at least, he had a job convincing the Baseball Ground faithful that his team could play as good a game as he could talk. In his first year, despite a splendid run in the League Cup that saw Derby reach the semi-finals before losing to Revie's high-flying Leeds United, the club actually finished a place lower – 18th – than in 1966–67.

But the supporters could sense that something was happening to this somewhat staid club with previously limited ambitions. Clough and Taylor had laid the foundations for a brighter future, acquiring the likes of Roy McFarland, an exceptionally promising young centre-half from Tranmere, John O'Hare, a solid centre-forward whom Clough had managed at Sunderland and rated very highly, and Alan Hinton, a brilliant left-winger of equal facility with left and right foot.

When, the following season, Clough and Taylor made their most imaginative signing in luring 33-year-old Dave Mackay – Double winner at Spurs – to the Baseball Ground and persuaded gritty little midfield player Willie Carlin to join them from Sheffield United for £60,000, they'd finally assembled the sort of side they wanted.

Promotion in 1968–69 never looked completely assured until Derby set off on an astonishing run of success on 15 March. They won their last nine games of the season to set a club record and thrust them to the top of the table, where they ended the campaign a clear seven points ahead of second-placed Crystal Palace.

There were outstanding partnerships in all areas of the pitch: McFarland and Mackay at the back, Carlin and Alan Durban in the middle, and O'Hare and Kevin Hector (20 goals in all matches) upfront.

Durban, a Welsh international from Bridgend, was a survivor of the previous era. Clough kept hold of him after noting his deft touch and feel for the flow of a game – not to mention his goalscoring instincts. Durban says that life under Clough was utterly different from anything he'd encountered anywhere before.

'Brian was just so unusual. It was all so new for us. It was like getting on a bus and going off for a magical mystery tour – you just never knew where the ride would take you. It was good fun, as well, because both Brian and Peter were good company. Brian liked a trip abroad, so whenever there was any frost or snow about we were off out of the Midlands and often out of the country.'

When Clough started out at Derby, he drew up a rulebook he called the 'Player's Ticket', a template for good behaviour that was handed to every new player when he joined the club. It wasn't dissimilar to Revie's manifesto, 'What I Expect from My Players'. It seems an old-fashioned sort of document now, and it didn't endure for more than a season or so. But it was his first attempt to impose a code of discipline on his players, before he was completely settled in his job and could rely purely on the strength of his own personality.

There were some obvious, practical rules about players having to be in the dressing-room one hour before kick-off and what time they should report for away games. More interestingly, there were strictures about their health and general behaviour. Rule 15 described in some detail when players were entitled to attend 'Dances': 'up to and including Tuesday (except where a Mid-week match is to be played), and also Wednesday, if permission is granted by the Trainer'. One rule said that 'Smoking on the Ground or in the Dressing Rooms during training hours [is] strictly forbidden', while others asked players not to ride 'motor-cycles' or have any connection with 'licensed premises' – whatever that meant, exactly.

Clough's management style was by now clearly formed. It revolved around ideas of simplicity and unpredictability, the former being the way he wanted his side to play their football, the latter the methods he used to run the players' lives and the club.

'Play the ball on the floor on the green grass, pass it to someone in the same shirt, and if you play in their half only we can score.' An ABC philosophy, perhaps condescending coming from someone else's lips, but these words with their touch of self-mockery drilled the message effectively into the players. John O'Hare certainly appreciated them. 'He made the game simple, yes. We all had jobs to do, basically doing what we were good at while at the same time trying to do the other bits as well as we could. But don't assume he didn't have a good eye for little tactical things, because he did.'

Team talks would be sharp and to the point, nothing over-elaborate. One day, his Derby side came in at half-time losing and waited for the reprimand that was sure to follow. Clough never even entered the dressing-room. Then, just as the players were leaving for the second half, he put his head round the door and said, 'It's not your fault – I picked the wrong side!'

Simple things can be remembered when under pressure, and when Clough did engage, that type of approach shone through, as Alan Durban explains: 'I can't remember too much ranting and raving at the interval. But there was always *one* thing that he would pick on to talk about that would set us straight – either to get forward earlier, or for the back four not to play so deep, just one improvement that he knew would be easy for us to absorb.'

The myth that grew up around Clough was that he was a manager almost by motivation alone. By whatever means, he would just send his players out onto the pitch feeling ten feet tall and the performances would follow. For Jack Charlton, this is nonsense. 'People talk about Brian's sides and their passing ability, but it wasn't just passing for passing's sake. He was very tactically aware. I remember going to see his side playing and I learned so much, particularly by the movement of the centre-forward that day. Brian was very good at getting his players to find space, run at the right time and pass at the right time. Sure, they did a lot of passing, but when it came to the end of the passing game, they were very positive.'

One of the unique features of Clough's management style was the way he would get his players to relax in the build-up to a game. Having been sent out 'on a downer' by Bob Dennison on his debut in 1955, Clough was determined he would not make the same mistake. In later years, he would send his Nottingham Forest side out to play a League Cup final at Wembley suffering major hangovers from the night before. Clough had insisted on the partying, and the effects were all too clear in a poor first-half display that left them 1–0 down to Southampton. Once the heads had cleared, however, Forest went out and played with great freedom, winning the game 3–2. A few beers, a cigarette, a sing-song, all of these sometimes just a few hours before the game; the nerves would vanish and the players would be frightened of no one by the time they started the match – that was Clough's theory, and it worked far more often than not.

Humour was another trait he would bring into play to reduce the tension. Here Clough had the perfect foil, as Peter Taylor was a natural comedian, disposing equally well of an awkward silence or a full-scale row with just an amusing expression or a witty one-liner delivered from the side of his mouth.

Clough varied training times and practices. He liked to keep the players guessing. They could never be sure from one day to the next what time they'd be training and whether their manager would be joining them. Some days, they'd be convinced he wasn't at the ground at all only to see him turn up at the very last minute and take the whole session. The next morning, the players might come in early to make sure they weren't caught out again – only for there to be no sign of Clough.

Later on, in his Nottingham Forest days, his attendance at training would be even more sporadic. He might wander into the ground with his flat cap and Wellington boots on and his dog by his side. But he'd watch intently and interrupt the session if he felt there was a useful point to be made.

He was an innovator in terms of rest and recuperation for players. In fact, making sure they received enough breaks became something of an obsession. After a good pre-season's work, he felt fitness levels merely needed to be 'topped up' from week to week. Besides, his teams were so successful they'd normally be playing two hard games every seven days.

Back in the late '60s and early '70s, it was unheard of for a manager to take his team off to Spain for a week's mid-season break. Geoffrey Boycott remembers discussing the idea with Clough. 'They would fly out on a Sunday – after the game on a Saturday – and he often wouldn't go with them. When I asked him about it, he said, "It's a long season, nine or ten months. I need a rest from them and they need a rest from me." It was very far-sighted in those days, and very few teams do it now. Peter Taylor would take them while Brian would stay here, resting his mind, walking on the beach, him and Barbara. Nobody would see him for a few days and he'd go back to work reinvigorated.'

If Clough allowed his players a degree of freedom of behaviour off the field, he played the puritan when instructing them what to do on it. Essentially, the referee was king and his word was law: don't argue with him, don't fall down when you've not been tackled, don't take advantage of the officials in any way, however small, and don't swear on the pitch.

Clearly, it was an attitude greatly appreciated by the referees. Clive Thomas was one of the strictest – and the best – in the country at that time, given the sobriquet 'The Book' for his rigorous interpretation of the laws. Born and brought up in the pit village of Treorchy in the Rhondda Valley, he had a rapport with Clough that would grow from mutual respect to friendship, culminating in him speaking at Clough's memorial service in 2004.

Their relationship began with a fascinating battle of wills during their first encounter in the late 1960s, when Thomas went to the Baseball Ground to referee a Boxing Day match. He and his linesmen entered the Derby County dressing-room before the game to check the players' studs and for him to say a few cautionary words about their conduct – a practice that was discontinued not long afterwards, much to Thomas's regret. Having finished the checks, he asked the players if they had any questions. When there was no reply, he remembers, he turned to leave the room only to hear a familiar voice

boom out. 'It was Brian, who said, "I've got something to say to you."
Now, the whole time I'd been in the dressing-room talking to the
players he'd been lying down on the table in the middle of the room.
So I replied, "Hold on. I'm assuming you're the manager. I would have
expected you to stand up or sit properly when asking me the question."
He said, "It's good enough for me to ask you like this," to which I
replied, "Unfortunately, it's not good enough for me," and I turned and
walked out.'

A few minutes later, Thomas's linesman told him – in a tone of some
trepidation – that Clough was on his way to see him. Soon afterwards,
the door opened and Clough marched into the referee's dressing-room.
'I said, "Stop. Mr Clough, you are the manager, you go outside and you
knock on that door and you wait for an answer." He replied, "It's my
club." I said, "It is your club, that's absolutely right, but when I set foot
in this ground, I'm in charge. And as far as I'm concerned, I want you
out of this dressing-room now. If you want to speak to me, you knock
on the door." Out he went, knocked on the door, and I called him in.
He then said to me, "I've just got this to say to you: if you're every bit
as good as the way you've handled yourself in the last few minutes, if
you can be like that you'll have a fantastic career. End of discussion."
And with that he walked out.'

Immense mutual respect flourished after that. Clough would ask
Thomas after games whether he'd had any problems with his players
on the pitch. The answer would invariably be no.

After the match, the post-mortems with the players and the media
concluded, Clough would retreat to his room and mull over the game
– and life – with some chosen friends. Lawrie McMenemy was often
one of them. He recalls: 'I was privileged to be within his inner sanctum.
If I was at one of his sides' matches as a neutral observer, he'd say,
"Hey, don't go off at the end, come and join me." Joining Brian was
very much like being in the famous boot room at Liverpool; you didn't
get in there easy – you had to earn the right. I spent many a time in his
office afterwards when he had the Ink Spots or Frank Sinatra on the
record player, with a nice glass of wine, and that's when the real
Cloughie came out, not the one who'd been in the spotlight for the last
couple of hours.'

It always hurt Clough to be reminded of his failure at the 11-plus.
But to watch him in those Derby days was to see a man of complete
natural intelligence, clever with words, comfortable in the company of
kings or paupers.

His innate psychological skills enabled him to quickly assess the character strengths and weaknesses of his players, which, once assimilated, he'd use to gain control over them. Fear – if it was necessary – respect and obedience would follow once he had the measure of the man.

In Boycott's view, you had to look beyond the blunt manner and the outspoken words for the real essence of Brian Clough. 'He was a genius at man-management. I wish I'd had Brian Clough as my manager. People who didn't know him thought he was just a loudmouth. But on the days he chose not to go into training he used to sit in his rocking chair by the fire at home and think about things, think about the formation of the team, about how he and Peter were going to deal with a particular individual. Everything about his approach was thoughtful, simple and uncomplicated. Of course, he couldn't have been a great manager on motivation alone, otherwise why not just employ a psychologist? But he was a genius at motivating people.'

Clough and Revie, then: dominant – but very different – personalities, working towards the same ends but using quite different means, masters of all they surveyed at their football clubs – dictators, if you like, but of the benign sort.

Revie was by now one of the masters of the management game, Clough the brightest pupil in the classroom. Admiration and respect were granted to the older man, but all that would change in the next few years.

Chapter 10

'Your Father's the Greatest of All Time'

One Saturday afternoon in the autumn of 1968, two fourteen-year-old boys left Repton School in the beautiful south Derbyshire countryside to make the twenty-minute journey to inner-city Derby and the city's incongruously named football stadium, the Baseball Ground.

They were excited by the afternoon's prospects. They had free tickets for the match, and they were looking forward to seeing for themselves how the home side had been transformed from Second Division also-rans into a team challenging for promotion under the guidance of their bright, inventive young manager, Brian Clough.

One of the schoolboys was Duncan Revie. It was to be an afternoon he wouldn't forget. 'I'd rung Dad up and said me and a pal would love to go and watch Derby County, would there be any chance of him getting us some tickets. Dad said, "I'll ring Brian and see what I can do." It was duly sorted out, and when we got to the Baseball Ground that day we knocked on the door at the main entrance and asked for our tickets. We were told to hold on, because Mr Clough wanted to speak to us.

'A few minutes later, Brian bounded down the stairs, greeted us warmly and said to me, "Duncan, young man, I want to tell you your father's the greatest manager of all time. Now come with me." He led us upstairs to the directors' lounge, gave us each a Coca-Cola and started to chat away.

'Now, for one thing, the time was 2.15. If that had been my dad at Elland Road, he would have told us to bugger off because he had important work to do preparing the team! But Brian just sat there with us, eulogising about my father, talking about him and Leeds United, how Derby aspired to be that good one day, and so on. He was fabulous company and made us feel so welcome.

'It gets to ten to three and I'm thinking, "This is ridiculous – doesn't he have work to do?" when suddenly he stands up and says, "Lads, I've got to go. I've got to go and talk to the lads downstairs. See you later." And that was my first meeting with Brian Clough.'

By the time Duncan Revie made that trip to the Baseball Ground, Clough and his father had already pitted their wits against each other three times that year – all of them cup ties and all in the space of just three weeks.

Derby, still in Division Two and being gradually moulded into a side in Clough and Taylor's image, had the misfortune to draw Leeds in both the FA Cup and the League Cup.

The latter was a thrilling adventure for them that season, with victories over Clough's old team Hartlepools United, Birmingham City, Lincoln City and Darlington propelling them towards the semi-final.

Clough's admiration for Revie and Leeds United knew no bounds, as was clear in an interview with the *Yorkshire Post* on the eve of the first of their semi-final encounters:

> They can teach my lads a lot – how hard they have to work, how much effort and dedication is required, in short, a complete picture of what we have to aim for in the future.
>
> Leeds must be the envy of nearly every club in the country with their spirit and running power and large pool of players. People tend to underestimate their individual ability, but make no mistake about it – these lads can play.

On the evening of 17 January, Derby's best crowd of the season, more than 31,000, watched the first leg and witnessed Clough's side test Leeds to the full. But their plucky effort was to no avail; centre-half Bobby Saxton needlessly handled from a corner in the closing stages, leaving Johnny Giles to coolly slot home the penalty to give the Elland Road side a narrow advantage.

Ten days later came the second instalment, this time an FA Cup third-round tie, and on this occasion nearly 40,000 spectators packed into the Baseball Ground. From start to finish, Revie's men mostly controlled a scrappy match, and goals from Lorimer and Charlton gave them a comfortable enough victory.

The third and final instalment – the second leg of the League Cup semi-final – came ten days later at Elland Road. Derby rattled Leeds with a goal from Kevin Hector in the first 15 minutes, but the home side recovered their poise with goals from Rod Belfitt (2) and Eddie Gray, before a late consolation goal from Arthur Stewart.

For now, Clough and Revie went their separate ways, Derby in pursuit of promotion, Leeds on the quest for silverware. Less than a month later, the Elland Road side finally acquired that elusive trophy when they beat Arsenal 1–0 in the League Cup final at Wembley. The gypsy curse that had so obsessed Revie had finally been laid to rest.

If truth were told, it was a drab affair for the large part, once Terry Cooper, in the 18th minute, had fired home a fierce left-foot volley through a crowd of players following a corner. Leeds were content to hold onto their lead, while Arsenal battled away ineffectually, the game punctuated by some tough tackling and ill-tempered exchanges.

No sooner did Leeds finally have one trophy in the bag than they picked up a second, just six months later. They reached the final of the Inter-Cities Fairs Cup, which in those days was held over from the end of one season until the beginning of the next.

Leeds faced Ferencváros of Hungary, widely recognised as one of Europe's finest and most cultured sides. Mick Jones, one of Revie's best – but perhaps least acclaimed – signings, a leggy, hard-working centre-forward with an excellent touch on the ball, gave the Elland Road side a narrow 1–0 lead in the home leg.

The expectation of most well-informed football experts was that Leeds would falter in the return leg in the Nep Stadium in Budapest. Ferencváros included in their ranks Flórián Albert, the reigning European Footballer of the Year, a dexterous, technically gifted player with excellent vision, superb passing skills of the Revie variety and an instinct for goal. Albert had almost single-handedly destroyed Brazil in Hungary's famous 3–1 victory in the 1966 World Cup.

But on the evening of Wednesday, 11 September, Gary Sprake turned in an inspired goalkeeping display and the Leeds defence stood firm, repelling wave after wave of attacks from Albert and co. A 0–0 draw meant Leeds were the first British winners of the trophy.

The celebrations went on long into the night, as Jeff Powell of the *Daily Mail*, who took part in them, recalls: 'We went to a nightclub after the game – players and football writers were much closer in those days. Anyway, I was there with Billy and Big Jack and all the boys, and it was champagne all round. Then, as the night drew to a close, a big dispute broke out over the bill. Big Jack was saying it's too much, we'll only pay for so many bottles, when a group of heavies arrived to "sort us out". Billy came out with the immortal line, "Everyone pick up a chair!" and all hell broke loose. There was a huge fight that spilled out onto the street.

'We all felt we'd acquitted ourselves pretty well and eventually headed back to the hotel, a few players with cuts on their heads, bruises, torn jackets and God knows what. Don was there to greet us at the door, and he surveyed the scene with some incredulity before turning to me and saying, "What have you done with my boys?" With a raised eyebrow, I replied, "Don, what have *I* done with your boys?"'

★ ★ ★

When Don Revie and Brian Clough next resumed their managerial duel, their status as the new power and the rising star in British football had been firmly established.

For Leeds, if 1967–68 was the Season of Achievement, with the League Cup and Fairs Cup triumphs, 1968–69 had been the Season of Destiny. Buoyed by their success against Ferencváros, they had started the new league season in awesome form, remaining unbeaten in the first twelve matches, with nine wins and three draws.

Everton, Arsenal and – above all – Liverpool valiantly kept up the challenge throughout winter and spring, but Leeds lost just two matches, and by 29 April, when they visited Anfield, only a point was needed to secure their first-ever league title.

It duly arrived after a fiercely competitive match, which ended in a 0–0 draw and The Kop generously saluting the enemy with a standing ovation. That great reception from the Anfield Choir was acknowledgement, finally, of Leeds' stature – and from some of the most partisan yet knowledgeable supporters in the country. It meant a lot to a club consistently criticised for its ruthless approach and tactics and all too rarely – in their eyes – applauded for the quality of their football.

Yet there had been nothing inevitable about the event. Don Revie had told his captain to take his side over to the Liverpool supporters if they triumphed, but Billy Bremner had been reluctant to do so when the moment arrived, as Eddie Gray recalled in his autobiography:

> As we approached the Kop end, the feeling that the gesture was
> going to blow up in our faces became increasingly pronounced.
> The Liverpool fans were clearly taken aback by it because you

could hardly hear a whisper from them. Their silence was almost eerie and it seemed to me to be only a matter of time before we were given an earful of abuse.

To our amazement, though, they suddenly started chanting: 'Champions . . . champions . . . champions.' The whole area seemed to explode. Those remarkable Liverpool fans were so enthusiastic in their applause that it was as if we had been transported back to Elland Road.

Six months later, on 25 October, Leeds were fifth in the league table when they took the field at Elland Road to face Derby County. Clough's side had made a coruscating start to their first season back in the top division and lay third, having been undefeated in their first eleven games, the last of the sequence a 5–0 trouncing of Tottenham Hotspur at the Baseball Ground.

That display, against Dave Mackay's old team, prompted the Spurs manager Bill Nicholson to describe Clough's side as a 'wonderful, wonderful team'. 'They humiliated us,' he confessed. 'They are very talented, and they don't just run, they know when to run and where.'

The clash of the champions and their potential successors was clearly the most attractive fixture on the list that day, and David Coleman and his BBC *Match of the Day* team joined more than 44,000 others in beating a path to Elland Road. They witnessed a game that lived up to its billing, both sides full of enterprise and speed, spreading the ball about in fluent, fluid movements involving defenders almost as much as attackers.

For Leeds, Eddie Gray that day lost nothing in comparison to George Best. A feint here, a shimmy of the hips there, and Derby's right-back Ron Webster was forever left trailing in his wake. Norman Hunter, too, had an exceptional game, displaying his more creative side, combining surging runs from defence with clever link-up play with Bremner and Giles.

For Derby, Dave Mackay strolled around the pitch playing his familiar role of headmaster to his younger players. Derby passed the ball neatly and cleverly, the man in possession always supported by two or three others, but they lacked a cutting edge.

Allan Clarke, Leeds' £165,000 signing from Leicester City at the start of the season, ultimately proved the difference between the two sides. He scored twice in the opening half, the first a simple header at the near post from a corner, the second when he latched on to a long pass from Mick Bates before rounding keeper Les Green and rolling the ball into an empty net.

It all left David Coleman in an almost euphoric mood. 'A first half of which English football can be proud,' he enthused. 'A wonderful, wonderful match – and the players so enjoyed it, too.'

There were no further goals in an equally entertaining second half, which ended with a rare tribute over the loudspeakers to Derby for 'playing football, which is more than can be said for some sides who come here'. One player was booked – Willie Carlin, Derby's terrier-like midfield player, for a pointless foul on Mick Bates.

After the match, Revie and Clough joined Coleman in the West Stand for a joint interview. It almost seemed as if they'd been placed in front of the cameras in positions that befitted their status in the game – Revie looking down on Clough, who stood several steps below him, with Coleman perched uncomfortably between them with the microphone.

The atmosphere was seemingly cordial, undoubtedly helped by Coleman's effusive introduction: 'I must say, I haven't enjoyed a match like that for a long, long time.' Revie was magnanimous in victory: 'Today, like all the times I've watched them on the box and on the field, they [Derby] played a lot of attractive football, and I think they're a very good side and a credit to the First Division.'

It's always been said on Clough's behalf that one of his great virtues was that he never criticised officials. Not so on this day, as he pointed the finger at the linesman who waved on Allan Clarke for the second goal. 'We felt he was a wee bit offside. The whole country will decide tonight when they watch it, and if he was offside like we feel, then Mr Barker might have an answer to give to the Football Association – like we have to when we drop clangers.'

The only frosty moment in the exchanges came with Clough's description of the Elland Road side: 'We've been through the Leeds machine today, came out of it quite well. I'm not quite sure why we didn't win. Perhaps it's because he [gesturing to Revie above] works harder than me or he's a better manager to me, because between the teams there was certainly nothing.'

Revie picked up on Clough's description of Leeds, irritated at the suggestion – not for the first time – that his team were mightily effective but functional rather than imaginative in their play:

Coleman: Now, you've often said that you wanted to be

215

respected for your football here at Leeds . . .
Revie: I just wondered what Brian was on about when he said
he'd been through the Leeds 'machine' . . . I wonder if he
meant footballing machine or what he meant . . .
Coleman: I was going to say – you've often said you want to be
respected as a football side rather than just efficient. But today
it was all there, wasn't it?

Revie's tetchiness came and went. The interview concluded with
Clough suggesting Leeds' 'talented side' could yet catch league leaders
Everton, while Revie was convinced the spectators would flock to
grounds 'if we turn on football like these two teams [have]'.

The men from Middlesbrough were at the height of their powers on
that autumn evening in 1969, comfortable enough in each other's
company and disposed towards mutual congratulation. Nobody would
suggest they were blood brothers – but no one could have predicted
the bitterness and recrimination that lay ahead in the coming years.

★ ★ ★

Years later, as they sat down with a drink on holiday in Portugal,
Duncan Revie asked his father what exactly had happened to sour his
relationship with Brian Clough. 'He just said, "I've got no idea what
happened there. None at all." He couldn't understand the antagonism
at the time, and he was still puzzled about it years later.'

One thing seems fairly clear from all the evidence available: the
antipathy that developed – which would have major consequences for
his career – was at Clough's initiation. Something – or some things –
that Revie did, real or imagined, wittingly or unwittingly, set Clough
off on a path from which he never turned back.

It's unlikely that the journey had started by 31 March 1970, the next
time Derby and Leeds clashed in the league. Clough could have been
forgiven for being put out when Revie turned up at the Baseball Ground
with a side composed entirely of reserves. The huge Easter crowd of
more than 41,000 certainly displayed their ire, jeering the Leeds side as
they ran out and booing them continually throughout a predictably
one-sided 90 minutes. They felt they had paid good money and been
cheated of a contest, and even a 4–1 win was no compensation.

Revie had rested his entire first team because he was overstretched
while battling on three fronts. Leeds faced a European Cup semi-final

against Celtic in just two days' time and then, twelve days away, an FA Cup final at Wembley against Chelsea.

Revie received staunch support from unlikely quarters. A *Times* editorial – perhaps guided by its football correspondent, the erudite Geoffrey Green, who was an admirer of Leeds – proclaimed: 'Small wonder if these commitments did not play some part in weighing the decision of whom to leave out and whom to include in a routine league match. The fact is that Leeds has made a great contribution to British football this season.'

As for Clough, if he felt any slight, he didn't betray any sign of it. 'They could have played their third team if they had wanted to – as long as we won.'

No, some time, somewhere, in 1970 or 1971 Clough's high regard for Revie began to disappear. There's almost something Shakespearian in this drama, the characters, the 'betrayal' and its consequences. Just as Brutus felt impelled to kill Julius Caesar once he believed he'd abandoned the high ideals of a republic and planned to make Rome into a monarchy under his own rule, so Clough would turn to verbal assassination after being convinced that Revie had betrayed the hallowed principles of the game he cherished.

Geoffrey Boycott likens Clough's attitude to Revie to his own towards Hansie Cronje when the South African cricket captain was found to have fixed matches. 'There was talk of underhand dealings in connection with Revie and Leeds,' he says. 'I'm in no position to say whether these stories were true or not. Now, I was friendly with Hansie Cronje, I liked him. We would go out together, he'd come and talk to me about his batting. When I found out what he'd done . . . oh my God, it wasn't just about what he'd done, it was about what he'd done to the game. He'd hurt the game we love, that we all care about. That's what Brian felt deep down about Don: this is our game, we love it, so how could you do something so underhand or demeaning?'

If the ill feeling Clough developed towards Revie can be attributed to one eye-opening moment, then Duncan Hamilton believes he may have the answer. Whenever the subject of Revie came up during the 20 years he knew Clough through his job as the reporter covering Nottingham Forest, the talk would often come back to one particular incident, as Hamilton recounts in *Provided You Don't Kiss Me*:

> Clough told me that he began to 'hate' Revie when he discovered
> him colluding with a referee after a match. Clough was

convinced that Revie had 'nobbled' the referee.

He had gone to watch Leeds and visited Revie in his office afterwards. He was standing behind the door, out of sight, when the referee tapped on it. Clough recalled: 'I heard the ref say to Revie, "Was that all right for you, Mr Revie?"'

Revie, Clough added, said a nervous 'marvellous' in reply, and waved him away, like a lord dismissing his butler. He carried on talking to Clough as if nothing had happened. 'There was something about it that told me the ref had been given something – and given Revie something in return,' said Clough. 'I knew Revie was bent.'

Firm evidence of corruption? Of match-fixing? Far from conclusive. Yet Clough was consistently adamant when discussing Revie with Hamilton that this was the turning point.

On a different scale of things, Clive Thomas felt uneasy about the way Leeds United dealt with referees. 'When you arrived at your dressing-room at Elland Road,' he remembers, 'you'd find on the table bootlaces, tie-ups, chewing gum, a bottle of liniment, all the little things you'd require for the game – although you'd probably have brought most of them with you. You might think, well, that's very good of them, and people might argue that's just being professional, but it wasn't to me. I felt there was a motive behind it.' Trying to get the referee on side with a gift or two? Or just proper preparation by the home side for the match, ensuring the officials could focus their minds on the decision-making to come?

A second theory about the Clough–Revie fall-out is proffered by Jeff Powell, chief sportswriter of the *Daily Mail*, a journalist who had an excellent working relationship with both men – especially Revie. Powell believes it dated back to a snub Clough felt he'd suffered at Revie's hands before a Derby v. Leeds match at the Baseball Ground.

'As an acknowledgement of the status of Leeds as champions, when they went to play a match at Derby Clough personally laid out the kit of the visiting side in their dressing-room. In the rush to get away after the game during a crowded period of important fixtures, Revie forgot to thank him and Clough took offence. Then, when Revie went to make amends with the gift of a bottle of vintage wine after Derby's return match at Elland Road, Old Big 'Ead ignored the gesture and The Don felt slighted.

'Don tended to breeze through everywhere, a great centrifugal force, and he'd not responded to Cloughie's romantic gesture in the way Brian probably expected. There he was, deferring to the man who had had all these great achievements, and I'm pretty sure he would have liked Don to come up and give him a bear hug. He was disappointed; it was a gesture that went more or less unrecognised, and he felt slighted.'

Hamilton's is the 'big bang' theory; Powell's episode is more a contributory cause to explain the rancour and suspicion that followed.

Johnny Crossan, a colleague at Sunderland and a good friend of his throughout his life, says Clough's view of Revie was straightforward. 'This whole Revie thing . . . talking to Brian, he would say, he stole all his bloody awards, he bought those awards. He would talk very calmly and openly about Revie. "He's a bloody crook," he used to say, "He's a bloody crook."'

Footballers are instinctively loyal to one another and the profession as a whole, even with the passage of time. Their equivalent of *omertà* descended on a few conversations about the reasons behind Clough's enmity towards Revie. The 'real story' is hinted at, but never disclosed.

On a broader front, others have claimed to have probed more deeply into allegations of corruption surrounding Revie. The most detailed of these was Richard Stott's investigation for the *Daily Mirror*, culminating in a series of articles published in September 1977. Stott claimed to have exposed five games Revie had allegedly tried to fix, and suggested that his investigation showed 'an overwhelming catalogue of bribery and double-dealing that went to the heart of the game in England'.

One of the games he claimed Revie/Leeds had attempted to rig was the Wolverhampton Wanderers v. Leeds league match at Molineux on 8 May 1972, the very last game of the season. Leeds had defeated Arsenal 1–0 in the Centenary FA Cup final two days earlier, so they went into the match at Molineux needing just a draw to win the Double – and deny Clough's Derby County the championship.

First, the match itself. Leeds were dogged by fatigue and injuries; they were without Mick Jones, who had been badly injured in the Wembley final, and a number of players including Clarke, Giles and Gray were carrying knocks that might have kept them out of a less important match. Wolves, mid-table and with only pride to play for, nonetheless displayed fierce commitment, and goals from Frank Munro and Derek Dougan put them 2–0 up midway through the second half. Billy Bremner pulled a goal back after latching on to a long pass from Paul Madeley, and Leeds launched a series of furious assaults on the Wolves goal in the dying minutes. Terry Yorath had a shot cleared off the line, and both Clarke and Lorimer had claims for penalties brushed aside. But Wolves held on, and the title went to Derby – with their team on holiday in Majorca and their manager in the Scilly Isles.

Then came the allegations. First, the *Sunday People* claimed that three Wolves players had been offered money to 'take it easy' and effectively throw the match. The Football League initiated an inquiry and the matter was referred to the Director of Public Prosecutions, but no further action was taken.

A few years on and the *Mirror* campaign hit the front page. When, soon afterwards, the *Sunday People*, the *Mirror*'s sister paper, returned to the fray, repeating the allegations about the Wolves game and adding some more, Billy Bremner decided to go to court.

Bremner sued the publishers of the *Sunday People* and ex-Wolves midfield player Danny Hegan, who had made the allegation that Bremner had offered him £1,000 to give away a penalty in the match on 8 May. The *Sunday People* had also claimed that Bremner had tried to fix games against Southampton in 1962 and Nottingham Forest in 1971.

Bremner won the day. After a six-day hearing in the High Court, the jury dismissed the *Sunday People*'s claims and awarded him £100,000 damages plus costs.

The lazy cliché 'There's no smoke without fire' is often trotted out when fresh – or recycled – stories about Revie and Leeds emerge. The plain fact of the matter is that no footballing body and no court has ever found the manager or his players culpable of any offence of corruption of any sort.

It seems that for a variety of reasons – envy of his achievements, distaste over the methods that took them to the summit, resentment over the way he would later leave the England job – Revie became fair game. More than that, he became the prey of choice.

Of course, it would be naive in the extreme to suggest that corruption didn't exist in the game to some extent in the 1960s and 1970s. We've already seen proof of the pudding with the 1965 trial in which Sheffield Wednesday players Peter Swan, Tony Kay and David Layne – and others – were jailed for conspiracy to defraud. In this period, more money was coming into the game and the stakes were higher in the struggle for promotion and relegation. Temptation will have trapped some players, managers and administrators. But the narrow, claustrophobic, often febrile world of football is a place where rumours abound, stories are exaggerated and people's motives need to be questioned very carefully.

Brian Clough's views about Don Revie may or may not have changed as a result of one Dasmascene moment. That aside, he was definitely starting to form a very different view of Leeds than the one he'd clearly held back in 1969. As Derby played Leeds more regularly, and as Clough also surveyed Revie's men from the vantage point of the television studios (where he was spending an increasing amount of time), admiration turned to distaste for what he increasingly believed was their cynical approach to the game.

As Peter Taylor commented: 'Brian was the first and foremost of Don's critics and made him the butt of such outrageous comments as "You have to listen carefully to what Don says, and think about it. Then either swallow it, or bring it up."'

Taylor shared his managerial partner's views about Revie and did little to discourage his growing obsession. He only started to worry when he felt Clough might be being distracted from his job, especially when Derby versus Leeds games came around. Years later, Clough made it perfectly clear what he had come to think about the Elland Road side:

> I despised what they stood for – systematically putting referees under intolerable pressure with their violent behaviour, both physical and verbal, their overreactions, and the unsavoury spectacle of skipper Billy Bremner running alongside the harassed referee, constantly yelling in his ear.
>
> They angered and offended me to such an extent that I took every opportunity to condemn their cynicism, which, for me, devalued so much of what they achieved and the marvellous football of which they were capable – a high level of skill and organised teamwork that I, like millions, admired. Leeds in those days cheated – and I was more than happy to draw people's attention to the fact.

But it has to be said that the simple fact of the matter was that Derby almost always came off second best as the two sides fought for supremacy – along with Arsenal and Liverpool – in the First Division.

In their six league and League Cup encounters from October 1970 to October 1972, Leeds won four, Derby one (in their championship-winning season of 1971–72) and there was one draw. At Elland Road in March 1971, Leeds won 1–0 with a Lorimer goal despite the absence – through sickness and injury – of Cooper, Gray, Bremner, Clarke and Sprake. Then, in October 1972, the new FA Cup holders (Leeds had deservedly defeated Arsenal 1–0 in the centenary final at Wembley in May) hammered Derby 5–0 at home, a masterful Johnny Giles establishing his side's superiority with penetrative passes and two goals before limping off in the fiftieth minute. Lorimer, who always performed well against Derby (and who would be the butt of Clough's jibes just three months later), scored the final goal.

That was a day when charges of foul play could be laid very firmly at the door of Clough and Derby. Eric Todd of *The Guardian* reported: 'The forces of evil were greater than those for good, so that at the end one was left not savouring the quality of so much fine Leeds football but contemplating sadly the deplorable cynicism with which one footballer can treat another.'

Of the four players booked, three were from Derby, including McFarland 'who almost sliced Lorimer in half', Todd 'for a squalid foul on Jones' and Durban; the other was Norman Hunter who 'did a sort of bicycle exercise into O'Hare's stomach'. McFarland, Todd and Hunter were 'lucky indeed to remain on the field'.

As Clough continued to snipe away at Leeds and Revie in print (where he was as prolific as ever) and on TV, so the heat simultaneously seemed to be turned up when their sides met on the pitch. Matches at the Baseball Ground started to become especially fierce encounters. The tight little stadium with the supporters close to the action – not to mention the cloying mud on the pitch itself, which often resembled a ploughed field – contributed to the intense atmosphere.

John O'Hare was usually in the thick of the action at centre-forward for Derby. 'I always got the impression from very early on that they [Clough and Revie] didn't like each other very much. Whether it was professional – I do feel there might well have been a bit of envy on Brian's behalf, because Leeds were a terrific team – or personal, I couldn't say. But those were real needle games, games with a hard edge to them. Leeds were the best and we at Derby were the upstarts. I would say there was generally no maliciousness. Hunter and Charlton were just hard guys who did their job. You expected to get kicked now and again. The ones who were a bit nasty were elsewhere on the pitch.'

Clashes between Archie Gemmill and Billy Bremner, two highly skilled but combative midfield players, were often explosive affairs, as Gemmill explained in his autobiography: 'It's true we used to be tigerish against each other at club level, but that was par for the course whenever Derby and Leeds met. The players carried on the ill-feeling that always seemed to exist between their managers, Brian Clough and Don Revie.'

From Eddie Gray's perspective at Leeds, it was Clough's frustration at so rarely being able to match Revie's side that led to the bitter atmosphere. 'I think Brian might well have been a bit envious of what Don achieved,' he says, 'plus the fact that when his side played against us they found it difficult to beat us. Yes, there was an edge to those games, but then again there was an edge to a lot of games in those days. They were a good side, Derby, but their pitch didn't help; the ball would always be sticking in the mud and players couldn't get away from their opponents as quickly as they normally could, so consequently there would always be collisions.'

Gray's wing partner Peter Lorimer, so often the scourge of the Derby defence, thinks Clough used his well-publicised rivalry with Revie and Leeds to motivate his players. 'Brian tried to make it that way. There's no question. We were the best team, and it was his way of trying to upset the apple cart, get the Derby fans wound up. That's just the way he was.'

As time wore on, referees who took charge of these games also sensed an added dimension to the normal top-of-the-table clash. Clive Thomas, for one, could feel it and it meant he needed to be on his mettle even more. He recalls: 'The personal animosity – why that was so I couldn't say – showed without a doubt when you refereed those two sides. Without any doubt, I sensed it every time. It conveyed itself on the field to the players, and you knew you had a tough game on when you had to deal with those two sides.'

Thomas, however, contrasts the behaviour of the two sets of players on the pitch: 'The Leeds players would react by trying to get anything out of you. Derby would not. You'd give a free kick against McFarland and his hand would go up – "Sorry, ref" – acknowledging and accepting the decision that had gone against him. You did that to Bremner and his arms would be up in the air as if he was on at the Palladium – "Why are you giving that, ref?" So you would begin to question yourself, and when you had to next take a decision against Leeds you would wonder, did I get it right the last time? Psychologically, you were under pressure all the time. Now, I never felt like that when making decisions on Derby.'

Thomas was – is – a particularly strong critic of Revie's Leeds. But his views weren't necessarily held by all of his colleagues at the time. The Durham-born referee Pat Partridge was one of the most respected of his generation, officiating in five Wembley cup finals, a European Cup-Winners' Cup final and a World Cup:

> The most frequent accusation against Bremner was that he tried to referee matches. That was rubbish at least when I was around. Sure, he yapped away all the time and he challenged decisions you made, but never in a way which you could send him off. It was all down to respect – if he had that for you, it was all right.

* * *

On Sunday, 28 January 1973, Clough travelled up to Leeds to be one of the special guests at an evening event at the Queens Hotel. Hosted by Yorkshire Television with the Variety Club of Great Britain, it was designed to celebrate the very best of international sport and for the county to select a sports personality of the year.

Five hundred guests took their seats in the elegant, art deco building. With speakers of the quality of Harold Wilson (former prime minister, then leader of the opposition), comedian Leslie Crowther and Clough himself, all was set fair for an entertaining evening. The chief constable of Leeds City Police, James Angus, was also among the audience.

Peter Lorimer had been forewarned that he'd won the coveted top award. Leeds had an FA Cup replay against Norwich City the following evening in Birmingham, but Revie was happy for Lorimer to stay and receive the trophy as long as a car was standing by to whisk him off to the Midlands straight afterwards.

Harold Wilson presented Lorimer with his award, the pictures were taken and the Leeds winger, thrilled to have followed in the footsteps of Jackie Stewart, left the room and headed for Birmingham. He never heard what followed.

Clough stood up to speak and promptly told his audience: 'I have sat here now for approximately two and a half hours, and I am not replying to anything or anybody until I have had a wee. And I'm being very serious – you get on your bloody feet and go to the toilet, you get a beer, and then if you've not got to get up early in the morning, get back and listen.'

Eleven minutes elapsed before Clough returned. He then launched into an astonishing tirade against the Leeds team. First of all, he informed the absent award winner that he'd won 'despite the fact that he falls when he hasn't been kicked, and despite the fact that he protests when he has nothing to protest about'.

Then he turned his fire on others, as John Helm, who covered the event for BBC Radio Leeds, recalls: 'He absolutely tore the Leeds players to shreds. This is where he first came out with his famous statement about Eddie Gray, that if he'd been a racehorse he would have been shot. He said Bremner was a little cheat. He said the side should be deducted ten points and relegated for all the cheating and cynical football they'd put on. Of course, everyone in the audience was just absolutely gobsmacked, because these players were idols to the Yorkshire public and here was someone lambasting them in front of them, when they didn't think he was a manager to lace Revie's boots anyway.'

Clough's outburst was greeted with shouts of 'get off' and 'sit down', but he merely responded to the hecklers by saying, 'I was not particularly glad with the idea of speaking to you lot. I have to stand up here, but you are sitting in the crowd, which hides you.' He then described one complaining member of the audience as a 'mumbler', adding, 'We are becoming a nation of mumblers. Stand on your feet if you have anything to say. Come up here and make the speech if you think you could do better than me.'

Eventually, he realised he had gone too far and told the crowd, 'If I have made a mockery of Yorkshire sport, I apologise. I was told before I came that no matter what I made of my speech, the dignity of the occasion would prevail.'

There had been little dignity in Clough's performance. He sat down to boos, then signed some autographs, while many guests decided they'd had enough and left the room.

When Yorkshire TV aired the programme, Clough was cut out of it. Lawrie Higgins, YTV's head of sport, explained, 'I wouldn't give this man a minute of our time. He was insulting to many people. It is always a gamble when you invite someone to speak – but responsible people don't usually act in this way.'

Clough was unrepentant in the following days. He told the *Daily Mirror*:

They didn't tell me beforehand it was being filmed. They didn't

brief me on what I could and could not say. And if in future they
want a puppet to get up and say something to please everybody
in the room, I suggest they invite Basil Brush, instead of asking
a football manager to give up his only day off of the week.

Clough suggested that the Leeds supporters in the audience had
behaved as they did 'because they still haven't forgiven Derby for
winning the League One championship'. Observers at the dinner noted
that Clough had been annoyed because his name on the toast line was
'Brian Clough, manager of Derby County', when he felt it should have
read 'Brian Clough, manager of Derby County, First Division
Champions'.

Later on, Clough would acknowledge that his behaviour that night
left something to be desired. The apology he offered, however, was to
Harold and Mary Wilson, not to anyone at Leeds United: 'I wrote to
the Wilsons, sending flowers to Mary and telling them that my rudeness
in Leeds all those years ago had been "on my conscience for too long".
They wrote back, a kind letter as always, and I'm glad I got it off my
mind.'

* * *

That evening would have far-reaching consequences for Clough's
career. In the short term, the developing acrimony between himself
and Revie – and their players – plumbed new depths in a quite vicious
encounter at the Baseball Ground just over a month later.

The match on 3 March was played on a pitch that resembled 'a
harbour at low tide' – as Eric Todd of *The Guardian* graphically
described it – and contained no less than 55 fouls in the 90 minutes, 29
of them committed by Leeds.

Referee Ron Challis booked just two players, Norman Hunter of
Leeds and Roger Davies of Derby County, but half a dozen others
could easily have been added to his list. If it had been played today, it
would probably have ended up as a four-a-side game.

The boots of Davies and Allan Clarke collided with the heads of
Paul Madeley and Roy McFarland; one of Gordon McQueen's first acts
on his debut was to cart John McGovern over the touchline and into a
low wall; Hunter mercilessly hacked down Archie Gemmill in the mud
in the centre of the pitch. The list of often quite brutal infringements
was endless.

In amongst it all shone some moments of exceptional football, none better than Alan Durban's curling right-foot free kick into the top left-hand corner of the net, which put Derby 1–0 up after 25 minutes. Durban was an old hand in these games. 'The one thing about Leeds was that if you upset one of them, you'd upset all of them,' he says. 'It was one for all and all for one, as far as they were concerned. They had six or seven who could really dish it out, and remember you could get away with a good deal more then than you can do now.'

Lorimer equalised with a dubious penalty before half-time, but Kevin Hector's header at the far post restored Derby's lead shortly after the interval. Another Lorimer penalty – again extremely doubtful, after Hunter went to ground in the penalty area after no more than a suggestion of a push – restored parity. Then Colin Todd left a back pass way too short and Allan Clarke nipped in to slot the ball past Colin Boulton for Leeds' winner.

In fact, there were a host of other fouls that went unpunished in this match, not to mention umpteen sly nudges and kicks. An FA Cup quarter-final tie between the two sides was scheduled for a fortnight's time, and Eric Todd caustically remarked, 'To be on the safe side, a knowledge of probationary work or guerrilla warfare would be an advantage to the referee appointed.'

The bitterness lasted long after the final whistle, as Clough and Revie sparred in front of the TV cameras. Revie was first off the mark: 'Who's Brian Clough kidding when he says Derby are skilful and entertaining? They're a bit tough. In fact, they're the toughest we've played this season.' Clough countered, 'I keep hearing Revie saying that Eddie Gray needs protection from referees. I'll endorse that and also say teams over the years have needed protection from Leeds.'

The row rumbled on for a few days before a truce of sorts was called. Revie offered some words of praise for Clough – although the criticisms remained: 'Brian Clough has done a great job at Derby. He's one of the best managers in the business. But I wish he wouldn't keep having a go at people like Sir Alf Ramsey and Matt Busby. Surely, they have proved themselves. As for attacking football, look at Derby's away record. They've only scored nine away goals all season.'

In fact, the FA Cup encounter on 17 March proved thankfully free of grudge and defensive belligerence. Clough was away at the time, spending time with his mother, Sally, at Eston Hospital, Middlesbrough, where she was dying of cancer.

After Lorimer volleyed home Mick Jones' downward header just before the half-hour, Leeds held on comfortably for a 1–0 win, which was crafted mainly by the dominance of Giles and Bremner in midfield but also fortified by the return of Eddie Gray.

The closing months of the 1972–73 season were amongst the blackest in the football careers of both Revie and Clough. For the latter, the disappointments on the pitch paled into insignificance beside the loss of his mother:

> Nothing prepared me for the news she had gone. I'm sure I didn't say a word for several seconds. I immediately saw her face. I thought about her in that little woolly hat. I thought about her cleaning all those pairs of shoes. I thought about her hanging out the washing and standing at the mangle and leading us like a row of little ducks to church on Sundays. I thought about her being always there when I returned home from school. And I cried a little.

On the pitch, Derby's brilliant European Cup run ended in acrimonious fashion when they lost their semi-final first leg tie 3–1 to Juventus in Turin.

To add insult to injury, McFarland and Gemmill were inexplicably booked (ensuring that both would miss the return leg), and Derby's suspicions about the German referee, Gerhard Schulenberg, were only heightened when he was seen in jocular conversation at half-time with his compatriot Helmut Haller, a Juventus substitute on the night.

Collusion? Corruption? No substantial proof, but Clough and Taylor were infuriated by that meeting and by events on the pitch. Taylor was even arrested – after a fashion – by police at the ground, who detained him for half an hour or so after a contretemps with Haller. After the game, Clough dismissed local journalists with the words 'I will not speak to cheating bastards' – making sure they understood what he was saying by getting writer Brian Glanville, an Italian speaker, to translate.

The return game at the Baseball Ground ended 0–0, Derby's chances fading away after Roger Davies was sent off. They finished their league season with three victories (and nine goals), but it couldn't disguise a disappointing campaign after the heady days of the previous spring. Seventh place in the table – despite the European triumphs – was unsatisfactory for Clough and Taylor.

If Derby had encountered the sometimes cynical world of Italian football, so did Revie and Leeds when they took on AC Milan in Thessaloniki on 16 May in the final of the Cup-Winners' Cup.

It was hard enough without the.services of Bremner, Clarke, Giles and Gray. But when Greek referee Christos Michas began to give a series of puzzling decisions – including turning down two obvious penalty claims – it became a well-nigh impossible task for Leeds.

AC Milan ran out 1–0 winners, thanks to a sixth-minute goal from forward Luciano Chiarugi. Chiarugi, an Italian international, who had the sobriquet 'Cavallo Pazzo' ('Crazy Horse'), was noted for his propensity to fall to the ground relatively easily. The Italian media created the neologism 'chiarugismo', a synonym of 'football diving'.

The reverberations from that game lasted long after the final whistle had gone; in 2006, Richard Corbett, Labour MEP for Yorkshire and the Humber, even tried – unsuccessfully, as it turned out – to get UEFA to look at the match again for evidence of match-fixing, following corruption scandals in Italian football involving Milan, Juventus, Lazio and Fiorentina.

But by far Revie's biggest blow in the 1972–73 season had come 11 days earlier at Wembley. Sunderland, then in the Second Division and managed by his long-time adversary Bob Stokoe, beat Leeds 1–0 in the FA Cup final at Wembley.

Rarely had there been stronger favourites. But, as the Leeds players admitted afterwards, it was their complacent approach that cost them dear, while the underdogs chased, harried and played with no little skill to earn their triumph.

Ian Porterfield scored the only goal of the game with a sweet volley with the foot – the right one – he normally just stood on. But the Sunderland keeper Jim Montgomery went down in Wembley folklore with a string of great saves, one of them from a point-blank shot from Lorimer that he somehow deflected upwards and onto the crossbar.

Stokoe had told all who would listen over the years that Revie had once tried to bribe him to throw a match when he was player-manager of Bury – an accusation, like all the others against the Leeds manager, that has never been proved. However, whatever the rights and wrongs of that, it spurred Stokoe on and made his victory all the sweeter.

With the summer break nearly over, it might have been expected that Clough would concentrate his thoughts and efforts on a fresh attempt to win back the championship title. Instead, he chose to go back into print with his fiercest attack yet on Revie's Leeds.

The back-page lead story in the *Sunday Express* on 5 August was headlined 'I Would Put Leeds in Division Two – Brian Clough lashes Soccer's bosses for letting off Don Revie's "bad boys"'.

What had angered the Derby manager was a Football Association disciplinary commission hearing the previous week. Leeds had been let off relatively lightly over their record of conduct on the pitch for the 1971–72 campaign. The punishment of a £3,000 fine had been handed down – but it was effectively suspended, as it wouldn't be collected from the Elland Road side if they showed a 'substantial improvement' in the coming season. Clough was apoplectic with rage:

> Leeds United should be starting the new season in the Second Division. The Football Association should have instantly relegated Don Revie's team after branding them one of the dirtiest clubs in Britain. As it is, the befuddled minds of the men who run the game have missed the most marvellous chance of cleaning up Soccer in one swoop.
>
> No wonder Don Revie was smiling broadly as he left the disciplinary commission hearing in London. I looked at his happy face staring at me out of my newspaper in Spain. It just about spoiled my holiday to read that the £3,000 fine has been suspended until the end of the coming season.

Clough went on to liken the punishment to 'breathalysing a drunken driver, getting a positive reading, giving him the keys back and telling him to watch it on his way home'. Later in the article, he attempted to head off the criticism he knew would come his way:

> There will be those who accuse me of having a go at Don Revie and Leeds because I envy them. That is nonsense. Sure I envy Don Revie's Elland Road set-up. More than once I have called him the shrewdest manager in the business. I will not retract from that.
>
> But I do not envy him his team's reputation and I feel strongly that the tuppence ha'penny fine is the most misguided piece of woolly thinking ever perpetrated by the FA – a body hardly noted for its commonsense.

Revie's response came quickly, and in language unusually blunt – at least in public – from him: 'We all know that he can walk on water. If he is not criticising Sir Alf Ramsey it has to be somebody else. This time he has chosen Leeds United. I think it is time he shut his mouth.'

More ominously for Clough, his own chairman, Sam Longson, agreed with those sentiments. 'It is time Brian made up his mind what he wants to do and to get on and do it,' he said. 'If he decides this time that he wants to get out of soccer, to give himself a free platform to speak his mind about the Football Association, Leeds United and just about everybody else, then I will not stand in his way.'

On the eve of the new season, Clough seemed almost out of control. His self-confidence, his ego, knew no limits, and it was dragging him into dangerous waters. He would also admit later that the death of his mother – to whom he'd been very close – had affected his thinking in this period.

His feud with Revie was at its height. He faced almost certain disciplinary action of his own from the FA after his comments about Leeds. His flirtation with the idea of a larger role as a media pundit was growing, and he was on the verge of fresh talks with ITV.

All of this infuriated Longson, who was dismayed that Clough was in the spotlight all the time, often, as he saw it, to the detriment of Derby County Football Club. A reckoning loomed.

Chapter 11

'He Won't Be There Long'

By the autumn of 1973, there was a growing sense that the Great BBC Television Revolution was over. All the pioneering work of director general Hugh Greene and controller of BBC1 Paul Fox from the mid-1960s onwards was gradually being cast aside in favour of blander, reassuring family-based programmes – a conservative schedule to suit the fourth year of a Tory government.

That would be the liberal interpretation anyway. For example, the days of cutting-edge political satire, in the form of *That Was the Week That Was*, appeared all but over. One of its successors, *Up Sunday*, was being carefully vetted by BBC executives and would prove to be a pale shadow of *TWTWTW*. John Wells, who worked on both, reflected that *Up Sunday* was 'something like a retreat from Moscow'.

Dissension had given way to deference. Controversial drama like *Up the Junction* and *Cathy Come Home*, with challenging social themes, was rarely commissioned. In its place, game shows, mildly diverting comedy and classic films won prime slots in the schedule.

Despite these changes, there was still much to admire. In the 'educate' category of John Reith's historic brief for the nation came *The Ascent of Man*, a brilliant 13-part series about the history of science and technology, written and presented with immense flair by the Jewish mathematician and biologist Jacob Bronowski.

Then there was Michael Parkinson. Such was the regard for his talents – and his ability to boost the ratings – that on the weekend of Saturday, 20 October and Sunday, 21 October he appeared on both evenings. On Saturday, he hosted his usual one-hour show at 11.15 p.m., following *Match of the Day*, while on Sunday at 11 p.m. viewers could watch a special hour-long interview he'd conducted with Hollywood actor Jack Lemmon.

Those tuning in on Saturday night were anticipating animated conversation – and almost certainly a touch of controversy – when two bright, young (relatively speaking), articulate Yorkshiremen, born just a week apart in 1935, sat down together.

Parkinson and his show's main guest, Brian Clough, settled back to discuss the nation's World Cup exit, managerial resignations, directors, politics and much more at the end of a day filled with depressing news, both foreign and domestic.

At the top of the bulletins were events in the Middle East, where the Yom Kippur War was entering its third week, the tide finally turning decisively in favour of the Israeli forces, which were now only 50 miles from Cairo. But a worldwide oil embargo would follow shortly, plunging Britain – whose coal stocks were rapidly dwindling due to a miners' overtime ban – into an energy crisis the like of which the country had never experienced before.

Then there were concerns much closer to home. As guests made their way to the Parkinson show's studio at BBC TV Centre in Shepherd's Bush, they might well have kept a wary eye out for loose bags and suspiciously parked vehicles. The IRA had made it clear that they were now concentrating their terrorist attacks on the mainland, with particular emphasis on London. In September alone, in the space of five days, bombs had exploded at Victoria Station and in two underground stations, and then – on the same day – large devices were detonated in Oxford Street and Sloane Square.

So, as Brian Clough walked down the curved stairway to the accompaniment of Harry Stoneham's jazzy signature tune, the packed audience in W12 – and several million watching at home – were looking for some lively, spicy exchanges to end their day on a more optimistic note.

Parkinson's 1973 series was arguably one of his best ever. Among the guests were actor and film director Orson Welles – who famously walked into Parkinson's dressing-room, ripped up his list of questions and told his host, 'We'll just talk' – Jacob Bronowski (Parkinson considered their interview to be his best ever, the highlight of which was Bronowski's poignant description of his visit to Auschwitz, where he had lost many relations) and the mercurial footballer George Best.

Parkinson, with his love of Yorkshire cricket and Barnsley Football Club, liked to feature sportsmen and sportswomen on his show as much as Hollywood actors like Bing Crosby or David Niven and writers like W.H. Auden. 'These days you have to be a disgraced footballer to get on, bragging about your sexual exploits,' he says. 'But then I could indulge my love of sport and have, I hope, more thoughtful and illuminating conversations with those I admired. I was always fascinated by Clough. In some ways, he was a strange, strange man. But he was absolutely made for television. He was opinionated, he was funny, he was irreverent, he was articulate and he was bright, too. In terms of his personality and outspokenness, you might compare him to Gordon Ramsay today. He was an easy choice for the show.'

Clough's journey to London was delayed by a puncture to his BBC limousine – symptomatic of the fraught week he'd endured. Typically, he'd just packed more turmoil and controversy into seven days than most football managers would fit into a lifetime.

On Tuesday, after six years in which he'd raised up not just a football club but a town and a whole community, Clough had left Derby County. Ironically, in view of where he was that Saturday night, it was television that had finally done for him. In August, he'd turned down the chance to succeed Jimmy Hill as ITV's soccer analyst, but he'd secured continuing employment with the company as a part-time pundit on his friend Brian Moore's show *On the Ball*, and chairman Sam Longson was far from happy about that.

There was a certain inevitability about what subsequently happened, as Peter Taylor recounted in *With Clough by Taylor*:

> Derby's board tried to gag Brian. He refused to be restrained, so the directors delivered an ultimatum, 'Stop engaging in literary work by writing articles in the press and stop entering into commitments with radio and television.'
>
> The letter was signed by Sam Longson. We read it together and immediately resigned together. I saw our position as the outcome of Brian's false relationship with the chairman, something I had warned Brian about for years.

Clough believed the chairman had used the issue as an excuse to get rid of him. 'Sam Longson was chuntering on, saying it could be detracting from my job and so on and so forth,' he recalled later. 'I was doing no more last year or the year before than I'd been doing five years ago. He used to loan me his car to go to the TV studios in those days!'

Taylor felt Longson had revelled in the exposure Clough had brought his club until he grew jealous of his manager's high profile in the game – and beyond it. Longson used to refer to Clough publicly as his 'adopted son', but the cracks in the Derby 'family' had, in truth, been developing for many months.

The day after Clough and Taylor handed in their resignation letter, Clough set off to Wembley in his new role as ITV chief pundit to comment on England's vital World Cup qualifying match against Poland.

His performance on that calamitous night for English football was bizarre. Before the game, he brandished a small object before the eyes of the audience and said provocatively, 'I've got a nail here in my hand and I want it to go in the Polish coffin – or perhaps it could go in Sir Alf's.'

He went on to describe Poland's goalkeeper Jan Tomaszewski as a 'clown'. Some clown. Clough was forced to eat his words – which he did with great reluctance – as Tomaszewski pulled off save after save, beating back waves of attacks from the likes of Allan Clarke, Tony Currie, Mick Channon, Colin Bell and then – most dramatically – Derby's own Kevin Hector in the last minute.

Then, on Saturday afternoon, just before he was set to travel down to London for the Parkinson show, Clough lit the fuse of rebellion at the Baseball Ground when he made an extraordinary appearance minutes before the kick-off of the Derby County v. Leicester City game.

The fans made their views crystal clear with a demonstration, banners proclaiming 'Clough In, Directors Out' and 'Clough Is King'. There was an uneasy mood inside and outside the ground, and extra police were employed, with plain-clothes men even guarding Longson and his colleagues on the board.

Then Clough made a remarkable, brief appearance, striding into the directors' box in much the same way as his hero Frank Sinatra might have stepped onto the stage in Las Vegas. Sitting just a few seats away from Longson, he stood and milked the resounding applause for several minutes. Longson responded by flinging his arms aloft as though the acclaim had been for him rather than Clough.

Pursued by the waiting press pack, Clough comfortably outpaced them all before reaching his chauffeur-driven Rolls-Royce, which then whisked him home. Soon afterwards, with Barbara and Peter Taylor, he set out from Derby and on the 130-mile journey down to London and *Parkinson*.

To watch Clough that October evening was to witness a man – despite the troubles of previous days – at the height of his powers.

Dressed immaculately in a fashionable light-grey suit with matching lilac shirt and tie, he was the very picture of health and vitality. The television studio was an environment in which he felt completely at ease. The audience expected much from 'The Great Chatsby' – as his principal impersonator, Mike Yarwood, had dubbed him – and rarely did he disappoint.

In many ways, his performance that night summed up his whole career in public – articulate, engaging, funny and just occasionally self-deprecating ('I accept without any shadow of a doubt that I talk too much') but with stinging, overblown attacks on those he felt had wronged him.

Longson's blood pressure must have shot up at much of the early conversation. 'I'm not leaving the town,' Clough told Parkinson. 'I would go back under one condition – the people who run Derby would have to be replaced with people of integrity.'

Asked if there was any validity in the argument of Longson and others that all his utterances on television and radio had brought the game into disrepute, he responded acidly: 'The very sight of them brings the game into disrepute – and when they open their mouths they kill it. These are the people who can't put two words together, and it's embarrassing that men like that will stop men like me talking to the likes of you.'

There was a dig, too, at the game's administrators – not a wise move for a man who, even then, aspired to become England manager. Reminded of Football League secretary Alan Hardaker's comment that disappointed English football fans would forget all about the World Cup in six weeks' time, he retorted, 'That is criminal. Get him on and ask him why he says silly things like that. It is silly, and it is wrong.'

In the discussion, there was a clue to Clough's volatile behaviour in the previous year. Responding to a question about the influence of his parents, Clough replied, 'I was very close to me mam and dad, very, very close. Me mam died nine to ten months ago, and this could have caused an upheaval with me, in actual fact, which I'm not aware of. I'm not quite sure if I've recovered from me mam dying.'

Public meetings, petitions, threatened strike action by the players – Clough's protracted departure from Derby dragged on for some time. He was behind much of the plotting, encouraging the official protest movement that would march through the town and using his contacts in the press to get the best possible coverage.

But eventually it became clear to Clough and Taylor that there was no way back. Longson, who had cleverly called their bluff, now played his next, decisive card by inviting Dave Mackay to be Clough's successor. The players respected Mackay and found themselves on the horns of a dilemma, bound by their loyalty and affection for Clough but wanting to get on with their careers, realising that the tough Scotsman would be the next best thing if they couldn't bring their old manager back.

Once the protests had started to fizzle out, Clough and Taylor had to think about fresh employment. Clough wanted to take some time away from the game, travel the world and see some of his heroes – sporting and otherwise – in the flesh; Taylor, kicking his heels in Majorca, wanted another job at once.

When the offer to return to management arrived for the two of them, it came within weeks and from the most unlikely of sources. Brighton & Hove Albion were in the lower reaches of the Third Division, a club with a congenial setting but absolutely no footballing pedigree. In some ways, it would be like returning to Hartlepools United – except this time the expectations on the two men would be much greater.

The big difference was the chairman of Brighton, the personable and highly persuasive Mike Bamber, and the financial inducements he could offer. The latter began with a £14,000 signing-on fee for Clough and Taylor. Clough was immediately impressed by his new chairman, and he recalled, 'He turned out to be the nicest and best chairman I ever worked with. Nothing was too much trouble. He looked after me like a king.'

But the reality was that Clough never saw Brighton as anything more than a temporary job until he could find something bigger and better. 'It was a case of football management or drive a lorry – I didn't have the O levels needed for working in a bank,' was the characteristic Clough summation of his situation at that time.

At first, it started promisingly. On the pitch, his new charges managed a win and two draws in the first three games. Off the field, there was encouragement as well, his intemperate remarks in the *Sunday Express* about Leeds United and Don Revie resulting in no disciplinary action against him.

'Carry On Talking, F.A. Tell Clough' was the *Daily Express*'s assessment of his 55-minute hearing on 14 November at the Association's headquarters at Lancaster Gate. In truth, the outcome wasn't a complete surprise, as Vernon Stokes, the retired solicitor who headed the disciplinary committee, was noted for favouring lighter punishments in these sorts of cases.

Even so, no penalty at all was the best result Clough could have expected, and he was hugely relieved. 'It was a superb discussion,' he enthused afterwards. 'If I had had the same type of talks with other directors, I might still be at Derby County.'

Back at the Goldstone Ground, the enormity of the task confronting him was starting to dawn on Clough. On Wednesday, 28 November, Brighton were dumped out of the FA Cup by the amateurs of Walton & Hersham, humiliatingly beaten 4–0 at home in front of a bemused 9,000 home crowd. The chief executioner was 26-year-old Clive Foskett, a joiner who had managed to get the day off from doing some restorative work to the Natural History Museum. He scored a hat-trick and made the Brighton defenders look as ponderous as some of the dinosaurs that surrounded him as he went about his day job.

It got even worse for Clough and Taylor three days later when Brighton lost 8–2 at home to Bristol Rovers in the league. Clough pulled no punches when he was interviewed by Brian Moore for *The Big Match* the following day: 'They [his players] just caved in. They were raw. They couldn't cope with this type of pressure. They've got to have more spirit and more heart to play professional football than they showed yesterday.'

As his frustration with the job grew, it was a refrain he would return to in the coming months. After a team meeting in early February, he told Steve Curry of the *Express*: 'The players have shirked all moral responsibilities and have not even attempted to learn their trade.'

The Brighton players were angry and perplexed. One of them – anonymously – told the same paper: 'We had this fairly stormy meeting but we never dreamed the manager would launch an attack like this against us. I don't think Clough has tried to get to know us.' Another added, pointedly, 'How can he say all that when he flies off to America the day before a match and doesn't reappear until the day before the next match?'

The trip to America referred to was Clough's visit to New York to watch Muhammad Ali's second bout with Joe Frazier at Madison Square Garden on 28 January 1974. There was a suggestion Clough might write a piece for the *Daily Mail* about the fight, but that came to nothing. He did, however, introduce himself to a puzzled Ali – who had no idea who he was – at one of the great man's press conferences. But the two big egos got talking, and when Clough explained what he did for a living, Ali replied, 'Football managers are grey men. You ain't old enough to be a manager – you should still be a player.'

His trip to America was typical of several he made around this time. He missed the glamour and performance levels of top-flight sport and went out of his way to catch the major events. Being kept apart from his family lowered his spirits, as did the travel to and from Derby to the South Coast.

'He used to talk [to me] about his days at Brighton. He'd recall driving all the way down from Derby to London, negotiating his way through the capital's traffic, and then seeing the sign, "Brighton, 50 miles". His heart would sink,' remembers Duncan Hamilton.

By this stage, early in 1974, Clough was already tiring of his managerial duties at Brighton. He had no appetite for coaxing performances from a mediocre side; at Hartlepools United, he'd been entrusted with a similar position, but then he'd been in his first job and on a mission. Seven years on, he'd lived at the quality end of the Football League and desperately wanted to return to it.

But in the meantime there was another major diversion from football in February 1974 in the shape of a general election. Prime Minister Edward Heath called for the vote on 7 February – well over a year before he was required to go to the country.

The oil embargo in the wake of the Yom Kippur War had strengthened the miners' hand as their overtime ban continued. By January, coal stocks had been reduced to such a degree that a state of emergency was declared and a three-day working week imposed. On 4 February, the miners voted 81 per cent in favour of a national strike, and Heath's patience finally snapped. He announced an election, determined to make it a single-issue campaign on the theme 'Who Governs Britain?' – the subtext being that the electorate had to decide between the political class and the trade unions, or, effectively, himself and the miners.

Clough threw himself into the short campaign with gusto. In the constituency of Derby North, Labour MP Phillip Whitehead was defending a nominal majority of 3,479 over the Conservatives. But there had been boundary changes that had increased the size of the constituency by 70–80 per cent, and the Liberals had also joined the fight this time. There was everything to play for, despite the obvious unpopularity of the Government in a largely, but not wholly, working-class seat.

Clough made appearances with Whitehead at two public meetings at Brakensdale and Derwent schools, as well as rolling his sleeves up and canvassing on doorsteps. It served a dual purpose for him. He was articulating and defending his socialist principles and doing his level best to help get a Labour government back in power, but at the same time he was also stoking the fire of the protest movement against Derby County, which had never completely gone out. The Goldstone Ground would see precious little of him during the week for the next 21 days.

His appearance at a packed house in Derwent Secondary School, on Beaufort Street, on Thursday, 19 February, was, inevitably, front-page news. Under the headline 'Ex-Rams Manager Makes a Plea', the *Derby Evening Telegraph* reported Clough's short (seven-minute) speech, interrupted by calls of 'Come back!' and, from one woman, 'We love you!'

Clough told his audience he wasn't there to talk about specific Labour Party policies because there was a lot he didn't understand. Instead, his belligerent rallying cry concentrated on a personal endorsement of the sitting MP – and a hint that he wasn't quite yet done with Derby County.

> I believe Phillip Whitehead is one of the best MPs Parliament ever had. He brings some integrity to a place where there is very little of it. Some of them get away with murder. We shovel them in and when they get there we wish we could shovel them out again. But this is one man we don't want to shovel. Let's get him back, then you can get me back.

In the campaign, the Tories' candidate David Penfold went on the attack over Rolls-Royce, far and away the town's biggest employer. He accused Whitehead of signing a House of Commons motion calling for a reduction in defence expenditure of more than £1,000 million a year – when close on half of Rolls-Royce's sales were to the Government.

But Clough was out 'on the knocker' day after day. Whitehead, who would later describe him as 'a more articulate version of Johnny Prescott', said he was like a Pied Piper on the council estates, attracting hordes of people – especially youngsters – to his campaign trail.

On polling day, Thursday, 28 February, Clough used his car to ferry voters in the Allestree area to the polling booths. Whitehead squeezed home, but it was close. He had a majority of 1,293 over Penfold, with the Liberals coming a respectable third. The turnout was 79.1 per cent, up nearly 15 per cent from 1970.

Who can say for sure if Clough's presence was crucial? There's certainly a strong case to be made for it. But no sooner had he helped secure the future of a democratic socialist government than he was given the opportunity to go and work – however inadvertently – for a monarch.

★ ★ ★

Shortly after his electioneering exploits, Clough received a visit in Brighton from two representatives of the Iranian Football Federation. The emissaries from the East came bearing gifts – specifically, a tempting offer for Clough, with Peter Taylor, to manage their national football side on a two-year contract at a salary of around £20,000 a year (tax free).

Mohammad Reza Shah Pahlavi, ruler of Iran since 1941, was determined to create a strong national side, and the building of a new £20-million sports complex in Tehran was a means to that end. Crowds of fifty, sixty and one hundred thousand were not uncommon for big club matches; the country regularly performed well in the Asia Cup but had missed out on qualification for the 1974 World Cup, and those in charge were determined that wouldn't happen next time. They were also keen to make an impression in the 1976 Olympic Games.

But the Shah's desire to make Iran a leading football nation had as much to do with politics as with sport. By 1974, the early, optimistic days of the 'White Revolution', with its emphasis on the modernisation and secularisation of the country, were but a dim, distant memory. The self-styled 'Guardian of the Persian Gulf' had turned from an enlightened despot into an increasingly autocratic ruler. He and his wide family had a grip on most levers of the state, and the secret police – SAVAK – ensured political dissent was either controlled or crushed. The following year, the Shah would abolish the multi-party system and rule through his own Rastakhiz (Resurrection) Party. A successful soccer team, then, was what bread and circuses were to the caesars of Rome – distractions for the masses from their dictatorial rulers.

All of this almost certainly hadn't filtered into Clough's mind when he opened the sliding doors of a first-class compartment on a Midlands train heading for London St Pancras on the morning of Monday, 11 March.

The Brighton manager, armed with a sturdy cooling box containing a bottle of Dom Perignon champagne, glanced at the man sitting in the corner and hailed him: 'Now then, young man, somebody's told me you're a young Labour MP who's football daft. I want you to join me in a drink, because I've got a momentous day ahead.'

The young man in question was 40-year-old Joe Ashton, MP for Bassetlaw, on his way down to Westminster for the week's parliamentary business – or so he thought. He recalls: 'He offered me a drink, but I declined, saying it was too early for me. He then explained that he was heading off to Iran that afternoon to talk terms with them about taking on the job as their national team manager. He was clearly very excited and thinking seriously about it. It wasn't working out for him at Brighton, the travelling was getting him down, and here was the opportunity to work on the international scene. He told me as well that his family would have their own private swimming pool, a Rolls-Royce with a chauffeur, and the kids would be allowed to feed the Shah's world-famous stallions! But before he travelled, he wanted to go and take advice at the Foreign Office – essentially to see if all this was kosher and to find out more about possible schools for his children. And as a favour he wanted me to accompany him to King Charles Street [Foreign and Commonwealth Office main building, just off Whitehall].'

So Clough and Ashton evaded the waiting press on the platform at St Pancras, jumped into a cab and headed off to the Foreign Office. If they were surprised by the unexpected appearance of one of the most famous faces on British television, the urbane diplomatic staff didn't show it and quickly sprang into action. The matter was dealt with in an hour, and the reassurances Clough required were delivered.

Clough spent most of that week in Tehran, where he examined the facilities and tried to get a feel for the country. He remembered being treated exceptionally well: 'The Iranians flew us out first class, put us up in the most sumptuous hotel, and served us the finest caviare until it was coming out of our ears.'

One of his hosts in the Iranian capital was Kambiz Atabai, president of the Soccer Federation of Iran, who had another, more exotic title: Master of the Horse. Mr Atabai, confidant of the Shah, thinks Sir Stanley Rous, then in his final months as president of FIFA, could have had a part to play in inviting Clough to Iran: 'But Mr Clough had come to our attention of course. We knew how successful he'd been with Derby County, he was very charismatic, he publicised himself well. He was a very strong personality with a lot of passion for the game and we thought he would be the right man for the job.

'We wondered – and he wondered – whether the job would be exciting enough for him. But we were very ambitious, the people were soccer-mad and we wanted to get the best person we could. We definitely wanted an English-speaking coach, which would have been easier for everyone around, the players and the people in the Federation.'

Not everyone was relaxed about Clough's potential arrival in Tehran. The new British ambassador, Sir Anthony Parsons – who had hosted a press conference by Clough at his embassy – told the Iranian Federation, 'If you employ him, I will not have any responsibility for the consequences.'

In any event, after mulling over the offer for a few days, Clough decided to remain at Brighton. Publicly, he said Brighton were holding him and Taylor to their contracts and that he was disappointed he couldn't go. 'I'm staying at Brighton to do a job. I'm not saying I'm happy here,' he told the *Daily Express*.

Privately, he would concede – as he did to Joe Ashton on another train journey down to London a few weeks later – that there were more prosaic reasons. 'Clough said he had been tempted, but he told me, "Oh, it would have been too much. I could tell I would miss it in the UK. I couldn't get a drink. I prefer the old wet and windy Derby ground to the heat of the Middle East."'

Clough was never short of offers. As far back as November 1969, when he was starting to make an impression at Derby, Barcelona came calling. In April 1972, he and Taylor took more seriously an approach from Coventry City, whose chairman, Derrick Robins, a former first-class cricketer, was a man they admired. After the Iran episode, there were tentative enquiries about their services from Ajax of Amsterdam, Aston Villa and Queens Park Rangers. But the two of them soldiered on until the end of the season, just about keeping Brighton afloat in the Third Division by finishing in 19th position.

Then, on Wednesday, 1 May, came the announcement that would change Brian Clough's football career – and that of Don Revie – irrevocably. Sir Alf Ramsey, manager of England for exactly 11 years and winner of the World Cup, was leaving his job.

★ ★ ★

According to Ted Croker, the new secretary of the Football Association, Sir Alf's fate had been effectively sealed on St Valentine's Day, 14 February, when the FA had decided to form a new committee called 'Future of Football', the brief being 'to consider our future policy in respect of the promotion of international football'.

Clearly, as far as the committee was concerned, Sir Alf was the past, not the future, the draw at Wembley in October and elimination from the World Cup making the decision more straightforward. He had carried on managing the side in a state of limbo for six months, but few in the football world doubted that his days were numbered.

It was at the second meeting of the committee, on 1 April, that it was formally decided to seek a new England manager and draw up a fresh list of responsibilities for the jobholder. On 19 April, Sir Alf was informed by FA chairman Sir Andrew Stephen that he was sacked, and the decision was made public on 1 May.

The newspapers soon settled into a game of speculation about his successor. Mentioned prominently in early dispatches were Gordon Jago of Queens Park Rangers, Gordon Milne of Coventry, Jimmy Adamson of Burnley and Jimmy Armfield of Bolton Wanderers. Trailing a little way behind were the promising youngsters Bobby Robson of Ipswich and Jack Charlton of Middlesbrough.

But there was one candidate who towered over all the others by virtue of experience and consistent achievement at club level. And, at that time, his side were enjoying their 'Golden Period'.

Just four days before Sir Alf's departure, Don Revie and his Leeds United side had rounded off their 1973–74 campaign with a 1–0 victory against QPR at Loftus Road. They were champions – for the second time – by a comfortable margin of five points over their nearest challengers, Liverpool, and they had lost only four matches all season, scoring sixty-six goals and conceding thirty-one.

Statistics were all well and good, but it was the manner of their triumph that impressed. This was the year when the Leeds players were encouraged to cast off caution and any preoccupation with opponents, to express themselves and parade their skills in a more expansive fashion.

Allan Clarke recalled an inspirational pre-season team talk. 'The Gaffer said, "Right, lads, we've been the best team for the last decade. I know we haven't won as much as we should have, but that's in the past. Now, I've had a thought in the close season – can we go through the whole campaign unbeaten?"'

For a while, it looked as if it might happen. Revie's men won their first seven games on the trot, and after the last of those, a 2–1 win at Southampton, that most eloquent of sportswriters, John Arlott, was moved to write: 'Wearing the white strip of a blameless life, Leeds moved in a ceaseless flow, back in packed defence, competing for the midfield, sweeping forward with backs overlapping. Yet it was all so controlled, so amiable . . . so free from the aura of violence they used to generate.'

It would be 8 October before they lost their first match, 2–0 away to Ipswich Town. After that, they stayed well ahead of the pack until March, when successive defeats at the hands of Liverpool, Burnley (4–1 at home) and West Ham caused some panic.

But they recovered their poise with a 2–0 home win against Clough's Derby County and any doubts were swiftly erased. A decade later, looking back, Revie regretted not allowing his players free rein for their ability much earlier: 'That season they started turning out some of the most fantastic football I have witnessed. I should have realised the talent they possessed much earlier. I really only started letting them off the leash for the last four to five years I was there.'

It was as good a time as any for Revie to bow out, with a convincing championship triumph and the reputation of his side as cynical professionals to a large extent repaired after a season of far fewer sendings-off and bookings.

Revie was alerted to the Football Association's potential interest in him over the England manager's job when he received an informal approach from a friendly intermediary – Tom Holley, a journalist on the *Sunday People*. Holley knew Revie well. He himself had played for Leeds United before turning to journalism; he'd been a stalwart centre-half with 169 appearances for the Elland Road club in the 1930s and '40s (excluding wartime games), many of them as captain, before being replaced by the great John Charles.

Revie told Holley he'd be keen to take over the national side – providing the terms and conditions were satisfactory. Soon after the England job was formally advertised, Revie put in a call to the Football Association, as Ted Croker remembered in his autobiography:

> 'I'm very interested in the job and I'd like the opportunity to
> talk to you about it,' he said. He explained he did not wish to
> apply in the normal way but could I tell the committee that he
> was prepared to put his name forward. I was excited because no

one on the short list had his qualifications. He was a proven winner at club level, both in England and in Europe.

Gordon Jago, Gordon Milne and Jimmy Bloomfield of Leicester City were the candidates on the shortlist. Revie was a different proposition altogether, and Sir Andrew Stephen, Dick Wragg – chairman of the international committee – and Croker immediately went up to Elland Road to see him. Croker remembered: 'Our initial meeting with Revie was a brief one. It was obvious that he wanted the job and we wanted him to have it. He did not want sweeping changes. He was sensible enough to appreciate how the system worked.'

Negotiations on a financial settlement with Leeds took a little longer. Eventually, Manny Cussins, the chairman, and Sam Bolton, senior director, told the FA team they wouldn't insist on full-blown compensation for the loss of Revie but would require a payment to assist in the expense of appointing his replacement. A figure was eventually agreed – still large, around £200,000, according to some reports – and Revie himself landed a five-year contract at £20,000 a year.

So, at just after 4 p.m. on Thursday, 4 July, in the Leeds boardroom, Revie was unveiled as the new England manager. Enthused by the performances of West Germany and Holland in the recent World Cup, he told the readers of the *Daily Express* that he wanted to unearth the young talent he felt sure was out there in the country: 'In the past, we produced players of the calibre of Cruyff and Beckenbauer, and I believe they are still there. I have to talk to schoolmasters to try and help them discover a new Cruyff, a Finney or a Charlton. The boys have got to go back to the basic skills and be encouraged at school level.'

Revie made his job sound like a crusade, and he called upon all the country, press, public and players to join him. The London-based media in particular had been critical, often viciously so, of his Leeds teams and he could expect no more than a short honeymoon period with them. As for the public, well, if you believed a poll conducted in the *Daily Express* in May, there was only really one man for the job: Brian Clough. The Brighton manager received an overwhelming 30 per cent of the votes cast in answer to the question of who should be Sir Alf's successor.

Coming in a creditable second with 20 per cent was Jackie Charlton, World Cup winner, whose Middlesbrough side had just been promoted from the Second Division by a staggering 15-point margin. Third was Sir Alf himself with 10 per cent, a clear indication that the footballing public felt his dismissal unjustified and crudely handled by the Football Association. As for Revie, he came in fourth with only 9 per cent of the vote.

'Tell the *Daily Express* readers they have good taste,' joked Clough on the phone from Majorca, where he was on holiday. 'That really is beautiful. An honour. I once told you I'd do that job for nothing. It is the most important job in English football.'

Despite public acclaim, Clough could never be a serious candidate in the summer of 1974. His age – 39 – would have counted against him with the elderly gentlemen at Lancaster Gate, despite his stunning achievements at Derby. Moreover, his regular, often barbed criticism of football's authorities from his high-profile position on TV and radio had irritated and embarrassed them.

However, Duncan Hamilton believes Clough, buoyed by public support, would have thought he had a chance of the top job: 'He definitely would have believed he was in the frame. He'd just won a league title with Derby and was up there with the brightest and the best. Practically, he would have thought that he could put a stop to all that travelling to Brighton; if he got the England manager's job, he wouldn't have to live in London.'

With Revie installed, attention now turned to who would be his successor at Leeds. Manny Cussins and Sam Bolton had just a month to find the right man before the curtain-raiser to the new season, the Charity Shield match against Liverpool at Wembley on 10 August. Powerful voices urged them to look within the current ranks at Elland Road – but they were minded to spread their net much wider.

* * *

Revie's initial recommendation to the Leeds board was that his fellow North-Easterner Bobby Robson – then fashioning a bright, young Ipswich side – should be his successor.

In his autobiography, Robson recounted how he took a call from Leeds' chief scout, Tony Collins: 'Don Revie has asked me to call you. He's proposing that you take over from him. Leeds United want you to come . . . We've got great players, and money to spend. You can step in and carry on Don's good work. You'd be a fool not to take it. It's a fabulous appointment.' Fabulous or not, Robson had an excellent contract at Ipswich and great freedom of action at Portman Road; he turned down the approach.

If the appointment was to be 'in-house', then Revie had no doubts about who was the best man for the job. He told Manny Cussins that he thought Johnny Giles had all the attributes necessary to carry on his legacy.

Giles, the oldest of the side at 34, had always seemed easily the best equipped for management. He was an intelligent, independent-thinking man off the pitch, with an astute football brain but also a tough, detached approach that would have commanded respect from his old colleagues.

At one point in those early days in July, Giles was confident he'd be chosen, according to Eddie Gray: 'At John's interview with the Leeds board, he was seemingly told the job was his. I learned about this while Peter Lorimer and I were doing some work together on the training pitch. John ran over to us and said, "I'm going to be the new manager – the club will be announcing it tomorrow."'

But all that changed when Giles' midfield partner started to make representations of his own to the board. Billy Bremner, a passionate, fiery individual but a leader to his fingertips, had credentials that contrasted sharply with Giles' but were compelling in their own right. The board started to be concerned that if they appointed one or the other, their relationship as players would be damaged and, by extension, team harmony disturbed. After some days' consideration, they decided to take a safer route and look for someone outside Elland Road.

In fact, in a remarkable coincidence, two of the best jobs in football had become vacant at almost exactly the same time. Just as Don Revie was saying his goodbyes at Elland Road, so his great managerial friend – and midnight confidant – Bill Shankly was making his departure from Anfield after fifteen successful seasons that included two league titles, two FA Cups and a UEFA Cup victory.

Revie and Shankly had almost identical records of achievement, the former's perhaps the greater for having been accomplished in a shorter space of time. There was great mutual appreciation, and the good relationship they developed over the years filtered down to their players, despite the ferocity of some of the encounters. There was no quarter asked and none given in Leeds–Liverpool encounters, but there were rarely any long-standing recriminations for rough deeds committed on the pitch. It was to one of the leading performers in those battles of the 1960s that the Leeds board turned next in their hunt for Revie's replacement.

Ian St John always seemed to be a thorn in the side of Leeds in those days, regularly scoring crucial goals – none more so than the flying whiplash header he sent past Gary Sprake to win Liverpool the FA Cup in extra time in 1965. Now aged 36, he was learning the managerial ropes back in his native Scotland with Motherwell, the side where he had started his playing career. In the middle of July, he received an unexpected call from the Celtic manager Jock Stein, then one of the great and good of British football, with connections at many Scottish and English clubs. Stein himself had been approached earlier about the Leeds job but quickly declined and instead extolled St John's virtues.

St John remembers, 'Jock asked me, "Would you like to go back to England?" I was quite excited and asked him, "Do you mean the Liverpool job?"

'"No," he replied, "Leeds have asked me to put your name forward as Don Revie's successor."

'Now, my wife hadn't quite settled back in Scotland and would have preferred to live in England, so there wasn't a problem on that front. Jock said, "A couple of the Leeds directors would like to meet you in a hotel at Scotch Corner," so I motored down there as soon as I could.'

St John felt the meeting on Monday, 15 July went well, and he was surprised by the amount of detail in the discussions – players, wages, club finances, the lot. He certainly felt that this was a serious approach and he was in with a very good chance of the job – although he was aware other candidates were being considered.

'When I got home that day from the meeting, Jock called me, having spoken to his man on the board. He said it had gone well, and he was sure the job would be mine. But the chairman had told him he still had one person to talk to.'

To the astonishment of everyone in Leeds – and the whole football world – that person was Brian Clough. St John was eventually cast aside – along with Jimmy Armfield, also on the shortlist – and Leeds set their sights squarely on bringing to Elland Road the man who had heaped scorn and opprobrium on them over the last four years.

As the news filtered out on 18 July, one Leeds supporter, George Hindle, launched an immediate petition to try to prevent Clough's arrival. He got more than four hundred signatures in just one evening spent in the town's Merrion Centre.

Bob Roberts, an influential figure at the club in the 1960s who had rejoined the board in 1973, was the director most enthusiastic about luring Clough to Elland Road. 'We should wipe the slate clean,' he said. Together with Cussins, he was able to persuade the board that despite everything that had happened in the past, the appointment of the charismatic, dynamic Clough would mark a sharp and significant change from the Revie era.

Clough was a brilliant motivator, the man who could manage the transition and keep the honours coming. That was the theory – as long as bygones could be bygones. But John Helm, who was able to test the mood at BBC Radio Leeds, just remembers the whole city being flabbergasted. 'It was the most amazing decision of all time, particularly gobsmacking after what he'd said at that Sportsman's Dinner 18 months previously. Everybody thought Giles would get the job – the recommendation from Revie was so strong, although Bremner had put a bit of a spanner in the works by applying himself at the last minute. But Clough?'

Events moved quickly, and Cussins – with Bob Roberts as his right-hand man – pursued Clough relentlessly over the next few days, eventually persuading him to break his contract with Brighton. But there was a major hitch in the closing stages.

What Cussins really wanted was Clough and Peter Taylor, the double act, the psychologist supreme and the best spotter of talent in the country. But after negotiations at a Hove hotel between Cussins, Clough, Taylor and Mike Bamber, the Brighton chairman, Taylor elected to stay at the south coast club.

He felt he owed them loyalty after they'd offered him work so soon after the Derby debacle and had provided him with such generous working conditions ever since. Bamber had denied Taylor and Clough nothing – he hadn't interfered in footballing matters but instead had provided money for transfers, put them up in the best hotels and laid on a new Mercedes coach for team travel.

Clough agreed the deal to come to Leeds in the early hours of Monday, 22 July. Ambition, it seemed, had overcome any doubts in his mind about the place to which he was headed. He was desperate to be back on the big stage. 'I'm delighted to take this challenge, but terribly, absolutely sad to be parting with Peter Taylor,' he said on that bright, hopeful morning. In the course of the next 44 days, he would quickly come to realise just how much he'd miss his old partner.

* * *

Ever master of the outrageous quote, Clough would later reflect, 'It didn't take me long to realise my being in charge at Leeds was like

Breshnev becoming Prime Minister of Britain with a Tory Government.' He certainly had a fondness for analogies with the Soviet Union, having previously compared Alan Brown's regime at Sunderland to the Kremlin.

On the day of Clough's appointment, the Leeds players had already been back in pre-season training for a fortnight. Instead of joining them to settle in good and early for the new season, he chose to fly back to Majorca and resume his family holiday. It would be nine more days before the employees at Elland Road saw their new manager.

Clough always valued his breaks away from the game with his family. He felt, with much justification, that they refreshed and reinvigorated him for the demanding season ahead. But his prolonged absence at this juncture immediately raised some eyebrows, as Peter Lorimer explains: 'He said he wasn't going to break his holiday to come to Leeds, and straight away that showed a bit of contempt. It was bad, because we were a professional club that tried to do everything right. His attitude was, I've got the Leeds job, I'll go when I'm ready. That was wrong.'

Typically unconventional, Clough brought his young sons Simon and Nigel along for the ride when he finally arrived at Elland Road on a wet morning on Wednesday, 31 July. 'I could sense the hostility in the air,' Clough wrote later. 'I should have known what to expect from the moment I drove my car through the gates and into the ground. A man, heavily built, red faced and aggressive – just a supporter, I assume – came striding up to the car and said: "You're bloody well late."'

Nigel was ordered to go off and join the first team on the training pitch, while his father disappeared into his office. It could have been a nice, human touch in other circumstances and surroundings, but to a sceptical set of players it was just more evidence of bizarre behaviour, according to Helm: 'The poor little kid was obviously overawed, and the players thought, what the hell is all this about? You've got Paul Madeley, Paul Reaney, all these internationals, and an eight-year-old boy training with them. What on earth was going on?'

Then Clough called a press conference that certainly wasn't out of the textbook, as Helm recalls: 'I'll never forget it. Cloughie grabbed hold of a coat hanger off a peg in the room immediately opposite the manager's office. When somebody asked him what he was going to do with the team, he grabbed the coat hanger and started sweeping it around, saying, "I'm going to get rid of so-and-so," and then he smashed one of the journalists across the knee – a chap called Ronnie Crowther from the *Daily Mail* – he physically hit him. He could have been had up for assault!'

With the atmosphere tense and a strange first day evolving in his new job, Clough was relieved to see a friendly face a little later. Geoffrey Boycott had been expecting to take to the field for Yorkshire at Headingley that day to play old rivals Lancashire in the quarter-finals of the Gillette Cup. But the game never stood a chance of getting under way because of the pouring rain, so unexpectedly Boycott had time on his hands. He decided to take the opportunity to head down to Elland Road and give his old friend some moral support. 'I had to wait until he'd finished talking to the chairman, but I was one of the few to see him that day,' he says. 'The first thing he said to me while he sat in his office was that he was worried about the age of his squad. It was still a good one, but he needed some fresh blood. The level of performances from the older players wouldn't last long – and he felt he needed to act very quickly.'

There was an early setback in that first week on the coaching side when Les Cocker announced he was rejoining Revie at England in a full-time assistant's post. Coach, trainer, physiotherapist, Cocker had been Revie's trusted lieutenant for 14 years, and the move wasn't unexpected.

Clough moved quickly to replace him and persuaded his old Derby colleague Jimmy Gordon to rejoin him. Gordon, a sage, always enthusiastic Scot, had been a decent wing-half for Middlesbrough after the war, supplying the great Wilf Mannion with good possession. After he'd stopped playing, he learned his trade as a trainer at Ayresome Park, which is where he and Clough first met. After the blow he'd suffered when Peter Taylor elected to remain at Brighton, Gordon's arrival gave Clough some reassurance.

The Leeds players were baffled because Clough said next to nothing to them in the first couple of days. They could see him observing them at training, but there was little direct contact. Then, on Friday morning, he called them all into the players' lounge for their first proper meeting. Of all the extraordinary moments in Clough's career, this would be perhaps the most astonishing of all.

First of all, he explained that he'd been silent up to then because he liked to watch, absorb and learn about a football club and its players from a distance. He wanted to trust the evidence of his own eyes before reaching any kind of initial conclusions. Then he gave the players those opinions – with both barrels, as Peter Lorimer recalls: 'Brian committed professional suicide at that meeting. He said he wanted to tell us – "you lot" – what he thought before we started working together in earnest, so he went from player to player, right through the team, being basically as nasty as he could about each and every one of us.'

Lorimer was told he was a 'diver' who made a meal out of tackles; Bremner was informed his fiery temper would be quickly curbed; Hunter that he'd got 'a terrible reputation in the game'; Giles was 'another with a bad reputation'.

The group as a whole was particularly angry when Clough finished his tour of the room by turning to his last victim, Eddie Gray, and telling him, 'If you'd have been a racehorse, you'd have been put down years ago. You're never fit.' Lorimer was outraged. 'Now that really upset us, because every player worries about injuries, especially if they're career-threatening, and you don't lay into them like that, because they're already going through torture. Eddie had been going through a bad time and that really offended us as a group. Clough had had his career ended by a bad injury himself, so he should have known better.'

Clough ended his diatribe with a flourish: 'I may as well tell you now, you may have won all the honours going – league titles, cup competitions, European competitions – but as far as I'm concerned you can throw every one of your medals in the bin, because you've never won any of them fairly.'

With hindsight, says Lorimer, there was really no way back after that: 'The lads basically stood up and walked out of the room, saying, "Ah f—, we don't need this." When you play for a football team – daft as it seems – you basically play for your manager, the man at the helm. You've got that feeling of obligation to perform for him. What Clough said was insulting Don, insulting us as a group of men, and really it has to be the most amazing thing I've ever heard in my time in football. Now, I'm an easy-going kind of guy and nothing much gets to me, but the Gileses, the Bremners, the Hunters – their hackles were up immediately. The season was going to start, but there was no passion there whatsoever, and you need that as a footballer.'

Perhaps Clough felt that although this approach was a gamble, it was a psychological trick he could pull off. He'd done this kind of thing successfully before with more pliant players, those he'd developed or bought himself. But if it was an attempt to draw a line under the Revie era and establish his own dominance, it had backfired horribly.

Clough wasn't finished that day. In the evening, he made his way to the studios of Yorkshire Television on Kirkstall Road, where he'd agreed to be interviewed by three leading sports journalists for a live programme entitled *Brian Clough Comes to Leeds: A Calendar Special.* With news presenter Austin Mitchell in the chair, Clough was questioned by John Sadler of *The Sun*, Peter Cooper of the *Daily Mirror*, and Keith Macklin, chief football correspondent of Yorkshire Television.

With the players still seething at home after the criticism thrown at them earlier in the day, Clough showed no reluctance in repeating it. Even if his language was toned down somewhat, the message was quite clear. He even alluded to the meeting:

> I said to Billy and the players this morning, 'Despite the fact that you are champions, people are still begrudging you it.' They've sold themselves short for ten years, and that's a tragedy. That's [the length of] a player's career.
>
> I would expect – and accept – a little strangeness, as there was a strangeness there as I discussed things with them this morning . . . I felt I was more wary of the Leeds players when I walked in on Wednesday morning than they were wary of me. It's a natural reaction to someone who comes in new, having to follow Revie. It's perfectly normal.
>
> I don't think it will take them long to realise that I am a very, very honest manager. I think they will have realised that already, and once having a basis of that understanding, the fact that I am honest and they are talented, then that has started already.

Honesty may have been the approach, but everyone associated with Leeds will have been gritting their teeth as, quite coolly and calmly, Clough used his answers to go through a list of reservations he had about the club and its achievements, and the remedies he proposed.

He said the players had been disliked because 'they were niggling and messing about and all that type of thing'; he wanted to incorporate 'a little bit of warmth' that had been missing from the set-up; he revealed he'd been left 'slightly over a barrel' by Revie because a lot of players' contracts had not yet been signed.

He mocked the value of the dossier: 'I think to a large extent it's been overplayed. Because if it's been done for ten years, we must know every single player . . . players that have played, players who are going to play, and players who have not even been conceived yet!'

He referred to the players on several occasions as 'talented' and Leeds as a 'top club', but he'd made his overall view crystal clear in almost his first in-depth answer: 'I think Leeds have always sold themselves short. They've been champions but not good champions in the sense of wearing the crown reasonably well. I think they could have been a little bit more loved.'

For Revie himself, he had a joke, although it will have sounded to the England manager like an out-and-out jibe. 'I had great fears of that bloody suit of his in the office when I walked in – you know, the one that he'd had thirteen years. I thought, if that's there it's going straight in the bin, not only because it's old but because it would smell.'

There are those who believe that Clough's approach wasn't just insensitive or a psychological strategy that went wrong. The theory is that it was nothing less than a systematic attempt to undermine not just Revie's reputation but the club itself. Jeff Powell believed that was the case: 'It was a deliberate attempt to wreck the club. To go into a group of players you're going to manage and tell them they're a bunch of cheats, you're clearly not going to have the dressing-room on your side from then on. He went to Leeds to destroy Leeds, there's no question of that.'

Eddie Gray wouldn't go that far. But he thought Clough had a clear strategy on arriving at Elland Road. 'He had an obsession about cutting us down to size and rebuilding us in his own image. I think Brian came to Leeds with a bit of a complex, and that complex was Don. He didn't want anything connected with Don round and about him.'

One physical manifestation of this fixation was Clough's desire to have all the furniture changed in his office so that all trace of Revie was removed. Visitors would also notice that – in a weirdly appropriate way – the new nameplate would never remain properly fixed to the door and would often fall down.

His preoccupation with Revie and his legacy showed itself again shortly before the Charity Shield match against Liverpool at Wembley on Sunday, 10 August. He'd been in the job a week and a half and Leeds had played – and won – a couple of pre-season friendlies by then, but as far as Clough was concerned it wasn't his team. Duncan Revie remembers his father receiving a phone call from Clough on the eve of the match: 'Brian was quite wound up. He said to Dad, "This is your side, I'd like you to lead them out." But Dad replied, "No, Brian. You're manager of Leeds United now, you're going to have to lead them out."'

Perhaps Clough's gesture had generosity attached, because if Revie had taken Leeds onto the Wembley turf he would have done so alongside his old friend Bill Shankly. Bob Paisley had effectively taken over as Liverpool manager by then, so Shankly's final appearance at the Twin Towers was purely for sentimental reasons.

Revie was, however, in the crowd, and once on the pitch the Leeds players all turned and waved to him in a gesture of affection and solidarity.

Clough and Shankly, the new boss and the departing maestro, looked on aghast as the two sides produced an ill-tempered contest that disintegrated into a series of niggling fouls and petty disputes. It culminated in a stand-up fist fight between Billy Bremner and Kevin Keegan, resulting in both of them being sent off. Both men petulantly threw their shirts to the ground as they left the field, an image that went around the world – it was the first Charity Shield to be shown live on television – and brought widespread condemnation.

The game ended in a 1–1 draw, but Liverpool took the prize by winning 6–5 on penalties. Even then, Clough was guilty of an eccentric decision, allowing his goalkeeper David Harvey, rather than new signing and forward Duncan McKenzie, to take a spot kick (which Harvey missed).

Instead of the usual one or two match ban, Bremner and Keegan were each suspended for eleven games and fined £500, a huge sum in those days. Clough's vision of a cleaner, more honest sort of football had been dealt a major blow.

As pre-season continued, Clough's behaviour and methods continued to perplex and irritate players and staff. He blotted his copybook at the club's big dinner at the Mansion House in Roundhay Park, as Gray recalls. 'Every year, eve of season, we'd have a big do, directors would be there, players, everyone from the club. It was a big get-together before the long, hard slog of ten months of football. It was supposed to be a seven thirty for eight start, yet Brian turned up at half past ten in his tracksuit! It didn't go down well with Manny Cussins, the chairman, or endear him to anyone else. But that's how Brian went about things at Leeds.'

The rigorous training regime that Revie had instituted from very early on in his time was cast aside in favour of a more relaxed routine. Clough himself would often arrive nearer 11 a.m. than 10 – Revie's starting time – with the excuse that he had been travelling up from Derby. In fact, he spent the bulk of his time at Leeds in the city's

Dragonara Hotel. Some of the players felt their fitness levels were dropping with less physical work.

As the season approached, Clough's preparation was hampered by a string of injuries and suspensions to key players, on top of the long-term absence of his captain. Gray and Jones were on the treatment table, while Clarke and Hunter were out for the first two games because of ill discipline at the end of the previous campaign.

Clough had already signed Duncan McKenzie, a skilful but unconventional striker, from Nottingham Forest for £267,500. But he desperately needed some other, experienced replacements – and a friendly face or two – so he turned to his old Derby stalwarts John McGovern and John O'Hare, buying them for £130,000.

The fact he'd been a teammate in Scotland sides with the likes of Bremner, Gray and Lorimer helped O'Hare to settle in well. But it was clear to him immediately that something was badly wrong. 'It was obvious when I got there that they didn't like him,' he says. 'We had team meetings about it and the three of us [O'Hare, McGovern, McKenzie] weren't left out, we were all involved. It became clear that he wasn't going to survive this, because the players wanted him out. I'd come home and tell my wife, "He won't be there long." I was actually going to buy a house in the Leeds area, but I calculated there wasn't much point because he wouldn't last.'

By the time O'Hare and McGovern arrived on 24 August, Clough's Leeds had already lost their first two matches – 3–0 away at Stoke City and 1–0 at home to Queens Park Rangers.

The Stoke match wasn't a complete disaster; Leeds created a few decent chances, which a sharper McKenzie – or Allan Clarke, if he'd been there – might have finished off. But they were undone by a typically elegant midfield display from Alan Hudson, once a Chelsea star but now settling in well in the Potteries under the sympathetic management of Tony Waddington.

The defeat at home to QPR was a different matter altogether. Gerry Harrison in *The Times* reported a 'warm reception for their new manager', but the cheers quickly faded as Gerry Francis gave QPR a 14th-minute lead, which they held on to comfortably until the end. Harrison observed ominously, 'Above all, his [Clough's] side lacked authority in the penalty area, but it is a change of character, indeed, to see a Leeds side outfought.'

With O'Hare and McGovern in place, and Clarke and Hunter back after suspension, Leeds beat Birmingham City 1–0 at Elland Road to raise the gloom. It was a sketchy display, but Clarke scored a characteristically opportunist goal, and O'Hare showed some nice touches alongside him in attack.

Three days later, Johnny Giles was back in the groove in the return encounter with QPR. He and Terry Yorath – who scored Leeds' goal with a clever lob – had their work cut out to match the skill and industry of Stan Bowles and Gerry Francis, but Clough's men hung on for a 1–1 draw.

That was about as good as it got. Four days later, they lost 2–1 away at Manchester City – for whom Colin Bell scored the winner – and then on 7 September, at home to Luton Town, the nadir was reached. They could manage only a nervous 1–1 draw with a side newly promoted – a result that left them stranded second bottom of the First Division.

The Elland Road crowd, a section of which had cheered Clough before the QPR game, now booed and jeered him before singing Don Revie's name. They also called for Terry Yorath to come off the substitutes' bench and replace John McGovern, who was having a torrid time and being heckled spitefully and unmercilessly.

Clough was furious at the treatment meted out to his former captain: 'To say the crowd gave him some stick is the understatement of the season. Their attitude to him sickened me. But though he is a boy in stature, he is a man there on the pitch and he won't allow it to destroy his game.'

Anger, frustration, isolation – Clough was experiencing all of them. 'Instead of unity and common purpose, there was animosity, unrest and suspicion. I have never experienced anything like it before and would never wish such dreadful circumstances against my worst enemy.'

One man who did his best to lighten Clough's mood was Hans Marsen, the 31-year-old assistant general manager of the Dragonara Hotel where Clough was staying. Marsen, Munich born, was an affable man who built up a good rapport with a number of the well-known individuals who came through the Dragonara's doors in those days. He befriended Stanley Baxter, Scottish comic actor and impressionist, and once lent Sir Hugh Fraser, owner of Harrods, £100 to visit the local casino. Clough got on well with Marsen, giving him tickets for the odd game, even allowing him to travel on the team bus.

'I liked Brian a lot,' he recalls. 'I came across plenty of guests with airs and graces who never spoke to you, but he was the opposite. He was a down-to-earth, unpretentious guy, very easy to talk to and relate to. He would just come back in the evenings, go to the restaurant and then retire for the night. He missed his family not being there, and I don't think he had much support. He was pretty much alone.'

Also staying at the Dragonara was Duncan McKenzie, who was startled to receive a phone call from Clough in the early hours, summoning him down to reception. They'd earlier returned from playing in a testimonial game at Southampton.

'Cloughie said, "Now then, don't let me see you get off a plane in that condition again."

'"What condition?" I replied.

'"You were drunk," he said.

'I denied the accusation, pointing out that I didn't drink at all anyway. We argued briefly, but it soon became clear he just wanted an excuse to talk to someone. He was a very lonely man, absolutely isolated, and he knew there would be no respite for him. He did want to know what the players were saying about him, but I made it clear he'd get my full support on the field but I couldn't – and wouldn't – tell tales off it.'

By the evening of Saturday, 7 September, Clough had just about reached rock bottom. The side had managed just four points in six league games, and the crowd was now turning against him. Something, it seemed, had to give.

Chapter 12
'Thank You, Manny Cussins'

Brian Clough was clearly feeling the strain. In a revealing interview with Don Warters of the *Yorkshire Evening Post*, he betrayed his anxiety and apparent paranoia when he spoke about the 'ghost' stalking the corridors of Elland Road.

In his office, in the changing-room, in the boardroom, in the car park, around every corner of the football ground, he sensed the massive presence of Don Revie. As the problems started to pile up, 'The Don' haunted him more and more, a constant reminder of his own failings and how he'd fallen so far below the standards expected of a manager of this great club.

Clough had also started to believe that this ethereal presence still had a physical manifestation in the running of Leeds United Football Club. He suspected that Revie, still in the very early days of his England job, had time on his hands and was spending some of it conferring with his old players. Put simply, he believed he was being plotted against.

In his wide-ranging and injudicious front-page lead interview with Warters – headlined 'I Am No Destroyer, Says Brian Clough' – Clough claimed, 'I am getting the support of the players. I have never been so convinced of anything in my life as that.' They would be words that would quickly be thrown back in his face. He also brandished a red rag to a bull when he asserted, 'The confidence of the players was destroyed a little when Don Revie left. That was nobody's fault other than Revie's.'

The week beginning Monday, 9 September got off to a bad start for Clough, with a further diminution of his authority. At the weekend, he'd reached an agreement with Nottingham Forest to sell them Terry Cooper, Leeds' England left-back, who'd played only a few games since breaking his leg in a league game against Stoke City in April 1972.

Clough's instinct to want to sell Cooper was a harsh but probably correct one, as the full-back, now aged 30, would never be the same player again after his very bad injury. But Cooper was a talismanic figure, the man who'd scored the winning goal in the League Cup final at Wembley in 1968 that brought Leeds their first trophy under Don Revie. Another complicating factor was that he would shortly be entitled to a testimonial.

But for the directors who had never been convinced about Clough's appointment – Sam Bolton, the vice chairman, being the chief amongst them – here was the opportunity to start to confront him about the problems building up at Elland Road. In a 90-minute board meeting on Monday, Clough was challenged about his decision, and ultimately told he couldn't sell Cooper.

The official word was that manager and board had concluded that the proposed transfer should be called off because the bid from Forest was not high enough. 'There was no pressure from the board for me to withdraw from the Forest bid,' Clough told the press. It was an untruth, uttered to buy him some time.

But time was running out for Clough. Five and a half weeks earlier, he'd held his first, extraordinary meeting with his new charges in the players' lounge, the occasion when he'd told them to chuck all their medals in the bin because they'd only won them by cheating.

Now, on Tuesday, 10 September, he was back in that same lounge with the players, in a meeting called by Manny Cussins and Sam Bolton to 'clear the air' over the difficulties that plagued the club.

Everything had changed in those 40-odd days. The power that Clough had wielded then had now almost completely ebbed away, leaving him utterly isolated and vulnerable. This was going to be less of a discussion, more of a trial.

Apart from the drama of the event, the meeting would prove to be historic because it was one of the few – if any – instances of sheer player power winning out in such a way at a major football club.

Manny Cussins started the meeting by asking, 'What's going wrong? Why are you players not playing for the manager?' The players began to give their views, but it was then suggested by one of them that it would be best if Clough left the room so they could express themselves freely.

But as Clough was about to depart, the man normally least likely to make a fuss stood up. Paul Madeley turned and said to Clough, 'The lads just don't think you can manage.' It was a telling blow, delivered by the quietest of men, and it set the mood for the rest of the meeting.

Duncan McKenzie, John O'Hare and John McGovern, all in the room but keeping their counsel, looked on as the grievances of their new colleagues then poured out. McKenzie had no doubts about who was directing this 'assassination'.

'This was Sam Bolton's moment,' he says. 'He was the one who was revelling in the mischief because he was the one who didn't want Clough in the first place. He'd now decided Clough was going. You felt the players were almost bullied into what they were saying by Sam – and he was delighted with what they said because it was his "I told you so" to the rest of the board.'

Once Clough was out of the room, criticism of him knew no bounds, recalls Peter Lorimer. 'The players said, well, the way the manager is behaving has been detrimental towards us all. He's been very critical of us, the club, Don Revie, everything. He's basically knocked the spirit out of the camp.'

Lorimer's recollection is that after the players had had their say, Clough was called back into the meeting. 'Sam Bolton then told him, "Well, we've had a meeting with the players and basically they think you're no good as a manager." Sam Bolton was a very direct guy. Clough replied, "That's their opinion, and I'll tell you why I think they're wrong." Soon after that the meeting broke up.'

John O'Hare had no doubts about what would be the consequences of that extraordinary hour. 'We were playing at Huddersfield in a League Cup game that night and Willie Carlin, my old Derby colleague, came up for it. I remember seeing Willie before the game and telling him, "I think he'll be gone by tomorrow, or if not then, the end of the week."'

Several hours later, Clough did indeed take his players – now openly in revolt against him – to lowly Huddersfield Town of the Third Division for a second-round match in the League Cup. His self-confidence had taken the severest of knocks, but, Clough being Clough, he wasn't yet ready to throw in the towel.

This was a night when he could have been forgiven for thinking that the gods had finally deserted him. With just ten minutes left on the clock, his fretful, stumbling side was drifting towards a humiliating defeat. The score was 1–0 to the home team, and to compound Clough's misery, the normally reliable Lorimer had missed a twice-taken penalty in the first half that would have given his beleaguered outfit a foothold in the game.

His career at Elland Road looked to be heading for an ignominious conclusion. Fifteen thousand spectators packed into the Huddersfield ground on a balmy autumn evening awaited the knockout blow.

As Clough sat back on the bench in the dugout, arms folded and face impassive, a familiar figure loomed large above him in the directors' box, barely 20 yards away. The ghost had appeared in person. Revie, in his familiar sheepskin jacket and driving gloves, was on the eve of announcing his first squad for a 'get-together' in Manchester in a couple of weeks' time.

He'd come to Leeds Road that night to watch the likes of Allan Clarke, Paul Madeley and Norman Hunter, but as he observed them struggling against inferior opposition, he would again have harboured thoughts of resentment against the man below, who had inherited his championship-winning team and now appeared to be leading them towards oblivion. To anyone who had talked to him in the previous month, Revie had appeared utterly distraught at the squandering of the golden legacy he felt he'd built up over a decade or more.

It had been a night when at least some sections of the Leeds fans had demonstrated their loyalty to Clough, chanting his name as he took his seat at the start of the match. But Leeds' former manager decided he'd seen enough after 80 minutes of football. Revie picked up his programme and walked out, keen for a quick exit from the ground after an unsuccessful night's scouting. All he'd discovered – as if he didn't know already – was that his former charges had been stripped of their normal ebullience and confidence.

Back on the pitch, the Leeds players had belatedly found some momentum and were pressing for a result. As the game entered the final minute, and with referee Pat Partridge looking at his watch, Lorimer was put through into the penalty area and, from an acute angle, managed improbably to lash a fierce shot past Huddersfield keeper Terry Poole and into the back of the net. 1–1.

Many of today's football managers rant and rave on the touchline, often making themselves hoarse through vocal entreaties to their players. Clough, throughout his coaching career, was not normally one of those who displayed a surfeit of emotion. On this night, it was different; the sheer relief of a rare moment of success, an indication that the players might just still be willing to give something for him, propelled him from his seat. He clenched both fists in triumphant salute and a smile lit up his face as he celebrated with his backroom staff.

After the game, Clough, typically, paid generous tribute to his opponents: 'I have never in my life seen a Third Division side play as well. They never stopped running from 7.30 until the final whistle. It was not just their running that caused us problems – it was their football that was superb.' On Lorimer's face-saving effort, he remarked: 'It was a goal good enough to win a cup final. After the misses it was going to take something like that to get us one.'

When Clough reflected on his situation as the team bus made the short journey back to Leeds, it may have seemed as if a glimmer of hope was emerging. Much of the day had been a dismal experience for him, but hadn't the players just shown him where it matters, on the pitch, that they were still prepared to fight for him? Given time, couldn't he still turn the season round?

But it was just a fleeting half-hour of satisfaction and respite. Peter Lorimer recalls, 'As we arrived back in Elland Road on the team bus from Huddersfield, the chairman was heard to say that he wanted a chat with the manager.' It sounded ominous to the players, given the events of earlier in the day. Clough travelled immediately to Manny Cussins' home in Alwoodley, Leeds, for yet another awkward meeting on a day he must have felt would never end.

★ ★ ★

Whatever Clough and Cussins talked about – or even agreed – late on Tuesday night, there was no immediate public comment or statement from either of them.

The pressure had certainly been building on Manny Cussins to act to stop the rot. The dapper, white-haired Jewish businessman began his involvement with Leeds United in 1961, when he joined the board having given the club an interest-free loan of £10,000 that had helped to keep it afloat.

Cussins had made his fortune in the furniture retail business, managing the John Peters Furnishing Group; his Waring & Gillow shops were on most UK high streets. But he also had a strong philanthropic streak; the Manny Cussins Foundation, established in 1962, gave large sums of money to the elderly and children at risk.

Cussins became chairman in May 1973, succeeding Percy Woodward. After his flirtation with the idea of appointing Johnny Giles, Cussins, bullish, headstrong and determined to make his mark as chairman, wanted the brightest and the best, and Clough headed the queue after his exploits at Derby County. The new chairman had pursued Clough relentlessly, persuading him to break his contract with Brighton & Hove Albion and come to Elland Road.

Now, just over 40 days later, it was down to Cussins to take responsibility and inform Clough that he had no future at Leeds United. What they discussed in Alwoodley that Tuesday night has never been disclosed, but two months later on *The Frost Interview*, Clough gave the viewers enough clues about how the evening went:

> FROST: Did he actually say – Mr Cussins – 'You're sacked'?
> CLOUGH: No, it's never done as brutally as that. That would be far too forthright, far too literally to the point. I could have coped with that kind of thing quite easily, because in football management you live with the sack, you live with the thought of it in the back of your mind . . . It's done a little more subtly, it's done with a smile, it's done with a [breaks off] . . . when you're sitting on a settee, perhaps in somebody's house. I'm assuming this is the way it's done – it's the first time it's happened to me.

Clough travelled back to the Dragonara Hotel that night knowing that this miserable episode in his life was very nearly over. But there was still plenty of hard negotiating to do to ensure it was, at least, financially worthwhile.

* * *

Wednesday, 11 September passed quietly enough. After the exertions of Tuesday night, the Leeds players had a day off ahead of Saturday's away match at Burnley. Rumours continued to circulate at Elland Road that Clough was in imminent danger of dismissal, but of the man himself nothing was seen or heard in public.

There was, however, a brief response in the press from his nemesis. Revie, irritated by Clough's comments about him in the *Yorkshire Evening Post*, contacted the paper to say, 'I do not wish to become involved in a slanging match, but I wish Clough would stop mentioning my name. A lot of things he has been saying about me are untrue.'

On Thursday morning, 12 September, the newspapers offered no fresh clues to the tumultuous events that lay ahead that day. The front pages continued to focus on the subject of troubled industrial relations, a perennial theme of the early 1970s.

The *Daily Express* carried news of a vital meeting due to take place later that day between the National Coal Board, led by Sir Derek Ezra, and a negotiating team from the National Union of Mineworkers. 'Miners: It's a Big Deal', the headline roared, and there were grounds for hope that the two sides appeared to be on the verge of agreeing a crucial multimillion-pound productivity deal.

Such a deal would banish the memory of the previous winter's fuel crisis and provide a welcome antidote to the slew of grim national news, including rising inflation (then at 16 per cent) and unemployment, and IRA attacks on the British mainland.

The sports coverage centred on another night's action from the League Cup. There was, however, an interesting development on one other managerial story, which had more than a passing link to Elland Road. Terry Neill, the former Arsenal centre-half currently in charge at Hull City, had been appointed manager at Tottenham Hotspur. The man who'd been in charge at White Hart Lane for the previous 15 years, Bill Nicholson, had recommended Johnny Giles as his successor – either on his own or in partnership with Spurs legend Danny Blanchflower. Don Revie had also, once more, put in a word on Giles' behalf. But Neill took over as Tottenham's youngest-ever manager, while the managerial ambitions of Giles were again put on hold.

Then there was a letter on the sports page of the *Yorkshire Post* from one Michael Pulford, of Priory Road, Cottingham. In it, he decried the 'selfishness, ignorance and bad manners by a large number' of the crowd at Elland Road the previous Saturday:

> Do the so-called 'supporters' not realise that when a new manager and new players come to the club it takes time for a pattern to be formed and perfected? Further, can they not imagine that this is particularly so when the new manager is following a legend in his own life, and when one of the new players [McGovern] is temporarily taking the place of the side's playing inspiration [Bremner]?

Such sentiments were probably still shared by a fair number of patient and faithful Leeds United fans. But perhaps more representative of the majority feeling was this letter in the *Yorkshire Evening Post* from L. Gregan, of Dewsbury Road, Leeds:

Come off it, Mr Clough. We supporters can criticise players if
we like. We are used to world-class players at Elland Road and
when we think players are below that standard, we are entitled
to have a go. Perhaps Mr Clough can explain why he has spent
£375,000 on new players who are no better than those in the
reserves?

* * *

At 9 a.m. on Thursday, 12 September, the BBC Radio Leeds sports
editor, 32-year-old John Helm, was arriving for work at his office at the
Woodhouse Lane studios, just down the road from Yorkshire County
Cricket Club's Headingley headquarters.

Helm had been taken under Revie's wing when he arrived at Radio
Leeds in May 1970 after 11 years in print journalism, first on the *Shipley
Times & Express* and then the *Yorkshire Post* and *Evening Post*. He quickly
discovered that the popular image of Revie as a dour, over-obsessed
man didn't match his own experience.

'He realised it was to his benefit to court the local media. But he was
extremely kind. He even sent a bouquet of flowers to my wife when
we had our second child, before he even knew me, really.

'I always say there were two Don Revies: the working DR, the
professional one at Elland Road, and the other one, at home and at his
golf club, where he'd got his sweater on as opposed to his superstitious
blue suit. Then he'd be full of bonhomie, pour you a drink, chat to you
and tell you anything.

'At the club, he knew everyone, down to the tea ladies and the man
administering the ticket office. He'd seek out tickets for the matches
for them, find hotels where they could stay – there was a very kind side
to him.'

On that Thursday morning, it was the ticket-office manager, Don
Tolson, who alerted Helm to the fact that something unusual might be
happening at Elland Road.

'Don knew everything that went on at the club. If not a mole, he
was a very good source of information for me. He rang me at 9.30 and
said, "Something's up," so I just headed down to the ground straight
away.'

Clough had started the day in an ordinary sort of way, out in his
shorts training with the players in preparation for Saturday's match
against Burnley.

But when Helm arrived, the reporter found the players hard at work with Jimmy Gordon, Clough's right-hand man, with no sign of the manager himself on the training ground. However, gazing up at the windows of the boardroom a little later, he could clearly see the figure of Clough flitting in and out of view. In the next few hours, as he began filing pieces into every hourly news bulletin at Radio Leeds, the national press pack began to join him, as anticipation of some kind of announcement began to grow.

* * *

As the journalists massed in the Elland Road car park like eager onlookers awaiting a public hanging, they weren't to know that Clough's fate had already been sealed long before Thursday lunchtime.

Of the ageing men who made up the Leeds board, Manny Cussins, together with Bob Roberts and Sidney Simon, were seen as pro-Clough. Sam Bolton and Percy Woodward (both former chairmen) had been against the appointment from the outset.

The arithmetic, then, would once have favoured Clough. But Roberts, who had gone to Majorca back in July to meet him and help wrest him away from Brighton, was now back on the Spanish island on his own summer holiday and effectively incommunicado. Bolton and Woodward had taken the opportunity to press the case for Clough's removal to Cussins, who had, by then, started to waver significantly.

The four men had held their first meeting that week in secrecy at Maenson House, off Whitehall Road, an office block just a mile and a half away from Elland Road. Maenson House used to be one of the symbols of Leeds' rich manufacturing past, a former clothing factory that was the home of manufacturers Joseph May & Sons, which specialised in ready-to-wear clothing and which had opened a showroom in London's Regent Street in 1936 to display their 'Maenson models'.

At Maenson House, the decision to sack Clough was briefly discussed and agreed; the news was then broken to Clough by Cussins on Tuesday night. Two of the board – Cussins and Woodward – reconvened at Elland Road on Thursday morning. There was the small matter of a pay-off to negotiate with Clough and his lawyer. Cussins said later that the objective of the day had been to achieve a 'parting of the ways with no unpleasantness'.

Clough, in his updated autobiography *Cloughie: Walking on Water*, published in 2002, described the afternoon's events as follows:

> Realising that the situation was reaching a head, I had Colin [Lawrence – his close friend from Derby] with me at Elland Road the day I was bombed out. I had no time for the legal profession in those days. I treated lawyers with contempt, believing that all they were good at was sending bills.
>
> Fortunately for me, Colin knew a solicitor called Charles Dodsworth, from York I believe. Colin asked him to come to the ground, and it was because of his presence and the legal document he helped to draw up that Leeds finished up paying off the contract and all the tax.
>
> I had signed a four-year contract and told Manny Cussins, 'You'll have to square it up.' 'Right,' Cussins replied, but I bet he didn't realise what he'd let himself in for: 'grossing up' I think it was called, or something like that. Whatever the term, what I do know is that Leeds signed an agreement that committed them to paying all my tax for the following three years. Instead of costing them £25,000 as a pay-off, it finally worked out at £98,000.

★ ★ ★

Benjamin Charlesworth Ralph Dodsworth, otherwise known as 'Charlie', is that lawyer credited with saving the day for Clough and, effectively, making him financially secure for life. Today, £100,000 translates into something akin to £700,000. But Dodsworth's recollections of that day are at variance with Clough's account.

Charlie Dodsworth, now aged 85, lives in a spacious bungalow near Malton in North Yorkshire, with splendid views of the Howardian Hills spread out before him as he gazes out of his sitting-room window. His family is firmly established in the Yorkshire gentry, and he can trace the line back to Norman times. Portraits of his ancestors, many of them with the same sturdy, ruddy features that he possesses, stare down from the walls.

He followed his father into the legal profession after the Second World War, but was something of an unwilling lawyer. 'I hated it really, to begin with, and I told my father, and he became quite upset. Gradually, though, I settled into it, dealing with wills, family settlements, trusts and that kind of thing. I did like fighting causes.'

Dodsworth's other role, which he combined with his legal work at the York-based firm of Gray, Dodsworth and Cobb, was that of Under-Sheriff of Yorkshire, an ancient office dating back to medieval times. In that role, he had a grisly duty – to arrange and supervise all the executions in the county, by then, of course, all carried out in private inside the jails.

'I must have seen half a dozen men hanged. I had to be there at the moment of execution with the governor and chief warden of the jail. I got quite friendly with Albert Pierrepoint, the hangman. It wasn't something that unduly perturbed me. I just had to say "now" to Mr Pierrepoint, he would do the job, and the man would disappear through a hole in the ground. I was never there for more than 25 seconds.'

Dodsworth, old-fashioned, garrulous, mildly eccentric, would have been an entertaining drinking companion if you stumbled across him in a bar. That's exactly what Colin Lawrence, Clough's friend and minder, did in the summer of 1974 at the Peacock pub on the Chatsworth estate in the Peak District.

Lawrence, a travelling nylon-stockings salesman, hit it off immediately with the avuncular Yorkshireman, and over games of darts and dominoes Lawrence told Dodsworth of the troubles his friend Brian was having reaching a settlement with Brighton Football Club, with whom he had just broken his contract in order to go to Leeds. 'Colin told me Brighton were suing Brian for damages, and would I act for him. I said no, it's not what I do, someone else should do that. But he was very insistent and I agreed to do it. As I say, I liked fighting causes – especially ones that appeared lost.'

Dodsworth entered into lengthy correspondence with Brighton, and ultimately – and this is after the Leeds episode – he secured a satisfactory outcome for Clough. 'I thought we were going to have a hell of a row. I'd written them several clever and perhaps devious letters, and it appeared that we might have to pay back something in the region of £20,000. Nobody was more surprised than me when the letter came from Brighton's solicitors, saying they had decided to settle. No money passed hands either way, and each side had to pay their own costs. I thought it was a miracle.'

What Dodsworth is less clear about are the events of 12 September and the key role that Clough has given him credit for playing. 'I certainly wasn't with him at the ground. I always took my holiday in September in the south of France, and I'm pretty sure I was in Villefranche that year. I do remember getting a phone call that week asking me if I would come back and see him [Brian], but I couldn't, I had friends staying with me at my holiday villa.'

The sequence of events was almost certainly something like this. With their principal man away, Gray, Dodsworth and Cobb contacted a Leeds firm, Jobbings, Fawcett and Grove, on Wednesday morning, and instructed them to act for Clough over his pay-off. So the man who entered the Leeds boardroom to do battle at Clough's side that day was not Charlie Dodsworth but 51-year-old David Somersall Creasey. The story he later told of what happened that day was a remarkable one of persistence and concentration on the job in hand on one side and rank incompetence on the other.

David Creasey died in 2009, but he recounted the afternoon's events to his son, Julian. 'Two things impressed themselves on my father that afternoon,' he relates. 'Firstly, that Cussins and Woodward had brought no lawyer to advise them and thought they could handle this all on their own; Cussins had a great belief in his own abilities as a businessman. But secondly, that they thought the proper way to conduct the negotiations was by drinking copious gin and tonics. They were getting steadily pissed as the afternoon wore on, while Clough and my father stuck firmly to cups of tea and water.'

The long and short of it was that the two directors just didn't grasp how much this pay-off was going to cost the club. According to David Creasey, the deal that was eventually agreed guaranteed Clough a six-figure sum after tax, plus he was allowed to keep the club Mercedes.

'They [Cussins and Woodward] just didn't appreciate the whack they were going to take. I got the impression from my father that Clough did most of the talking. As you know, he was very bright. He knew what he wanted, but he actually ended up with more than he'd asked for! My father certainly felt he'd been part of a good deal, and at the end Clough came and put his arm round him and said, "Now, David, there's a tale to tell your grandchildren!"'

Clough, then, far from feeling chastened and resentful at his impending dismissal, was, in fact, experiencing a massive surge of relief mixed with no small measure of elation. What was, in many ways, the worst day of his professional career was also turning out to be the most productive in financial terms.

Charles Dodsworth kept in touch with Clough for many years afterwards and even drew up a couple of wills for him. Clough would ring him up and ask him to meet at a restaurant in Walshford Bridge, near Wetherby, where there would invariably be a bottle of champagne on ice. 'He rather disappeared out of my life in the late 1980s. Brian was a card, a rogue, but an absolute charmer. I had a cottage in Welbeck, in Nottinghamshire, where an old nanny who came to us in 1915 and a parlour maid who came in 1919 lived together in retirement after my mother died. Brian used to pop in and visit them now and again, have a drink with them, pull their legs, and they adored him. So did lots of people from all walks of life.'

★ ★ ★

It was around 6 p.m. when the two parties left the boardroom after striking the deal. Word was starting to filter out that Clough's tenure was over even before Manny Cussins came out to make the official announcement. The first wire-service alert read simply: '6.15 CLOUGH FLASH: BRIAN CLOUGH SACKED AS LEEDS UNITED MANAGER.'

At Yorkshire TV headquarters in Kirkstall Road, John Wilford, the editor of programmes, had just finished producing the evening edition of *Calendar*, the regional news programme. Having got wind of the Clough story, he set out to cover it as best he could. In that task, he was helped by an outstanding team of reporters, producers and executives, all of whom went on to make names for themselves in broadcasting in the 1970s, '80s and '90s.

They included Paul Fox, previously controller of BBC1 and later chairman of ITV and managing director of BBC Network TV, who was then director of programmes for Yorkshire Television; Nick Gray, a talented 27-year-old programme director recruited by Fox who later created and produced the groundbreaking hospital drama series *Jimmy's*; Sid Waddell, the charismatic Geordie who would transform the coverage of darts on TV but was then a junior producer in the newsroom; Michael Wood, 26-year-old cub reporter, later to become an outstanding historian and broadcaster; and Kevin Sim, who became executive producer of David Frost's popular daytime programme *Through the Keyhole*.

Wilford himself had a strong background in both sports and news. He had played semi-professional football for Morecambe before turning to football writing and reporting. He reported on the 1966 World Cup for ATV, then became news editor at Yorkshire TV in 1968 before moving up to become editor of programmes.

'Kevin Sim and I were heading off to the bar after *Calendar* finished, pondering what to do on the Clough story,' he recalls. 'Kevin said, "Wouldn't it be great if we could get Clough and Revie together?" I said, "Yes, that would be terrific, but what are the chances?" He said, "I'll go down to Elland Road if you get someone to track down Revie."'

Barely minutes later, Kevin Sim had phoned back, saying Clough had agreed to take part – but wanted paying in cash. Then, almost immediately afterwards, another producer, John Meade, said he'd located Revie in a restaurant in Roundhay Park, one of the more fashionable areas of Leeds. 'I think he'll come,' he said.

'I then phoned Paul Fox,' says Wilford, 'who was still at work, and said, "We're going to have to open up the bank because they both want paying and they both want cash." And, contrary to what has been said since, they both knew they were coming on the programme with each other.'

* * *

Back in Beeston, Manny Cussins and Brian Clough emerged from the Elland Road boardroom bathed in light amid a phalanx of television cameras and the clicking of dozens of flashbulbs. The worst-kept secret of the day was out, and both men looked surprisingly relieved and determined to put the best face on it.

Clough, buoyed up by the scale of his pay-off, could barely contain his glee. 'It's a very sad day for Leeds and for football,' he told the waiting media scrum. 'But I'm feeling very friendly towards Mr Cussins. Everything is fine between him and I.' To demonstrate his affection, he placed an arm round the shoulder of the somewhat embarrassed Leeds chairman.

Cussins said, 'What has been done is for the good of the club. The club and the happiness of the players must come first. Nothing can be successful unless the staff is happy.'

He elaborated in the course of a short, impromptu press conference: 'The feelings of the players influenced us a little, although I must point out that two or three of the established players were of the opinion that Clough should be given [more] time. In general, we have to be big enough to know if we have gone wrong and, in coming to that conclusion, to act to put things right.'

On Clough's golden handshake, he admitted, 'I will not give you the figure, but it was reasonably substantial. No contract has been signed, but there was a moral agreement.' With that, his Rolls-Royce drew up and he headed for his home in Alwoodley. Clough disappeared back to the manager's office.

Meanwhile, John Helm's day was far from done. He wanted the first interview with Clough and made his way towards the East Stand, near the corner flag and adjacent to the car park. The secretary Maureen Holdsworth let him into Clough's office, and he waited for him to come and clear his desk.

Clough arrived, and Helm had his scoop. 'His mood was cocky, defiant, he felt he'd done nothing wrong and couldn't understand it, really. He said he'd been let down by the board [and] even more by the players and that Manny Cussins and Sidney Simon should have had stiffer backbones.'

Bizarrely, Helm and Clough then found themselves locked in the ground; Maureen Holdsworth had gone home and shut the offices up. 'We went back to his office, where he did have access to a phone, and he made the call to get us let out. While we waited, I remember Cloughie ringing the Dragonara Hotel, where he'd been staying, and ordering a crate of champagne. That was his typical response to the day's events!'

Before he left Elland Road, Clough made an unexpected appearance at a meeting that was taking place at the ground about Norman Hunter's testimonial. Those attending – none more so than Hunter himself, who had never seen eye to eye with Clough – were startled when the departing manager popped his head round the door, walked in and handed Hunter a bottle of champagne from the crate he'd just had delivered.

He then turned to Hunter's committee members and said, 'You lot who are looking after this lad – work as hard as you can to earn him as much money as you can. There is no one else deserves it better than he does.' Clough then reclaimed the champagne from Hunter and walked out. To the last, he was nothing if not unpredictable.

* * *

While events were unfolding at Elland Road, back at Kirkstall Road the *Calendar* team were preparing for the Clough–Revie showdown. Paul Fox had successfully applied to ITV's television network centre to 'open up the slot' at 10.30, after *News at Ten*, for a special half-hour programme devoted to Clough's sacking.

At that time, Yorkshire TV was a company riding the crest of a wave. For it to have been able to attract executive talent of the calibre of Fox – the man responsible for bringing to television such classic programmes as *Dad's Army* and *Monty Python's Flying Circus* – showed how highly rated it was by those in the industry.

In 1974 alone, YTV had launched the situation comedy *Rising Damp*, which still stands the test of time; an outstanding drama series, *South Riding*, with Dorothy Tutin as a feminist headmistress; and another sitcom that demonstrated the talents of writer Alan Plater, *Oh No, It's Selwyn Froggitt*. For good measure, comedian Les Dawson, with his deadpan style and curmudgeonly persona, was still going strong with his series *Sez Les*.

Now its main news programme, *Calendar*, was on the verge of a remarkable scoop. Clough and Revie had been trading insults in the media for a number of years, but they'd never been brought together in the same studio. Revie was to claim in that night's debate that he had phoned up the programme after their interview with Clough at the start of the season and asked if he could go head to head with his successor the following evening. He said he had received no reply to that inviting request.

Whatever the truth of that, events were now moving inexorably towards a unique public confrontation between the two rivals. Such a spur-of-the-moment decision to put the programme out live, after *News at Ten*, would be unlikely to happen today. Then, ITV companies had great flexibility about programming and scheduling in their own areas; nowadays, programme output is tightly controlled from the centre.

The presenter entrusted with the task of conducting the debate was 39-year-old Austin Mitchell, co-host along with Richard Whiteley (later of *Countdown* fame). Mitchell had been on the books of Yorkshire TV since 1968, first as a reporter and then as a presenter. A West Yorkshireman by birth, he went to Bingley Grammar School before further education at first Manchester University, then Nuffield College, Oxford. From 1959 to 1967, he lectured in history and sociology at Otago and Canterbury universities in New Zealand.

Later, he would graduate into politics, becoming Labour MP for Great Grimsby, a constituency he still represents today. Affable, gregarious, with an enquiring mind and an acute social conscience, Mitchell possessed all of the attributes required to be a successful constituency MP. Many of those skills apply equally to the job of a reporter/presenter, and in 1974 he was one of Yorkshire TV's rising stars.

Mitchell had chaired that discussion with Clough early in August, and his experience then led him to predict troubles ahead. 'Clough made what I regarded as some daft pledge that he was going to tighten up Leeds' act, and have a much cleaner team,' he recalls. 'It was ill-advised stuff. What he wanted to do was make the point that his would be a brand-new approach, vastly different from that of his predecessor. But, in my opinion, it's best to work your way in rather than barge down the door. So, like everyone else, I was a fascinated observer of the next seven weeks, which proved more and more miserable for him and Leeds.'

At 6 p.m. that day, Mitchell presented a *Calendar* programme with a varied diet of news. There was no conclusion yet from the vital talks between the NUM and the Coal Board. But on the industrial front there was good news to report by way of a big investment boost for Sheffield Steel. Elsewhere in the south of Yorkshire, a tanker had rammed into a cottage at Hatfield, while gypsies were disturbing the peace in Dinnington. And to the east of the county, in Bridlington, a brief thaw in the Cold War, as a contingent of Russian industrialists visited the Satra Motor Car Importation and Preparation Centre – home to the Lada 1200 and Moskvich 1500, perhaps a cheap alternative for British car-owners in that time of recession.

Mitchell recalls, 'At the end of *Calendar*, people normally hung around to have a few drinks to unwind, or just buggered off. I happened to be still around, and then John [Wilford] approached me and said we've got this interview with Clough, and hopefully Revie too – or perhaps it was the other way around, Revie and hopefully Clough.

'Anyway Wilford was in charge and arranging it all, and asked me to hang on and not go home. I did as I was instructed, but I told him I wasn't enthusiastic as I knew so little about recent events, and about Clough and Revie, and frankly I didn't really feel up to the job.'

Nick Gray, who'd been in charge of *Calendar* that day, was asked to stay on and direct the special. To keep the studio open until eleven o'clock meant that the crew of fifteen would need to be paid substantial overtime – some had started the day at nine in the morning. Gray gave them orders to break for supper and meet back at the studio at 9 p.m. Some of them repaired to the YTV bar, where they celebrated their financial windfall, returning two hours later somewhat the worse for wear.

Mitchell was undoubtedly nervous about chairing the discussion,

276

because of his relative lack of knowledge of the subject matter at hand. But he was reassured by Wilford's promise to keep feeding him questions through his earpiece. 'In those days, we all had long hair, so an earpiece could be easily concealed, and I knew John would keep giving me all the relevant prompts.'

Mitchell may have had only a limited grasp of football matters, but it was his unobtrusive style that mattered more. He explains his philosophy: 'My interviewing technique was just to put the pennies in the jukebox, sit back and listen to the records play. Just occasionally, I'd push somebody for an explanation or guide the debate into a new quarter. Interviewing was very different then to the type of aggressive, inquisitorial approach adopted by the likes of John Humphrys today. The interview wasn't about me, it was about them and their views and the interplay between them. I would ask a question and then let it develop.'

Wilford believes that his decision to choose Mitchell to do the interview, rather than expert sports presenter Keith Macklin, was one of the best he ever made in his journalistic life. 'Keith was furious, absolutely furious, but I was quite clear in my mind that this was nothing to do with football. I didn't want a football man talking about keeping it tight at the back and formations up front. I just didn't want that. I wanted this to be about them as people. And I told Austin as we went on air, "If you don't have to speak, don't." And he didn't.'

* * *

On that day on the other side of the Atlantic in San Clemente, California, a depressed Richard Nixon was pondering his future. Just a month earlier, on 8 August, the 37th president had been forced to leave office in disgrace after the truth about the Watergate cover-up emerged. His downfall had been the news story of the summer, indeed the year, a long episode of revelation that had transfixed America and captured the attention of the rest of the world.

As Mitchell contemplated the evening ahead and the nature of the men he would soon be dealing with, a straightforward comparison emerged in his mind. Don Revie and Brian Clough were Yorkshire's very own Richard Nixon and John Kennedy. The fact that the two American presidents had pioneered the live television debate in 1960 lent greater weight to his observation. He was about to embark on a similar project, even though an audience of 66 million was obviously beyond the hopes of Yorkshire TV executives.

Nixon and Kennedy had once been firm friends in Congress across the political divide. But the early fondness between the two degenerated into distrust and paranoia. As Mitchell saw it, those words could equally describe the prevailing nature of Clough and Revie's relationship – if you could call it that. The two men, both desperate to reach the very pinnacle of their world of professional football, had rubbed along without apparent rancour in their early years, but had been at each other's throats in recent times.

Physical and behavioural comparisons were valid, too. Revie, particularly under pressure, possessed the dark, brooding, saturnine countenance and hostile manner that Nixon so often presented. Clough's youthful face, his effervescence and optimism, together with a punchy vocal delivery, were all out of the Kennedy mould.

Although Clough was a manager on the make and had one league championship under his belt, it was Mitchell's belief that he was certainly jealous of the older man's achievements. 'I also felt that the fact that they came from the same area heightened the challenge, in the sense that Clough felt Revie should behave differently coming from the North-East, that rather than exhibit its dourness, he should express its interest and excitement.'

As Clough arrived at the Kirkstall Road studios for the interview, word had filtered back to Mitchell and Wilford about his buoyant mood. 'In the car, he'd kept saying, "This is the big one," clearly a reference to the pay-off he'd just secured,' says Wilford. 'He was certainly bouncy and showy on arrival, and the thought occurs to me now that maybe he was a little bit drunk.'

Clough himself, in his autobiography, confirmed that money was uppermost in his mind that evening. 'I was preoccupied by thoughts of only one place – the bank. I wanted to get the Leeds cheque into my account as quickly as possible.' He recalled that later, after the debate had finished, 'As I lounged in the back seat of the car for the final few miles home, I put my feet up, stretched my arms behind my head, and said: "Gentlemen, we've just won the pools."'

Revie's mood was somewhat less euphoric. He was now England manager, of course, just two months into the job and starting to contemplate a European Championship qualifying match against Czechoslovakia the following month. He was excited at the prospect of revitalising the national team, but the bonds with Leeds United, strengthened over 13 years, were proving hard to shake off. He had looked on aghast over the previous seven weeks as Clough had – as he saw it – wrecked his team, his legacy to the city of Leeds. He had a festering sense of resentment.

* * *

Both men arrived at the Kirkstall Road studios 'loosened up' – Clough from drinking his celebratory champagne at Elland Road, Revie from the effects of a good meal in Roundhay. Revie, as befitted his status as England manager, was shown upstairs to Paul Fox's office, while Clough was taken downstairs to the green room, the main hospitality suite.

Fox, aged 49, was already well on the road to legendary status in the broadcasting industry. His stewardship of BBC1 in the late 1960s had seen the flowering of exceptional dramatic writing talent, notably Harold Pinter, Dennis Potter and David Mercer. On the sporting front, he'd invented the BBC Sports Personality of the Year competition and persuaded Roger Bannister into the studio just hours after he'd run the first sub-four-minute mile.

Fox had got to know Revie back in 1956 when the England manager, then a Manchester City player, gave him two tickets for the FA Cup final at Wembley – in which Revie had a starring role in Manchester's 3–1 victory over Birmingham City, a match best remembered for the bravery of the badly injured goalkeeper Bert Trautmann. 'After that, we became friends. I didn't have many footballers as friends, but I liked and admired Don. I had a great deal of time for him, and I knew that all those stories about how greedy he was were unfair. He told me why he was always preoccupied with his finances – because in addition to supporting his wife Elsie and children Duncan and Kim, he also had to provide for two invalid aunts.

'When I chatted with him, it was enjoyable, like chatting to a mate. And in the days when most football players were monosyllabic, Don could speak eloquently and explain how football was played and his philosophy for the game.'

Revie's and Clough's fees for their TV appearance that night required a bit of hasty work on his behalf. 'I knew they had to be paid in cash, but I didn't have any, so I had to ring up the secretary of the company, Leslie Formby, who was at some kind of bowls night somewhere, and get him to drive straight back to Leeds and open up the safe in my secretary's office and get the money out! It was highly unusual and highly unorthodox – but this was a great coup, and we wanted to make it happen.'

Fox's recollection is that the two men were paid around £150 each. Wilford believes the sum was much higher: £400, which would be worth around £2,700 now. Fox handed one envelope to Revie, Wilford the other one to Clough.

Wilford remembers a little encounter with Clough before final preparations for the show began that was illustrative of his complex character. 'Clough said brusquely, "I'd like 40 Senior Service," and I said, "Did I hear you right, or did you say, please, John, would you be kind enough to get me 40 cigarettes?" And at that he put his arm around me and said, "John, I'm sorry, I don't know why I behave like this."'

* * *

Just before 10 p.m., as *Calendar* were finalising their preparations, a call came from ITN asking if Clough could be put into a studio to do a quick 'down-the-line' interview. *News at Ten* wanted to do it at 10.10, an indication that it was far more than just a big sports story but was rated as one of the main news stories of the day.

It was very nearly a disaster, as Nick Gray recalls: 'ITN warned us over the talkback that they would be coming to us shortly for the interview with Clough. He was brought in, looking very merry and eating a cheese sandwich to soak up all the champagne he'd been drinking that afternoon.

'As studio director, I heard the ITN control room counting down to us. I yelled at the floor manager to get the sandwich out of Clough's mouth. The floor manager lunged into shot, grabbed the cheese sandwich from the Clough mouth, removing it at the exact moment that ITN cut to our output, and I cued into the short interview.'

* * *

After his *News at Ten* appearance, Clough was taken along the corridor to Studio 2, and ten minutes later, just a minute before the start, Revie was led in and shown to his seat next to Clough.

The scene was now set. The final advert after *News at Ten* faded away, to be replaced by the familiar *Calendar* music played out over the title 'Goodbye Mr Clough', with some scenes of the recently departed Leeds manager in a tracksuit top and club shirt, one of them amongst a crowd of apparently adoring fans.

The set was minimalist. Against a stark blue-grey background, three basic chairs were arranged together in a semi-circle around a clear table with three glasses of water placed on top of it.

The three men's appearance and apparel spoke eloquently about their character and personality. Mitchell's hair did indeed disguise his earpiece, but his Beatles-style mop looked a touch old-fashioned, more '60s than '70s. He wore a dark-blue suit, light-blue shirt and a wide, green and blue patterned tie.

Clough wore a close-fitting light-grey suit – wide-lapelled, as was the fashion – accompanied by a striped blue and white shirt and a diamond-patterned blue tie. His hair was immaculately coiffured, with a modest quiff in place. He looked utterly relaxed and at ease for a man who'd been through a traumatic day – but then the television studio had become almost a second home for him.

Revie wore a bright royal-blue blazer, a white shirt, his dark England tie (with the three lions emblem) and light-grey trousers. His hair was slicked back and his sideburns were long; the face, on this occasion, was austere and unsmiling. No description of Revie has ever bettered that by Arthur Hopcraft in his seminal book about soccer, *The Football Man*: 'He is a big, flat-fronted man with an outdoors face, as if he lives permanently in a keen wind.'

Wilford had been deliberate about the seating arrangements. 'I didn't put them on either side of the table, I put them side by side, so they didn't need the interviewer and could turn and talk to each other more naturally. It worked very well in making them engage with each other.'

Mitchell introduced the programme in suitably dramatic fashion:

> Tonight the football world has been stunned by the shock news that after only seven weeks in the job Brian Clough has been sacked as manager of Leeds United. It's been claimed that the footballers passed a vote of no confidence in him, and certainly today the board took the shock decision that Clough must go. Tonight on the live *Calendar* special, we're talking not only to Brian Clough himself, but also to the man whom he succeeded as the manager of Britain's most successful football team, to Don Revie, the England manager. But Brian Clough: first of all, Brian, what's your reaction to being booted out in this fashion?

Clough responded easily and fluently. He said he was very sad but suggested that seven weeks was hardly a long time to be given to prove yourself in any kind of work. 'I would hope that Mr Revie would get a lot longer time in his job,' he added. The old arrogance was on show; he said he had always been convinced it was going to work out, and claimed, 'I don't want to be blasé or conceited, but I'm not sure who they could have got to improve his [Revie's] record.'

Mitchell then threw the ball into Revie's court, asking him if he thought it was possible for Clough – for anyone, indeed – to step into his shoes at Leeds. Revie's response was that it would have been a very, very difficult job for anyone to do. As Mitchell then cut in to ask whether Brian Clough was the man he would have wanted to succeed him, Revie's tetchy mood exhibited itself:

> Austin, Austin, don't start jumping the gun. You asked me a question – I'm going to answer it . . . last season we had an awful lot of injuries and suspensions, and we played without four and five and then six players, right from the very first match. I knew the players. Clough – because he calls me Revie – didn't know them. And I knew how to handle them, to juggle them about, and he didn't have the time to do that.

While Revie worked through a long, ponderous answer, the camera panned to Clough's face, where, chin in hand, he suddenly looked up to give a cheeky, schoolboyish smirk to the viewers. Indeed, the debate at this stage felt as if one was watching from within a headmaster's study, with an errant boy explaining his misdemeanour and why he'd committed it, and the teacher being rather disdainful of the explanation. Clough was trying to justify his short tenure at Elland Road, and Revie wasn't having any of it.

The five or six minutes that followed were for the footballing connoisseur. With Mitchell holding the ring effectively, Clough and Revie argued over players and tactics, from the minutiae of midfield player Terry Yorath's enteritis to the broader question of whether full-back Frankie Gray merited the description 'world-class'. There was even a fleeting alliance between the two men when the hapless Mitchell dared to suggest to Clough that the players might not have been trying for him out on the pitch. The exchange – and the revelation from Clough that followed – moved the programme into another gear:

AM: Well, let's look. Are you sure the team was playing its best for you?

BC: Oh, I'm absolutely certain.

AM: With results like that?

BC: Oh, results like that [loud and dismissive]! Of course they were playing their best.

DR: Austin . . .

BC: They couldn't do anything else. It was second nature to them . . .

DR: Thank you, Austin. Let me ask you a question. How long have you lived in Leeds?

AM: Five years. And I've never seen such a disastrous start to the season.

DR: Have you ever seen a Leeds United team not try? They might have had bad times, they might miss open goals, but never, ever should you accuse or insinuate that a Leeds United side never tried, because there's never been a player who's gone out on that pitch in a white shirt who didn't try. They might have had a bad game, they might miss open goals, they might do bad things, but never not try.

AM: OK, I accept that, but there have been claims that there was in fact a vote of no confidence, or something amounting to that, passed by the players. Is that correct?

BC: That is absolutely correct.

AM: Well, how did you react to that?

BC: Oh, I wanted to be sick. Oh, I wanted to be sick. If you had a vote of no confidence from the people you'd worked with, I would assume you'd react the same way. I felt sick.

AM: What was the main reason for it, do you think?

BC: I don't know what the main reason was. I think, you know, I didn't have time to get to know them, and that type of thing. I do believe honestly, whoever had walked in would have had the same problems. Plus the fact that all the other incidentals went against us, i.e. results and that type of thing.

With that, the programme stopped for a half-time break and adverts. Clough's admission that his players had passed a vote of no confidence in him was confirmation of the rumours that had been swirling around Elland Road that day – but no less startling for that. A feeling of freedom was clearly coursing through his veins after the day's events, and he seemed unworried by what might be regarded by others as loose talk.

Clough's supremely relaxed, disarming approach, combined with an innate fluency and articulacy, had been in sharp contrast to the ponderous, at times hectoring approach of Revie. But if it was a boxing match, you might have scored them level on points. Clough had been on the defensive right from the start because of his failure at the job; Revie had made it clear – if not explicitly, then implicitly – that it had been a foolish appointment, and there was plenty of evidence to back him up.

The fierceness of the rivalry was, even in the first half-hour, self-evident. Occasionally, each man seemed to reach out to the other just for a moment, like a recently divorced couple put together in a room and hesitantly, occasionally a little wistfully, trying to recapture old understandings.

But the depth of their animosity had yet to be laid bare. It started to surface soon after the break, as Revie finished a long answer responding to an accusation by Clough (in his previous *Calendar* interview) that he had failed to sort out the players' contracts before he left to take up the England job.

> DR: Now, on that same programme, Brian said there was no warmth in the club. Now, that really shook me.
> BC: Did I say no warmth?
> DR: You said no warmth in Leeds United [slight apologetic grimace by Clough]. Now [what I had] was the closest thing any group of players and staff have ever had.
> BC: Did I say no warmth? Did I say no warmth between me and them, or no warmth in the club?
> DR: No, you said no warmth in the club, Brian.
> BC: I don't remember. If I did say it, then obviously the warmth that you generated between you and the players – that can't be taken away.
> DR: Never, ever [hint of a smile at Clough's climb-down].

Austin Mitchell took this exchange as his cue to pursue the reasons for the personal antagonism. What follows encapsulates perfectly Clough's football philosophy and why he believed it to be superior to Revie's; it also captures Revie's deep-seated enmity for a man who had taunted him mercilessly in the media in recent years.

AM: You have different styles as managers and it's generally believed – with some accuracy – that you don't get on particularly well. Now, why is that? Brian Clough?

BC: Well, when I was manager of Derby County I was in direct conflict with Don Revie and his Leeds side, and it's natural I didn't get on with him, because invariably they were above us. Er, that's the flippant answer. Having said that, I believe in a different concept of football to Don. I believe it can be played slightly different to the way Don plays it, and get the same results. Now, that may be aiming for Utopia, and it might be me being a little bit stupid, but that is the way I am. I'm a little bit stupid regarding this type of thing. I'm a little bit of an idealist, I do believe in fairies and that is my outlook. Now, Don's slightly different, and his record proves, over results, that he's actually right. But having said that, I want to be like me. And Don obviously wants to be like him.

AM: Don Revie, is this a question of style, why the two of you don't get on?

DR: Well, I don't know . . . I think that, truthfully, Brian is a fool to himself. I must be very honest here. I honestly feel he's criticised Matt Busby, Bertie Mee, me personally, Peter Lorimer, Norman Hunter, Billy Bremner, Peter Storey. He's criticised so many people in the game whose records are there for all to see. He's criticised so many people. This is his style, and if that's his style, fair enough, but I think that is totally, totally wrong for the game of professional football. He says about honesty and things like this, but when you talk about honesty, if honesty is going to destroy the game then you're in all kinds of trouble. I think you're doing the game a disservice.

For Revie, the programme was proving, in one sense, cathartic. He was tired of the constant goading by Clough, and determined to have his say. But he remained flat-footed in contrast to Clough's nimble verbal dexterity. The logic that Clough provided for his notion that he would win the league 'better' than Revie escaped him completely.

BC: I said I want to win the league, but I want to win it better. Now, there is no other reply to that question, because you had won the league.

285

> DR: No, there's no way you could win the league any better . . .
>
> BC: Why not?! [making a sweeping gesture with his arm]
>
> DR: No, no, no. We lost only four matches . . .
>
> BC: Well, I could lose only three!
>
> DR: No, no, no.

The programme had now moved into completely new territory. It was an arena where Austin Mitchell was completely redundant, because for three to four minutes he asked no questions but sat back as Clough and Revie probed each other's defences.

One very long exchange revealed differences in their management style: Revie was baffled as to why Clough hadn't made a morale-boosting address to the whole Leeds United staff on his first day; Clough said he'd concentrated on training with the players. They even, bizarrely, tried to outdo themselves as to who had – literally – the most hands-on relationship with the players:

> BC: I took their shirts off their backs after they'd finished training.
>
> DR: I used to do that, and massage them on a Thursday.

Underneath it all, the bad feeling, the edge between the two men, quietly simmered away, occasionally nearly boiling over:

> DR: I never got close to Ramsey. He was a cold man.
>
> BC: I think you are!
>
> DR: A cold man? Oh, don't ask our players that or they'll laugh their socks down.
>
> BC: That's opinion.

When Mitchell finally returned to the fray, it was to wrap up the programme. Clough reached out to Revie in a playful way:

> AM: What's going to happen now to Brian Clough?
>
> BC: Oh, many things are going to happen to Brian Clough. Er, I'm going to have forty-eight hours, or three days, I don't know, to think things over. I think – and please don't think I'm being flippant – I've got many ambitions in life, and one of my ambitions is – and I wanted this when I was manager of Leeds and Derby – I want to coach the England youth! I might just

apply to this guy! [gesturing in the direction of a stony-faced Revie]

Revie was having none of this peace offering. Invited by Mitchell to make the final remarks, he said this in response to the question of how he felt about Clough's personal situation:

> Well, naturally, anyone who's been sacked in football, you feel a little bit sad for. But whether Brian's gone about it the right way, I don't know, because I wasn't there. But if Leeds United players have had a meeting with Brian, and the chairman, then there must have been something totally wrong.

The credits rolled and the two adversaries shuffled off the set without a word to each other. Revie didn't loiter, and as he headed off into the night no doubt his mind was starting to turn towards the England challenge awaiting him. Six weeks later, he got off to the perfect start with a 3–0 win over Czechoslovakia at Wembley in front of 76,000 appreciative fans.

Clough was driven back to his home in Derbyshire, stopping off there briefly before heading back out to the Queen's Hotel in Quarndon for a drink with friends and footballing colleagues.

He'd phoned Duncan McKenzie and asked him to join the party. McKenzie remembers, 'The first thing he said to me was, "I'll mark your card. You're the worst-paid player in the club!" Then he gave me a bit of advice: "Another thing: all your nutmegs and your back-heels, all your clever flicks – never change."'

The next morning, Friday, 13 September, Clough, barely able to believe his good fortune, still had the matter of his pay-off cheque on his mind. In his autobiography, he recalled:

> I'd been in touch with my own bank manager, who advised me that the quickest way of steering the Leeds cheque into my account in Derby was to present it at the issuing bank, next morning. So Colin drove back to Leeds and handed in the cheque, which was then expressed into my personal account. Thank you very much, Manny Cussins – wherever you are.

For Austin Mitchell, there were no feelings of elation about the events of that Thursday night. It was an opportunity they'd grabbed – and

287

grabbed very successfully. 'It was one of those accidental achievements, from my perspective,' he reflects now. 'I felt it was a cathartic interview because it summed up the basic tensions and the basic characters of those two men at a moment of strain which heightened everything. Their real characters shone through, and that's the whole purpose of a television interview, to me – to show what people really are.'

He believed, like many people watching, that Clough was the clear 'winner'. 'Revie was always much better on his own. I was, I suppose, basically on Clough's side, as a person. I thought he was a likeable, outgoing guy in nearly every way. He could use bullying tactics, but he was essentially honest and open and articulate.'

A head-to-head debate between the two leading football managers of the day could never happen in today's climate, where big money rules and the top football clubs – which are effectively businesses – are controlled so tightly. Alex Ferguson and Arsène Wenger locking horns in a half-hour special is but a dream.

For Clough and Revie, all roads now led to Lancaster Gate. Revie would spend the next three years trying to make a success of the 'impossible job' of England manager. Clough would bide his time, rebuilding his reputation at Nottingham Forest before waiting for the opportunity to fulfil his own lifetime's ambition.

Chapter 13
'Not Worth the Aggravation'

Despite his humbling experience at Leeds, it wasn't in Brian Clough's nature to go away and hide while he attempted to rehabilitate his reputation. Just two months after walking out of Elland Road, he was back on television, talking about life, football – and Don Revie.

This time he was the guest of that other consummate chat-show host, David Frost. *The Frost Interview* in those days went out at 9.25 p.m. on BBC2, sandwiched on this occasion between a music programme called *Colour My Soul* and a late-night film, *Poor Cow*, a typically stark story of a working-class girl forced to turn to crime from Ken Loach, the master of British social-realist cinema.

Clough had been enjoying his new-found freedom after the experience at Leeds, able to relax in the knowledge that he was now, effectively, financially secure for the rest of his life. But clearly the wounds left from those calamitous 44 days were still raw enough. Asked by Frost to reflect on his time at Elland Road, Clough wasted little time in launching yet another verbal assault on his predecessor:

> CLOUGH: Perhaps I didn't give them [the players] enough time to get over the guy who was there before me – because he was there for a long, long time. Perhaps I wanted to get with them the same feeling that they'd had with the other guy. I'm loath to mention him, you know, and if we can refrain from doing it, [I hope] we'll do so [Clough smiles and laughs].
>
> FROST: It's really like the House of Commons, isn't it? You hate to mention him – why?
>
> CLOUGH: I hate to mention him. Why? Because he's a very talented man and I don't like him. Don't ask me why . . . that's

how it is. He's a very, very talented man and his record is unsurpassable. But I just don't happen to like him, and I don't like the way he goes about football either.

FROST: Why don't you want me to ask you why you don't like him?

CLOUGH: Because I can't tell you. It's impossible. We'd get closed down, David [laughter from audience].

FROST: Do you want to experiment?

CLOUGH: No [more laughter, as he sips from a glass of water].

It was another indication from Clough that it wasn't just Revie's methods at Leeds United that he disliked so intensely – that there was some other reason, some accusation, that was lurking in the background, too dangerous to mention because of potential legal pitfalls.

He wasn't quite finished with his attack. Frost asked Clough about his aspirations for the England job and his disappointment at not being considered six months earlier. He replied, 'It was a possibility, because everyone has got a chance. But I do feel envy when this particular man has got this particular job. And this is the thing I must dismiss from my mind. Very important.'

Later on in the interview, Clough did concede that Revie had done 'a superb job' in guiding England to their 3–0 victory over Czechoslovakia at Wembley two weeks earlier. But in the course of the half-hour interview, he steadfastly refused to mention Revie even once by name, instead referring to him as 'that man' or 'that particular guy'.

The depth of Clough's ill feeling was relayed to Revie by journalists while the England manager was scouting in Berne, Switzerland. He replied succinctly yet sharply, 'Brian Clough has to earn his living somehow, and I don't wish to say anything which may stop him from doing so.'

Just over seven weeks later and Clough was back collecting a wage for the job he did best, that of managing a football team. Now he'd had to lower his ambitions and hope to work his way back to the top from the lower divisions – in this instance from Division Two, with Nottingham Forest.

At first glance, the City Ground was an unpromising place from which to resurrect his faltering career. Very much as at Derby County, the side was languishing near the bottom of the table, the team a mixture of experienced players who had failed to fulfil their potential and younger ones who had yet to realise theirs. Home gates averaged not much more than 10,000 and many of the club's brightest prospects had had to be sold to keep the finances on an even keel. 'They didn't just need a new manager – the bloody place was so dead it needed the kiss of life,' was Clough's characteristically blunt assessment.

In fact, he got off to the best possible start with two wins in London in the first few days. On his third day in charge, Wednesday, 8 January, his Forest side beat Tottenham Hotspur of the First Division 1–0 in an FA Cup replay at White Hart Lane, centre-forward Neil Martin scoring the header for a notable upset in front of 27,996 spectators. Forest then remained in London for a Saturday league encounter with Fulham at Craven Cottage, again achieving a narrow but important 1–0 victory. This time Barry Butlin scored the vital goal.

But that was as good as it got, and Forest slowly sank back into the mire, finishing sixteenth, just six points clear of the relegation places. Clough had identified the problem areas and had at least started to put them right in the three months at his disposal, helped by two of his old favourites, John McGovern and John O'Hare.

McGovern had now been with Clough throughout his entire managerial journey, while O'Hare had joined the train just one stop down the line at Derby County in 1968. They now rejoined Clough from Leeds, where they'd remained, largely unused, after their master had quit the scene. Clough took great delight in buying them back at reduced transfer prices, thus ensuring that Leeds had done very badly out of the deals involving the two men.

As the 1975–76 season started to unfold, these two were the undoubted backbone of a developing side, which also featured improved displays from the likes of Martin O'Neill and John Robertson (who'd been on the transfer list for a long period under previous manager Alan Brown), with Ian Bowyer and a promising young full-back called Viv Anderson also making crucial contributions. Clough's shrewdest signing for the new season was probably the experienced Newcastle full-back Frank Clark.

Clough rejuvenated Forest to the extent that they rose eight places in the table, finishing strongly with nine wins and just two defeats in their last fifteen games of the campaign. He was satisfied – but only up to a point. 'I weeded out those who couldn't do it, encouraged those who could, made sure the directors knew their place, and guaranteed we figured in the papers on a regular basis with more than our fair share of back-page leads.'

Down in Division Three, his old friend and colleague Peter Taylor had narrowly missed out on promotion with Brighton & Hove Albion. With just four games to go, Brighton stood in the third promotion place, only for a disastrous run-in of one defeat and three draws to see them pipped at the post by Cardiff City.

Taylor, initially loyal to Brighton and their likeable chairman Mike Bamber when Clough walked out, now felt the moment had come and gone for him on the south coast. He was ripe for a change, and ready for an approach to call him back to his home-town club . . .

* * *

Don Revie had thrown himself into the England job – on and off the field – with enthusiasm, hard work and his familiar meticulous attention to detail.

In a letter to one of his new bosses, Professor Sir Harold Thompson (soon to be chairman of the Football Association), on 31 March 1975, he sent him his diary for the previous few months so that Thompson could see just what he'd been doing, day by day.

It had been a punishing schedule. Aside from all his footballing commitments with the full England team, the Under-21s, youth and schoolboy sides, plus any number of corporate events he had to attend, Revie was taking a particularly close interest in commercial activities associated with the national side.

He believed there was scope for exploiting the England 'brand', thus bringing in extra sources of income for the Football Association that could be ploughed back into the game at all levels. His critics saw it as another example of his obsession with money, but in fact he spotted these business opportunities long before they would become commonplace in football. He told Thompson:

> Mr Croker [FA Secretary] will be informing you of all the discussions we have had with Austen Reeds, Courtauld, the Milk Marketing Board, Stylo Football Boots and Thomas Cooks. The MMB and Austen Reed have offered us certain sums of money over a period of five years which you have to decide on in the near future whether to accept or not.

At this stage, Revie and Thompson were managing to maintain a cordial enough working relationship. They were both stubborn Yorkshiremen, but that's almost where the comparisons end. Thompson, the son of the chief executive of a colliery, was a brilliant scientist, an Oxford don who had moved in the highest circles of his profession, rubbing shoulders with the likes of Albert Einstein, Erwin Schrödinger and Max Planck.

Thompson himself was a chemist who numbered Margaret Thatcher among his students. His chief passion away from the classroom had always been football, and in 1948 he was one of the founders of the Pegasus team, an amateur side that drew players from Oxford and Cambridge. In 1950–51, in only their third season, Pegasus beat Bishop Auckland 2–1 in the final of the FA Amateur Cup final at Wembley.

Thompson extolled the Corinthian ideals of soccer, which, regrettably but inevitably, seemed out of place in the modern game. But despite having the best interests of the game at heart, his commendable philosophy on football and life was not always matched by his own behaviour. He was an autocrat, treating some of his staff as a Victorian gentleman might treat visiting tradesmen. He regularly referred to Ted Croker, the affable secretary of the FA, not by his Christian name or even as Mr Croker but merely as 'Croker'.

With his imperious, often rude manner, this middle-class Yorkshireman from a privileged background and the prickly Revie from his working-class milieu always seemed likely to clash at some point. Yet when Thompson replied to Revie's letter of 31 March, his sympathy and appreciation were evident: 'I thought that I lived a mad, hectic life, but I think yours is even more gruelling and complex. At any rate, I am sure that everybody is grateful for the effort you are putting in, and I hope that in due course it will be properly rewarded.'

By the end of June 1976, two years into his job, you could put forward a convincing argument on Revie's behalf. The bare statistics showed that England had played eighteen, won eleven, drawn four and lost three – a solid enough record.

World champions West Germany were beaten 2–0 at Wembley on an entertaining if rain-soaked evening in March 1975, with the extravagantly gifted Alan Hudson – on his debut – and the effervescent Alan Ball controlling much of the play against a side that boasted the likes of Franz Beckenbauer, Rainer Bonhof, Berti Vogts and Sepp Maier.

Then, in May, Scotland were trounced 5–1 at Wembley, the highlight of which was a coruscating performance in central midfield by Gerry Francis of Queens Park Rangers, a player recommended to Revie at Leeds a few years back but whom he had declined to bring to Elland Road.

The good run continued on 13 June 1976 in the Olympiastadion, Helsinki, where England comfortably disposed of Finland 4–1 in their first qualifying match for the 1978 World Cup, regulars Kevin Keegan (with two) and Mick Channon (one) providing three of the goals.

But in amongst the highlights were some major disappointments – and some worrying trends. The critical defeat had come in a vital European Championship match in Bratislava on 30 October 1975 against an extremely capable Czechoslovakian side.

The match was first played on Wednesday, 29 October, but abandoned because of fog after just 17 minutes. When the teams reconvened the following night, Mick Channon gave England the lead after 26 minutes only for Zdenek Nehoda to pull the home side level on the stroke of half-time.

Peter Gallis added a second just after the interval and the Czechs comfortably held on for a deserved victory. Their inspiration that night was 27-year-old Jaroslav 'Bobby' (his nickname after his idol, Bobby Charlton) Pollak, whose technique and strategic thinking in midfield outfoxed Gerry Francis, Kevin Keegan and Colin Bell.

Czechoslovakia went on to win the final in Belgrade the following June, defeating West Germany on penalties after extra time. With hindsight, then, not a loss to be ashamed of, but at the time the media were quick to fault Revie's tactics, particularly his decision to play Keegan in midfield rather than in his normal striking role.

Revie's relationship with the national media had always been a spiky one. He was quick to take offence – there had been plenty of that during the Leeds years – and wasn't averse to ringing up individual reporters and editors when they'd written something of which he disapproved.

Nevertheless, it came as a surprise to Brian Glanville of the *Sunday Times* when two days after the Czech game Revie came on the BBC's *Sports Report* radio programme to discuss the match with him. Perhaps it was a gesture of openness worth applauding; but can you imagine Fabio Capello, Sir Alex Ferguson or Arsène Wenger slugging it out with the leading sportswriters of the day in a free-for-all debate?

In actual fact, Revie did himself few favours by confronting the urbane Glanville on air. There were some lively enough exchanges on the tactics of the match (the Keegan role), but Revie was clearly seething at Glanville's previous criticism of him and allowed himself to appear undignified.

> REVIE: It's a little bit disturbing when you get fellows as intelligent as Brian Glanville writing articles like he did on Sunday, saying that I'd become isolated, pompous, one thing and another . . .
> GLANVILLE: I didn't say you'd become pompous, Don . . .
> REVIE: Ah, well, you insinuated that, and I think you know me better than that. And then another thing you say in your article, that my tactics were wrong against Czechoslovakia. At least I went for an attacking policy that everybody's been screaming about, and you've been screaming about, Brian. Now you've turned the tables on me and said I should have played defensive.

The problem was that Revie did increasingly appear to be swayed by public opinion – as reflected in the press – rather than backing his own judgement about individual players and systems, as he would have done in his Leeds days.

He admitted as much a few years later: 'Where I went wrong was not following Ramsey's example. He picked a squad he thought was the best and stuck by them. I was trying to find talent like I had at Leeds with Billy Bremner and Johnny Giles, but it wasn't really there. I do blame myself for chopping and changing too much.'

In fact there was some talent available for Revie and England, perhaps not quite in the Bremner and Giles class, but nonetheless there. Yet the likes of Alan Hudson, Charlie George, Frank Worthington and Tony Currie were either used briefly and then discarded or, in the case of Stan Bowles, not played at the right time or in the right position.

Revie found it hard to come to terms with the transitory nature of the job, only being able to bring his players together for a few days before matches. Working with his players at Leeds six days a week, he'd been able to build up a unique spirit, camaraderie and sense of loyalty that he couldn't hope to replicate with England. He wasn't able to exert the same sort of control over the playing or the administrative side that he'd had in the past, and it left him frustrated.

Trevor Brooking, West Ham's skilful playmaker, had made his

England debut against Portugal in the dying days of the Ramsey era. By the summer of 1976, he had forced his way back into the international reckoning and was an impressive performer in a tournament in America in which England beat Italy and America and lost narrowly to Brazil. He was also in the side that beat Finland 4–1 in Helsinki, giving England's World Cup campaign the ideal start.

But Brooking could sense that, by then, what had worked well at Leeds was becoming counterproductive at England – and that Revie was starting to lose the respect of a large section of the team:

> The dossiers were certainly something I'd never experienced at West Ham. But I remember, playing Finland, you might have thought from reading them that we were playing some sort of world-beaters, because they were emphasising what you had to be wary of and be careful of, preparing us for the worst when we should have been building ourselves up. They were a little bit OTT.

By then, the extracurricular activities that had suited the Leeds players fine had also become the object of derision from the England squad:

> We would have the indoor putting and the bingo, with sessions when we'd all put money into a kitty and play out the winners. Now, it was to encourage togetherness, and I can understand the idea, but, you know, there were some seasoned pros who, I think, wondered what on earth was going on. They'd deliberately lose in the putting competition so they could get upstairs, rest up and watch the TV.

England's inadequacies, papered over to a large extent up until then, were well and truly exposed by a fluid Italian side at the Stadio Olimpico in Rome on 17 November 1976. It was the crucial match of the whole World Cup group, the game from which England needed at least a point to make them feel qualification was realistic.

Revie played Stan Bowles despite the QPR player having just recovered from flu, but he primarily opted for caution, with defensively minded midfield players Brian Greenhoff and Paul Madeley winning places in the line-up.

Giancarlo Antognoni's deflected free kick gave the Italians a fortuitous lead in the 36th minute and they rarely looked back after that. The clinching goal, a diving header from Roberto Bettega, was a masterpiece of intelligent, flowing football.

'Bankrupt' was the headline in the next day's *Daily Express*. 'No amount of talk of early resistance, a near recovery, a chancy first goal, can obscure the basic truth that much of English Soccer remains naive compared with the leading exponents,' wrote David Miller.

'World's Apart' was the view of the *Daily Mirror*. Frank McGhee reported:

> It wasn't manager Don Revie's fault that England lost a vital World Cup qualifying match in the Olympic stadium here yesterday. It was the failure of English football as a whole.
>
> We have men who can run and chase, battle and work – something they all did manfully, sweatily in this match. But the Italians have men who can really PLAY.

Any England manager knows he's in trouble when football writers – as they did then – start to make comparisons with 1953 and the lessons Billy Wright's England side were taught by the Hungarians at Wembley. The gulf in class between the England side and the best of the Europeans was further illustrated in England's next game on 9 February 1977.

The great Johan Cruyff brought a young Dutch side to Wembley for a friendly match and it was all over by half-time. Two beautifully taken goals from Cruyff's protégé, 20-year-old Jan Peters of Nijmegen, the product of Total Football, left the likes of Dave Watson and Mike Doyle, good honest triers but no more than that at international level, floundering. England were lucky to trail by just two as they were torn apart by a dozen or more magically constructed, defence-splitting manoeuvres.

Again, memories of 1953 were revived. David Miller wrote:

> The sumptuously skilful Cruyff, wearing the number 9 like Hidegkuti 24 years ago, like Revie himself for Manchester City, helped destroy England from deep midfield.
>
> A Wembley full house paid £260,000 to see England play humble mouse to Holland's strolling, arrogant cat. The Dutch . . . displayed positional switching and silken control that utterly baffled their conventional, groping opponents.

Revie was under no illusions:

> The Dutch had great control, a wonderful feel for the ball.
> They seemed to control it in just one second. This match shows
> just how far we have to go in terms of world football. The
> lesson for us, for the whole of English football, is that we have
> to go right back to the bottom and start again, especially on
> skills.

Almost certainly out of the World Cup for the second time in a row
and now humiliated by Holland, Revie knew the vultures would be
circling. His honesty that night about the problems in the English game
might have been refreshing in another context; then, it just seemed to
imply that the game was up and there was little he could do in the
short to medium term to turn things around for his country.

The pressure was starting to take its toll on him and his family. Revie
was now starting to think about finding a way out.

* * *

While his great rival was contemplating a bleak future with England,
Brian Clough's fortunes had markedly changed for the better and he
was anticipating a likely return to Division One by Nottingham Forest.

By the night of the England–Holland match on 9 February, Forest
lay fourth in the Division Two table, just a point away from a promotion
place. They'd entertained the City Ground crowd royally with a series
of thumping victories, including over Carlisle (5–1), Sheffield United
(6–1) and Burnley (5–2).

Two men had made the difference – one off the field and the other
on it. The former was Peter Taylor, reunited with his Middlesbrough,
Hartlepools and Derby colleague, providing tactical expertise, a genius
for spotting and developing good players and a touch of humour to
alleviate his old colleague's darker moments.

Clough had flown to Majorca pre-season to try to re-establish the
old partnership and sensed immediately that Taylor was ready to
resume work with him. 'I could see the enthusiasm light up his
suntanned face. I saw an immediate twinkle in his eye. He couldn't
ever hide his enthusiasm from me, no matter how hard he tried – and
he tried again on this occasion.'

Taylor needed little coaxing but knew the two of them needed to learn the lessons from events at Derby and – for Clough – at Leeds. 'Our show was back on the road, but the old arrogance had been tempered by a new realism; we meant every word when warning players. "Produce the goods or you're out. It's our neck or yours in this business – and there's no way that we'll go before you."'

The second man to make the difference was John Robertson, Forest's naturally talented but wayward left-winger. Don Revie, for one, had spotted his ability even back in the summer of 1974, and had included him in his first get-together with 85 England players in Manchester. The only problem was that Robertson was Scottish – so Revie had reluctantly to cross him off his list!

Despite his obvious skill – immaculate ball control, passing and crossing – at that stage of his career the clever little winger was off the rails. He was lazy and ill disciplined. Clough put it even more brutally: 'He was fat, often unshaven, dressed like a tramp, and smoked one fag after another.'

But both Clough and Taylor knew Robertson had it in him to be a minor genius. Even when fit, there appeared to be nothing particularly outstanding about him. He had no searing pace with which to scare full-backs, he could dribble but not with the style or effectiveness of a Best or Gray and he didn't possess a fierce shot in the Lorimer mould.

But what he did was to make the very best use of every blade of grass down the left wing. He would mesmerise defenders with his control of the ball, which never seemed to slip away from him. His calculation of the space and time needed to race away from a tackle and send across a perfectly flighted centre was invariably, utterly precise.

Robertson drew defenders to him like bees to honey. While they were buzzing around him, his teammates benefited from the wide open spaces they left behind. Attacking or defending, he was always Forest's outlet, the man who would give them time to regroup.

No one played more games – 56 – than Robertson in the 1976–77 season. He scored eleven goals, five of them from the penalty spot, and created many more. Forest now had a strike force – Peter Withe, signed from Birmingham, and Tony Woodcock, rehabilitated at Forest – able to capitalise on Robertson's brilliant work, and the goals consequently flowed.

O'Neill, McGovern, Clark, Bowyer, Anderson and O'Hare were the other mainstays of the side. Taylor was responsible for taking a gamble on Larry Lloyd, a big, powerful former England centre-half who had been consigned to the reserves at Coventry.

Clough and Taylor found Lloyd a difficult character to deal with, on and off the pitch, in the first months after he'd been signed on loan. Off it, he tended to speak his mind, which wasn't sensible given the nature of the regime. On it, his sometimes reckless tackling and occasional feuds with centre-forwards meant he was clocking up a large number of disciplinary points.

But the managerial duo eventually settled him down with their usual formula of threats and enticements. Lloyd's place at the 'spine' of the side was crucial, and he had a leading role in Forest's successful run-in to the end of the season, playing in all of the last 13 matches. He was also a part of Forest's cup-winning side – not one of the main trophies, but the much-derided Anglo-Scottish Cup.

In fact, after nine games and some decent opponents along the way, it was a trophy worth having, if only to mark Forest's new status as a competitive, exciting side on the rise. Leyton Orient were beaten 5–1 over two legs in the final, with West Bromwich Albion, Bristol City, Ayr United and Kilmarnock having been disposed of in earlier rounds. It was Forest's first trophy since their FA Cup final victory over Luton Town at Wembley in 1959 – Forest having been sent on their way that day with a goal from Reg Dwight, Elton John's uncle, before he was carried off with a broken leg.

Victories over Plymouth Argyle away on 2 May and Millwall at home five days later in the last match of the season put Forest on the brink of promotion. But in a strange quirk of fate, they had to wait for another Wolves result to decide their fate while they were heading away on holiday in Majorca.

In 1972, Wolves had beaten Revie's Leeds to give Clough and Taylor's Derby their First Division title. This time round, they needed Wolves to do them a favour yet again by beating their chief promotion rivals, Bolton Wanderers, who required just a point to deny Forest elevation.

The news came through just as Forest's holiday-bound plane landed in Palma. Wolves had obliged, just as they'd done almost five years before to the day. Kenny Hibbitt scored the only goal of the game – and he'd been as influential as anyone in the defeat of Leeds on 8 May 1972.

So Clough was back in the top flight of football again. But history was soon to repeat itself in another way, courtesy once more of Don Revie. Clough would, for the second time, have the chance to follow in The Don's footsteps, this time not for club but for country . . .

★ ★ ★

Nowadays, it's becoming almost commonplace to see the wealthy potentates and businessmen of the Middle East investing directly in the English game – indeed, they're buying major chunks of it, as in the case of Sheikh Mansour bin Zayed Al Nahyan and Manchester City.

Back in the 1970s, when the game was in its infancy in the United Arab Emirates, Sheikh Mansour's father, Sheikh Zayed bin Sultan Al Nahyan, was merely looking to import footballing expertise from the United Kingdom. He had noted what had taken place across the Persian Gulf in Iran, where the Shah's men had attempted to persuade Brian Clough to take the job of national coach before settling for Frank O'Farrell, former manager of Leicester City and Manchester City.

O'Farrell had done a good job in guiding Iran to victory over Kuwait in the final of the 1976 Asian Cup. The UAE ruler, through his persuasive emissary Qasem Sultan, general secretary of the UAE Football Association, now also decided to turn to England for a manager who could not only take charge of the national side but transform the coaching and administration of football in his country from top to bottom.

The Arabs had kept a close eye on the fortunes of the England side, and in March, not long after that humbling defeat by Holland at Wembley, they calculated it was the right time to make an approach to an increasingly disenchanted Don Revie.

He was clearly intrigued and obviously flattered, but at that stage he turned down their advances. When they persisted in the course of the next few months, however, he began to have second thoughts.

A short conversation high up in the stands at Wembley at around 7.50 p.m. on Wednesday, 30 March, may well have gone further in helping him make up his mind. It happened minutes before England's World Cup qualifying match with Luxembourg (which they won 5–0), and the participants were Lord Harewood – former president of the Football Association, president of Leeds United and Revie's close friend – and Sir Harold Thompson. As the two men passed on their way to and from the toilet, Lord Harewood expressed the hope that England would have a good win. Thompson's reply was, 'Or a loss – which would settle it all.'

The meaning of Thompson's reply became a matter of some debate in the later High Court case. Thompson maintained there was nothing sinister about the words – they were a clear summation of the situation, which was that if England lost to Luxembourg they would, as a matter of simple arithmetic, have finally been dumped out of the World Cup.

Lord Harewood put a very different interpretation upon them. He felt it was a hostile and disloyal reference to Revie and that the manner of it made it clear that Thompson was almost hoping a loss would take place so that Revie could be removed from his post.

For Lord Harewood, Thompson's remark was not the only evidence that he wanted rid of Revie. 'I knew how much the FA were conspiring against Don as England manager,' he says. 'How did I know? Because John Cobbold, the chairman of Ipswich, told me they had talked to him about getting Bobby Robson in as manager; he said they were interested in him. So I knew there was a conspiracy afoot.'

Lord Harewood would undoubtedly have relayed all this on to Revie, fuelling his suspicion and concern over his future.

Whatever the truth of the motives behind Thompson's remarks that March evening, Revie's mood wasn't helped two months later when the two of them boarded the plane returning to London from Belfast, where England had just scrambled a 2–1 win over Northern Ireland. 'What a load of rubbish that was,' was Sir Harold's verdict to his manager. Revie gritted his teeth and agreed it hadn't been the best of displays, but inwardly he felt the slight deeply, such was his mounting anxiety.

By now, the Revie–Thompson relationship had all but broken down. Duncan Revie puts it bluntly: 'Dad hated Thompson, and Thompson just thought Dad was a bricklayer.'

Revie admitted that he 'used to bristle' when he got into conversation with Thompson. The FA chairman would regularly and provocatively mispronounce his name as 'Revvie' when he knew it to be 'Reevie'. Later, he would recount a conversation he had with his employer over dessert at an FA lunch. 'When I get to know you better, Revie,' said Thompson, 'I will call you Don.' To which, after a long pause, the England manager replied, 'When I get to know you better, Thompson, I will call you Sir Harold.'

With the UAE still hovering in the background and after much discussion with Elsie, Revie decided they should both pay a visit to Dubai to get a feel for the place and whether they thought they could live out there permanently. Elsie flew out on Thursday, 2 June, two days before England's home international match against Scotland at Wembley. She rang her husband at the team hotel at West Park Lodge on Saturday morning and pronounced herself very satisfied with what she'd seen so far. Armed with that encouraging news, Revie set about preparing his team for the clash with the old enemy.

It was a weekend when events dictated that a move to the Middle East became a distinct probability. At Wembley, Revie watched while his England side stumbled to another embarrassing defeat, losing 2–1 to a compact, confident Scottish team managed by Ally MacLeod. Goals from his Leeds centre-half Gordon McQueen and Kenny Dalglish were no more than the visitors deserved, and a Mick Channon penalty in the closing minutes was a consolation goal England hardly deserved.

The ecstatic Scottish supporters then invaded the pitch, sitting and swaying on the crossbar at one end before tearing down the goal posts. The 'tartan hordes' then proceeded to rip up large sections of the turf to take home as souvenirs. Throughout the 1970s, the problem of football hooliganism had been growing in significance and becoming an increasing worry for the authorities. This was perhaps the most naked example of the problem, portrayed for the entire nation to witness on TV on a summer's afternoon.

The next morning, at 9 a.m., Revie followed in his wife's footsteps to Dubai. He caught a plane from Heathrow to Amsterdam and from there on to the UAE capital. Later, some over-imaginative reporters would claim that the England manager had been disguised in dark glasses, cap and muffler for his clandestine trip – like a spy in a Frederick Forsyth novel. Most of what they wrote was incorrect, although he did wear the shades. They didn't, however, stop him from being recognised by one journalist.

His discussions with the UAE Football Association were detailed and fruitful. By the end of the day, Revie had been offered a deal that would eventually amount to an annual salary of £60,000 for four years, plus an additional £100,000 cash payment – all tax free – plus free accommodation and other fringe benefits.

Qasem Sultan and his colleagues were keen for Revie to pledge his future to them there and then, but he told them he couldn't – and wouldn't – make a final decision until after 16 November, the date of England's final World Cup qualifying match with Italy.

But the UAE officials had good cause to be very optimistic. 'He was completely honest and said that although he believed England would beat Italy at Wembley, they would not qualify on goal difference,' Qasem Sultan wrote in a subsequent letter to Ted Croker. 'He informed us that if we were prepared to wait until November, he may then be in a position to join us.'

In early June, the England team set off to South America for what would ultimately prove to be a successful tour, with creditable performances against Brazil (0–0), Argentina (1–1) and Uruguay (0–0). However, probably more important than the football for Revie – at this stage – was a conversation he had in a Buenos Aires hotel room on 11 June with Dick Wragg, chairman of the FA's international committee, and his closest confidant at Lancaster Gate.

Revie told Wragg that the poor displays from his team and the unremittingly hostile press that accompanied them were depressing him and his family. He floated the idea of resigning, if the FA would pay out the remaining two years of his salary, amounting to £50,000. Wragg and fellow board member Peter Swales – to whom Revie also put the suggestion on another occasion – would later say he had asked for an extra £5,000 tax-free, something Revie firmly refuted when asked about it in the ensuing High Court case.

Wragg tried to reassure Revie about his position but also promised to ask for the opinions of his committee members before the England manager met them again at the FA's summer conference in Bournemouth on 25 June.

By the time of that conference, Jeff Powell, the *Daily Mail*'s football correspondent, had been told by one of his sources that Revie had been offered a job in the Middle East. When it was confirmed, Revie asked Powell not to publish anything for the moment, with the quid pro quo that he promised the reporter the exclusive story of his resignation and move to Dubai – if and when it took place.

By now, though, Revie's mind was firmly made up. He tried to have a chat with Sir Harold Thompson on the Sunday night of the Bournemouth conference – the same night he'd spoken to Jeff Powell – only to be told that Thompson had an engagement with the mayor that he couldn't break. The two men didn't speak again until they confronted each other in an FA disciplinary hearing the following year.

By this stage, Revie and Powell were working closely together in planning the moment and method of his departure. Powell's advice had been blunt from the outset. He recalls: 'The first thing he asked me when we had our initial conversation about this was did I think he was going to be sacked. I said yes. It was my job to know. The results weren't fantastic; there could be little doubt about it. I told him it was 99 per cent certain he was going to get the push.

'We were sitting in his house in Leeds, and he outlined the offer he'd received and asked, "What should I do?"

'I said, "From a financial point of view it's the only thing to do, but you must understand what the reaction will be if you go in this manner before you're pushed." We had a long chat about the ramifications of it all.'

The two men carried on as normal for the next week or so. They both attended the Open golf championship in Turnberry, Scotland, on Thursday, 6 July, watching Tom Watson and Jack Nicklaus begin one of the greatest head-to-head confrontations in the history of the game, the so-called 'Duel in the Sun'. Then, that weekend, the plan was hatched for Revie to announce his resignation – first on the front page of the *Daily Mail* – and for the contract to be signed with the UAE.

'Don called me to say, I think I'm going to do this but I've got to get to Switzerland to make sure the Emirates will bank the money, I've got to decide how to handle the FA and so forth. I said I'm happy to help, and I rang the office to tell them I had a big story and that they had to give me carte blanche to do everything I needed to do around and about it. We thought that by going through Switzerland we would also manage to throw people off the trail, so we booked tickets for Zurich, on to Geneva, back to Athens and then on to Dubai.'

Powell started to work on his exclusive story, to be written before he and Revie set off on their circuitous journey to Dubai. He left three envelopes at the *Daily Mail*, with strict instructions for the order in which they should be opened and the day on which they should be published. Envelope 1 was 'Revie Quits', the basic story of his departure, to run on Tuesday, 12 July. Envelope 2 was 'The Deal with the UAE' to run on Wednesday, 13 July, and Envelope 3, 'The Big Interview', would feature on page one on Thursday, 14 July. On subsequent days, there would be more colour and interviews from Dubai.

Revie, meanwhile, wrote his formal letter of resignation to the Football Association, sending copies to Sir Harold Thompson, Dick Wragg and Ted Croker. He put them in the FA internal postbox late in the day on Monday, 11 July, thus ensuring that they would reach their recipients only after the story had come out first in the *Daily Mail* the following morning. The letter read:

> Private and Confidential
> Dear Sir Harold,
> It is with deep regret that I tender my resignation as England Team Manager, to take effect forthwith.
>   You and your committee are aware of the many reasons I have

found my job intolerable. I was aware of the difficulties when I accepted the post, and did not expect it to be an easy job. I realised that help and co-operation from all sections of the Football Association would be necessary if we were to make progress in present day football, and I naturally assumed that this would be given. This was not the case. The job of England manager is a difficult enough one when everyone is pulling in the right direction. It is an impossible task under the present set-up.

The constant criticism I have had to withstand has not only affected my wife and family but has also, I fear, rubbed off on the players. They have been magnificent. Many of them have been upset on my behalf and have tried too hard to get results for me, and the pressure has sometimes produced the wrong results.

In addition to all these facts, it has been brought to my notice that enquiries have been made of another manager and his club concerning the England job.

I would like to convey my thanks to the International Senior Committee. They have been wonderful to me and I have enjoyed working with them. I have written to Mr Wragg and Mr Croker, informing them of my decision.

I wish the England team and the Football Association every success in the future.

Yours sincerely,

Don Revie

So while Revie and Powell were in Dubai, the rest of Fleet Street was left looking on enviously at a sensational scoop. In Tuesday's story, Revie confided to *Daily Mail* readers that he'd left the job principally because of the pressures on his family:

I sat down with my wife Elsie one night and we agreed the job was no longer worth all the aggravation. It was bringing too much heartache to those nearest to us.

The past three years have been very rough for my family. The criticism aimed at me has clearly affected my wife and children. It reached a point that almost every time my name was mentioned it was coupled with criticism.

It was rough on my son and daughter. It's not very pleasant to hear your father constantly attacked.

Revie knew he would face censure and it duly followed. If there was a general mood that could be gauged, it was one of disapproval at his resignation and failing to see the job through but greater revulsion that he was now in the – very lucrative – pay of another country while leaving England rudderless.

Amid the swirl of condemnation, Frank Butler's was a voice of reason in his column in the *News of the World* at the end of that tumultuous week. Under the headline 'Goldfinger', he wrote:

> A long admirer of Revie as player, tactician, manager and well-organised family man, I'm disappointed he walked out on a job he had contracted to finish. He is the captain – or rather – the Admiral leaving a sinking ship.
>
> Yet for all this, there has been a sickening amount of hypocrisy, sour grapes and envy behind the vitriolic attacks on Revie. Some by people once sycophantic disciples of the man, genuflecting in his presence, grateful to be included in his company and swearing allegiance until death do us part.
>
> How many businessmen wouldn't stretch their loyalty if tempted with a more lucrative income from a rival company? Wouldn't they slip off to some meeting place hoping not to be seen?

There was, of course, precious little sympathy from Sir Harold Thompson, rather a cold fury at the manner of Revie's going. However, his response, six days later, was fairly measured – to a large extent for legal reasons:

> Dear Mr Revie,
> I have received your letter of resignation dated 11 July. It was discussed at a meeting of the FA on July 15 and is being considered further in consultation with the FA's legal advisers.
>
> Your earlier letter, dated July 7, apologising for failing to keep our meeting fixed for July 4 and saying that you would telephone me next week (i.e. beginning July 11), was addressed to the FA and posted on July 7, arriving July 8, but only given to me on July 12.
>
> I was not aware of what you call the 'many reasons' why you have 'found the job intolerable' and not clear either which 'sections of the FA' did not cooperate with you. I had the

impression you had been well paid, and had received liberal expense allowances, and certainly the FA has never before spent such a large sum on the general preparation and costs of the England team squad. It would help me if you can be more specific in regard to your complaints about lack of co-operation, which are serious and should not be made without better evidence.

You also state that 'enquiries have been made of another Manager and his Club regarding the England job'. By whom? I know nothing whatever about this, and as I have told you at Bournemouth on June 25, neither the International Committee nor any other FA committee has to my knowledge ever considered the matter of your dismissal. I think that you have a responsibility to give the facts about this particular charge, or withdraw it.

I will only, at present, make one further comment. If the public statements about your negotiations with the United Arab Emirates at the precise time when the England team was on its way to South America without you are true, or if any such negotiations took place prior to that, negotiations which you deliberately did not mention to the Chairman of the International Committee when you saw him at your request, then this was not the kind of behaviour which I would have expected of you, nor of anyone who regarded duty, loyalty and integrity as important personal qualities.

Yours sincerely,

H.W. Thompson

It was no surprise when a month later the FA decided to charge Revie with bringing the game into disrepute, accusing him of a 'flagrant' breach of contract, 'acting deceitfully', 'debasing your position in English football', and telling the *Daily Mail* before the authorities about his resignation.

But before any commission could sit in judgment on that – with or without Revie present – another newspaper muddied the waters for the FA and lowered his reputation even further in the public estimation.

On Tuesday, 6 September, the *Daily Mirror*'s front page screamed 'World Exclusive – Revie – The *Mirror*'s disturbing dossier on his rise to fame'. Over the next five days, Richard Stott and his investigative team published details of Revie's alleged involvement – directly or indirectly – in four or five cases of attempted match-fixing and bribery.

One of them suggested he'd directly bribed Bob Stokoe, then player-manager of Bury, in 1962, to 'take it easy' in a crucial relegation match with Leeds; another supposedly involved Revie recruiting a 'middleman' to influence Wolves players to throw a vital championship game with Leeds United in 1972; another that he had acted to influence an end-of-season match against Nottingham Forest in a bid to win the Football League championship.

Stott stated that Revie had known about his investigation since May, before the Home International Championship. He also claimed in his 2002 autobiography *Dogs and Lampposts* that Revie had left for the UAE when he did because he was 'terrified' of what Gary Sprake, Leeds' goalkeeper, was about to reveal about him.

There is no evidence to back up his latter claim. And although Stott claimed to have submitted to the FA what he described as a '315-page dossier of statements, names, dates and witnesses, an overwhelming catalogue of bribery and double-dealing that went to the heart of the game in England', no charges were ever brought in any civil or criminal court against Don Revie in respect of any of the *Mirror*'s allegations.

On the one occasion a newspaper – the *Mirror*'s sister paper the *Sunday People* – was taken to court over a matter relating to one of Stott's allegations, it lost the case, to Billy Bremner, Revie's captain.

Stott's autobiography is a brilliant portrait of Fleet Street in the 1960s and 1970s. But when you read the scornful conclusion to his chapter on the Revie investigation, that 'the only good thing to come out of it was that life with the Arabs for Revie was, by all accounts, pretty dreadful' – patently untrue, according to family and friends – you start to wonder a little about his motives.

Stott suggested that the FA didn't want to pursue Revie because officials were worried about what a wide-ranging inquiry might throw up, that he might be just 'part of a new breed who became managers after playing in the shadow of the minimum wage, when footballers were paid a pittance for entertaining 50,000 crowds every weekend'. There's clearly something in this latter proposition, as the match-fixing trials of the early 1960s would indicate. As for the former, Sir Harold Thompson, for one, wanted to check with the Director of Public Prosecutions whether there was a case to prosecute against Revie over the *Mirror* stories.

The reply came back swiftly from Raymon Anning, deputy assistant commissioner of the Metropolitan Police's Criminal Investigation Department. In a letter to Sir Harold dated 16 September, Ted Croker informed him that Commissioner Anning felt 'it was not their practice to take action based on newspaper articles and it seemed extremely unlikely that this would be an exception'.

Two days after that pronouncement from the DPP, Brian Clough emerged from his public silence – partly self-imposed, partly at the urging of his eminently sensible chairman Brian Appleby – to rail against his old rival.

In a *Sunday Mirror* article under the headline 'Revie – By Clough', his language was, even by his standards, colourful and vituperative:

> Don Revie could have ordered champagne and caviare at breakfast this morning. One telephone call in Dubai's £50-a-night Intercontinental Hotel would have been enough. And a fat lot of good it would have done him.
>
> The taste, I suspect, would have been like the porridge at Wormwood Scrubs or water from a dirty stream.
>
> Why? Because I'm convinced Revie will find Dubai the most luxurious prison in the world. I'll share the sadness because he has left me feeling like a spiv outside Wembley Stadium on Cup final day.
>
> He has left us wearing a black armband for football. I'm carrying a millstone round my neck. I'm a professional man and he has sold me short by quitting England as he did. He has sold football short. What's worse, he has sold himself short.

After this opening flourish, he went on to accuse Revie of 'degrading' English football and suggested that his own directors looked at him with a little less respect after Revie resigned.

What would the senior figures at the FA make of that kind of public outburst, however sympathetic they might be to the sentiments contained in it? Because Clough, whose Nottingham Forest side had made a storming start to their first season back in Division One, was high up on their list of candidates to replace Revie.

* * *

While Harold Thompson continued to contemplate sanctions of some kind – it seemed any kind – against Revie, he and his committee turned their attention to electing his successor.

Thompson was clear about the sort of man he wanted. He told Dick Wragg, 'Above all, I want somebody who has character and principles of honesty, devotion and can co-operate dutifully. The new man should deal with the team and its coaching. He should not have authority to commit the FA financially or otherwise, as has been happening recently.'

The final sentence was a clear reference to Revie's commercial activities, which had, in fact, brought in thousands of pounds for the FA. Dutiful? That word didn't augur well for Clough's chances, as he was anything but.

In the short term, the FA turned to Ron Greenwood to steer them through a friendly match against Switzerland in September and the final two World Cup qualifying games, away in Luxembourg in October, then at home against Italy at Wembley on 16 November.

Greenwood was Thompson's kind of man, steady, sober and an FA insider through his close connections with the Association's coaching scheme. Aged fifty-five, he had been West Ham's general manager for the previous three years, relinquishing the day-to-day management of the side after thirteen years in charge.

Under Greenwood, the Hammers had won the FA Cup in 1964 and the European Cup-Winners' Cup in 1965. He could take immense credit for overseeing the development of three of the 1966 World Cup winners: Bobby Moore, Martin Peters and Geoff Hurst.

If England wanted a dynamic young coach to revitalise the team and enthuse the country, he wasn't the man. To use the old expression, he was a 'steady pair of hands', a man with an astute soccer brain who would at least, his advocates claimed, steer the nation's football team into calmer waters.

In the first two of his three games in charge, however, Greenwood did nothing to put himself out ahead of the pack. England stuttered to a lacklustre 0–0 draw against Switzerland, then barely managed to dispose of little Luxembourg, needing a last-minute goal from Ipswich's Paul Mariner to make the game safe.

However, he did his candidacy a power of good when England beat Italy 2–0 on an exciting Wembley night, with goals from Kevin Keegan – who produced a hard-running, inspirational display – and Trevor Brooking.

It was too little, too late, of course; England would have needed to win 6–0 to qualify for the World Cup, so it was really a question of playing for pride. But England fizzed and sparkled, with clever wing play from new caps Steve Coppell and Peter Barnes (from Manchester United and City respectively) providing the experienced Italian defensive trio of Claudio Gentile, Marco Tardelli and Romeo Benetti with an uncomfortable night.

Back at Lancaster Gate, Harold Thompson and his colleagues first of all invited suggestions about who should be the new manager from all the FA Council members around the country.

Bob Lord, one of Thompson's influential colleagues and the man Arthur Hopcraft memorably described as the 'Khruschev of Burnley' in *The Football Man*, was one of the first off the mark. In a letter to Thompson on 27 July, he declared, 'Pardon me if I'm overstepping the line as a member of the Council, but please do not fall for either Clough or [Jack] Charlton.'

But there was plenty of support coming in for the Forest manager. Ernest Smith, of Cumberland Football Association, wrote: 'I take him [Clough] as the "Long Term Policy". He is the person who I think will make some of our England players toe the line, and in my view has a talent for spotting young, promising players.'

H.L.P. Holmes, secretary of Derbyshire County Football Association, recommended Clough's management – on and off the field: 'As a motivator of players I do not believe that there is anyone more capable than this man . . . His discipline as a club manager with his players is superb. He has complete authority and the players accept it, even over such trivial things as length of hair etc.'

There were also some – uninvited – opinions from England supporters with passionately held views, invariably advocating Clough. 'Stop sitting in FA Headquarters like little tin gods,' wrote D.J. Saunders from Market Harborough on 17 October. 'Start doing something constructive for the 1982 finals by appointing Brian Clough, who instead of being your slayer could become your saviour.'

As the FA called for applications for the job and put out their own feelers for some of the serious candidates, Clough was doing his prospects no harm through the performances of his buccaneering side. By the end of October, Forest stood proudly at the top of the First Division table, four points clear of their nearest challengers, Liverpool. In thirteen matches, the league newcomers had won ten, drawn two and lost just one away, at Arsenal; they'd scored twenty-eight goals and conceded just eight.

In 1974, newspapers had conducted polls to assess the public mood. Then, Clough was comfortably the favoured candidate, with around 30 per cent of the votes of the *Daily Express* readers, for example. A similar poll in the same paper three years on gave the Forest manager more than double that vote – 67 per cent – to make him undeniably and overwhelmingly the 'people's choice'.

The FA did consider, momentarily, appointing one of their own rather than a club manager, after what they considered to be the disaster of Revie. To that end, both Allen Wade, director of coaching, and Charles Hughes, assistant director of coaching, were informally interviewed. Hughes, in his letter of application, emphasised his technical knowledge, pointing out the success his book *Tactics and Teams* (and the 11 films that accompanied it) had had worldwide. He also pointed out that they had brought in £40,000 to the FA coffers. Wade, the football academic par excellence, influenced several generations of bright young managers like Bobby Robson, Don Howe and Dave Sexton with his books such as *Positional Play* and *Soccer Strategies*.

But Thompson and his colleagues, some of them no doubt grudgingly, had to acknowledge that the job of England football manager in the late twentieth century involved more than being a good classroom teacher.

As they sifted through the letters of application, they came across an interesting range of approaches. Billy Wright, the first footballer in the world to win 100 international caps (nearly all of them as England captain), was put forward – by his wife! Joy Beverley Wright, eldest of the popular vocal trio of sisters in the 1950s and 1960s, told the committee her husband was too modest to approach them but that he had a great heart for football and a great deal still to offer the game. Wright, aged 53, was head of sport at ATV Midlands at the time.

Mrs Wright wasn't the only woman to write on behalf of her husband. Doris Mee, the wife of Bertie, Arsenal's manager, who had stepped down the previous year after a decade of success at Highbury, also sent in an application.

Harry Catterick, who had just stepped down from managing Preston North End (following 12 years in charge of an attacking, cultured Everton side), wrote simply: 'I am 57 years of age and unmarried. Should you favour me with an interview I am sure I would convince you of my suitability for the job.'

Bobby Moore had played his final professional game (for Fulham) in

England in May. In his letter of application, he didn't need to make mention of his long and illustrious international career, but chose instead to emphasise his coaching qualifications, with preliminary and full FA badges. He did tell the committee, however, 'how proud I was of my association with the England team' and concluded, 'I feel that the experience and knowledge I have gained at this level of football over the years has provided me with the ideal background for the specialised demands of the job.'

It would be difficult to disagree with that assessment, and in the more modern era the great, recently retired player might be looked upon more favourably as a candidate for international manager. Moore never seriously expected to be a candidate for the main job but hoped his application would at least bring him into the England coaching set-up. He was mortified not to receive even a reply from the FA.

Moore's 1966 defensive colleague Jack Charlton suffered similar disappointment. He was out of a job, albeit temporarily, having just left Middlesbrough after four very successful years in which he'd won them promotion and been voted Manager of the Year.

Charlton recalls being asked to apply for the post: 'I got a call from a man at the FA who said, would you be interested in the England job? Then, a couple of days later, I got a similar call from a second man at the FA asking me the same question. I said, yes, but what should I do? Just write a letter and apply, they said, so I wrote the letter, in my own handwriting, outlining my qualifications – staff coach with the FA, etc., my management of Boro – put it in an envelope and sent it off. I never got a reply, not even an acknowledgement.'

Charlton's letter was posted on 25 July. When Ron Greenwood was asked to submit a list of names of potential candidates to the FA, Charlton's was on it (along with Clough's). But when Charlton heard nothing over the summer, he started considering other offers and was finally appointed manager of Third Division Sheffield Wednesday in October. The FA's apparent indifference to his application would always rankle with Charlton.

Others to write included John Bond (Norwich City), Jimmy Bloomfield (Leyton Orient, formerly Leicester City) and Ken Furphy (head coach of Team America, formerly Sheffield United). Jimmy Armfield (Leeds United) and Gordon Jago (Tampa Bay Rowdies, formerly Sheffield United) submitted 'verbal applications'.

Gradually, though, the field was whittled down until it contained just four names: Ron Greenwood, Bobby Robson, Brian Clough and Lawrie McMenemy.

Don Revie had always believed the FA had made approaches of some kind to Robson while he was still manager – indeed, he'd referred to this belief in his letter of resignation to Sir Harold Thompson. On 31 October, Robson's name was on the shortlist the FA's electoral committee decided to call for interview on Monday, 5 December.

In public, Robson sounded enthusiastic about the job. 'To stay here [at Ipswich] I've turned down other clubs, big clubs,' he told the *Daily Express* on 4 November. 'But the England job is the most important, the most significant there is. It's the only one I would consider leaving Ipswich for.'

Privately, however, the FA were being told a different story by the board at Ipswich Town. Ten days after Robson's comments in the press, Ted Croker wrote to Sir Harold:

> I received a telephone call from Mr Patrick Cobbold, the chairman of Ipswich Town Football Club, in response to my letter regarding Bobby Robson.
>
> He said they would agree to us interviewing Bobby Robson, but that he could not be available on 5 December, as they have a match on that day. He also said that they would be very loathe [*sic*] to lose him and that he had talked to Bobby Robson and he was not very keen on the England job, although no doubt he would be prepared to put his point of view to us.

Ipswich were clearly fighting to hold onto their man, and perhaps being a little disingenuous over his true feelings about England.

Meanwhile, over at the City Ground, Nottingham Forest were also keen to keep their manager, and Brian Appleby was somewhat irritated by all the press speculation. He described as 'disgraceful' the leaking of the FA's plans to approach Clough for an interview. 'If I had read that another club wanted Brian, I would have complained to the FA to whom I am now complaining. It is an Alice in Wonderland situation.'

The match Patrick Cobbold had referred to in his letter was Ipswich's UEFA Cup return tie with Johan Cruyff's Barcelona in the Nou Camp, which they lost 3–0, thus drawing on aggregate before succumbing 3–1 in a penalty shoot-out.

Robson's interview had therefore been brought forward to Monday, 21 November. It went well, and the likes of Sir Matt Busby, Bert

Millichip and Peter Swales in particular were impressed by his articulacy and his vision for reviving the English game, as well as being mindful of the impressive displays of Ipswich against the best Continental teams.

Now the committee prepared to meet the three other candidates on Monday, 5 December. Greenwood was still in the box seat, but the FA were keen to see the two other young North-Easterners and learn their views on England's future.

★ ★ ★

'It's a bit cold lads, isn't it?' was Brian Clough's greeting just after nine o'clock to the group of cameramen and reporters who had camped outside the Football Association's genteel west London headquarters at 16 Lancaster Gate.

It was a clear winter's morning on Monday, 5 December. Clough was due to be interviewed at 9.30, Lawrie McMenemy at 10.15 and Ron Greenwood sometime after 11 a.m.

Clough was in an upbeat mood. 'I've always liked the England job and I'm delighted to be associated with it,' he said before disappearing past the white stucco pillars and into the hallway. 'I didn't even get to this stage last time.'

He had taken his preparation for the board seriously. A few days before, he'd rung Gerald Mortimer, football correspondent for the *Derby Evening Telegraph*, to ask him to mark his card.

'Brian phoned up and said almost accusingly, "You went to Oxford, didn't you?"' remembers Mortimer. 'He wanted to know more about Harold Thompson. I said, well, I didn't know him from personal experience because "Tommy" was a chemist and I read English, so our paths didn't really cross. But of course I knew about his history with the Pegasus football team, and I told Brian about that. I did warn Brian, "I'm not sure you'll like him because he's an intolerant bugger and he'll probably call you 'Clough', without any 'Mr' beforehand, and he expects people to bow and scrape to him."'

It was reassuring for Clough to be sat in the waiting room alongside his fellow North-Easterner and good footballing friend. McMenemy, aged 41, was the youngest of the candidates. Manager of Southampton since 1973, he'd guided the Second Division south coast team to an improbable FA Cup final win against Manchester United the previous year. Southampton's 1–0 win, courtesy of a late goal from Bobby

Stokes, was on a par with Sunderland's victory over Don Revie's Leeds United three years previously.

In the wake of the euphoria following that triumph, McMenemy had the difficult task – just like Sunderland's manager Bob Stokoe before him – of trying to fulfil the heightened expectations of supporters and get his team straight up into the First Division. McMenemy chose to do so partly by encouraging youth but also by recruiting a group of very good players in the twilight of their careers, rekindling their enthusiasm and making the best use of their vast experience.

So by 1977 he'd brought to The Dell men like Peter Osgood, Alan Ball and Chris Nicholl; later, Kevin Keegan and Charlie George would arrive. McMenemy was an exceptionally good man-manager and seemed to be able to coax the best out of these 'difficult' stars.

As he and Clough sat waiting to be interviewed, the Forest manager spotted an elderly man about to mount the staircase. 'He was a real old-timer,' says McMenemy, 'and Cloughie called out in a jocular fashion to him, "Hey, young man, are you bloody sure you're going to make them stairs? Don't you think you should be getting the lift?" I thought, oh, bloody hell, that's one vote gone for Brian, and, sure enough, he turned out to be on the panel. It was a typical Brian moment.'

Once in the interview room, McMenemy was confronted by a disparate group of FA councillors, some of them 'football people' like Busby, Swales and co., others from the ranks of local and regional football who sat on the association's committees. The average age of the group was probably somewhere around 60.

'They gave you a good listening and plenty of time to answer questions, and to ask them yourself. Quite honestly, I took it very much in my stride because I never really thought I had a real chance. I was the outsider of the three of us [Clough, Robson and himself]. Looking back afterwards, I dropped one clanger, when I said I would be honoured and delighted to be offered the main job, but I wasn't looking to get involved in any others – Under-21s, youth team, whatever. That wasn't what they wanted to hear. But generally I felt quite comfortable in there with some of the types of people sitting in judgment on us – public-school, landowner types of gentlemen – because my chairman, Sir George Meyrick, was from that sort of background, Eton and so on.'

Clough himself felt he'd done well. He knew he'd crossed swords in the past with some of the club chairmen on the panel – Sir Bert

Millichip of West Bromwich Albion, for one – and he was on his guard with Sir Harold Thompson.

'He was an academic, a stroppy know-all bugger who in my view knew nothing about my game. If he was such a brilliant mathematician, he figured it wrong when the FA got rid of Alf Ramsey. I was wary of the Mad Professor and he was wary of me.' The colourful recollections came later, but at the time Clough kept his feelings very much to himself, and he relaxed and charmed many of the committee men.

'When I went striding out of the interview, across Lancaster Gate, to an hotel where Peter Taylor was waiting, I felt as if I was walking on air . . . "I'll tell you, pal," I said, "if that job depends on the interview, if interviews mean anything at all, I've pissed it. Can't miss. Assuming it's not bent, of course."'

After listening to the sitting candidate, Ron Greenwood, following after McMenemy, the FA's seven-strong electoral committee went away to consider their verdict before reconvening a week later, on Monday, 12 December.

Seasoned watchers believed it might be a tight decision. Sir Harold Thompson and William 'Tagge' Webster were reckoned to be firm Greenwood supporters. Sir Bert Millichip and Sir Matt Busby were thought to lean more towards Robson, although not being averse to Greenwood. Clough might be able to count on the votes of Dick Wragg and R.H. Speaks (Kent County). It was believed the seventh member, Peter Swales, would plump for either Robson or Clough.

Whatever happened, Clough had given himself every chance. In December 1977, he was at the height of his powers, still young, still dynamic, still occasionally outspoken, yet maturing all the time as a football manager. His Nottingham Forest side had just embarked on one of the greatest runs of results ever produced by a First Division side – 42 games without defeat.

Don Revie had taken the job Clough had coveted – but for which he was perhaps not quite prepared – back in July 1974. Now he was ready and able to succeed the man in whose footsteps he'd followed for so many years.

Epilogue

12 December 1977–13 December 1979

Sir Harold Thompson and his seven-man international committee gave themselves a week to consider their choice. They'd been particularly impressed by the passion and vision shown by two of the three North-Easterners: Brian Clough and Bobby Robson. If ever there was an opportunity to take a bold leap forward and give one of the talented next generation a chance to revitalise the national side, then this was it.

But they considered themselves badly burned by their experience with Don Revie and caution, not boldness, was their guiding principle. England's 2–0 victory over Italy the previous month had done Ron Greenwood's cause much good, and despite the performances of Robson and Clough at interview, Sir Harold felt he wanted to be sure he had a man who would 'restore moral behaviour into the game . . . a man of high standards, moral principles, ethics, integrity and honesty'.

Ron Greenwood was that individual in his estimation, and Thompson was able to carry the committee comfortably enough with him. The West Ham man's appointment, on a three-year basis, was announced on Monday, 12 December to no real surprise from the football world, only regret in some quarters at an opportunity missed.

Clough was bitterly disappointed he didn't get the job. 'My rejection by the FA is one of my great regrets in life,' he wrote later in the *Sunday Express*. 'I was the best man for the job they gave to Ron Greenwood, but they didn't want me.'

He wondered whether his answer at the interview to a final question from Sir Matt Busby might have cost him his chance. He recalled the exchange like this: '"One moment, Brian," Sir Matt called. "When you said you would take the job, did you mean it?" "Of course," I said, "any job. Any job at all."'

Clough believed that his apparent enthusiasm encouraged the committee to offer him a position in the England set-up but allowed them to pass him over for the main job. Clough – along with Peter Taylor – was appointed England youth-team manager, a job he carried out relatively successfully for six months before he resigned, mainly because his club responsibilities meant he couldn't give the work his undivided attention.

Those commitments at the City Ground were massive, because Clough and Taylor had entered their golden period as club managers. Forest's run of unbeaten Division One games, which started on 26 November 1977, continued for 42 matches (the length of a full season) until they were finally defeated 2–0 by Liverpool at Anfield more than a year later, on 9 December 1978. This astonishing achievement would last 26 years before Arsène Wenger's Arsenal side overturned it in August 2004, eventually setting a new record of 49 games without defeat.

If the England manager's job had fallen vacant anywhere between May 1978 and May 1979 it's almost unthinkable that Clough wouldn't have been chosen if interested, such was the scale of his achievements.

The hors d'oeuvre was the League Cup, captured in March with a 1–0 win – courtesy of a Robertson penalty – in a replay against Liverpool at Old Trafford after the first match at Wembley finished goalless. Few games ever gave Clough as much pleasure as the two-legged semi-final victories over Leeds, 3–1 at Elland Road and 4–2 at the City Ground.

Then to the main course, with Forest carrying off the league title by seven points from Liverpool, wrapping up their triumph four games from the end of the season.

A year later, they had to settle for the runners-up berth behind the Merseysiders, just before they took on Malmö of Sweden in the European Cup final at the Olympiastadion in Munich. It was an undistinguished match, with the tall, imposing Swedish defence desperately attempting to stifle the creativity of the English champions.

But it was settled by a superb goal, fashioned by the unrivalled John Robertson. Picking the ball up on the left touchline midway into the

Malmö half, he glided towards the edge of the area, taking two
defenders with him, before accelerating past them to find a yard of
space in which to arc a perfect cross beyond the goalkeeper to the far
post.

There, rushing in to duck and head the ball into the net from just a
few yards out, was Trevor Francis, Britain's first £1 million player, in for
his first European game after being cup-tied all season. The goal was
scored in injury time in the first half and Forest were never seriously
troubled after that.

Clough and Taylor's feat in taking this small, provincial English side
to the European summit remains one of the greatest achievements in
club football – bar none.

For Clough, John Robertson's cross was the single most satisfying
moment in his whole career:

> When I sit in my garden and close my eyes I can still see that
> moment in Munich when Robertson made his move. Peter
> Taylor stiffened beside me and grabbed my arm. Robertson is
> not far from the corner flag. There are half a dozen Malmo
> players in the box. Trevor Francis is hurtling towards the far
> post, and Robbo sends over the perfect cross. One–nil. Pass me
> the European Cup. Thank you.

* * *

While the legend of Clough was growing, Don Revie's reputation as a
manager and as a man would be sorely tested in a series of acrimonious
confrontations with the Football Association.

The first encounter came at Lancaster Gate on Monday, 18 December
1978, when a special disciplinary 'commission' of the Football
Association heard the case against Revie of bringing the game into
disrepute through the way he left his job with England.

On the same day, they also had before them Alan Ball, Revie's one-
time England captain. He also faced a disrepute charge, arising from
his recently published autobiography, in which he'd admitted receiving
payments – from Revie – as an inducement to leave Blackpool and join
Leeds United back in the mid-1960s.

Sir Harold Thompson, having failed to find a way to pursue Revie
through a court of law, had set up this 'tribunal', but to all intents and
purposes he was the judge and jury. Just in case he needed support, he

had on his right-hand side Bob Lord, chairman of Burnley FC, who had constantly feuded with Leeds United during Revie's time there.

Gilbert Gray, QC, Revie's counsel, took early exception and made representation about Lord's demeanour, sitting as he did with his arms folded, glaring at the 'defendant'. Gray also heard Thompson say to his client before proceedings got under way in earnest, 'Now then, Don Revie, you've pulled some strokes on me in the past – it's comeuppance time now.'

The three other members of the tribunal were Lord Westwood of Newcastle, president of the Football League, 'Mac' MacMullen, vice chairman of the Football Association, and Richard Strachan, a York City director and lawyer – men of unimpeachable character.

Gilbert Gray, a fellow Yorkshireman, was the ideal man for Revie to have at his side. Called to the bar in 1953, he spent many of his early years in the profession as a prosecutor in Middlesbrough. He had developed into one of the most skilled defence barristers, taking on some of the hardest high-profile cases, like John Poulson, 'the Black Panther' and, later, Matrix Churchill and *Spycatcher* (Peter Wright).

Gray was in the classic tradition of the advocate, persuasive, witty and persistent. On this occasion, he let Sir Harold Thompson know he thought he was a less than impartial head of the hearing. In particular, he made play of Thompson's critical comments about Revie in the press, telling him, 'This commission has been presided over by you – against whom I make no personal comment – but who has apparently got into the press making observations which seem to pre-judge one aspect of the matter that says that he – Mr Revie – has behaved disgracefully.'

The essence of the Alan Ball case was that Revie was supposed to have met the (then) Blackpool player clandestinely somewhere halfway between Yorkshire and Lancashire – Saddleworth Moor was suggested – and handed over payments of £100 on three occasions to 'bribe' him to come to Leeds. The assignations were alleged to have taken place in 1966, before the World Cup.

Revie denied ever having met Ball on the moors, and apart from Ball's word, there was of course no other evidence for Thompson to 'prosecute' the case against Revie. Nevertheless, Revie was asked if he would give evidence in the Ball case. Gilbert Gray's response to this request was withering:

> What I say is this. That until there is evidence against Mr Revie

> on the first principles of English justice, he is not called upon to make any answer . . . It is like putting a man in a magistrates' court and saying, "Stand up there and prove that you were not driving under the influence of drink." You have got to have evidence to show that he was.

But all Gray's robust defence and incisive comments about Thompson's methods and motives were to no avail. The FA chairman was determined to have Revie 'convicted' and punished, and the penalty duly came in the form of a ten-year ban from all football in England, until July 1987. Alan Ball was fined £3,000 for accepting financial inducements from Revie.

The penalty was so harsh, and there was so clearly a prima facie case of restraint of trade, that Revie couldn't let the matter rest. He fought on for his reputation and his livelihood, and his second – and final – battle with Thompson and the FA came nearly a year later, on 26 November 1979, in the High Court of Justice.

The case of *Revie v. Football Association Ltd* lasted 14 days, and much of the evidence that had been presented against Revie at the commission was on show again in front of the judge, Mr Justice Cantley.

Joseph Donaldson Cantley, a small man possessed of an infectious laugh, but also with a slight speech impediment, was a product of Manchester Grammar School and widely respected in his years on the Northern Circuit. He'd been catapulted to national fame just six months earlier when he presided in the sensational trial of former Liberal leader Jeremy Thorpe, who was accused of attempting to murder former male model Norman Scott, who had professed to be Thorpe's lover.

His handling of the Thorpe case was criticised for his pro-Establishment bias. Certainly, he did little to hide his contempt for the quality and character of the main prosecution witnesses, describing Scott as a 'crook, a fraud, a sponger and a parasite', and dismissing Andrew Newton, the erstwhile airline pilot who shot Scott's dog, Rinka, as 'that awful man' and 'a conceited bungler' who 'might have been inspired to take a little more care' if he had, in fact, been intent on murder.

He kept amused those in court for the Revie case by his complete lack of knowledge of the contemporary game of football and the characters who populated it. When Kevin Keegan appeared before him, he seemed blithely unaware of who he was – something akin to a judge failing to recognise David Beckham today. Even on the one occasion he could claim recognition of a famous England player, he got the wrong man:

> JUDGE CANTLEY: Jack Charlton? He's one of the few that I
>   have heard of. He behaves so well.
> ROBERT JOHNSON, QC: I wonder if your lordship isn't
>   thinking of the one with no hair, called Bobby Charlton?
> JUDGE CANTLEY: Oh, that may be so.

Unfortunately for Revie, Cantley's predisposition towards the authorities was as much in evidence in this case as it had been in Jeremy Thorpe's six months earlier. Sir Harold Thompson, in his estimation, was a man who could do little wrong, and in his summing-up he described him in glowing terms that caused a few eyebrows to be raised:

> Sir Harold is a gentleman with a distinguished past in amateur football, as well as a long experience of the Football Association. To him, English football is or should be a national sport, and a healthy one, and not, as it sometimes seems, merely a prosperous and influential and noisy part of the flourishing entertainment industry. He deplores the coarse commerce and materialism and the selfish greed which, from time to time, obtrude in professional football, and he wants to make a change for the better.

For anyone who had watched the case over the two weeks, it was clear that, in contrast, the judge attached motives of selfishness and greed to Don Revie. The former England manager had brought many of the leading figures associated with the game to speak on his behalf – Jock Stein, Jimmy Hill, Lawrie McMenemy, David Coleman, Johnny Giles, Lord Harewood – but when Cantley delivered his character assessment of Revie, it was a brutal one.

The judge accused Revie of telling a 'direct lie' when he'd gone to Peter Swales, hinting of resignation but telling him nothing about the interest from the United Arab Emirates, and he called him a 'prima donna' who resented anything that could be interpreted as criticism. 'He is a very prickly man who has been brooding on imagined wrongs.'

After accepting that the Football Association had every right to charge Revie with harming the game, Cantley went on: 'Mr Revie was the English team manager. He held the highest post of its kind in English professional football, and he published and presented to the public a sensational and notorious example of disloyalty, breach of duty, discourtesy and selfishness. His conduct brought English professional football at a high level into disrepute.'

But, 'with regret', Cantley overturned the ten-year ban on Revie. He made it clear that it was no longer than he would have thought proper, but it was 'likely' that the FA's disciplinary hearing was biased because of Sir Harold's appearance at the head of it following his widely publicised remarks about Revie. 'Things would have been very different if Sir Harold had stood down from the hearing,' Cantley remarked.

The judge granted the FA nominal £10 damages for Revie's breach of contract. But he refused to grant Revie damages, only ordering the FA to pay a third of his costs.

Gilbert Gray had jousted amicably with Cantley throughout the High Court hearing, occasionally introducing sporting metaphors that left the judge perplexed and a little irritated. In general, Gray liked and rated highly the man who had actually supported his own application to be a QC back in the early 1950s. 'But,' he says, 'I was disappointed he saw fit to make some of those closing remarks about Don. Joe was a jury advocate; he would always overstate any case that he came across. He was the sort of man who liked to play for the press, and he certainly did that in this case.'

Neither Revie nor Thompson was in court on Thursday, 13 December to hear Cantley's judgment. Duncan Revie, at the time a young articled clerk at the London firm of Lovell, White and King, had been working on his father's legal team and was there to hear it. 'The first thing I'm going to do is to ring Dad in Dubai and tell him he's won,' he told the media defiantly. The FA indicated they might appeal, but it was an option that was never seriously contemplated. Too much dirty linen had already been aired in public.

As for Don Revie, he had (figuratively) walked from court free to pursue his managerial career where and when he wanted, but hardly without a stain on his character. The newspapers, which were by now almost universally against him, carried headlines the next day like 'Revie's Hollow Win' (*Daily Express*) and 'Branded But Not Banned' (*Daily Mirror*).

Revie returned to Dubai to continue his job for the football-mad sheikhs of the UAE, trying to transform an infant soccer nation into one that could compete on the world stage. Whether he would ever want to return to England to ply his trade was a question that stretched out far into the vast desert that surrounded his white-walled villa.

Afterword

B rian Clough never did manage England. But on 28 May 1980, in the Santiago Bernabeu Stadium, Madrid, he reached the pinnacle of the game when his Nottingham Forest side won their second successive European Cup final by defeating Hamburg 1–0, through a goal from John Robertson.

Clough remained at Nottingham Forest until 1993. Although never league champions again, they were runners-up once, third three times, fifth twice, and only once outside the top ten; under his management, there were also four League Cup victories between 1978 and 1990. In his final season, 1993, Forest were relegated from what had by then become the Premier League.

The partnership with Peter Taylor ended in 1982 when Taylor returned to Derby County. The rift that developed between the two of them was not repaired before Taylor's death in 1990.

In 1991, Clough was awarded the OBE. Two years later, he was given the freedom of the city of Nottingham, followed by that of Derby in 2003. Increasing drink problems meant he suffered from liver disease, and in January 2003 – having been given only months to live – he underwent a liver-transplant operation. He died, aged 69, from stomach cancer on 20 September 2004 in Derby City General Hospital.

There are now three statues of Brian Clough: one in Albert Park, Middlesbrough, a second in central Nottingham and a third (with Peter Taylor) outside Derby County's Pride Park stadium.

★ ★ ★

In the end, Don Revie served out three years of his four-year contract as coach to the United Arab Emirates national side. He left to become manager of the UAE First Division team Al Nasr, where he remained until 1984 before moving to Egypt for a brief stint as coach to their leading club side, Al Ahly.

He came back to the UK on a permanent basis in 1984, initially looking to get back into management. At one point, he was lined up to be coach at Queens Park Rangers, but the deal fell through and he never managed a football club again.

In May 1987, specialists diagnosed Revie as suffering from motor neurone disease, an incurable muscle-wasting disease. In May 1988, he made his last visit to Elland Road, in a wheelchair, for a benefit match in his honour. He died, aged 61, on 26 May 1989 in Murrayfield Private Hospital in Edinburgh.

Barnsley-born sculptor Graham Ibbeson has been commissioned to produce the first statue of Don Revie, in bronze and seven feet high, and it will be sited somewhere in Leeds in 2012.

Notes on Sources

Prologue

We can, of course, never know exactly what Don Revie was thinking as he contemplated a move back to Middlesbrough in September 1958. But from many conversations with his footballing contemporaries and knowledgeable commentators and a careful reading of all the published remarks he – and others – made, we do have a very clear idea of the factors that would have influenced his decision. So Revie's thoughts in this chapter, while imagined, are well rooted in fact.

Chapter 1 'An Infant Hercules'

Much of the history of Middlesbrough in this chapter, from the early nineteenth century through to the mid-twentieth, is informed and guided by Asa Briggs' magisterial book *Victorian Cities*. In particular, the brilliant passage about Middlesbrough steel coiling itself round the world 'like a strong and invincible serpent' is quoted in that book, and many of the facts and figures about the growth of the town and its social make-up come from it, too, including the quotes from Ravenstein and Bell.

Other history books that contributed significantly to my portrait of the town and the period were Richard Overy's *The Morbid Age*, together with Martin Pugh's *We Danced All Night* and Roy Hattersley's *Borrowed Time*. I also quote from George Scott's evocative 1956 memoir *Time and Place* at p. 33 ('eerily quiet streets'), pp. 35–6 and pp. 43–4, because it is the book that captures best the spirit of the town in the 1950s and the impact the football club had on its people.

On my walk between Brian Clough's and Don Revie's homes, Paul Stephenson of the Cleveland and Teesside Local History Society was my guide. I'm indebted to him for his sharp insights and extensive factual knowledge, and to Mavis Barwick and Kathleen Stevens for allowing me to interview them.

Don Revie's memories of his childhood are drawn from his autobiography *Soccer's Happy Wanderer*, published in 1955 when he was just 28. Except where stated, the quotes from him in this chapter are taken from that book. The television interview from which I quote is *Personal Choice* (with Mike Barrett), that went out on the BBC on 22 November 1974, and the radio interview quoted was with Ron Jones for a BBC series in 1974. In addition, I've drawn on some reflections Revie made in a BBC radio programme broadcast in September 1998 in the series *Master Managers*.

Brian Clough's recollections of his youth are taken from his autobiography published in 1994 (with John Sadler), although the memories of other family members come from a series of excellent podcasts (on the Middlesbrough Council website) that were made to mark the erection of the Clough statue in 2007 and the establishment of the 'Brian Clough Trail' across all his old haunts.

The *Evening Gazette* (Middlesbrough), *The Times* and the *Daily Mirror* all reflected what was happening in the world at that time. Finally, *The Boro Bible* (Harry Glasper and Chris Kershaw), 1999, was an invaluable source for statistics on Middlesbrough Football Club.

Chapter 2 'This Boy Can Play'

On the historical front, Bill Norman's *Luftwaffe Over the North* provided all the information I needed about Middlesbrough's place in the front line in the early years of the Second World War. I read the logbooks of Archibald and Marton Grove schools on a visit to the Teesside Archives in Middlesbrough. George Scott's *Time and Place* is back again, for his pithy observation on the impact – or rather lack of it – of the bombers on the town.

Don Revie's autobiography *Soccer's Happy Wanderer* was a vital source in charting his development as a young footballer in his time with Middlesbrough Swifts, and, except where stated, the quotes from him in this chapter are taken from that book. I interviewed his son Duncan in June 2010 and the first of his recollections about his father – his capability as a bricklayer and his insistence that his son should do some manual work – appears here. I also spoke to Ken Mothersill and Frank Stephenson for this chapter.

The photograph of Revie with the Boro Swifts side discussed here comes from the *Evening Gazette*, and I refer to a number of articles from that newspaper about him. Peter Thomas's recollection of Revie's signing to Leicester comes from an article he wrote for the *Daily Mail* in 1978.

Revie appeared on ITV's *This Is Your Life* on 24 April 1974 – the day Leeds United clinched their second league title; the quote from his sister Jean is from that programme.

On the Clough side, I discovered the picture of the Marton Grove side discussed here on Friends Reunited, where it had been uploaded by George Hindmarsh, brother of one of the players in the photograph, Lol Hindmarsh.

Clough's autobiographies were invaluable in tracing his progress through adolescence. The quote from him on p. 58 ('I enjoyed being head boy') is from *Cloughie: Walking on Water* and those on p. 59 ('I turned up for my first day') and p. 63 ('I'd known for a long time') are from *Clough: The Autobiography*. Keith Harkin and George Littlefair spoke to me in May 2010, and the quote from Peter Lax is from a *Northern Echo* article. I had a fascinating trip to Billingham Synthonia in May 2010, where Dave Lealman and Jackie Weatherill gave me chapter and verse on Clough's stay with the club. The reminiscences of Barbara Clough and Brian's sister Doreen are from those Middlesbrough Council podcasts.

The story about how Ray Grant persuaded Middlesbrough to sign up Clough comes from Tony Francis's *Clough: A Biography* – quite possibly the best book ever written about the man.

Chapter 3 'I'll Be That Man in a Thousand'

The descriptions of Revie's match-winning performances in the Portsmouth v. Leicester FA Cup semi-final, and the Manchester City v. Birmingham FA Cup final, were greatly aided by British Pathé News and MCFC videos respectively.

Once more, *Soccer's Happy Wanderer* was my source for much of the description of Revie's career at Leicester City, Hull City and Manchester City. Except where stated, the quotes from him in this chapter are taken from that book. Revie told Mike Barrett (*Personal Choice*, BBC TV, 1974) about his eating habits as an apprentice footballer, Johnny Duncan (p. 68) and the influence of his wife Elsie (p. 70). Elsie's comments on their wedding were made on *This Is Your Life*.

Ernest Hecht, publisher of Souvenir Press, was a friend and business associate of Revie's (he published his – and Leeds United's – football annuals in the 1960s) and he spoke to me about his memories of Revie, as did Brian Glanville.

Eric Thornton knew Revie well in his time at Manchester City. His account of Duncan signing Revie to Leicester City and his vivid recollection of events on the eve of the 1956 cup final, from *Leeds United and Don Revie*, are quoted here.

I interviewed Brian Pilkington in May 2010 about his one and only cap for England, and the experience of playing alongside Revie. He was part of a very successful Burnley side at that time.

Some of the detail of that momentous England v. Hungary match in 1953 is derived from Norman Giller's *Footballing Fifties*; Billy Wright's reminiscences are taken from Giller's biography of him, entitled *A Hero for All Seasons*. *The Times* was the principal source for coverage of other England games in this chapter.

Chapter 4 'Clough Must Change His Style'

Lindy Delapenha, Brian Phillips and Alan Peacock were all teammates of Clough's in the 1950s. I interviewed them between January and May 2010. Delapenha, aged 83, is retired and living back in Jamaica; for many years, he was director of sports at the Jamaican Broadcasting Corporation. Brian Phillips, aged 79, lives in Mansfield these days, while Alan Peacock, the youngest at 73, does much excellent work for the Middlesbrough Former Players Association. Rolando Ugolini, Middlesbrough's goalkeeper and the life and soul of the team in the 1950s until Peter Taylor replaced him, is now 86. I interviewed him in February 2010.

Clough's other teammate from that period who features in this chapter is, of course, his best friend and colleague Peter Taylor. The quotes from him in this chapter are from his autobiography *With Clough by Taylor* (with Mike Langley). Once more, I've drawn on Clough's own book for his early days in a Boro shirt. The quotes from him on p. 96 ('I loved the feeling') is from an interview with the *Sunday Express*, 4 February 1958, and those on p. 90 ('At the very moment') and p. 101 ('Derek Kevan was') are from *Clough: The Autobiography*.

The son of 'Big Astor', Garth Garriques, talked to me about his father's extraordinary life as comedian and football fan. Duncan Hamilton, author of the memoir *Provided You Don't Kiss Me: 20 Years with Brian Clough*, assessed Clough's view of Revie in those days. I spoke to Alan Keen about his memories of Clough as a player in February 2010.

As ever, I was guided by coverage in the *Evening Gazette*, especially by its enthusiastic football correspondent (and confidant of Clough) Cliff Mitchell. The *Daily Mail*, *Daily Express* and *Daily Mirror* were other useful sources.

Finally, that picture of Wilf Mannion and Rolando Ugolini, taken by George Douglas, featured in *Picture Post* and is the property of Getty Images.

Chapter 5 'Give It a Real Go for Walter'

In the autumn of 1958, three of the big newspapers in the North-East – *Evening Gazette*, *Northern Echo* and *Sunderland Echo* – were extremely interested in the story about whether Don Revie would join Middlesbrough, his home-town club. It featured on both front and back pages, and I quote from all of those papers.

Exactly what Revie was thinking as he made his decision is a matter of conjecture. But all the thoughts I have him entertaining here have, once more, clear factual basis.

My report on the Middlesbrough v. Sunderland game in October 1958 is an amalgam of match reports from the *Sunderland Echo* and *Northern Echo* – mainly the former – with player interviews interspersed throughout. The *Yorkshire Post* features towards the end of the chapter, reporting on Revie's start at Elland Road.

I interviewed Middlesbrough players Billy Day, Alan Peacock and Carl Taylor for this chapter – although Billy's description of his walk to Ayresome Park comes from one of the podcasts made for the unveiling of the Brian Clough statue and trail that appear on Middlesbrough Council's website.

I also spoke to two of the Sunderland players who featured in the game on 11 October – left-winger Colin Grainger and goalkeeper Johnny Bollands. The interviews were conducted between April and August 2010. I also spoke to Sunderland full-back Colin Nelson.

The story about Len Shackleton and Don Revie comes from an interview Brian Leng (the editor) conducted with Len for theRokerEnd. com, the official website for the Sunderland Former Players Association. I'm very grateful to be able to use it in its entirety, with kind permission from Len's son Roger Shackleton. Charlie Hurley's memories of playing against Clough are also from theRokerEnd.com.

I didn't personally interview Sunderland's defender Len Ashurst, but I have quoted his autobiography *Left Back in Time* on Don Revie and Alan Brown.

Norman Giller's *Footballing Fifties* and *The Boro Bible* once more helped with match reports and statistics. Clough's comment on Dennison is taken from *Clough: The Autobiography*.

Chapter 6 'Some of the Lads Don't Like You'

Rolando Ugolini gives his recollection here about how Clough met his wife Barbara; Clough's memory, from *Cloughie: Walking on Water*, completes the story. *Clough: The Autobiography* is quoted at pp. 127, 129, 130–1 and 140.

To paint a picture of Clough's two appearances in an England shirt, I drew on the memories of his forward colleague John Connelly, whom I interviewed in June 2010. The *Evening Gazette*, *Daily Express*, *Daily Mail*, *Observer* and *Telegraph* provided the match reports.

Alan Peacock, Brian Phillips and Derek McLean provided me with first-hand recollections about the story of discord within the Boro dressing-room over Clough's captaincy; Peter Taylor's autobiography fleshed out more details, as did my interview with Ray Robertson in May 2010. *Ron Reynolds: The Life of a 1950s Footballer* (Dave Bowler and David Reynolds) is a splendid portrait of the decade, and I quote from it here. Simon Inglis's *Soccer in the Dock* tells the story of corruption in the game in that period.

Personal Choice (BBC TV, 1974) provided me with the story about Revie and Billy Bremner's first game for Leeds. I interviewed Jack Charlton and Lord Harewood in May 2010, and their reflections on Revie start here. The quote from Revie on his managerial aspirations is taken from Eric Thornton's *Leeds United and Don Revie*. Matt Busby spoke about his meeting with Revie on *This Is Your Life*.

I relied on two Leeds United websites – The Mighty Mighty Whites and WAFLL – for much factual and analytical information in this chapter.

Chapter 7 'From Butlins to the Kremlin'

Clough's autobiography informs much of this chapter, especially his crystal-clear memory of his serious injury against Bury in 1962 (p. 159) and his state of mind afterwards (p. 160). But his recollections of joining Sunderland and his association with Alan Brown (p. 156) and his realisation that his time at Sunderland was over (p. 161) come from a *Sunday Express* interview in 1968.

Ron Reynolds' memories of the lifting of the maximum wage are from Dave Bowler and David Reynolds' *Ron Reynolds: The Life of a 1950s Footballer*.

Brian Leng, editor of theRokerEnd.com, recalls watching Clough as a teenager. I interviewed Johnny Crossan, the gifted Northern Ireland player and one of Clough's best friends, in June 2010.

The account of the second pitch encounter between Clough and Revie is an amalgam of match reports from the *Sunderland Echo* and *Yorkshire Post*. The Mighty Mighty Whites (from which the quote from Eric Smith is taken) and WAFLL were again invaluable in piecing together events in this period. Colin Nelson also provided his perspective, and Len Ashurst's *Left Back in Time* is again quoted here.

For Revie, his son Duncan gave me that clear memory of his father's vision for the future of football. Eddie Gray's autobiography *Marching on Together* is quoted on Albert Johanneson, while the quotes from Johnny Giles (about Alan Peacock) and Bobby Collins (about Don Revie) came from Jason Tomas's book *The Leeds United Story*.

Jack Charlton told me of his duels with Clough on the pitch (although his thoughts on Bobby Collins' addition to the team are taken from *Jack Charlton: The Autobiography*), while Alan Peacock remembered how impressed he was by the Leeds 'method'. I introduce Peter Lorimer for the first time in the book here, recalling his debut at the tender age of 15; I interviewed him in Leeds in May 2010.

Chapter 8 'It's Us Against the World'

The information to illustrate Revie's dilemma over whether or not to take the Sunderland job comes principally from reports in the *Yorkshire Post*, although Lance Hardy's book *Stokoe, Sunderland and '73* and Jason Tomas's *The Leeds United Story* helped me glean more details. Once again, Revie's imagined thoughts were meticulously drawn from these and other accounts from the time.

My account of Clough's forays into politics was helped by articles in the *Evening Gazette*, Ben Pimlott's *Harold Wilson* and Peter Taylor's autobiography.

To flesh out the character of George Hardwick I'm indebted to Ron Darby, proprietor of the Blue Bell Lodge in Acklam, Middlesbrough, and to Hardwick's autobiography *Gentleman George* (edited by John Wilson). The quotes from him on being offered the manager's job at Sunderland and on Clough at the club are taken from that book.

John O'Hare was one of Clough's favourite players; he took him to Derby, then to Leeds, and finally to Nottingham Forest when he became manager there in 1975. I interviewed John in June 2010 about Clough's spell as Sunderland youth-team manager – and much else besides.

Geoffrey Boycott appears for the first time here. I spoke to him in July 2010; he was a friend of Clough's, and he describes here how they met in the early 1960s.

The quote from Revie about 'playing for results' comes from the ITV duel with Clough (see Chapter 12). Jack Charlton and John Connelly recall Leeds v. Man United encounters, and Eddie Gray – whom I interviewed in May 2010 – describes how Revie recruited him to Leeds. Lord Harewood remembers the solidarity of the club in that period.

I took the quote from Billy Bremner from *Bremner! The Legend of Billy Bremner* by Bernard Bale. As ever, The Mighty Mighty Whites and WAFLL helped fill in the gaps.

For Clough's time at Hartlepools, In the Mad Crowd website proved an indispensable source of facts and figures. For Clough's view of his time at Victoria Park, I was aided by interviews he gave to *The Journal* in 1965 and to Michael Carey of *The Guardian* in September 1968 (p. 176), as well as his autobiography (pp. 174–5, 175 and 190) and Peter Taylor's (p. 178). I interviewed Mick Somers in July 2010.

Chapter 9 'The Most Superstitious Man in the World'

Revie's credo 'What I Expect from My Players' (published in 1970 in *The Park Drive Book of Football*) forms the starting point for an assessment of his managerial style. Eddie Gray provided more insight, partly through his interview with me but also in the programme *Master Managers*, presented by Bryon Butler on BBC Radio in 1998 (the flicking back of the hair). Norman Hunter's contribution to that programme is also featured here.

Revie's own contributions to *Master Managers* (pp. 193 and 194) and *Personal Choice* (pp. 195 and 196) are also quoted.

I interviewed Ian St John and Tommy Docherty in May 2010. I spoke to Alan Keen about the influence of Revie's dossier. The actual excerpts from one of those dossiers come from Jason Tomas's *The Leeds United Story*.

Duncan Revie talked to me about his father's motivational ability and his determination that his son should have the education he never had.

The story about the gypsy curse is well known, but I'm indebted to that *Yorkshire Evening Post* article of June 1971 for the only interview ever recorded with Gypsy Laura Lee.

For an appraisal of Clough's character, his friends and colleagues Michael Parkinson, Geoffrey Boycott, Clive Thomas (interviewed in

July 2010), Lawrie McMenemy (spoken to in May 2010) and Jack Charlton were all full of acute observations. I spoke to Alan Durban in May 2010, and I drew once more on my interviews with Duncan Hamilton and John O'Hare.

I felt the novels by John Braine, Alan Sillitoe and David Storey captured the mood of the time and the type of working-class heroes – like Clough – who were coming to the fore. I quote briefly from *Room at the Top* and *Saturday Night and Sunday Morning*.

Chapter 10 'Your Father's the Greatest of All Time'

Duncan Revie's fascinating story about meeting Brian Clough came from our interview in June 2010. Clough's laudatory comments about Revie were published in the *Yorkshire Post* in January 1968.

Derby County: The Complete Record by Gerald Mortimer, helped with the accounts of the Derby v. Leeds encounters in 1968. Jeff Powell provided the reminiscence of the aftermath of the Ferencváros match when I talked to him in March 2010.

I watched BBC's *Match of the Day* (Saturday, 25 October 1969) to see Clough and Revie interviewed together by David Coleman.

Duncan Revie, Jeff Powell, Duncan Hamilton, Geoffrey Boycott, Eddie Gray and Johnny Crossan all had various interpretations of the developing Clough–Revie rivalry.

For accounts of the Leeds v. Derby encounters in the early 1970s, I turned to John O'Hare, Peter Lorimer, Clive Thomas and Alan Durban. I quote Archie Gemmill from his autobiography *Both Sides of the Border*, Eddie Gray from his, *Marching on Together*, and Pat Partridge from his, *Oh, Ref. The Guardian* – usually Eric Todd – had the best match reports of those games and I quote widely from them.

For a detailed account of Clough's performance at the Sportsman's Dinner in January 1973 I turned to the *Yorkshire Post*. John Helm, who was there, also gave me his account, and Clough referred to it in *Clough: The Autobiography*, which I quote at pp. 221, 226 ('I wrote to the Wilsons') and 228.

I record Clough's attack on Revie from the *Sunday Express* on 5 August 1973, and Sam Longson's comments about Clough were taken from the *Yorkshire Post* a couple of days after that article.

Chapter 11 'He Won't Be There Long'

The *Daily Express* was an excellent source for the story of Clough's final days at Derby, his period at Brighton and his move to Leeds. I quote from the newspaper at the time, although Clough's comment that his taking over at Leeds was like 'Breshnev being Prime Minister of Britain with a Tory Government' came from an article he wrote for the paper on 24 April 1980.

The opening part of the chapter involved viewing Clough's appearance on *Parkinson* on 20 October 1973, and I also drew on my interview with Michael Parkinson. My reflections on the state of British television are partly drawn from personal experience – I was 16 then – but Brian Viner's *Nice to See It, to See It, Nice* also proved of immense help.

For another of Clough's political adventures, in the general election of February 1974, I again drew on Ben Pimlott's *Harold Wilson*, with reports from the *Derby Evening Telegraph*.

Joe Ashton provided me with the colourful story about Clough's visit to Iran when I interviewed him in February 2010. Mr Kambiz Atabai shared his memories of Clough's time in Tehran in an interview with me in March 2010. My source for the comment by the late Sir Anthony Parsons must remain anonymous.

I called on Ted Croker's autobiography *The First Voice You Will Hear Is . . .* for an FA view of Revie's appointment as England manager.

Revie's quote about 'letting them off the leash' is from *A Word with Williams*, BBC Radio, 2 February 1984. He discussed the lessons to be learned from the Dutch national team in the *Daily Express* in February 1977.

The quote from Allan Clarke appears on the Mighty Mighty Whites website. Eddie Gray is quoted both from his *Marching on Together* (p. 248) and from my interview with him (pp. 255 and 256). John Helm recalls the surprise of Clough's appointment as Leeds manager, while Ian St John, in an interview in May 2010, told me how close he was to getting the job. Bobby Robson's quote about his approach from Leeds is taken from his book *Farewell But Not Goodbye: My Autobiography*.

For Clough's first 40 days at Elland Road, I was guided by reports in the *Yorkshire Evening Post* (reporter Don Warters usually to the fore). Peter Lorimer, Geoff Boycott, Duncan Revie and John O'Hare had varying recollections of that period. *Clough: The Autobiography* is quoted at pp. 237 ('He turned out' and 'It was a case of'), 242, 251 ('I could sense the hostility') and 258 ('Instead of unity').

Brian Clough Comes to Leeds: A Calendar Special was essential watching for gauging the attitude of Clough in those days, and I quote from that compelling programme.

I interviewed Hans Marsen in September 2009 about Clough's stay at the Dragonara Hotel, and I spoke to Duncan McKenzie – who also stayed there – in May 2010.

Chapter 12 'Thank You, Manny Cussins'

The *Yorkshire Evening Post* was my principal source for the story of the first three days of Clough's final week at Elland Road, although I refer to the *Yorkshire Post* and *Daily Express* as well.

Peter Lorimer, Duncan McKenzie and John O'Hare were all at the meeting of players and directors when Clough's fate was effectively decided, and I've called on their memories of that extraordinary occasion and its aftermath.

Clough's reference to his meeting with Manny Cussins on the same day comes from his appearance on *The Frost Interview* on BBC TV in December 1974.

As for Thursday, 12 September, when Clough was sacked, my aim was to talk to as many people as I could who were involved in the events of that day. I interviewed John Helm, Charles Dodsworth and the *Calendar* team of Austin Mitchell, John Wilford, Sir Paul Fox and Nick Gray between August and October 2009. I spoke to Julian Creasey, son of David (Clough's lawyer on the day) in August 2010.

I drew on Clough's updated autobiography *Cloughie: Walking on Water*, and Norman Hunter's memory of Clough barging into the committee meeting brandishing a bottle of champagne comes from his autobiography *Biting Talk* (with Don Warters).

The centrepiece of the chapter is *Calendar*'s special programme *Goodbye Mr Clough*, and I quote widely from it.

Chapter 13 'Not Worth the Aggravation'

The main source of much of this chapter is the Thompson Papers, kept by the Royal Society in London. The collection includes correspondence between Sir Harold and Revie (including the latter's letter of resignation and the ensuing reply), the debate within the FA and the Football Council on who should succeed him as England manager and the letters of application for the job.

In addition, two particular documents in the collection helped me piece together a narrative of events between March and July 1977. The first was the full transcript of Revie's appearance before an FA disciplinary committee on 18 December 1978, when he was charged with bringing the game into disrepute; the second was the record of the subsequent High Court judgment from Justice Cantley. Lord Harewood, in my interview with him, fleshed out the evidence he gave to Justice Cantley in December 1979. The Thompson papers also made reference to the Metropolitan Police's assessment of whether Revie could be prosecuted over corruption allegations, and I have reproduced that here.

I quote from Clough's appearance on *The Frost Interview* on 13 November 1974 on his continuing bitterness towards Revie.

The website Englandstats.com helped me with accounts of the England games in Revie's reign as manager, together with match reports from the *Daily Mirror* and *Daily Express*. The spat between him and Brian Glanville was on BBC Radio's *Sports Report* on 1 November 1975. Revie talked about not having enough quality players in his *A Word with Williams* interview, and Trevor Brooking's insights into his managership came in the *Master Managers* programme.

Clough's autobiography and Taylor's *With Clough by Taylor* (pp. 298–9) help tell the tale of Forest's rise in 1976 and 1977, and the website www.bridportred.co.uk has all the relevant statistics.

Jeff Powell was the man who broke the story of Revie's resignation, one of the biggest sporting scoops of all time, and his story features prominently here; I interviewed him in April 2010. I quote from Richard Stott's autobiography *Dogs and Lampposts* about the allegations of corruption made against Revie in the *Daily Mirror* in September 1977.

For the story of Clough's attempt to become Revie's successor at England, I talked to Gerald Mortimer, football correspondent of the *Derby Evening Telegraph*, in July 2010. My interview with Clough's fellow candidate Lawrie McMenemy was done in May 2010, and Jack Charlton remembered his experience of applying.

Clough's attack on Revie in the *Sunday Mirror* (September 1977) is quoted. I've used quotes from Clough's autobiography about the day he was interviewed by the FA.

Clough: The Autobiography is quoted at pp. 291, 298, 299 and 318.

Epilogue

My account of Revie's FA disciplinary hearing in 1978 and his appearance in the High Court a year later again benefited from seeing the full transcript of the former and the judge's summing-up in the latter.

But my principal, human source for those events was Revie's renowned defence barrister, Gilbert Gray, QC. Called to the bar in the 1950s and still in practice today in his 80s, he was involved in some of the most famous trials of the twentieth century: the Birmingham pub bombings, 'the Black Panther', *Spycatcher* and Brinks Mat.

Nottingham Forest's rise to glory comes partly from my own recollections and partly from viewing match reports in the *Daily Telegraph*, *The Times* and *The Guardian*.

Clough's autobiography has the last word on his failed attempt to become England manager (p. 320) and captures his elation at winning the European Cup (p. 321).

Books

Ashurst, Len, *Left Back in Time: The Autobiography of Len Ashurst*, Know the Score Books, 2009

Bale, Bernard, *Bremner! The Legend of Billy Bremner*, Andre Deutsch, 1998

Banks, Gordon (ed.), *The Park Drive Book of Football 1970*, Pelham Books Ltd, 1970

Bowler, Dave, and David Reynolds, *Ron Reynolds: The Life of a 1950s Footballer*, Orion, 2003

Bowles, Stan, with Ralph Allen and John Iona, *Stan Bowles: The Autobiography*, Orion Books, 2004

Braine, John, *Room at the Top*, Penguin Books, 1981

Briggs, Asa, *Victorian Cities*, Penguin Books, 1990

Charlton, Jack, with Peter Byrne, *Jack Charlton: The Autobiography*, Corgi Books, 1997

Clough, Brian, with John Sadler, *Clough: The Autobiography*, Corgi Books, 1994

Clough, Brian, with John Sadler, *Cloughie: Walking on Water – My Life*, Headline, 2002

Croker, Ted, *The First Voice You Will Hear Is . . .* , Willow Books, 1987

Edwards, George, *Right Time, Right Place: The Inside Story of Clough's Derby Days*, Stadia, 2007

Francis, Tony, *Clough: A Biography*, Stanley Paul, 1987

Gemmill, Archie, with Will Price, *Both Sides of the Border: My Autobiography*, Hodder and Stoughton, 2005

Giller, Norman, *Footballing Fifties*, JR Books, 2007

Giller, Norman, *Billy Wright: A Hero for All Seasons*, Robson Books, 2002

Glasper, Harry, Dave Allan, Peter Harris, Mark Hooper and Dave Robson, *The Boro Alphabet*, Middlesbrough Football and Athletic Club, (1986) 1999

Glasper, Harry, and Chris Kershaw, *The Boro Bible*, Middlesbrough Football and Athletic Club, (1986) 1999

Gray, Eddie, with Jason Tomas, *Marching on Together: My Life with Leeds United*, Hodder and Stoughton, 2001

Hamilton, Duncan, *Provided You Don't Kiss Me: 20 Years with Brian Clough*, Harper Perennial, 2008

Hardwick, George (ed. John Wilson), *Gentleman George: The Autobiography of George Hardwick*, Juniper Publishing, 2001

Hardy, Lance, *Stokoe, Sunderland and '73: The Story of the Greatest FA Cup Final Shock of All Time*, Orion Books, 2009

Hattersley, Roy, *Borrowed Time: The Story of Britain Between the Wars*, Abacus, 2009

Hopcraft, Arthur, *The Football Man*, Aurum Press, 2006

Hunter, Norman, with Don Warters, *Biting Talk: My Autobiography*, Hodder and Stoughton, 2004

Inglis, Simon, *Soccer in the Dock: A History of British Football Scandals 1900 to 1965*, Willow Books, 1985

McKenzie, Duncan, with David Saffer, *The Last Fancy Dan: The Duncan McKenzie Story*, Vertical Editions, 2009

Mortimer, Gerald, *Derby County: The Complete Record*, Breedon Books, 2006

Mourant, Andrew, *Don Revie: Portrait of a Footballing Enigma*, Mainstream Publishing, 1990

Norman, Bill, *Luftwaffe Over the North*, Leo Cooper, 1993

Orwell, George, *Keep the Aspidistra Flying*, Penguin Classics, 2000

Overy, Richard, *The Morbid Age: Britain Between the Wars*, Allen Lane, 2009

Partridge, Pat, with John Gibson, *Oh, Ref*, Souvenir Press, 1979

Peace, David, *The Damned United*, Faber and Faber, 2006

Pimlott, Ben, *Harold Wilson*, Harper Collins, 1992

Priestley, J.B., *English Journey*, William Heinemann, 1994

Pugh, Martin, *We Danced All Night: A Social History of Britain Between the Wars*, Vintage, 2009

Revie, Don, *Soccer's Happy Wanderer*, Museum Press, 1955

Robson, Bobby, with Paul Hayward, *Farewell But Not Goodbye: My Autobiography*, Hodder and Stoughton, 2005

Scott, George, *Time and Place*, Staples Printers, 1956

Sillitoe, Alan, *Saturday Night and Sunday Morning*, Harper Perennial, 2006

Storey, David, *This Sporting Life*, Vintage, 2000

Stott, Richard, *Dogs and Lampposts*, Metro Publishing, 2002

Taylor, Peter, with Mike Langley, *With Clough by Taylor*, Sidgwick & Jackson, 1980

Thornton, Eric, *Leeds United and Don Revie*, Robert Hale and Company, 1970

Tomas, Jason, *The Leeds United Story*, Arthur Barker Ltd, 1971

Varley, Nick, *Golden Boy: A Biography of Wilf Mannion*, Aurum Press, 1997

Viner, Brian, *Nice to See It, to See It, Nice: The 1970s in Front of the Telly*, Pocket Books, 2009

Ward, Andrew, and John Williams, *Football Nation: Sixty Years of the Beautiful Game*, Bloomsbury, 2009

Newspapers

Evening Gazette (Middlesbrough)
Northern Echo
Sunderland Echo
Yorkshire Post
Yorkshire Evening Post
Derby Evening Telegraph
The Times
The Guardian
Daily Express
Sunday Express
Daily Mail
Daily Mirror
Daily Telegraph

Television and Radio

BBC Television and Radio Archive
This Is Your Life (ITV, 1974)
Brian Clough Comes to Leeds: A Calendar Special, Yorkshire TV, 1974
Calendar: Goodbye Brian Clough, Yorkshire TV, 1974

Websites

The Mighty Mighty Whites: The Definitive History of Leeds United
WAFLL (Leeds United statistics)

theRokerEnd.com (Sunderland Former Players Association)
www.bridportred.co.uk (Nottingham Forest statistics)
In the Mad Crowd (Hartlepool United statistics)
Middlesbrough Council
Englandstats.com

Other
Sir Harold Thompson papers (Royal Society)

Index